AUGUSTAN STUDIES

IRVIN EHRENPREIS
1920–1985

AUGUSTAN STUDIES

Essays in honor of IRVIN EHRENPREIS

Edited by
Douglas Lane Patey and Timothy Keegan

NEWARK: UNIVERSITY OF DELAWARE PRESS
LONDON AND TORONTO: ASSOCIATED UNIVERSITY PRESSES

© 1985 by Associated University Presses, Inc.

Associated University Presses
440 Forsgate Drive
Cranbury, NJ 08512

Associated University Presses
25 Sicilian Avenue
London WC1A 2QH, England

Associated University Presses
2133 Royal Windsor Drive
Unit 1
Mississauga, Ontario
Canada L5J 1K5

The paper used in this publication meets the minimum
requirements of the American National Standard for
Permanence of Paper for Printed Library Materials Z39.48-1984.

Library of Congress Cataloging-in-Publication Data
Main entry under title:

Augustan studies.

Includes bibliographies.
1. English literature—18th century—History and
criticism—Addresses, essays, lectures.   2. Ehrenpreis,
Irvin, 1920–1985—Addresses, essays, lectures.
I. Ehrenpreis, Irvin, 1920–1985.   II. Patey, Douglas
Lane.   III. Keegan, Timothy, 1949–   .
PR442.A917   1985   820'.9'005   85-40084
ISBN 0-87413-272-X (alk. paper)

Printed in the United States of America

Contents

Preface

This volume is offered in honor of Irvin Ehrenpreis by his friends, colleagues, and students in the study of the literature of the Augustan age. It does not encompass the range of his interests, which is suggested by the concluding list of his published works. There such names as Wallace Stevens, T. S. Eliot, and John Berryman jostle with Dryden and Pope, Fielding and Austen, all of whose works Professor Ehrenpreis has illuminated. Here we honor his distinguished contribution to the twentieth century's understanding of the eighteenth.

Throughout his career Irvin Ehrenpreis taught us that to see the literary work clearly we must look to its *relationships.* As biographer, scholar, and critic, he was concerned to explore those entanglements, personal, literary, and historic, that give works their deepest meaning and value. At a critical juncture in the development of modern literary thought, his influential essay "The Cistern and the Fountain" demonstrated that topical reference and historical context, what used to be called the "external" circumstances of a work, may compose a poem's very structure and meaning—that the external may also be internal. His well-known essay "Personae" clarified and corrected our understanding of the relation between the author and his work, freeing a generation of readers to penetrate more deeply the meaning of Augustan satire. More recently, his study of "Explicitness in Augustan Literature," with the scrupulous and elegant management of particulars for which Professor Ehrenpreis was distinguished, has pointed us to a deepened understanding of the interactions of Augustan writers with their literary contexts and works with their literary heritage. All these concerns unite in his magisterial life of Swift, a strikingly coherent achievement of critical biography accurately subtitled "The Man, His Works, and the Age." There as elsewhere, in his readings of poems, novels, and plays, Professor Ehrenpreis has shown how a criticism alive to literature's informing relationships may enrich, not detract or distract attention from, the work of art, while more recently still, in *Acts of Implication,* he shows how such criticism may lead us to an understanding of those literary procedures that characterize the Augustan age as a whole.

The essays which follow span the Augustan period, from commentaries by Mary Lascelles on seventeenth-century epitaph and elegy and by Christopher Ricks on Clarendon's style in the *History of the Rebellion* to G. A. Starr's discussion of the sentimental novel and Rachel Trickett's of the transition from classic to romantic aesthetic theory. The essays follow no narrow topical programme, yet each is concerned with informing literary relationships: of individual works to genre, to other works, to the shape of their authors' lives, to contexts material and intellectual. Thus Emrys Jones and Margaret Doody explore the meaning for Dryden and Swift of two ancient sources of diction and vision, Lucretius and Virgil's *Georgics*, while Timothy Keegan, Roger Lonsdale, and Leopold Damrosch, Jr., find the meaning of three groups of works in their place in the lives of their creators: Swift's autobiographical verses, Jonathan Richardson's collection of *Morning Thoughts,* and Samuel Johnson's *Rasselas.* David Wykes accounts for features of the first English "she-tragedy" by reference to the transmission of its story through various seventeenth-century modes of literary production, while Maximillian Novak traces Defoe's concern with "sincerity" to the role of that concept in contemporary moral and theological debate. Susan Staves explains the assimilation of elements of Restoration plays into eighteenth-century novels by attending to the relation of literary forms to social forms, and Ralph Cohen outlines a comprehensive theory of literary history based on generic transformation, instanced here in the conversion, from ballad to chapbook to tragedy, of the story of George Barnwel.

The volume contains as well Peter Steele's lively reconsideration of Sterne's voice in *Tristram Shandy* and a bibliographic list assembled by J. D. Fleeman of the prospectuses and proposals in which Samuel Johnson had a hand. Of course, not all those who would wish to honor Professor Ehrenpreis can be found here; the editors regret particularly that, as a result of ill health, Professor Louis Landa was unable to complete a paper planned for this book. But we know that the many who have been enriched directly and indirectly by the contribution of Irvin Ehrenpreis to our understanding and appreciation of the Augustan age—and of our own—join us in celebrating his distinguished critical achievement.

Irvin Ehrenpreis died in an accident in Münster, West Germany, on 3 July 1985, while this book was in the final stages of production. The editors join his family and many friends in mourning his untimely loss; and they hope that this book, which was originally intended to be presented to him as a mark of esteem, will serve instead as a tribute to his memory.

Douglas Lane Patey
Timothy Keegan

Abbreviations

CE	*College English*
CJ	*The Classical Journal*
EC	*Essays in Criticism*
ECS	*Eighteenth-Century Studies*
HLQ	*Huntington Library Quarterly*
JEGP	*Journal of English and Germanic Philology*
JHI	*Journal of the History of Ideas*
MLN	*Modern Language Notes*
MLR	*Modern Language Review*
MR	*Minnesota Review*
NR	*The New Review* (London)
NYRB	*The New York Review of Books*
N & Q	*Notes & Queries*
PQ	*Philological Quarterly*
REL	*Review of English Literature*
RES	*Review of English Studies*
SAQ	*South Atlantic Quarterly*
SEC	*Studies in the Eighteenth Century*
SECC	*Studies in Eighteenth-Century Culture*
SEL	*Studies in English Literature*
SP	*Studies in Philology*
TLS	*Times Literary Supplement* (London)
VQR	*Virginia Quarterly Review*

AUGUSTAN
STUDIES

1

Literary History and the Ballad of George Barnwel

Ralph Cohen

In 1979 René Wellek published an essay that he called "The Fall of Literary History." It was a sad essay by one of our most distinguished and knowledgeable critics; in it he declared that the

> attempts at an evolutionary history have failed. I myself have failed in *The History of Modern Criticism* to construe a convincing scheme of development. . . . Croce and Ker are right. There is no progress, no development, no history of art except a history of writers and institutions or techniques. This is, at least for me, the end of an illusion, the fall of literary history.[1]

The idea of progress as a linear development in critical theory or in the writing of poetry or prose fiction is an illusion that needed to be discredited. And it is to the credit of René Wellek that he is ready to abandon it. But it has never even been held by a number of contemporary critics, because they do not identify history with progress or with linear continuity. For example, Michel Foucault, in urging a concept that he calls "effective history," writes:

> History becomes "effective" to the degree that it introduces discontinuity into our very being—as it divides our emotions, dramatizes our instincts, multiplies our body and sets it against itself. "Effective" history deprives the self of the reassuring stability of life and nature, and it will not permit itself to be transported by a voiceless obstinacy toward a millennial ending. It will uproot its traditional foundations and relentlessly disrupt its pretended continuity.[2]

The history that Foucault seeks to write deals precisely with those unique characerics of events that characterize literary texts. "Effective" history "deals with events in terms of their most unique characteristics, their most acute manifestations" (154). It deals with these by opposing the idea that the past is recognizable, by opposing continuity as representative of a tradition, by opposing history as the will to knowledge "by risking the destruction of the subject who seeks knowledge."[3] Foucault's history when applied to the study of poetry or other texts has no illusions about "progress." But it has its own difficulties with reference to literary study.

Literary history that studies the "unique" characteristics can only do so by reference to the non-unique. The very language of history that Foucault offers implies certain continuities in the study of discontinuities. His history correctly opposes the idea of continuity as representative of tradition because tradition is normally based not on the uniqueness of the individual text but on its similarity to other texts. But neither of these options is desirable, since it is characteristic of texts to be like as well as unlike others. Indeed, in order to explore the relation between continuity and discontinuity, it seems necessary to assume some continuity—whether of kind, style, or subject—and some possible range of discontinuity. This indicates why Foucault's "effective" history is ineffective in dealing with types of change or types of uniqueness, whether trivial or radical. Change can only be charted by contrast with continuity, and different types of change result in different charts. But underlying the charting is the assumption that some changes do not alter an episteme, while others do. For Foucault, history as the study of uniqueness is opposed to, rather than evidence of, accumulated "knowledge." A history that is identified with dispersal of events, with discontinuities and randomness, cannot provide knowledge in the sense of continuity or covering laws or generalizations that are transhistorical. *Knowledge,* like most terms, has been used in many different ways, and a theory of literary history that does not take the amplifications, reductions, and contradictions of its concepts into account will either discover endless repetitions or endless change.

This essay is part of a larger project proposing a literary history based on a theory of genre and generic transformation. It is an attempt to analyze textual uniqueness in terms of textual continuity and discontinuity. But first it is necessary to reexamine what a verbal text is and how it is related to other texts. I cannot in this essay present the entire theory; I have taken instead a single text to illustrate the possible range of inquiry that such a literary history offers. Since this text is an early seventeenth-century broadside ballad—"An Excellent Ballad of George Barnwel Who Was Undone by a Strumpet, that caused him thrice to Rob his Master and to Murder his Uncle"—I explore its relation both to the genre-term "ballad" and to other seventeenth-century ballads. I offer some historical explanations for the clustering of ballads in the new eighteenth-century genre, the ballad opera. And I indicate some of the possibilities that flow from such a new approach to genre. I study the ballad itself and the commercial and moral consciousness it represents. How this consciousness undergoes change is part of the larger story. My aim here is to offer an example of how this new literary history might be written.

It may be argued that a discussion of relations among works—intertextuality—is not particularly new, no more than is the analysis of a text. I am prepared to grant this claim, since any theoretical uniqueness must be accompanied by some theoretical continuity. But the chief claim of *this* new literary history is that it explains how texts are dispersed as well as what is continuous in them and why. It offers—perhaps *attempts* is a better term—a reconstitution and reinterpretation of some subjects central to literary history: *genre, literary relations,* and *history.*

My history concerns the genre called "ballad," and it is based not on the study of all ballads within the genre but of a single ballad that is an instance, a single example, of ballad composition in the early seventeenth century. The subject of this essay is how this "generic instance" can be understood in its uniqueness, its contradictions, its continuities and discontinuities with other ballads, its interrelations with texts from other genres, its historical ramifications in eighteenth-century writing.

≈≈≈≈≈≈≈≈

In the Stationers' Register of 14 December 1624 is recorded the licensing of a collection of ballads, one of which is "George Barnwel." Copies of this ballad in the seventeenth century contain the notation that the tune is that of "The Merchant" or "The Rich Merchant Man," a ballad by Thomas Deloney licensed in 1594 with the note that it was "A most sweet Song of an English Merchant, borne at Chichester. To an excellent new Tune."[4] But as C. M. Simpson remarks, "Despite the popularity of Deloney's ballad and the frequent use of the tune associated with it, no music has survived which can be confidently identified."[5] Since the tune of the Barnwel ballad was that of "The Rich Merchant Man," no original tune survives for it either. The date of Deloney's ballad, however, permits us to place the production of the Barnwel ballad between 1594 and 1626. *1624?*

The absence of Deloney's tune prevents a discussion of the relation of words to music in "George Barnwel," but it does permit a comparison of the Barnwel text with others that shared its music. Not only did "The Rich Merchant Man" and "An Excellent Ballad of George Barnwel" share the same tune, but at least two other seventeenth-century ballads joined their company: "The Unfaithful Servant" (Pepys's Collection) and "The Kentish Miracle" (1684). These four ballads are representative of a ballad proce- *a conscious* dure: a single tune with which are paired quite different lyrics. Underlying *attempt?* this procedure is an attempt to associate different events by providing a shared tune for presenting them. Thus "The Rich Merchant Man" is about a merchant who, in a quarrel, kills a man in Germany and is condemned to death. He is redeemed by a woman who shows her love by offering to die with him. The Barnwel ballad deals with a harlot who seduces the youth who falls in love with her, making him first a liar, then a thief, and finally a murderer.

The rich merchant refuses offers of marriage from women who are after his money, whereas Barnwel, the young apprentice, only too readily succumbs, providing money to his harlot. So, too, "The Unfaithful Servant" deals with a poor serving maid who permits herself to be debauched by her master and with him poisons his pregnant wife. Sexual debauchery, desire for money, and readiness to commit murder or betrayal are thus the intertwining themes. We have here examples of transformation procedures within a genre: the tune with which the lyrics are paired is a constant, while the different narratives are the selected variables to which the constant is applied. "The Kentish Miracle," the fourth ballad in the group, is about a poor pious widow who is refused food and finally receives bread for her seven children which lasts seven days. The biblical allusions provide a religious allegory as a text for the tune, and they contrast the impious narratives with those of the suffering Christian or the honorable merchant.

"The Kentish Miracle," which was printed after the Civil War, may be seen as advocating acceptance of a moral norm regardless of the suffering it causes, whereas two of the other ballads present villainy as forms of personal pleasure or gain, as deliberate attempts to flout the moral order and escape punishment—even though they fail to win out in the end. The ballad about George Barnwel, the merchant's apprentice, initiates another perspective on seduction and villainy. The Barnwel ballad, therefore, can be seen as part of a process of perspective-making in seventeenth-century texts, not merely ballads. *Don Quixote,* for example, becomes a model for prose fiction by providing multiple perspectives. The dominant plot is interrupted by inset stories, not unlike the invariable tune to which are set variable lyrics. The process is connected in the novel to a rejection of a certain type of narrative—romance—and in the broadside ballad to an affirmation of initiative within imitation, the retention of some of the features of an older, oral ballad form in a printed one.

The pairing of words to music to which I have referred was not, of course, begun in the eighteenth century, but inherent in the setting of different ballad subjects to the same tune was the leveling of low, religious, and high subjects. This leveling indicated the possibility of parody, of mixing the fantastic with the real, the merry with the mad. The grounds for this variation in the seventeenth century can be identified with the tactic of play, for there are songs sung in the streets as well as those sung at home. But this is a special kind of folk play; it belongs to the principle of pleasing different groups within the populace. Thus the stable tune and the unstable words can be the occasion of authentic variety as well as variety that could be used to cozen or manipulate the buyer.

The broadside ballad was an object of merchandise sold by chapmen,

Cf. novel inset stories

and the ballad of George Barnwel provides an excellent example of how sex could be merchandised. It involves a youth's financial manipulation by a strumpet and carries as its subject and in its imagery that very merchandising which underlies the distribution of this genre in the seventeenth century.

The term *ballad* (or *ballade*), according to George Gascoigne (in 1575), referred to poems that have "sundrie sortes" of verse:

> for a man may write ballade in a staffe of six lines, euery line conteyning eighte or sixe sillables, whereof the firste and third, second and fourth do rime acrosse, and the fifth and sixth do rime togither in conclusion. You may write also your ballad of tenne sillables, rimyng as before is declared; but these two were wont to be most commonly vsed in ballade, which propre name was (I thinke) deriued of this worde in Italian *Ballare*, whiche signifieth to daunce. And in deed those kinds of rimes serue beste for daunces or light matters.[6]

In tracing the name *ballad* to the Italian *ballare*, to dance, Gascoigne indicates its origins as a poem about light matters. It is important, for generic procedures, to understand how a name given to a unique instance comes to include numerous other unique instances that constitute a genre. In the seventeenth century, *ballad* referred not only to light subjects, but to criminal, romantic, and aristocratic subjects as well. Ballads were included in the seventeenth-century poems that told stories of knights, of ghosts, of common folk. The broadside ballads of which "Barnwel" is one were poems about contemporary events and politics.

But the term *broadside ballad* also referred to a method of production. "Ballad" was "a piece of paper printed on one side only,"[7] so that the term came to refer to broadside ballads as disposable objects. In *The Compleat Angler* (1653), Izaac Walton mentions "an honest ale-house, where we shall find a cleanly room, lavendar in the windows, and twenty ballads stuck about the wall."[8] This process of sedimentation by which the generic name comes to refer to different and even previously absent features of works is a historical one. It does not matter that *ballad* is not derived from the Italian; what does matter is that Gascoigne at a particular time should identify a certain kind of verse and a certain kind of thematic material with it. The term eventually refers to a process of production, that is, broadside printing, and also to a process of distribution, as when Autolycus peddles his ballads in *A Winter's Tale* (1611; 4.4). A ballad was a folk poem paired to a tune (although who the creative "folk" were was not known). Although the earliest ballads were oral, the broadside ballad was a printed text; it became, indeed, a subgroup within the term *ballad*. The broadside served as a news carrier; its subjects were contemporary events, and when the newspaper and the periodical papers displaced it as news carriers, this ballad underwent a process of change.

subgenre: "broadside ballad"
folk poem → news

The process by which broadside ballads were elevated from baker's dish to literary artifact involves social and literary transformations. The few seventeenth-century collectors of ballads—"like Selden and Pepys, Bagford and Anthony Wood, who rescued copies while they were still obtainable"[9]— were educated men who for one reason or another preserved this ephemera of their times. Although in the eighteenth century some dictionaries continue to link *ballad* with trivial writing—Bailey's *Dictionary* (1730) defines *ballad* as "a Song commonly sung up and down the streets," and Johnson (1765) quotes Isaac Watts's statement, "Ballad once signified a solemn and sacred song, as well as trivial, when Solomon's Song was called the ballad of ballads; but now it is applied to nothing but trifling verse"—Addison redefined "Chevy Chase" as an example of the epic.[10] And in 1731 the Barnwel ballad was transformed into a tragedy, one of the most elevated of genres, following in the steps of Nicholas Rowe. By this act a broadside ballad, among the most ephemeral of genres, became the basis for a new conception of tragedy. In a generic sense, a common theme was rendered polite, and the bathetic and carnivalesque passages were rewritten as pathetic and tragic.

ballad opera

The transformation of this ballad into a tragedy occurred contemporaneously with the transformation of the ballad into a new genre in which ballad tunes were combined with new words and fitted into a drama: the ballad opera. This "new" kind was born in the early eighteenth century; its model is *The Beggar's Opera* (1728). But the procedure of incorporating an ephemeral form into a more enduring one—here, ballads into comic drama—is not new, but is a repetitive pattern in literary history; note the movement from short fiction to collections of such fictions, from proverbs to books of proverbs, from sonnets to sonnet sequences. The ballad sung in *A Winter's Tale,* for example, does not make that play a ballad opera, but it does indicate that the play, which is generically a dramatic romance, mixes characters from the lowest and highest classes and is comprehensive in the sense that it includes other genres within it.

dramatic romance

Ballad clusters—that is, ballads with different words paired to the same tune—metamorphose into a dramatic genre in the ballad opera. The pairing procedure is retained, but it now functions as part of a narrative that is expressed in dialogue and addressed to an audience in a theater rather than the random street audience. Why did the ballad take this historical direction? The answer given in the early eighteenth century is that it served to parody the songs in the newly imported Italian opera, and, at the nationalistic level, this seems a reasonable answer. But there are other, more pertinent literary explanations.

parody of Italian opera

The broadside ballads are street literature—in our terms, "popular" literature—and they are combined with a comic genre that satirizes romances and parodies a foreign but polite genre. A procedure thus operates in this new genre that makes the lower genre—ballad—part of a higher one and

low genre (ballads) + high genre (opera, drama)
⇒ ballad opera (Beggar's Opera)
or ⇒ tragedy (The London Merchant)

that compromises the higher by having it include the lower. In this new art form, the genres create a mixture, the responses to which differ from those accorded individual ballads or comedies. This procedure of relating higher forms to lower is analogous to the new commercial enterprise of bringing "civilization" *to* uncivilized countries and taking raw materials *from* them. This exploitative "commerce" for self-interest is what Pope satirizes in a passage in *The Rape of the Lock:*

> Unnumber'd Treasures ope at once, and here
> The various Off'rings of the World appear;
> From each she nicely culls with curious Toil,
> And decks the Goddess with the glitt'ring Spoil.
> This Casket *India's* glowing Gems unlocks,
> And all *Arabia* breathes from yonder Box.
> The Tortoise here and Elephant unite,
> Transform'd to Combs, the speckled and the white.
>
> (1.129–36)

While Pope is using commercial imagery to indicate the misuse of religious, reflective (artistic), and personal values, so that comprehensiveness becomes a personal trait of acquisitiveness, the ballad opera suggests the internalizing and manipulation of the ballad. It becomes a song of personal expression, or an allegorical reflection, or a narrative within a narrative. Thus the absorption of the ballad into the drama produces a genre in which song functions to make sophisticated what was unsophisticated, to bring to artistic unity what in street literature was inconsistent, even contradictory. There are other commercial aspects to this interchange. In the seventeenth century, *commerce* was a term for intellectual as well as economic exchange. The inclusion and exploitation of ballad in the ballad opera can be understood as a generic transformation analogous to economic "civilizing" procedures. The elevation of genres constitutes a process of elevating the audience's consciousness of class change; here what it justifies, of course, is the shift in the role of the merchant. In *The Beggar's Opera* Peachum is a merchandiser of criminals and stolen goods, and he is both against and for the law. He is thus held up to ridicule as the unprincipled man of principle: the principle being his own self-interest. Only three years later the ballad of George Barnwel was made into a tragedy, *The London Merchant,* in which the merchant's principles are identified with the moral and economic interests of the state:

I have observ'd [says Trueman] those countries, where trade is promoted and encouraged, do not make discoveries to destroy, but to improve, mankind by love and friendship; to tame the fierce and polish the most savage; to teach them the advantages of honest traffick, by taking from them, with their own consent, their useless superfluities, and giving them, in return, what from their ignorance in manual arts, their situation, or some other accident, they stand in need of.[11]

In *The London Merchant* (1731), the ballad disappears as a form, only to be replaced by one of the highest genres of the eighteenth century. The tragedy did not incorporate the ballad but, rather, rewrote it in language no longer identified with that of traditional tragedy, since such a tragedy dealt only with affairs of state.

Broadside ballads were usually anonymous; the ballad opera, by providing authorship, helped give them a status they had not previously enjoyed. The ballad opera also reveals another characteristic of intertextuality: the tunes of its ballads were usually composed in times earlier than the texts and the dramatic action. The ballad opera, therefore, indicated a particular interweaving of time past with time present and in its own way established a correspondence to the procedure of "imitating" (as Dryden used the term)—of rewriting and loosely translating classic texts from Horace, Juvenal, Lucretius, and others, in order to indicate artistic and educational continuity.

The Beggar's Opera, the most successful of the ballad operas, addressed audiences more variegated than those reached by the ballad-mongers. It thus provided a public precedent for altering and intermingling popular and polite art. Joining ballads into ballad operas, moreover, served varied, even contradictory political purposes. On the one hand, as critics have pointed out, the narrative of informers, highwaymen, and prostitutes suggests an allegory of upper-class behavior, and on the other hand, because the ballads used were composed in the past, the continuing consciousness of allegorical interpretation is affirmed, so that such behavior (on the part of lower and upper classes) seems a "law of nature."

Fred Kidson points out that many of the tunes in *The Beggar's Opera* were taken from Henry Playford's *The Dancing Master,* which first appeared in 1650, and from Tom Durfey's *Wit and Mirth, or Pills to Purge Melancholy* (volumes published from 1698 to 1720), although dates do not represent the date of composition of the ballads.[12] In the introduction to the play, the Beggar indicates that the play was originally an epithalamion: "This piece I own was originally writ for the celebrating the marriage of James Charter and Moll Lay, two most excellent ballad singers."[13] This ironic statement underlines the reversal of values in a play that supposedly honors or praises the bride and groom. Not only does *The Beggar's Opera* deny to marriage the praise such "celebrations" imply; it shows marriage as a commercial enterprise. Moreover, in this opera, commercial consciousness, including romantic possessiveness, is what makes the world—as well as the underworld—spin.

❧❀❧❀❧❀❧❀❧❀

This consciousness appeared early in the broadside ballad, and the ballad of George Barnwel exemplifies it. This ballad belongs as well to the genre of criminal confessions, and, as such, it narrates the seduction, crimes, and punishment of Barnwel. It is apparent that a text can belong to more than one genre, but can one distinguish between a *text* and what might be merely a *compositional trait?* I am committed to a genre theory in which any trait or traits can become genres when an author uses them and the critic considers them as entities. It is, after all, the critic or theorist who groups such traits and distinguishes them from other groups (or genres). Thus a proverb may be an entity or genre when considered as individual statement or part of another genre when used, for instance, in a Shakespearean play. One can note the contrary procedure, namely, that a form like the epic may lead poets to remove features of the epic which have no status as genres and make them independent entities, which become genres. Such a procedure was noted by John Dryden in his description of the origin of drama.

> For the original of the stage was from the epic poem. Narration, doubtless, preceded acting, and gave laws to it: what at first was told artfully was, in process of time, repeated gracefully to the sight and hearing. Those episodes of Homer which were proper for the stage, the poets amplified each into an action; out of his limbs they formed their bodies; what he had contracted, they enlarged; out of one Hercules were made infinite of pigmies, yet all endued with human souls; for from him, their great creator, they have each of them the *divinae particulam aurae.*[14]

My aim here is not to develop a theory of genre but to indicate how such a theory might explain generic innovation. The critic who applies generic theory to literary history will want to explain why a poem that is an instance of a ballad genre should also be a confession. He will want to explain the values such a literary history has for our time. Such a critic will not consider genre as fixed but rather as groups of texts that constantly undergo some changes in features and in interrelations with other genres. The reasons for these changes may be social, technological, philosophical, or literary. But the purpose of applying this reconstituted generic theory to texts is to provide explanations of change and continuity, explanations that are appropriate to a history concerned with beginnings, interrelations, discontinuities, dispersals, while not ignoring continuities.

It is, therefore, not surprising that the term *genre* should itself undergo changes of meaning just as the term *ballad* does. Nor is it surprising that there should be different theories of genre, since the aims of applying such a theory may vary.

I have referred to *narrative* in this essay. Considerable disagreement exists about the uses to which the term is put. Narrative can, of course, be used as a synonym for *epic,* or *novel,* or *plot.* Such uses make it a genre or part of a genre. But narrative is sometimes considered a genre irrespective of whether one discusses a poem as a "narrative," a tragedy as a "narrative," a novel as a "narrative," or a short story as a "narrative." Such a view of genre disregards or subordinates the formal features that compose a text. It posits a metaphysical or other absolute that supposedly underlies all members of the genre. Such a theory of genre is antithetical to the version I offer, and it provides insufficient discrimination for the literary history I am proposing.

I shall use *narrative*, therefore, as the name of a part of (a feature of) a genre and shall make distinctions of continuity and change by attending to the language of specific texts. Since I shall be discussing a plot that has survived despite changes for more than two hundred years, I shall, in my own statements, extrapolate the series of actions that persist. These will then permit me to distinguish how the language and other textual features are continued or discontinued. (It should be noted that the statements are an abstraction offered in the words of the critic-historian. They are intended to make distinctions apparent, not to identify actual continuities.)

The actions are as follows:

> George Barnwel, a youth apprenticed to a merchant, is accosted by a woman, Sara Milwood.
>
> She is an experienced harlot and seduces him.
>
> As a result of his infatuation with her, George is persuaded to embezzle his master's money.
>
> He flees to her and she incites him to murder and rob his rich uncle.
>
> When the money is spent, she betrays him to the authorities.
>
> He escapes and betrays her to the authorities in turn; she is hanged.
>
> He flees to Poland and is hanged for an unrelated murder.

This bare plot does not indicate who is speaking, nor does it indicate that the text before us is a poem, nor does it suggest interrelations within the poem. But if we turn to the text, we note that it opens with an exhortation to the youths of England in a manner typical of confessional ballads:

> All Youths of fair England, that dwell both far and near,
> Regard my story that I tell, and to my song give ear.
> A London lad I was, a merchant's 'prentice bound;
> My name *George Barnwel* that did spend my master many a pound.
> Take heed of harlots then, and their enticing trains;
> For by that means I have been brought to hang alive in chains.[15]

The ballad concludes with Barnwel's hanging in chains "in Polonia":

> For murder in *Polonia* was Barnwel hanged in chains.
> Lo, here's the end of wilful youth, that after harlots haunt,
> Who, in the spoyle of ther men, about the streets do flaunt.
>
> (2.194–96)

The shift in narrator is obvious, since the poem begins in the first person and concludes in the third. There is here a narrative disruption, actually one of several, narrative disruptions. For example, in line 83 Barnwel says to his mistress, "Ten pounds, nor ten times ten, shall make my love decay," and suddenly the autobiographical narrator is displaced by an impersonal one:

> Then from his bag into her lap, he cast ten pounds straight way.
> All blith and pleasant then to banqueting they go,
> She proferred him to lye with her, and said it should be so.
> And after that same time, I gave her store of coyn. . . .
>
> (1.84–87)

The first-person narration is then resumed, only to be interrupted again a few lines later as the first part of the ballad ends.

These discontinuities may very well be the result of hasty composition or of multiple authorship (resulting from the artistic disregard in which broadsides were held). The narrational shifts can be understood as disjunctive, and, in this sense, they add to the multiple voices in the ballad—that of Barnwel, of Sara Milwood, of the third-person narrator (who may or may not be the same narrator who concludes the ballad with a moralistic warning similar to that with which Barnwel began). The narrational shifts can indicate shifts in tone, as in the passage quoted above, which depicts Milwood hypocritically lamenting her lack of money; when Barnwel provides it, "All blith and pleasant then to banqueting they go." The third-person narrator seems to be commenting ironically on their behavior, while making clear the connection between sex, subsidy, and stealing. Narration, in other words, takes place in the ballad within the dialogues of Milwood and Barnwel, even though all these are being reported by a narrator—Barnwel and an impersonal speaker or speakers.

The narrative procedures include the pseudo-lament of Milwood, the carnivalesque dialogue, and autobiographical seriousness; a mixture of the serious and the pseudoserious, they are frankly outspoken about sensual and sexual pleasures. This ballad, for all the crudity of its structure, displays in its organization the reversal of values that the story narrates. It is, after all, the story of an innocent youth who becomes corrupted by a prostitute, deserts the norms of behavior, robs his master, abandons his moral and sexual purity, and murders his uncle. Such a situation creates an upside-down world, and the broadside ballad in the second part exemplifies this inversion.

One of the strategies by which the world upside-down is depicted in the ballad is by the transfer of terms of endearment. Milwood refers to Barnwel as "sweet Barnwel" (32, 64), "sweetest George" (43), "Sweet George" (65, 80); Barnwel begins to refer to Sara as "sweet Mistress" (54) and "my sweet Sara" (68, 99). The same interchange occurs with "dear" and "dearest." Sara Milwood's use of the terms are strategies of seduction—"Her words bewitcht my childishness, she uttered them so kind" (66). Barnwel's use results from his falling under her spell. Thus the ballad indicates through such terms the contrary implications of the same language.

Ian Donaldson has characterized the "upside-down world" in literature:

> The first, more broadly farcical element arises largely out of a comic principle which Henri Bergson described as *inversion,* a term which significantly coincides with the old rhetorical term we have already met. Inversion involves a sudden, comic switching of expected roles: prisoner reprimands judge, child rebukes parent, wife rules husband, pupil instructs teacher, master obeys servant. . . . The second and more complex comic principle might be described as *levelling.* Here the emphasis is not so much upon the reversal of roles or the triumph of a natural underdog as upon the artificiality of all social distinctions in the face of human passion and incompetence. Fielding is one of the masters of this kind of comedy.[16]

In her introduction to *The Reversible World* (1978), Barbara A. Babcock discusses the numerous explanations that anthropologists and others give to the process of inversion and remarks that an important form of adult play involving reversal is "linguistic and literary gaming."[17] The role of repetition as reversal in the ballad enacts both a form of play and a reversal of values. And in the second part of the ballad we have an example of disorderliness and filth:

> "Tush, 'tis no matter, *George,*" quo' she, "So we the money have,
> To have good cheer in jolly sort, and deck us fine and brave."
> And thus they liv'd in filthy sort, till all his store was gone,
> And means to get them any more, I *wis* poor George had none.
> (171–81)

The commentator voices the standard moral attitude about criminals, but quite other social attitudes are voiced: the division of riches, the leveling of family wealth, the dominance of money over morals; of theft, even murder, as an equalizing procedure.

> "My father's rich, why then," quoth I, "should I want any gold?"
> "With a [rich] father indeed" (quoth she), "A Son may well be bold."
> "I have a Sister, richly wed, that I'le rob e're I'le want;"
> "Why then," quo' *Sara,* "They may well consider of your scant."
> . . . .
> "Nay more than this, an Uncle I have, at *Ludlow* he doth dwell
> He is a Grazier, which in wealth, doth all the rest excell.
> E're I will live in lack" (quoth he) "And have no coyn for thee,
> I'le rob the churl and murder him!" "Why should you not?" (quoth she)
> E're I would want, were I a man, or live in poor estate,

On father, friends, and all my kin, I would my talents grate."
"For without money, *George*," quo' she, "A man is but a beast;
And bringing money thou shalt be always my chiefest guest."

(143–54)

Barnwel refers to Milwood as a "wanton" at his first meeting, though he does not learn that she is a "wanton" until much later. She greets him first with the utmost politeness and later addresses him in billingsgate—"paltry Jack." At first she welcomes him effusively to her home; after the stolen money is gone she throws him out of the house: "And therefore now in railing sort she thrust him out of door" (181).

It is important to note how the concept of time in the poem is related to commerce and love. There is no knowledge of the total time involved in the actions, but specifications are often very precise. Barnwel returns to Milwood's home "next Sunday" (67). He stays with his uncle "A se'nnights space," seven nights and days. Time is thus made pertinent as a detail insofar as it supports the realistic imitation of actual experience.

This can be confirmed by the suddenness of Barnwel's change from innocence to desire. It stems from the mixture of Milwood's confession of love, and her pretense of lack of control: "With that she turned aside, and with a blushing red,/A mournful motion she bewray'd, by holding down her head" (47–48). Milwood uses a handkerchief (merchandise) "all wrought with silk and gold" (49) to wipe her (contrived) tears of love for Barnwel: "This thing unto my sight was wonderous rare and strange;/And in my mind and inward thoughts it wrought a sudden change" (51–52). The sight of the "wrought" handkerchief "wrought" an inward change; Milwood's external show of pretended love leads to Barnwel's inward transformation, an arousal of desire. She declares: "If thou would'st here alledge thou are in years a Boy,/So was *Adonis*, yet was he fair Venus' love and joy" (57–58). The reference to the story of Venus and Adonis suggests some knowledge of pagan lore even in the readers of a broadside ballad, and it serves here to stress the prurient rather than the pedagogical function of the classics. Once Barnwel is seduced, he becomes contaminated with the vicious moral attitudes of Milwood, and the fact that he comes to know her wiles and falsehoods does not lead him to control his sexual desires. Since his behavior is first governed by "sudden change" of mind and thought, the implication is that he is overpowered by a sexual drive that conquers his knowledge of virtue and obligation. Barnwel cannot put aside his attraction to Milwood: "Thus I that was with Wiles betwich'd, and snar'd with fancy still,/Had not the power to put away, or to withstand her will" (135–36). The ballad begins and ends with a warning to youths to avoid harlots, but in the second part it recounts the pleasures of debauchery, the joys of disobedience and sexual carousing. Exhortations to order are at the borders; disorder is at the center. The two parts can be

understood as a progress into wickedness and as a reversal of softness and
gentleness to viciousness, criminality, and treachery.

It is paradoxical that in referring to Barnwel's youth the ballad should
allude to an ancient myth. The point is, however, that the ballad itself is
sedimented, that is, it alludes to works and to aspects of previous ballads
that refer to different time schemes. The confessional exhortation is a
typical contemporary rhetorical feature of ballads about criminals; the inclusion of the narrator's reflections is a part of an oral tradition; the myth
of Venus and Adonis a classical pagan allusion. This reference by Milwood
is intended to provide a precedent for seduction and a stimulus and entice-
ment for sexual pleasure.

ɞ҂ɞ҂ɞ҂ɞ҂ɞ҂ɞ҂ɞ

There is a distinctive subject matter in this ballad that relates the dialogues between Milwood and Barnwell to commerce and to Barnwel's ap-
prenticeship to a merchant. Barnwel, at the beginning of the ballad,
gathers money for his master, but after meeting the harlot, he reverses his
values and gathers (or embezzles) it for her. So Milwood becomes his "master" and functions as a merchant who sells her affections. The diction of
counting, courting, and merchandising suffuses the ballad. The original
ballad, on the title page, refers to Barnwel who "thrice" robbed his master,
and the first stanza refers to one who did "spend [for] my master many a
pound." When Milwood first kisses Barnwel, he remarks that she said, "If I
would come to her, I should have more than this." And when Barnwel
leaves with a promise to return, he explains, "Thus parted we in peace, and
home I passed [went] right, / Then went abroad and gathered in by five
o'clock at night / A hundred pounds and one. . . ." And when Milwood
welcomes Barnwel she exclaims, "Welcome, ten thousand times, more welcome than my brother." And when he refuses her invitation for supper, she
asks if he would not "one hour or two abide?" And when she confesses
(falsely) her love, she urges, "Let not affections force be *counted* lewd desire" (emphasis mine). She claims to honor him until "her life doth end"
despite the fact that he is "in years a Boy." He stays and sups with her "with
joys that did abound": "And for the same paid presently, in money twice
three pound./Then from his bag into her lap, he cast ten pounds straight
way"; after he lies with her, he declares, "I gave her store of coyn,/Yea,
sometimes fifty pounds at once, all which I did purloyn." When his master
calls for a reckoning, Barnwel declares, "Full well I knew that I was out, two
hundred pounds that day." The narrator remarks in the imagery of money
as food that Barnwel "did her necessity so oft with money feed."

Barnwel comes to Sara Milwood for protection, explaining, "And I am
found behind the hand, almost two hundred pound." When she rejects
him he prepares to leave: "Therefore, false woman, now farewell, while
twenty pound doth last/my anchor in some other Haven I will with wisdom

cast." When George speaks about money in what seems a state of drunken joy, he says: "A fig for care or careful thought, when all my gold is gone,/In faith my girl, we will have more, whoever it light upon." And she promises him protection whenever he brings money:

> "For say thou should'st pursued be, with twenty hues and cries,
> And with a warrant searched for with *Argus'* hundred eyes:
> Yet in my house thou shalt be safe, such privy ways there be,
> That if they sought an 100 years, they could not find out thee."
>
> (155–58)

George goes off to murder his uncle in Ludlow, and "once or twice he thought to take his Father by the way." He goes on to his uncle, who entertains him for a "se'nnight's space," and rides with him to the market. On the way home, in a wood, he kills his uncle, and "fourscore pound in ready coyn, out of his Purse he took." Together with Milwood he spends the money "till all his store was gone."

The counting and accounting diction of the poem indicates the merchandising nature of the harlot in her behavior toward the merchant's apprentice. It is not merely that as a harlot Milwood sells her affection but that the use of the language of computation can function to support or to undermine sincerity, beauty, and honesty. In this respect, the language and imagery function as a *subtext*, that is, they tell a story that is a narrative about the overt narrative. Barnwel counts out money, Milwood counts out affection, kisses, lewd desires. Later they come to share their roles as counters and merchandisers. The letter that Barnwel writes when he is thrust out of doors and flees London has the language of a legal accusation or a commercial contract, as well as a confession. It results in the apprehension of Milwood.

> Unto the Mayor of *London* then, he did a Letter write,
> Wherein his own and *Sara's* faults he did at large recite.
> Whereby she apprehended was. . . .
>
> (189–91)

The driving forces in the story are sex and greed—the satisfaction of the apprentice's desire depends upon his satisfaction of the harlot's greed. In this criminal economy, when the money is spent, no sexual satisfaction is given. To rid herself of an unproductive burden, Milwood betrays Barnwel; then he betrays her. Protection is thus replaced by exposure.

Still another reversal is found in the term *apprentice*. In *The Apprentice's Vade Mecum* (1734), Samuel Richardson explains the term as follows: "The word *Apprentice* is derived also from the French *Apprentisse*, from the Latin *Apprehendere*, which signifies to *apprehend* or to *learn*, which is the Duty of a young Man entering into an Engagement to *learn* or *apprehend* the Art or Mystery to which he is bound *Apprentice*."[18] *Apprentice* and *apprehend* have the same source; they both relate to getting or seizing. In one sense an apprentice is apprehending knowledge, but in another he is apprenticed or bound to a master. Milwood calls upon the law to apprehend Barnwel; he, in turn, calls upon the law to apprehend her, though this time his conscience as well as his fear make him apprehensive.

> And to the Constable she went, to have him apprehended,
> And shew'd in each degree how far, he had the law offended,
> When *Barnwel* saw her drift, to sea he got straightway,
> Where fear and dread, and conscience sting, upon him still doth stay.

> Unto the Mayor of *London* then, he did a Letter write,
> Wherein his own and *Sara's* faults he did at large recite.
> Whereby she apprehended was, and then to *Ludlow* sent,
> Where she was judg'd, condemn'd and hang'd for murder incont'ent [*sic*];
> And there this gallant quean did die, this was her greatest gains.
> For murder in *Polonia* was Barnwel hang'd in chains.
>
> (185–194)

The reversals, the commercial consciousness, the plot of desire, murder, and betrayal, the narrative disjunctions constitute a broadside ballad that begins as a seventeenth-century imitation of reality but becomes a text with its own history of dispersal. I offer three examples of this. At the end of the seventeenth century the ballad is published with a brief prose biography of George Barnwel called: *The Prentice's Tragedy: or The History of George Barnwell: Being a Fair Warning to Young Men to avoid the Company of Lewd Women.*[19] This generic transformation may be considered a biographical supplement to the ballad. While addressed to a similar audience, it supplies some of the omissions of the ballad. The biographical genre identifies the parents of "Barnwell" and provides an explanation for his "sudden change." He was vulnerable because "he had read diverse Love Romances and found that a Queen fell in love with a *Crispine* that was but a Shoe-maker, and why might not some great Lady (as by her Garb he took her to be) fall in Love with him." The readiness to be deceived was prepared by romances that had become for him a substitute for the Bible. Other omissions or puzzles are also filled in: the kind of "wiles" that Milwood practices and the actions that make Milwood a murderer.

I refer to this biography written by a narrator with strong Puritan feelings and antifeminist prejudices as "dispersing" the ballad because it adds, supplements, and even rejects some of the plot and because it is a different genre; it supplants verse features and oral features by prose meant to be printed. The study of the ballad as literary history thus involves interconnections between a ballad and a brief biography: the forms can be seen as sharing certain moral, religious, and thematic values while, at the same time, becoming differentiated in respect to these values. Also, as a result of the generic shift, it can be seen that the biography introduces the life history of an individual, an attempt to identity "Barnwel" as a person with his own identity.

The generic transformation of the ballad into a tragedy in 1731 by George Lillo, possesses an ideological function. *The London Merchant: or, The History of George Barnwell* not only elevates the character of Barnwell and introduces the merchant as a man concerned with affairs of state; it sets up the behavior of merchants and their apprentices as models of virtue. The play—and George Lillo notes this in his dedication—alters the idea of tragedy:

> tragedy is so far from losing its dignity, by being accommodated to the circumstances of the generality of mankind, that it is more truly august in proportion to the extent of its influence, and the numbers that are properly affected by it: as it is more truly great to be the instrument of good to many, who stand in need of our assistance, than to a very small part of that number.[2]

The literary history that I am writing will, therefore, distinguish between instances of a genre and generic interrelations that share an ideology and those that replace one. And it will demonstrate that each text possesses features that can only be understood critically by being related to the text's own and other genres. The Barnwel ballad, for example, contains dialogues that the narrator presents as direct discourse, but these function within the framework of a song addressed to the youth of England for their edification. In any drama, dialogue becomes the manner in which description, narration, and any other linguistic feature is presented. Moreover, the shift from street song to theater performance is a shift in the nature of the audience and in the artificiality of the presentation. Literary history should offer reasons for this shift, and these reasons will have to explain the simultaneous existence of a past text and its present transformation. The process of understanding will involve, at the very least, a recognition of continuities and discontinuities, of variations within a genre and rewritings of it in other genres.

The process of variation within a genre is most obvious in the versions of the ballad that are published in the eighteenth century and especially in Bishop Thomas Percy's *Reliques of Ancient English Poetry,* published in 1765. This collection included a version of the Barnwel ballad, but this edited version published the poem in quatrains, removed many narrative irregularities and repetitions, and smoothed the rhymes. The effort to create uniformity and correctness at the expense of authenticity is another example—the tragedy is the first—to make a "literary" text out of what was considered a nonliterary street text. The reasons for this are many, and a literary history will have to propose them.

I conclude by noting that literary history is itself a genre. My example has sought to suggest the kind of interweavings that take place within it.

Neither evolutionary development nor endless disruptions are its constituents. Literary history possesses multidimensionality: it reveals formations, transformations, deformations. It seeks to explain relations, interrelations, integrations and disintegrations. The literary historian, as I conceive him, is of his time and so, too, is his history. For this reason, the modern literary historian ought to posit as his aim the history of continuities and changes.

NOTES

1. *New Perspectives in German Literary Criticism*, ed. Richard E. Amacher and Victor Lange (Princeton: Princeton University Press, 1979), 431.

2. Michel Foucault, *Language, Counter Memory, Practice*, ed. Donald F. Bouchard (Ithaca: Cornell University Press, 1977), 154.

3. Ibid., 160–64.

4. *The Works of Thomas Deloney*, ed. Francis O. Mann (Oxford: Clarendon Press, 1912), 599.

5. C. M. Simpson, *The British Broadside Ballad and Its Music* (New Brunswick: Rutgers University Press, 1966), 603. There are numerous discussions of the ballad and its music in books and essays by B. H. Bronson and Cecil Sharp. For a useful and concise statement, see M. J. C. Hodgart, *The Ballads* (New York: Norton, 1962), chap. 3.

6. George Gascoigne, "Certayne Notes of Instruction," in *Elizabethan Critical Essays*, ed. G. Gregory Smith (Oxford: Clarendon Press, 1904), 1 : 54–55.

7. Cyprian Blagden, "Notes on the Ballad Market in the Second Half of the Seventeenth Century," *Studies in Bibliography* 6 (1954): 164. Blagden notes, however, that there are ballads printed on both sides but finds these primarily at the end of the century.

8. Quoted in Alan Bold, *The Ballad* (London: Metheuen, 1979), 71.

9. Victor E. Neuberg, *Popular Literature* (Harmondsworth: Penguin, 1977), 60–62.

10. Samuel Johnson, *Dictionary of the English Language*, 6th ed. (1785); for Addison, see Albert B. Friedman, *The Ballad Revival* (Chicago: University of Chicago Press), chap. 4.

11. "The London Merchant: or, The History of George Barnwell," in *The Plays of George Lillo* (1775; rpt., New York: Garland, 1979), 1 : 139 (act 3, scene 1).

12. Fred Kitson, *The Beggar's Opera* (Cambridge: Cambridge University Press, 1922), 64–79. For a study of ballad opera, see Edmond M. Gagey, *Ballad Opera* (New York: Columbia University Press, 1937), and Joseph S. L. Lowry, "A History of the Introduction and Development of Italian Opera and its Burlesque in England, 1705–1745" (Ph.D. diss., University of Texas at Austin, 1975), chap. 3.

13. I take my text from *British Dramatists from Dryden to Sheridan*, ed. G. H. Nettleton and A. E. Case, rev. G. W. Stone, Jr. (Carbondale: Southern Illinois University Press, 1969), 530.

14. John Dryden, *Of Dramatic Poesy and Other Critical Essays*, ed. George Watson (London: Dent, 1962), 2 : 226.

15. Lines 1–6. I take my text of the ballad from the definitive edition in *The Roxburghe Ballads*, ed. J. Woodfall Ebsworth, 8: First Division (Hartford: Printed for the Ballad Society, 1897). Slightly different versions of the ballad can be consulted at the Houghton Library (Harvard University) and at the British Library. See, for example, a version of the ballad printed in the chapbook "The 'Prentice's Tragedy: or, The History of *George Barnwell:* Being a fair Warning to Young Men to avoid the Company of Lewd Women. Printed for W. O. and sold by the Booksellers of *Pye Corner* and *Londonbridge*" (n.d.; the British Library suggests 1700). Note also the spelling of "Barnwell": after *The London Merchant*, "Barnwell" becomes the standard spelling and is even used by Thomas Percy in his edition of the poem.

16. Ian Donaldson, *The World Upside-Down* (Oxford: Clarendon Press, 1970), 5–6, 7. See also Christopher Hill, *The World Turned Upside-Down* (London: Temple Smith, 1972).

17. *The Reversible World,* ed. Barbara A. Babcock (Ithaca: Cornell University Press, 1978), 25. See also David Kunzle, "World Upside Down: The Iconography of a European Broadsheet Type," in ibid., 39–94.

18. Samuel Richardson, *The Apprentice's Vade Mecum* (1734; facs. rpt., Los Angeles: Augustan Reprint Society, 1975), 2.

19. See n. 15.

20. "The London Merchant," Dedication.

2

Some Patterns in Epitaph and Elegy

Mary Lascelles

The seventeenth and eighteenth centuries comprise the great age of epitaph and elegy in England. Even though the soaring eloquence of the early seventeenth century is ruled out by the plan of this volume, we still have plenty, variety and, at the summit, splendor. This abundance imposes on the rash critic the necessity of choice. Selection entails an endeavor at definition; but these two terms did not always denote what we understand by them now, and their meaning was even then mutable. To offer a wholly satisfying definition of either asks more than I can afford; but I may—indeed, must—circumscribe my undertaking. It is only good manners to tell the reader what not to expect.

Both terms carry the burden of a long and intricate history. Epitaph, originally words spoken at a burial or inscribed on a tomb, has now expanded to include such a composition as this, framed *as though* it were intended for inscription on memorial stone or brass—whereas it has in fact been preserved in manuscript or print. Surviving thus, it may conveniently be distinguished as a *literary epitaph.* The varied and often elusive meanings of elegy, as it has come down from the ancient world and developed since the Renaissance, yield a sense that would be generally recognized in our day as *commemorative verse,* imbued with a sense of personal loss. Thus the epitaph will not be a satirical piece, whose inscription on a tomb is inconceivable, nor will the elegy be pure fiction. There is, moreover, one cupboard door that I have chosen not to open, knowing what would tumble out: a multitude of broadside ballads—popular clamor at the death of notable persons, or muddled morality on the topic of death.

One further explanation, or apology, is due. Although I have kept within the period 1660–1800 in my choice of elegy and literary epitaph, diverging only for an occasional analogue, I have not always been able to follow this course in exemplifying the epitaph proper. Even before the blight of the Victorian monumental mason fell upon church and churchyard, it was perishable: outside, at the mercy of weather; inside, of restoration and even bombing. So, for an apt and vivid illustration to my argument, I sometimes leave Restoration and Augustan decades and range among the centuries before and after.

It may seem strange not to give central place to the most memorable elegy in the English language; but the complexity of Gray's major recasting and manifold revisions, like underwater reefs, forbids direct approach. I must be content, in this brief comparative study, to acknowledge the supremacy of the *Elegy in a Country Churchyard,* leaving interpretation and appreciation in the capable and sensitive hands of R. W. Ketton-Cremer and Dr. Roger Lonsdale.[1] And if I am sometimes impelled to peer between their fingers, that is because the poem says many different things to many different people; and every one of them, to the attentive ear and candid mind, rings true and reverberates.

જાજાજાજાજાજા

To begin with a comparison: if the epitaph and the elegy are set one on either hand, a curious distinction will appear. Of the epitaph alone we are bound to ask: Who is speaking? To what voice must our mind's ear be attuned? Sometimes we are to suppose ourselves listening to the dead man, in earlier centuries imploring the Divine mercy, or asking us to pray for the repose of his soul. Even as late as 1565, traditional piety is perpetuated in Richard Fenn's declaration:

> Of alle I hadde here onlie now I have
> Nine akers wch unto ye poore I gave.[2]

The supposed first person, the voice from beyond the grave, carries an authority very apt for admonition, to which the writers of earlier epitaphs are prone: the age-old theme, *memento mori,* is reduced, in many a country churchyard, to the "uncouth rhymes" that moved Gray's pity:

> Walk softly by and cast an eye
> See how the grass doth grow
> Remember Friend thy life must end
> And here with me you must lay low.[3]

The use of a first-person voice being an understood convention, it can serve various purposes—for example, an affirmation of faith on behalf of the dead:

> Let the wind rage and billows roll
> Hope is the Anchor of my Soul
> It fastens on a land unknown
> And moors me to my Fathers throne.

These words are given to Robert Randell, "lost at sea aged 26."[4] In church-yards round the coast there will be found memorials to those who perished thus. Many of them are stoical in tone, as though recording a natural hazard; but death "at the hands of treacherous pirates" stirs a resentment in which we may surely hear the voices of shipmates.[5]

Epitaphs that make use of the terms of a man's trade or calling suggest some intervention by a fellow craftsman. But who wrote, or prompted, this memorial for "Peter Gedge, Printer"?

> Like a worn type
> He is returned to the Founder
> In hope of being recast in a better and more perfect mould.[6]

Despite the use of the third person, those technical terms are applied with such nicety as to allow a surmise that the printer chose them for himself.

Anyone who has ranged among these inscriptions will have noticed the prevalence of word-play, even simple puns. In a broader style, the black-smith, keystone of the village arch, is made to play merrily on his own predicament in verses which, reported from many parts of the country, have become a favorite with anthologists.

Walter de la Mare, that master of the imaginary epitaph, apologizes for the playful tone heard in many actual epitaphs: "The truth is, times change. What is common human nature in one age is unbecoming levity in another."[7] I would plead rather that grief and affection working on one another can issue in a playfulness that disconcerts the outsider. Some such mood may account for the singularity of a memorial tablet, which shows a man kneeling in prayer, his hat and a key (much the same size) on the ground beside him, and this inscription underneath: "Honest Thomas Cotes, that sometime was porter at Ascot Hall, has now (Alas) left his key, lodg[e], fyre, friends and all to have a roome in heaven This is that good mans grave Reader, prepare for thine, for none can tell but that you two may meet tonight. Farewell. . . . Set up at the app[o]intment and charges of his friend Geo. Houton."[8]

It is time to move on to a further question. No matter who is speaking, to whom are the words addressed? *Siste viator!* In the wayside graveyard of the ancient world as well as the church and churchyard of our own, inscriptions are usually framed as though for the benefit of the passer-by. Wordsworth imagines him pondering a tribute that is "the joint offspring of the worth of the dead and the affections of the living."[9] Johnson, while admitting that such a record must be allowed to err on the side of generosity—"In lapidary inscriptions," he told Burney, "a man is not upon oath"[10]—was provoked by the uniform extravagance of Pope's eulogies to his own sort of exaggeration: "The difficulty in writing epitaphs is to give a

particular and appropriate praise. This, however, is not always to be performed . . . for the greater part of mankind 'have no character at all' . . .
and therefore nothing can be said of them which may not be applied with
equal propriety to a thousand more."[11]

Although reluctant to differ from good authorities, I find Pope's
epitaphs frigid and fanciful—not unlike those vainglorious inscriptions on
the sculptured monuments of that age. As Prior says, "we teach marble to
lie." Such claims indeed did not go unchallenged, whether in the grave
remonstrance of Gray's *Elegy*—

> Nor you, ye Proud, impute to these the fault,
> If Memory o'er their tomb no trophies raise . . .
> Can storied urn or animated bust
> Back to its mansion call the fleeting breath?
> Can Honour's voice provoke the silent dust,
> Or Flattery soothe the dull cold ear of death?

or the plangent defiance of this epitaph:

> If breath were made
> For every man to buy
> The poor man would not live
> The rich would never die.
> Life is a blessing can't be sold
> The ransom is too high.[12]

Happily, not all inscriptions are aimed at astounding and subduing the
reader. The voice supposed to address us from headstone or mural tablet
may "implore the passing tribute of a sigh"—often with the conjuration: "if
you have suffered, or fear to suffer, a like loss, think on mine."

It is not, however, always the passer-by, the living reader, to whom the
words are addressed. The message may be framed as though spoken to the
dead. As in the elegy, with its traditional promise of consolation, it may
carry reassurance, though seldom with such poignant tenderness as in
Henry King's "Exequy." In the Christian centuries, passages from the Bible
are most often used: "many a holy text around she strews."[13] In our century, reassurance may be offered in terms of such Lucretian comfort as
Housman chooses for his literary epitaph, "Wake not for the World-heard
Thunder"—less famous but perhaps more moving than his "Epitaph on an
Army of Mercenaries." The dead soldiers are assured that, having given
their all, they may sleep forever:

> Sleep, my lad; the French are landed,
> London's burning, Windsor's down;
> Clasp your cloak of earth about you,
> We must man the ditch without you,
> March unled and fight short-handed,

> Charge to fall and swim to drown.
> Duty, friendship, bravery o'er,
> Sleep away, lad; wake no more.[14]

Prior may have thought like this about his own death, but he is not so explicit as to the mortality of the soul.

Matthew Prior's verses "For his own Epitaph" are among the strangest and most subtle in that small but notable group of literary epitaphs composed by poets for themselves. These epitaphs appear to be prompted by a variety of motives, variously combined: "this is how I would wish to be remembered"; "this is my claim to honorable discharge"; "this is what I find when I take a last look into myself." Thomas Hardy's "Afterwards" alone is simple; he is concerned with impressions left on those who knew him. Robert Louis Stevenson's "Requiem" survives in so many states that the simplicity of the final version (for which it is remembered) may be deceptive.[15] Walter de la Mare's "The Last Chapter" subtly and delicately avails itself of that traditional vein of humor latent in language drawn from the dead man's former profession:

> I am living more alone now than I did;
> This life tends inward, as the body ages;
> And what is left of its strange book to read
> Quickens in interest with the last few pages.
>
> Problems abound. Its authorship? A sequel?
> Its hero-villain, whose ways so little mend?
> The plot? still dark. The style? a shade unequal.
> And what of the dénouement? And, the end?[16]

I have not found, nor do I expect to find, many of these literary "epitaphs for the poet himself" in the period under review, but two are discoverable, and (though in very different measure) memorable. Edmund Waller's quiet voice and unassuming manner are out of fashion now except with the common reader, who cherishes the few lines he chooses to retain from a single poem:

> The Soul's dark Cottage, batter'd and decay'd,
> Lets in new Light thro' chinks that time has made.
> Stronger by weakness, wiser Men become
> As they draw near to their Eternal home.

Its original title, "Of the Last Verses in the Book," and the endorsement preserved in the family, "The last verses my dear father made,"[17] qualify it for inclusion under this head. Waller looks into himself and across the threshold, and comes to terms with what he discovers.

Prior's epitaph for himself has not haunted the popular imagination as have lines from Waller's "Last Verses" and Stevenson's "Requiem," but, once known, it is not easily forgotten. He begins airily borrowing for his opening a canceled line from the mock-epitaph he had written some fourteen years ago for his "Joanna or Janneton, Jinny or Joan": "Doctors give physic by way of prevention."[18] He will write to forestall "False Witness at Court." His life, precarious in more than one sense, has taught him to look warily forward: in its "party-colour'd" course, "High Hopes he conceiv'd, and he smother'd great fears." Looking backward, he sees those mingled strands of dangerous diplomacy and carefree privacy, and essays a self-portrait. He does not summon witnesses—as Swift does, only to flout them, in his elaborate *apologia*, *Verses on the Death of Dr. Swift.* He has rather the air of the painter alone in his studio, intent on his face in the looking-glass, contemplative and quizzical.

Presently, hovering overhead like Chaucer's Troilus, he looks down on the earthly life of man:

> And whirl'd in the round, as the Wheel turn'd about
> He found Riches had wings, and knew Man was but Dust.

Of a resting place, even for this dust, he cannot be certain: there are too many hazards in life and in death:

> If his Bones lye in Earth, roll in Sea, fly in Air
> To Fate We must yield, and the things are the same,
> And if passing Thou giv'st Him a Smile, or a Tear
> He cares not—Yet prythee be kind to his Fame.

In its idiosyncratic treatment of traditional themes, the literary epitaph draws near to the elegy.

❧❧❧❧❧❧❧

I suggested at the outset that the word *elegy*, for present-day readers, will signify commemorative verse, imbued with a sense of personal loss; but personal need not mean peculiar to the speaker. There is a great tradition, running from Simonides at Thermopylae, through Abraham Lincoln at Gettysburg, to the war poets of our own tragic century, in which the single voice expresses for many a shared grief. This voice falls silent in Restoration and Augustan England—not only because church and churchyard epitaphs usually commemorate those men who came home one by one to die. The soldier who "fought in all Queen Anne's wars" and those that followed is remembered as a solitary figure.[19]

In the elegy that does express peculiar loss, it is remarkable how often, and how strongly, this loss is associated with a sense of place. Not only does the strain "We were together here, and happy; I am here alone" recur; it lies at the very heart of the poem. This is confirmed by its survival in anthologies and popular recollection. Thus the Cambridge memories that

Johnson chose for commendation in Cowley's "On the Death of Mr William Hervey"[20] retain their place, no matter how the poem is pruned of less memorable stanzas:

> Ye fields of *Cambridge,* our dear *Cambridge,* say,
> Have ye not seen us walking every day?
> Was there a *Tree* about which did not know
> The *Love* betwixt us two?[21]

Likewise, Gray, discussing Lyttelton's *Monody* with Walpole, discriminates in favor of the lines that associate past happiness with place: "If it were all like the fourth stanza, I should be excessively pleased."[22]

> In vain I look around
> O'er the well-known ground,
> My Lucy's wonted footsteps to descry;
> Where oft we us'd to walk,
> Where oft in tender talk
> We saw the summer sun go down the sky;
> Nor by yon fountain's side,
> Nor where its waters glide
> Along the valley, can she now be found . . .[23]

This association of past happiness and present loss with a remembered place is the great tide on which *Thyrsis* rides, as does passage after passage of *In Memoriam.* It cannot, of course, carry the elegy whose freight is a fictitious tragedy, such as Pope's "Verses to the Memory of an Unfortunate Lady."[24] Yet something of its power may be felt in that strange poem found among Prior's manuscripts by A. R. Waller, and called by him "Jinny the Just": the woman and her manner of life are by no means a figment of the imagination; only her death is imaginary.

Neither personal loss nor its association with place is to be looked for in those poems that I can only call commemoration by request, such as Dryden's *Eleanora: a Panegyrical Poem dedicated to the Memory of the Late Countess of Abingdon.* Formal panegyric is no substitute for the claim that the dead man or woman is missed somewhere. Even Anne Killigrew performs her prodigies in a void. These "funeral poems," to borrow Johnson's designation of Tickell's "On the Death of Mr. Addison,"[25] are, however, not likely to make part of our idea of elegy, if only because nothing resembling them is written now; and that is surely no loss. Not all Dryden's versatile brilliance, nor his excellence in other poetic kinds, can reconcile me to the tradition in which so much of his commemorative verse is written.

Notwithstanding his admiration for the poetic technique of the poem that he calls "the *Ode on Killigrew*," Johnson found much to disquiet him in this tradition.[26] His condemnation of imagery drawn from pagan myth, especially in a Christian context, hardly needs illustrating: it plows a straight furrow from the early "Essay on Epitaphs" to the *Lives of the Poets.*[27] It may be objected that one such vein of imagery, the pastoral, had once served poets well and was presently to be recalled into service; but the pastoral elegy, having its own clear idiom, must be distinguished from the sort of diffuse paganism that perplexes by its ambiguities and perturbs by its evasions in the typical funeral poem of this age. Heaven is frequently and familiarly spoken of, but appears to be the residence of a patron, to whom favored clients have access. There is no appeal to divine mercy; these paragons do not require it. Johnson may be thought to press too heavily his objection to an accepted convention, but I cannot dissociate myself from his judgment: "In the monkish ages, however ignorant and unpolished, the epitaphs were drawn up with far greater propriety, than can be shown in those which more enlightened times have produced."[28]

Among the literary epitaphs of that age there is one that is neither peculiar to it nor constricted by its conventions. Represented in the earlier years of the seventeenth century by the rhetoric, or eloquence, of the panegyrics on Shakespeare and Donne, it had since then become more circumspect: I mean, tributes paid to a dead poet by his fellows. The loss they express may be in some sort personal, as it is for Dryden writing on John Oldham, but, beyond that, these writers claim that this man's death has impoverished their own community: he will be missed in the commonwealth of letters. Such a tribute is often associated with the idea of unfulfilment: Oldham, Keats, Clough are inheritors of unfulfilled renown. But whether the poet has died young or in the fullness of years, fellowship prompts the endeavor to characterize his genius in a literary portrait. Such is the aim of Cowper's "Epitaph on Dr. Johnson":

> Whose prose was eloquence by wisdom taught,
> The graceful vehicle of virtuous thought;
> Whose verse may claim—grave, masculine, and strong,
> Superior praise to the mere poet's song. . . .[29]

Johnson is portrayed as a great prose writer and powerful in his own kind of verse, which is not lyrical.

To discover how far the elegy, at its greatest, can transcend the literary epitaph—and by how much further the mere obituary—we need the guidance of Gray and Johnson, their theory and their practice. Johnson's gravest charge against Dryden's "Threnodia Augustalis," that "it has neither tenderness nor dignity," implies that these are, for him, indispensable qualities.[30] Gray, in the letter to Walpole from which I have already quoted, maintains that "Nature and sorrow, and tenderness, are the true genius of such things . . . poetical ornaments are foreign to the purpose; for they only show a man is not sorry;—and devotion worse; for it teaches him, that he ought not to be sorry, which is all the pleasure of the thing."[31] Johnson would have concurred as to Nature; but not, judging by his own practice, as to devotion. In their opinions on this subject the two men come closer together than either might have been willing to admit. Seriousness of feeling is at the center of an elegy; the frivolity of display is banished to the circumference, or further still. Something more may be learned from Johnson's concession, when he was rasped in argument by claims for Gray's odes: he could find "but two good stanzas in Gray's poetry, which are in his 'Elegy in a Country Churchyard.'" This was one:

> For who to dumb Forgetfulness a prey,
> This pleasing anxious being e'er resigned,
> Left the warm precincts of the cheerful day,
> Nor cast one longing lingering look behind?

The other he said he had forgotten.[32] The remark, agreeing left-handedly with his final tribute to the *Elegy* in his *Life of Gray*,[33] may be allowed to count rather for what it gives than what it withholds; and the choice of stanza for praise implies assent to a significant position. If it is, as Johnson stipulates, to wake an echo in the mind and heart of the reader, the elegy must resound in a wider context than is signalized by the death of an individual: it must have something to say about the human predicament in relation to death—not as a topic for trite moralizing but as an experience that it is our business to contemplate. In that stanza of Johnson's choosing, and in the one that follows, Gray dwells on its loneliness—a condition that he knew only too well, but does not appropriate to himself. Man appears, in one respect, less fortunate than the other creatures: they are either gregarious or solitary and, to judge by their behavior, in no doubt as to where they belong. It is the supposedly rational being who can unite in himself fears alike of company and solitude, the latter often prevailing in the hour of death. Our peculiar consciousness makes the change mysterious to us. Though nowhere so explicitly as in our own age,[34] this sense of bewilderment in face of a mystery pervades the *Elegy*. For Gray, a childless man—one, moreover, who has been truly called "a solitary living shoot from a weakening stock"—it issues in the desire to be remembered, which he attributes to the generations of village people whose poverty had hindered them from achieving anything memorable.[35]

At first sight, the *Elegy* and Johnson's poem "On the Death of Dr. Robert Levet" seem to lie far apart: the one so complex, the other a simple piece of commemorative verse for a single, and singular, individual. At a deep level, however, there is a notable affinity between them. Both have the power to evoke response beyond the apparent reach of either subject. Both are moving and therefore must be reckoned approachable. Successive generations of common readers have borne witness to the authenticity of Gray's approach. Johnson's poem reaches the heart, not only of the faithful but even of those to whom it is presented without ascription or comment. This is surely strange: the personifications are as far from our idiom as the conceits of the seventeenth century were from his. Some of the language has proved perishable—the vocabulary, not the syntax. Johnson does not, like Gray, appear to pine for the more highly inflected Latin; but in the phrase "social comforts," for example, we must beware of the change that has degraded "comforts" to mere things. "Officious" still kept for Johnson its benign meaning and had not come to suggest that good offices may be inopportune. The *Dictionary* takes account, as though reluctantly, of impending deterioration in both words, but for his part, Johnson holds to the original and etymologically justified meaning.[36] And if, for this reason, the language is no longer fully charged with pathos, neither were the circumstances of Levet's death pathetic: he had died as the man Johnson portrays would have wished to die:

> The busy day, the peaceful night,
> Unfelt, uncounted, glided by . . .
>
> Then with no throbbing fiery pain,
> No cold gradations of decay,
> Death broke at once the vital chain,
> And free'd his soul the nearest way.

Even the sense of loss is not unassuageable for Johnson: he knows that he will miss his old companion, but it cannot be for long. Nothing matches the poignancy of Gray's lament for Richard West: "My lonely anguish melts no heart but mine." Indeed, Johnson evidently took pleasure in circulating the poem among friends.[37] For whom, then, do we grieve? I suggest that, even as Gray's melancholy sense of his own situation overflows into compassion for the country poor starved of opportunity, so Johnson's response to his own predicament overflows into sympathy with the sick poor of London, to whom Levet had ministered, and of whom, Saunders Welch once told him, more than a thousand died yearly from starvation and neglect.[38] It was where

> . . . hopeless anguish pour'd his groan,
> And lonely want retir'd to die

that Levet would be missed.

ช่างช่างช่างช่าง

It is time to gather up the threads of this brief and slender argument. I have tried to trace patterns of likeness and difference among these kindred sorts of writing rather than pursue the particular resemblances that suggest indebtedness. Two instances must serve to indicate the direction such pursuit would take.

I mentioned earlier a minatory epitaph from Berwick-on-Tweed. Versions of this theme appear in various places: one is reported from Elgin Cathedral; one occurs in *Folk Songs of the Upper Thames*.[39] All contain in some form lines that seem to derive from a distich to be found on the last page of the 1651 *Reliquiae* of Sir Henry Wotton, where they are called an "Epigram":

> If breath were made for every man to buy
> The poor man could not live: the rich would never die.

This alone remains constant, though—allowing for defacement—the opening and close appear to vary. I surmise that a rhyming couplet can easily be carried in the average human memory and so become current, whether in popular ballad or epitaph.

In my other example, while the sentiment remains constant, the verbal echo is faint and fitful. Pope's Victorian editors observed, regarding two lines in his epitaph for Simon Harcourt,

> Who ne'er knew Joy, but Friendship might divide,
> Or gave his Father grief, but when he dy'd,

that the "conceit" in the second was already well worn, giving numerous parallels, some not very close.[40] When John Booth died at the age of seven, his parents found expression for their sorrow in this couplet:

> To him a Length of days in mercy God denied
> Who never gave his parents pain but when he died.[41]

The later version may be less elegant, but it is appropriate to the loss of a child and moving in its simplicity. If the resemblance is not coincidental, then I surmise that, in popular thought and practice, "what I can carry in my head is mine." Sir Henry Wotton's justly celebrated couplet,

> He first deceas'd; she for a little tri'd
> To live without him; lik'd it not and di'd,

is said to have been used in like circumstances to those of Sir Albert Morton and his wife.

I am not, however, concerned with the dull subject of plagiarism. Coincidence and indebtedness are to be expected where countless people, ranging from the most to the least articulate, respond to a common prompting. The proper analogy is surely musical: these are variations on a theme, though without the acknowledgment customary among musicians. I have noticed but one intimation of indebtedness, and that tacit: a line borrowed from the epitaph that Johnson, with good-natured professionalism, improved for Claudy Phillips,

Till angels wake thee with a note like thine,

is set within quotation marks, when it is borrowed for a Vicar-choral of Lichfield Cathedral.[42] Perhaps variations on a traditional air would be the right musical parallel for many of these echoes.

Wherein lies the power of one or another among these variations on theme or air to engage the sympathy and linger in the memory? Tenderness, dignity, simplicity—we acknowledge these requirements, mindful that the simplicity of one age will not always be that of another. Can anything further be inferred from my small assembly of illustrations?

The great poets are often found to be more illuminating in their practice than in their theory. Gray discounts devotion in this kind of writing, only to vindicate its presence in both versions of his *Elegy*. Johnson, young and angry, defies the writer of an epitaph to convey the uniqueness of the individual and, when old and benignant, shows not only that it can be done but also how to do it: by dwelling on one particular endowment or achievement, "the single talent well employ'd." For a humble counterpart to Levet's service to the sick poor, consider that given to Durham Cathedral by John Brimley (1576):

> Who praysed God with hand and voice
> By musickes heavenlie harmonie
> Dull myndes he made in God rejoice
> His soul into ye Heavens is lyft
> To prayse him still that gave ye gyft.

These were men who will be missed *somewhere*. Finally, there must be a sense of wider implications: Prior's speculative curiosity, the sympathy of Gray and Johnson, thoughts reflected in

> an eye
> That hath kept watch o'er man's mortality.*

NOTES

*While I owe thanks to friends for help with this little undertaking, I wish particularly to acknowledge that of my sisters, who shared with me their collections of church and churchyard epitaphs.

1. R. W. Ketton-Cremer, *Thomas Gray: A Biography* (Cambridge: Cambridge University Press, 1955), and his British Academy lecture, *Lapidary Verse* (Oxford: Oxford University Press, 1959); Roger Lonsdale's British Academy lecture, *The Poetry of Thomas Gray: Versions of the Self* (Oxford: Oxford University Press, 1973). See also Lonsdale's edition of the *Poems of Gray, Collins and Goldsmith* (London: Longman, 1969), the text I have used in quoting Gray.

2. Inscription at Foulsham, Norfolk; brass. This is the theme of the famous *Lykewake Dirge*.

3. Bintree, Norfolk, 1758.

4. Cley, Norfolk, 1821.

5. E.g., David Bartleman, St. Nicholas, Great Yarmouth, Norfolk, 1781; David May, Southwold, Suffolk, 1819.

6. Bury St. Edmunds, Suffolk, 1818. He "first established the Newspaper published in this town."

7. Walter de la Mare, "Strangers and Pilgrims," in *Ding Dong Bell* (London: Faber and Faber, 1936), 87. An old verger is supposed to be speaking.

8. 1648; a brass plate, informally but not unskillfully engraved, in Wing Church, Buckinghamshire.

9. "Essay upon Epitaphs," in Wordsworth, *Literary Criticism*, ed. Nowell Smith (Oxford: H. Mitford, 1925).

10. *Boswell's Life of Johnson*, ed. G. B. Hill and L. F. Powell (Oxford: Clarendon Press, 1934), 2:407.

11. *Lives of the English Poets*, ed. G. B. Hill (Oxford: Clarendon Press, 1905), 3:263–64 (reprinted from *The Universal Visitor*, May 1756, and appended to the *Life of Pope*).

12. The English Church, Berwick-on-Tweed, 1794. For further consideration of these lines, see p. 43 above.

13. "She" is "the unlettered muse," presiding genius of the churchyard.

14. A. E. Housman, *Last Poems* (London: Richards Press, 1922), xxix.

15. See the notes to Stevenson's *Collected Poems*, ed. Janet Adam Smith (London: Rupert Hart-Davis, 1950).

16. Walter de la Mare, *The Complete Poems* (London: Faber and Faber, 1969), 380.

17. See Edmund Waller, *Poems*, ed. G. Thorn Drury (London: Lawrence and Bullen, 1893), notes on this poem. Anthologists miss the point when they alter the title.

18. *The Literary Works of Matthew Prior*, ed. H. B. Wright and M. K. Spears (Oxford: Clarendon Press, 1959), 1:461.

19. E.g., Sir William Goode (1681–1751), St. Nicholas, Great Yarmouth.

20. *Lives of the English Poets*, 1:163. Admittedly, Johnson is here intent on an invidious comparison with the pastoral disguise under which Cambridge appears in "Lycidas."

21. Abraham Cowley, *Poems*, ed. A. R. Waller (Cambridge: Cambridge University Press, 1905), 34.

22. Thomas Gray, *Letters*, ed. Paget Toynbee and Leonard Whibley (Oxford: Clarendon Press, 1935), 1:288–89.

23. George, Lord Lyttleton, "To the Memory of a Lady, lately deceased. A Monody," in *The Oxford Book of Eighteenth-Century Verse* (Oxford: Clarendon Press, 1926); the poem opens with this stanza.

24. See Ian Jack, "The Elegy as Exorcism: Pope's 'Verses to the Memory of an Unfortunate Lady,'" in *Augustan Worlds: New Essays in Eighteenth-Century Literature*, ed. J. C. Hilson et al. (Leicester: Leicester University Press, 1978), 69–83.

25. *Lives of the English Poets*, 2:310.

26. Ibid., 1:439.

27. In *The Gentleman's Magazine*, 1740.

28. "Essay on Epitaphs," in *Literary Works of Matthew Prior* (Oxford: William Pickering, 1825), 5:264.

29. William Cowper, *Poetical Works*, ed. H. S. Milford (London: Oxford University Press, 1967), 363.

30. *Lives of the English Poets*, 1:438.

31. Gray, *Letters*, 1:289.

32. *Boswell's Life of Johnson*, 2:327–28.

33. *Lives of the English Poets*, 3:441–42.

34. E.g., in Robert Bridges, "On a Dead Child":

     Unwilling, alone we embark,
     And the things we have seen and known and have heard of fail us. . . .

35. Ketton-Cremer, *Thomas Gray,* 2.

36. The new meanings follow the definitions and illustrations.

37. See Johnson, *Poems,* ed. D. Nichol Smith and E. L. McAdam, 2d ed. (Oxford: Clarendon Press, 1974), notes to this poem (233).

38. *Boswell's Life of Johnson,* 3 : 401.

39. *Folk Songs of the Upper Thames,* ed. Alfred Williams (London: Duckworth, 1923).

40. Alexander Pope, *Works,* ed. W. Elwin and W. J. Courthope (London: John Murray, 1871–89), 4 : 383.

41. St. John's, Stamford, Lincolnshire, 1799.

42. John Saville, "48 years vicar-choral of this Cathedral," 1803.

3

A "Perpetual Torrent": Dryden's Lucretian Style

Emrys Jones

Dryden's translation of a few passages from Lucretius appeared almost exactly midway between his two chief religious poems, *Religio Laici* and *The Hind and the Panther.* The conjunction provokes thought. Lucretius was notoriously the great poet of doctrinaire materialism and atheism, so that, poetically speaking, in passing from his Anglican poem (November 1682) to his Catholic poem (April 1687), Dryden chose to travel via the most coherently argued, most intransigent, and greatest anti-religious poetry of the Western tradition. That he freely chose this route should be stressed. His Lucretius, which appeared in *Sylvae* in January 1683, was no externally imposed task, reluctantly undertaken and languidly performed. Dryden chose both the poet and the passages. He wrote with evident pleasure, even delight; and in the preface to *Sylvae* he speaks of the finished product with undisguised satisfaction.

His Lucretius was not only voluntarily undertaken; it engaged the full weight of his poetic attention. It is a great success, and the California editor rightly claims it to be "one of Dryden's masterpieces." Although neglected by the poetry-reading public, its quality has not gone unrecognized in the present century: the editor mentions T. S. Eliot and Geoffrey Grigson, though he fails to name Mark Van Doren, whose book (1920) prompted Eliot's essay and who singled out the Lucretius along with the Juvenal as Dryden's great triumph in verse translation. More recently, Charles Tomlinson has included a long section of the Lucretius in his *Oxford Book of Verse in English Translation* (1980), and says in his introduction: "If I had to give my vote to our greatest translator, it would go to Dryden."[1]

In this essay I want to describe a few of the qualities that distinguish these Lucretian poems. They have never attracted much close critical attention and have obviously suffered from the assumption that verse translations are in some way not really poems at all but an inferior order of production. But Dryden's practice as a translator, departing boldly from the original when it suited him, and intent above all on making a new and independent English poem, should long ago have shown up that assumption for the irrelevance it is. Dryden's Lucretian style has never been much discussed; indeed, the brilliant and diverse stylistic inventions of Dryden's translations are still generally under-described, although stylistic appropriateness was a matter to which Dryden clearly devoted a great deal of thought.

There is, however, one account of the Lucretian poems which I must glance at first before I proceed with my own. This is an essay by Norman Austin, still the most ambitious treatment of the subject, called "Translation as Baptism: Dryden's Lucretius."[2] This essay contains much valuable information concerning Dryden's use both of earlier editors of Lucretius and of earlier English translators, notably his immediate predecessor Thomas Creech. (Creech's heroic couplet version of the complete poem had appeared only a couple of years previously: Oxford 1682, London 1683.) Nonetheless, the argument put forward by Austin, as indicated by his title, seems to me wholly misleading; and it is, at the very least, regrettable that his views should have been taken over wholesale by Earl Miner, the California editor of these translations. No one who uses Miner's edition can overlook Austin's views, which are presented at the head of the commentary as if they were self-evidently true.

Mr. Austin believes that Dryden, a convinced Christian himself, was perturbed by Lucretius's programmatic atheism and that he sought a way of softening the impact of his poetry by "Christianizing" him. What Dryden did, according to Austin, was so to intensify the horrific bleakness, the unmitigated desolateness, of Lucretius's view of life as to make his pessimistic Epicureanism undermine itself: "Dryden has used Lucretius to expose the destitution of pagan philosophies." For Lucretius, "Every man enters the world under a curse"; and Austin quotes one of the passages translated by Dryden on the helpless newborn baby crying in an alien world:

> From the first moment of his hapless Birth,
> Straight with forebodeing cryes he fills the Room:
> (Too true presages of his future doom.)
>
> (5. 6–8)

"Dryden's Lucretius," Austin goes on, "yearns, albeit in pagan ignorance, for the event [i.e., the Redemption] which will remove that original curse. Was ever pagan poet closer to Christian revelation?" Austin's argument reaches its rhetorical climax in the final paragraph of the essay:

> Under Dryden's guidance Lucretius has become one of the best arguments for the positive ethical value of the classics. For Lucretius, the Epicurean, the atheist, the poet of the secular, once baptized by Dryden

in the English Thames, rises up from the waters one of the strongest of Christian apologists from pagan antiquity. His is a soul in anguish awaiting the Christian vision. (600–1)

I doubt if I am the only reader to have been startled by this passage: Lucretius, of all poets, "a soul in anguish awaiting the Christian vision"!

It may be asked how Dryden effects his "baptism" of Lucretius—about which he is altogether silent in the preface to *Sylvae*. Austin can point to nothing unequivocal in the text of the translations but has to rely on minute departures from the Latin: a "slight excision" (381), "one small expression" (592), "the discreetest implication" (599). That is to say, Austin brings to a few of Dryden's unobtrusive distortions of the original his own tendentious "Christianizing" interpretation, which ignores any of the other possible ways of interpreting these same departures from the original. If Dryden heightens the vehemence of Lucretius, intensifying (for example) the scorn with which Nature upbraids old men who are unwilling to die, or increasing the rabid ferocity of the sexual drive as described in the fourth book, he must do so because he is trying to show the untenability of a materialistic outlook and not because (as a less tendentious reader might argue) he is trying to communicate Lucretius's own characteristically vehement manner as vividly as possible. Certainly there is nothing explicit in Dryden's text, no overt distortion of doctrine, to which Austin can appeal as conclusively establishing his "baptismal" reading. Yet this misinterpretation, as I see it, has infected the California edition, as for instance in its note on Dryden's line: "A Soul serene, a body void of pain" (2.23). The note reads: "A Christianizing of Lucretius. Cf. Creech: 'A body free of pains.'"[3] The innocent reader may wonder where the "Christianizing" appears, for although there is nothing corresponding to this line in the Latin, Dryden is merely amplifying Lucretius, not distorting him in the interests of a Christian reading. No reader, I think, unprompted by this note, would think of taking the line in any other than a pagan—that is, "Lucretian"—sense.

It is in any case unfortunate that neither Norman Austin in his 1968 article nor Earl Miner in his 1969 edition should mention the most scholarly study to date of the subject of Lucretius in English in the early Augustan period: W. B. Fleischmann's *Lucretius and English Literature 1680–1740*. This book painstakingly locates Dryden's Lucretius in its full seventeenth-century context of other Lucretian writings: "Dryden's view of Lucretius coincided with the traditional humanistic acceptance of Lucretius the poet and rejection of the Epicurean metaphysics".[4] Fleischmann takes a judicious commonsense view of what Dryden was doing: Dryden as a Christian himself deplores Lucretius's dogmatic insistence on the mortality of the soul and the nonexistence of a future life (as is clear in Dryden's preface) but makes no attempt to disguise these doctrines, accepting that they are the essential foundations for his entire system. What we are concerned with, then, is not a "Christianized" poem but a translation or, rather, a recreation, of a pagan—a very pagan—poem by a poet who happened to be a practicing Christian.

It is, I think, unreal to talk of Dryden's Lucretius in isolation from the substance and quality of Lucretius's own poem. If Dryden's translation is a "masterpiece," it is so largely because the *De rerum natura* is itself a very great poem—"the greatest poem in Latin," according to one classical scholar who has shown himself to be especially responsive to poetic values.[5] According to this view, Lucretius is greater even than Virgil: he has a greater subject, and he brings to it more urgency and a more wholehearted commitment to his undertaking. Lucretius is the most serious of all the Roman poets, and his seriousness is inseparable from an inquiring, skeptical, exhilarating sense of actuality. Van Doren has praised Dryden's Lucretius and his Juvenal as his two great triumphs of translation. Yet alongside Lucretius, Juvenal must be shown up as a magnificently resourceful performer rather than as someone genuinely grappling with the world as it is; Lucretius's concern is not with rhetorical themes, however grandly conceived, but with fundamental realities that must be faced by the entire human race.[6] Juvenal is certainly entertaining: he gives Dryden at any rate "as much pleasure as I can bear." Lucretius, on the other hand, engages the reader in a way that almost transcends what he ordinarily expects of literature. In one respect, Lucretius seems positively unliterary, in that he deals with matters usually considered beyond the range of literary treatment.

But Lucretius's unliterary sense of reality was, one may conjecture, exactly what appealed to Dryden. And it is in this respect that his Lucretian versions may be said to have an affinity with *Religio Laici* and *The Hind and the Panther*. They are all about matters of urgent import; they all have a bearing on a man's stance with regard to ultimate reality. From this point of view, Lucretius's poem is not at all out of place in the company of the other two poems. So when in *Religio Laici* Dryden writes,

> For MY Salvation must its Doom receive,
> Not from what OTHERS but what *I* believe,
>
> (303–4)

he is speaking with the unqualified urgency and sincerity—a religious sincerity—that is everywhere to be found in the atheistic *De rerum natura;* indeed, like Dryden, with his weighted use of "must," Lucretius is also centrally concerned with necessity, with what is objectively so in the universe and therefore with what men *must* do. Dryden in short found Lucretius congenial because he was on the one hand scientific, rationalistic, and this-worldly (all qualities attractive to Dryden), and on the other intensely religious in the quality of his seriousness; scientifically frank about man's sexual nature, yet high-minded and high-principled: a zealously devout atheist.[7] If Dryden could not accept Lucretius's atheism, he must intuitively have found his materalism at least not difficult to entertain, for his own sensibility had a strong materialist strain to it.[8]

It must be stressed, then, that Dryden responded profoundly to Lucretius and that his translation was not a matter of merely turning Latin hexameters into heroic couplets but of ingesting as completely as possible his philosophical outlook, his personal temperament, his artistic sensibility, and his more narrowly poetic way of handling words. The year before Dryden translated Lucretius, the Earl of Roscommon had justified a methodical cultivation of empathy in his *Essay on Translated Verse* (1684), a poem to which Dryden appeals three times in his preface to *Sylvae:*

> Examine how your Humour is inclin'd,
> And which the *Ruling Passion* of your Mind;
> Then seek a *Poet* who *your* way do's bend
> And chuse an *Author* as you chuse a *Friend:*
> United by this *Sympathetic Bond,*
> You grow *Familiar, Intimate,* and *Fond;*
> Your *Thoughts,* your *Words,* your *Stiles,* your *Souls* agree,
> No longer his *Interpreter,* but *He.*[9]

Translation gave Dryden the opportunity to assume, if only temporarily, a different poetic identity. His own personal identity may have been, or may have seemed to him, a very fluid one; if so, it would have given him a powerful satisfaction to become for a time someone whose sense of self was more stable than his own, more aggressively or obdurately fixed, more confident of its own right to exist.

All this is made clear in Dryden's remarkable portrait of Lucretius's literary personality in the preface, which shows how consciously Dryden strove to recreate Lucretius in his own English terms:

> If I am not mistaken, the distinguishing Character of *Lucretius;* (I mean of his Soul and Genius) is a certain kind of noble pride, and positive assertion of his Opinions. He is every where confident of his own reason, and assuming an absolute command not only over his vulgar Reader, but even his Patron *Memmius.* For he is always bidding him attend, as if he had the Rod over him; and using a Magisterial authority, while he instructs him. From his time to ours, I know none so like him, as our Poet and Philosopher of *Malmsbury.* This is that perpetual Dictatorship, which is exercis'd by *Lucretius;* who though often in the wrong, yet seems to deal *bonâ fide* with his Reader, and tells him nothing but what he thinks; in which plain sincerity, I believe he differs from our *Hobbs,* who cou'd not but be convinc'd, or at least doubt of some eternal Truths which he has oppos'd. But for *Lucretius,* he seems to disdain all manner of Replies, and is so confident of his cause, that he is before hand with his Antagonists; Urging for them, whatever he imagin'd they cou'd say, and leaving them as he supposes, without an objection for the future. All this too, with so

much scorn and indignation, as if he were assur'd of the Triumph, before
he enter'd into the Lists. From this sublime and daring Genius of his, it
must of necessity come to pass, that his thoughts must be Masculine, full
of Argumentation, and that sufficiently warm. From the same fiery temper proceeds the loftiness of his Expressions, and the perpetual torrent
of his Verse, where the barrenness of his Subject does not too much
constrain the quickness of his Fancy. For there is no doubt to be made,
but that he cou'd have been every where as Poetical, as he is in his
Descriptions, and in the Moral part of his Philosophy, if he had not aim'd
more to instruct in his Systeme of Nature, than to delight. But he was
bent upon making *Memmius* a Materialist, and teaching him to defie an
invisible power: In short, he was so much an Atheist, that he forgot
sometimes to be a Poet.

(10–11)

Dryden is under no illusions as to the wrongness of Lucretius's beliefs; but
that is not going to deter him from striving, as strenuously as he can, to
assume the personality of that same Lucretius. At any rate, immediately
after the passage just quoted, he goes on to say: "These are the considerations which I had of that Author, before I attempted to translate some parts
of him. And accordingly I lay'd by my natural Diffidence and Scepticism
for a while, to take up that Dogmatical way of his, which as I said, is so
much his Character, as to make him that individual Poet." And so, in the
five extracts that follow, Dryden lays aside his own "Character" to take up
that of Lucretius.

The salient features of Dryden's Lucretian style can all be studied in the
most impressive of the extracts, that from the third book, "Against the Fear
of Death," and in what follows I shall confine myself to this extract. In his
valuable edition of the Latin text of book 3,[10] E. J. Kenney shows that the
book can be analyzed into three parts: (1) Introduction (1–93); (2) Argument: the soul is (a) Material, and (b) hence mortal (94–829); and (3) Conclusion (830–1094): death is not to be feared. Dryden chose to translate
only the concluding section, which can stand on its own as a complete unit.
This section forms what is technically known as a diatribe. As Kenney
brings out clearly, Lucretius used two distinct styles in the *De rerum natura,* a
scientific or expository style (represented in book 3 in lines 94–829) and a
non-expository style that, unlike the first, is emotional and suasive (represented in lines 830–1094). For this second style Lucretius used the methods
of diatribe, the sermon-lectures of the popular preacher-philosophers who
harangued audiences on large philosophical and ethical themes. Vehemence was, says Kenney, "an essential feature of the diatribe style"; and just
as the satirical element was an important part of the diatribe mixture, so
satire is "a profoundly important characteristic" of Lucretius's poem. Indeed, "it was, it seems, Lucretius who first harnessed the power of satire
and applied it to the systematic exposure of error, folly, and superstition"
(11). Furthermore, by combining the partially satiric diatribe style with the

main literary tradition of literary epos, Lucretius, argues Kenney, "laid the foundations of a tradition of satirical writing that has flourished down to modern times" (15).

In view of the highly emotional qualities of those parts of the poem translated by Dryden, the brief characterization of Lucretius given by Earl Miner in the California edition must be found somewhat inadequate and even misleading: "That blending of moral philosophy, science, and reasoning poetry which is characteristic of Lucretius" (277). This is misleading in that it quite fails to prepare the reader for the high emotional temperature, the essentially vehement address, of the extracts that follow. It would be more helpful to bear in mind Kenney's description of the *De rerum natura* as "the most passionate didactic poem ever written" (1); in any case, this is how Dryden himself saw Lucretius, as is clear from the preface, with its talk of his "sublime and daring Genius" and his "fiery temper." Nor does the California description alert the reader to the satirical component in the poem, a propensity to treat themes that have always attracted formal satirists from Juvenal onwards, so that Lucretius's treatment of (for example) greed for life (book 3) may be seen as anticipating Swift's Struldbrugs and his savagely unromantic picture of women in their private closets (book 4) as a possible source for Swift's scatological dressing-room poems.

Whether or not he knew of the diatribe background of Lucretius's poem, Dryden responded to many of its effects in the section of book 3 he chose to translate. He noticed certain recurrent features of the style and heightened them, whether or not there was any precise verbal equivalent in the Latin text. He brilliantly took over the posture of the diatribe-writer, a manner constantly veering between, on the one hand, ironical or sarcastic reproof or even jeering denunciation and, on the other, indignant or fervently exalted exhortation, the transitions between them coming abruptly or even fusing imperceptibly together, so that a certain bass note persists composed in part of a harsh impatience with human weaknesses and in part of a nobly aspiring hope of bettering the human lot; contempt and compassion mingle their satiric and tragic strains throughout. These abrupt shifts of tone and attitude were certainly closely observed by Dryden, as he shows in the preface: "he [Lucretius] seems to disdain all manner of Replies, and is so confident of his cause, that he is before hand with his Antagonists; Urging for them, whatever he imagin'd they cou'd say, and leaving them as he supposes, without an objection for the future." This use of an imagined interlocutor is a feature of the diatribe style noted by Kenney, whose description is, however, more attentive to generic considerations: "The style of the performance was semi-dramatic; the interlocutor of the Platonic dialogues survived in an attenuated form as an anonymous butt, whose objections, invariably futile, were prefaced merely by a φησί, 'he says,' and afforded opportunities for the speaker to display his wit and sharpen his point" (18). Lucretius's adaptations of these devices, adapted further by

Dryden, can be studied in full in Dryden's third extract at lines 76–107, 121–66, and 236–70.

In order to convey to an English reader Lucretius's personality and outlook, Dryden was impelled to resort to a special stylistic strategy. The first impression made by this Lucretian style is one of simplicity, though of a special kind; to describe this style, one might borrow a phrase Geoffrey Grigson uses of Dryden himself, and call it a "tremendous simplicity." Certainly it has at times an elemental, a hugely primitive, force. Dryden uses a conspicuously small vocabulary for these translations: he confines himself, evidently of set purpose, to a relatively small and narrow set of words, deliberately abstaining from the profuse and luxuriant and sometimes even boldly eccentric turns of phrase that he thought suitable (for example) for Juvenal or for Virgil's *Georgics*. The general effect is one of unadorned bareness. Many single lines have none but monosyllabic words; many more single lines admit one word of two syllables but are otherwise made up entirely of the simplest one-syllable words. Syntax is similarly controlled, with a view of maintaining an utterly direct mode of address: antithesis, and other figures of speech that might make for a neat or witty effect, are sparingly used, or if they occur, they seem to occur spontaneously, hit upon in passion rather than contrived by art. And there is, throughout, a strong tendency to repetition: the chief points of the argument are relentlessly, even repetitiously, hammered home, in keeping with the manner of a preacher in the full flood of his harangue.

Essential to the style is its apparent artless spontaneity, its headlong speed. And in this last connection a certain formal peculiarity of Dryden's Lucretius may be noted, although, as will be seen, the inferences we draw from it must be tentative and provisional. His Lucretian translations are undivided into paragraphs. The effect in this long (321 lines) extract against the fear of death is that Lucretius's weighty, impassioned flow is allowed to rush on with no interruption whatever. A reader fresh to this translation will (in my experience) not at first notice the source of this felt peculiarity, this seemingly endless outpouring. What he will notice is the sense of being carried away by an irresistible flood of argument and eloquence. However, the absence of paragraph divisions may be explained by Dryden's own sense of Lucretius's special qualities of unstoppable volubility: "From the same fiery temper proceeds the loftiness of his Expressions, and the perpetual torrent of his Verse." "Perpetual torrent": this phrase catches precisely the impact of Dryden's own verse, so that the reader feels overwhelmed, overborne, by the sheer massive onslaught of Lucretius's "fiery temper." What makes this argument problematical, however, is the fact that Dryden's other couplet poems in the *Sylvae* volume are also without paragraphs: these include versions of Virgil and Theocritus, in which paragraphing has no discernible expressive value.[11] It is just possible, I suppose, that there was a misunderstanding between Dryden and the printer, who instead of printing only the Lucretius without paragraphs printed all Dryden's couplet poems in this way. Whatever the explanation, I maintain that the undivided format of the Lucretian passages reinforced the effect of "perpetual torrent" for which Dryden was undoubtedly striving. It also contributes to a slightly primitive feel about the verse, a rough, impatient, unliterary quality, which is entirely consonant with Dryden's conception of Lucretius—as if what he has to say is much too urgent to allow for fussily peripheral "literary" considerations of that sort.

Within the impetuous flow of this diatribe against the fear of death, there are of course rhetorical divisions of a kind that modern editors recognize when they print the Latin text in conventional paragraphs. The first section (1–120 of Dryden's text) is on the nothingness of death and is taken in two parts, the first on atoms and void (1–48), the second on bodies and feelings (49–120); the next (121–62), in what Dryden calls "the *Prosopopeia* of Nature," imagines how Nature herself would upbraid the aged who are unwilling to abandon the feast of life, and so on. Each of these divisions treats its own topic within the larger theme of the fear of death, but although the transitions from one to the next are made with an imperious abruptness, so that it is at first easy to miss the joins between one section and another, each section nonetheless has its own dominant style and tone, its own rhetorical peculiarities.

The opening section is especially strong and tensely argued; it draws from Dryden a finely poised tone of address:

> What has this Bugbear death to frighten Man,
> If Souls can die, as well as Bodies can?
> For, as before our Birth we felt no pain
> When Punique arms infested Land and Mayn,
> When Heav'n and Earth were in confusion hurl'd
> For the debated Empire of the World,
> Which aw'd with dreadful expectation lay,
> Sure to be Slaves, uncertain who shou'd sway:
> So, when our mortal frame shall be disjoyn'd,
> The lifeless Lump, uncoupl'd from the mind,
> From sense of grief and pain we shall be free;
> We shall not feel, because we shall not *Be*.
>
> (3.1–12)

The first couplet, a complete sentence, states the theme—the mortality of the soul and consequent certainty that death entails nothing to be afraid of. The second sentence fills five couplets and uses a full-blown simile in order to make the point, simple to state but immensely difficult to imagine adequately, that just as we knew nothing of what was happening before we were born, so we shall know nothing of what will happen after we die. And with the tenth line of this ten-line sentence, the theme of the entire diatribe is epitomized: "We shall not feel, because we shall not *Be*." The simple

words are used with the fullest possible emphasis, particularly the last
word. They complete the thought of these opening lines, the effect of
conclusiveness given extra weight through the sonic iteration of "*because
. . . Be.*"

Feeling and being, or rather feeling and not-being, are the two opposing
ideas on which the first 120 lines are organized—in other words, the mortality of soul as well as body, the folly of imputing sensation to a corpse or of
supposing that consciousness can be prolonged after the body's dissolution.
Anyone who thinks otherwise is no more than "an unsincere, unthinking
Ass," "nor can/Distinguish 'twixt the Body and the Man." Non-being, nothingness, are the notions, or non-notions, to which Dryden's Lucretius
strives to give shape in these opening lines, and there can be little doubt
that Dryden himself was excited by the imaginative effort involved. Images
of matter, of inertia, of dragging mindless weight were always stimulating
to him; while a vivid interest in nonbeing was something he shared with
others of his literary contemporaries, notably Rochester.[12] Like Rochester's
famous poem, Dryden's is also to a large extent "upon" Nothing. At the
same time, Dryden betrays the extreme imaginative difficulty of making
vacancy tangible ("After Death nothing is, and nothing Death" was Rochester's way of putting it, translating Seneca, who was in turn following Lucretius), the difficulty of conveying by sensuous means the cessation of
sensuousness or of capturing in sound the annihilation of sound.

Dryden follows Lucretius closely through the insistent repetitions, the
almost hectoring pedagogical emphases, of his discourse; one device in
particular may be singled out. Lucretius at one point (3.860) uses the
phrase "vitai pausa" to express what happens when a creature dies: "a
stoppage of life" (Rouse, in the Loeb translation), "a break in existence"
(Kenney). (*Pausa* is not a common Latin word: "After Lucretius, *pausa*
disappears from Latin except for an occasional antiquarian revival.")[13]
What Dryden does in translating line 860 is to render Lucretius's phrase
literally, despite the oddity of its usage in English in this context: "Because a
pause of life, a gaping space" (38), where the second phrase—which has no
equivalent in the Latin—is added by Dryden as a gloss on the first. This is
the first time that Dryden has used the phrase "Pause of life," though he
has prepared the reader for it earlier by introducing the word "pause" in
line 25, again where there was no equivalent in the Latin:

> When once an interrupting pause is made,
> That individual Being is decay'd.
>
> (3.25–26)

In all, Dryden uses "pause of life" three times as well as this more idiomatic
"interrupting pause" (whereas Lucretius uses "vitae pausa" only twice in

book 3, at lines 860 and 930)—and he does so presumably in order to express, by means of a quasi-technical term, the pure vacancy, the hiatus or gap, in consciousness that we must imagine death to be. Moreover, like an experienced teacher careful to take his listeners with him, he distinguishes between each of his three uses of the phrase: the first is "a pause of life" (38), the second "that pause of life" (47), and the third simply "the pause of Life" (120), as if by the third time it can be taken as an established term that the listener will understand. And in fact the third occurrence comes in the final line of this long opening movement on the nothingness of death:

> . . . For then our Atoms, which in order lay,
> Are scatter'd from their heap, and puff'd away,
> And never can return into their place,
> When once the pause of Life has left an empty space.
>
> (3.117–20)

As a verbal device this quiet, weighted phrase seems to me wholly successful, its slightly un-English strangeness serving perfectly as a formula, a kind of opaque symbol, for death, the impenetrably unknowable experience.

The following phrases in the diatribe deal with the more centrally human, instinctively emotional revulsion against death, a set of responses among which two basic motives can be distinguished: first, an insatiable appetite for life; and second, a fear of what death may bring in the form of eternal punishments in an afterlife. Lucretius treats the first of these in his "*Prosopopeia* of Nature," and the second in his denunciation of the "Bugbear dreams" that delude men into thinking that they can continue to exist after death. For want of space I shall pass over these sections, powerful though they are, in favor of the briefer section on the indiscriminateness of death—an utter commonplace both of consolatory and of satirical moral writing, yet as treated by Lucretius in his unswervingly direct, passionately serious way made new, purged of any suggestion of triteness. The transition to this section is made with Lucretius's usual abruptness, and with a sudden switch to aggressive second-person address. Since I want to bring out something of the massive impetus and flow of Dryden's rendering, I shall quote extensively:

> Mean time, when thoughts of death disturb thy head;
> Consider, *Ancus* great and good is dead;
> *Ancus,* the better far, was born to die,
> And thou, doest thou bewail mortality?
> So many Monarchs with their mighty State,
> Who rul'd the World, were overrul'd by fate.
> That haughty King, who larded o're the Main,
> And whose stupendous Bridge did the wild waves restrain,
> (In vain they foam'd, in vain they threaten'd wreck,

While his proud Legions march'd upon their back:)
Him death, a greater Monarch, overcame;
Nor spar'd his guards the more, for their immortal name.
The *Roman* chief, the *Carthaginian* dread,   ⎫
Scipio the Thunder Bolt of War is dead,   ⎬
And like a common Slave, by fate in triumph led.   ⎭
The Founders of invented Arts are lost;
And Wits who made Eternity their boast;
Where now is *Homer* who possest the Throne?
Th' immortal Work remains, the mortal Author's gone.
Democritus perceiving age invade,
His body weaken'd, and his mind decay'd,
Obey'd the summons with a chearful face;
Made hast to welcome death, and met him half the race.
That stroke, ev'n *Epicurus* cou'd not bar,   ⎫
Though he in wit surpass'd Mankind, as far   ⎬
As does the midday Sun the midnight Star.   ⎭
And thou, dost thou disdain to yield thy breath,
Whose very life is little more than death?
More than one half by lazy sleep possest;   ⎫
And when awake, thy Soul but nods at best,   ⎬
Day-Dreams and sickly thoughts revolving in thy breast.   ⎭
                                                          (3.236–66)

Lucretius's diatribe has moved into a region more familiar to the dispen-
sers of funerary eloquence. But it should be noted first that this set-piece is
not ostensibly spoken in the poet's own person; rather, he tells his listener
to repeat over to himself the following thoughts, beginning, in Lucretius's
Latin, with a quotation from Ennius about Ancus, who was for the Romans
the archetypal good king. (Dryden naturally makes no attempt to reproduce the effect of quoting from a well-known earlier poet.) As Kenney puts
it: "This introductory use of a quotation is quite in the manner of the
diatribe: 'You know, of course, Ennius' famous line about Ancus; well, he is
not the only great ruler who has died'" (233). So the entire set-piece is as if
in quotation marks, at one remove from the austere person of the poet
himself. Dryden's free version necessarily sacrifices much of the tonal variation of the original (see Kenney, 27–28, 232–38); he puts a premium
instead on maintaining speed and impetus, and especially on reproducing
the piercing directness of Lucretius. At the same time, Dryden uses more
rhetorical figures than usual, which have the effect of giving the plain
diction an extra charge, increasing (so to speak) the volume of sound and
endowing the words with a kind of three-dimensional solidity.

The case histories are reviewed rapidly—the men of virtue, power and
glory, creative genius, and wisdom—with both Lucretius and, to a remarkable degree, Dryden managing to make it seem as if this most commonplace of themes were being sounded for the first time.

> Consider, *Ancus* great and good is dead. . . .

The expression strikes to the bare essentials, the epithets denoting elemental categories. Lucretius's lines on Xerxes (1029–33) constitute a complex periodic sentence with subject and predicate separated by three lines. Dryden contrives an arrangement at least comparable to this in his six-line sentence whose grammatical progress is delayed by a two-line parenthesis; its effect is closely similar to that of Lucretius's involved construction— namely, to make Xerxes' collapse into death seem more abject. Moreover, Dryden, unlike Lucretius, makes the whole passage (240–49) turn on ideas of kingship and rule and enriches it with a set of oppositions and parallels ("Who rul'd the World, were overrul'd by fate," "Him death, a greater Monarch, overcame"), the use of anaphora ("In vain . . . in vain") to evoke the marching army, as well as more quietly sardonic sonic reinforcement ("Nor spar'd his guards the *more,* for their im*mor*tal name"). For his triplet on Scipio, William Frost observes, after quoting the Latin—

> Scipiadas, belli fulmen, Carthaginis horror,
> ossa dedit terrae proinde ac damul infimus esset—

"Dryden's version manages to keep the phrase translating 'belli fulmen' at the center of a line and that translating 'Carthaginis horror" at the conclusion of one."[14] For his Homer couplet, Dryden, if anything, outgoes his original:

> Where now is *Homer* who possest the Throne?
> Th' immortal Work remains, the moral Author's gone.

He has taken over Lucretius's mortal/immortal antithesis from an earlier line where it was used of death ("mortalem vitam mors cum immortalis ademit" [when death the immortal has taken away his mortal life], 869), and applied it to Homer in order to secure a greater emphasis and climax; arguably the antithesis is more effective here than it was in the Latin. Lucretius keeps to the last Epicurus, his philosophical master and for him the greatest of men, and endows him with the image of light. He was the sun of men and was yet mortal: "Epicurus himself died when the light of his life had run its course, he whose intellect surpassed humanity, who quenched all lights as the risen sun of heaven quenches the stars" (Rouse). Dryden attempts to match the Latin phrasing with his own antithesis—"the midday Sun the midnight Star"—which works effectively, except that the verbal opposition is slightly misleading: it suggests that the star would be weakest at midnight just as the sun is strongest at midday, whereas of course the star might well be at its brightest at midnight and weakest at twilight and dawn. This kind of antithesis, however, verbally exact but illogical or misleading in sense, may be characteristic of Lucretius in other contexts.[15]

In Lucretius the great kings, generals, poets, and philosophers are contrasted to the recipient of the harangue, a supposedly cringing wretch, the "tu" of Lucretius, the "thou" of Dryden; and it is entirely in keeping with the diatribe form of address that Dryden, departing from the Latin, should invent a refrain-like line to frame the passage as a whole ("And thou, dost thou bewail mortality?", "And thou, dost thou disdain to yield thy breath?"), which catches perfectly Lucretius's unique personal tone in which contempt and pity are sometimes so mixed as to be indistinguishable. What was perhaps especially congenial to Dryden here was the fusion of satire and consolatory elegy, the impatience with human weakness and at the same time the sense of involvement with it, feelings that in Lucretius (as in Dryden's rendering) are so often registered in the switch from second-person singular address to first-person plural.

Lucretius's third book ends with a resumé of earlier arguments in which once again the verbal form is first-person plural—the "we" of human solidarity rather than the "thou" of impatient harangue. The theme is again the refusal, or inability, of human beings to surrender their precious identities to the impersonal order of the universe. But the familiar arguments are now expounded with a difference. The human urge to self-preservation, unavoidable though irrational, is now seen more from within and felt more as a tragic fact of life than as an absurd weakness to be excoriated. The personal feeling, as far as Dryden is concerned, is betrayed in the close resemblance between this passage and the most famous in all his plays: "When I consider Life, 'tis all a cheat." Both passages turn on the deceitfulness of hope and the tedium of life's endlessly circling process ("the dregs of life" is a phrase that occurs in both); indeed the speech in *Aureng-Zebe,* which has always been felt to express a deeply personal mood for Dryden, is essentially a free variation on the passage in Lucretius:

> When I consider Life, 'tis all a cheat;
> Yet, fool'd with hope, men favour the deceit;
> Trust on, and think to-morrow will repay;
> To-morrow's falser than the former day. . . .
> Strange cozenage! None would live past years again,
> Yet all hope pleasure in what yet remain;
> And, from the dregs of Life, think to receive
> What the first sprightly running could not give.
>
> (*Aureng-Zebe,* 4.1)

> Besides we tread out a perpetual round,
> We ne'er strike out; but beat the former ground
> And the same Maukish joyes in the same track are found.
> For still we think an absent blessing best;
> Which cloys, and is no blessing when possest;
> A new arising wish expells it from the Breast.

The Feav'rish thirst of Life increases still;
We call for more and more and never have our fill:
Yet know not what to morrow we shall try,
What dregs of life in the last draught may lie.

(3.305–14)

It would be too much to say that Lucretius positively acquiesces in, or excuses, the human refusal to be rational about its inordinate appetite for life, but the poetry itself proclaims the extreme difficulty of the human situation.

The closing lines of Book Three again treat the featurelessness of death, but again with a difference:

> Nor, by the longest life we can attain,   ⎫
> One moment from the length of death we gain; ⎬
> For all behind belongs to his Eternal reign.   ⎭
> When once the Fates have cut the mortal Thred,
> The Man as much to all intents is dead,
> Who dyes to day, and will as long be so,
> As he who dy'd a thousand years ago.

The Latin text ends quietly, so quietly in fact that it has been criticized as an inadequate ending to the book: "he will be no less long dead who has died with today's sun than he who died many months and years before" (Rouse). Dryden, however, has fashioned a far more sonorous conclusion.[16] Here, as in so many other passages, he owes something to Creech's 1682 translation:

> What though a *Thousand* Years prolong thy Breath?
> How can this shorten the long state of Death?
> For tho thy Life shall numerous Ages fill,
> The state of Death shall be *eternal* still.
> And he that dies *to day*, shall be no more,
> As *long* as those that perish'd *long* before.[17]

Creech's feeble last couplet must have showed Dryden that a strong ending was essential. What at any rate he did was to take over "a *Thousand* Years" from Creech's earlier line and bring it into the last couplet, so juxtaposing it with "to day." He dispensed with the relatively weak word "before" (which Creech had quite properly used to translate Lucretius's "ante") in favor of the far more emotively powerful, dramatic "age." "Age" instantly brings the speaker into our presence. Kenney remarks of the Latin text: "In using this final argument to ridicule those who cling to life, Lucretius rides roughshod over human psychology: it would be an oddly constituted man who received any real comfort from such reflections" (243). But these lines are perhaps not meant precisely to offer "comfort" but rather to startle the reader into doing (once again) the more-or-less impossible—imagining his own extinction. And he is made to do so by seeing just how long death's no-reign is. Certainly in Dryden, it seems to me, the effect of his splendidly reverberant yet chillingly hollow close, by bringing "to day" into juxtaposition with "a thousand years ago," is momentarily to annihilate history—as a thousand years are collapsed into a moment—shocking us into a glimpse, or an imagined glimpse, of the extrahistorical, timeless realm where death lives. Once more, as at moments throughout this death-meditation, we hear, or think we hear, the silence of

> That never changing state which all must keep
> Whom Death has doom'd to everlasting sleep

—the soundless, godless void that is altogether beyond language.[18]

NOTES

1. (London: Oxford University Press, 1980), xvii.
2. *Arion* 7 (1968): 576–602. See also Mary Gallagher, "Dryden's Translation of Lucretius," *HLQ* 28 (1964): 19–29.
3. *Poems 1685–1692*, ed. Earl Miner et al., vol. 3 of *The Works of John Dryden* (Berkeley and Los Angeles: University of California Press, 1969), 282. All subsequent quotations from Dryden's text are cited by book and line number from this edition.
4. W. B. Fleischmann, *Lucretius and English Literature* (Paris: Nizet, 1964), 227.
5. David West, *The Imagery and Poetry of Lucretius* (Edinburgh: Edinburgh University Press, 1969), vii.
6. For the estimate of Juvenal implied here, see H. A. Mason, "Is Juvenal a Classic?", in *Arion* 1 (1962): 8–44, 2 (1963): 39–79; rpt. in J. P. Sullivan, ed., *Critical Essays on Roman Literature: Satire* (London: Routledge and Kegan Paul, 1963), 93–172.
7. William Myers finds Dryden's fourth extract *"Concerning the Nature of Love"* "especially satisfying": "There is a sense of intellectual release in Dryden's implacable exposition of the inexorability of process" (*Dryden* [London: Hutchinson, 1973], 149).
8. See D. W. Jefferson, "Aspects of Dryden's Imagery," *EC* 4 (1954): 20–41. I have touched on the same subject in "Dryden's Sigismonda," in *English Renaissance Studies*, ed. John Carey (Oxford: Clarendon Press, 1980), 279–90.
9. In J. E. Spingarn, ed., *Critical Essays of the Seventeenth Century* (Oxford: Clarendon Press, 1908), 2:300.
10. E. J. Kenney, *The "De rerum natura" of Lucretius. Book Three* (Cambridge: Cambridge University Press, 1971).
11. Elsewhere in the 1685 *Sylvae* volume (406–17) is another translation from Lucretius "By a Person of Quality," namely, Sir Robert Howard (see Fleischmann, *Lucretius,* 145). This passage, which is in heroic couplets, is divided into paragraphs. Two other translations in this volume, one from the *Georgics*, the other from the *Aeneid*, are also paragraphed. Only Dryden's heroic couplet poems are left undivided.
12. See Barbara Everett, "The Sense of Nothing," in *Rochester: Spirit of Wit*, ed. Jeremy Treglown (Oxford: Basil Blackwell, 1980), 1–41. In this context one inevitably recalls Johnson's remark on Dryden: "He delighted to . . . hover over the abyss of unideal vacancy" (*Lives of the English Poets*, ed. G. B. Hill [Oxford: Clarendon Press, 1945], 1:460).
13. Kenney, *The "De rerum natura,"* 197.

14. William Frost, *Dryden and the Art of Translation* (New Haven: Yale University Press, 1955), 5.

15. As West suggests (*Imagery and Poetry of Lucretius*, 99–100).

16. Certainly Pope remembered it and echoed it twice (*Essay on Man*, bk. 1, 75–76, and *Epistle to Arbuthnot*, 123–24), the second a brilliant adaptation of Dryden's general effect to a totally different context and mood.

17. *Titus Lucretius Carus, His Six Books of Epicurean Philosophy, Done into English Verse, By Thomas Creech*, 3rd ed. (Oxford, 1683), 101.

18. Paul Hammond's article "The Integrity of Lucretius," *MLR* 78 (1983): 1–23, appeared too late for me to be able to refer to it. Among other things, it admirably fills out the Epicurean background for Dryden's translations.

4

The Wit and Weight of Clarendon

Christopher Ricks

Roguish Auden put in some words "in defence of gossip":

> And as for books, if you had to choose between the serious study and the amusing gossip, say, between Clarendon's History of the Rebellion and John Aubrey's Scandal and Credulities, wouldn't you choose the latter? Of course you would! Who would rather learn the facts of Augustus' imperial policy rather than discover that he had spots on his stomach? No one.[1]

Fortunately, in the real world, as against the world of bluff broadcasting, we do not have to choose between Clarendon and Aubrey. Yet we must admit that in one respect their very different styles invite the same question: are we delighting in an inadvertence, a fluke, rather than in any intended effect? Those who still hold to the belief that it is possible for a reader to take an unwarrantable pleasure in a writer's words are not obliged to equate intention with fully conscious decision; felicities are a coinciding of the happily unplanned with the deliberated. But Aubrey thrusts upon us the choice between apprehending his prose as genius or as ingenuousness. Consider this death sentence for the life of Sir William Davenant:

> He was next a servant (as I remember, a Page also) to Sir Fulke Grevil, Lord Brookes, with whom he lived to his death, which was that a servant of his (that had long wayted on him, and his Lordship had often told him that he would doe something for him, but did not, but still putt him off with delayes) as he was trussing up his Lord's pointes comeing from Stoole (for then their breeches were fastned to the doubletts with points; then came in hookes and eies; which not to have fastened was in my boyhood a great crime) stabbed him.[2]

The flashing naked surprise of those last two words—"stabbed him"—is a reenactment of the crime, made the more horrible by the juxtaposition of a truly great crime with the observations about tailoring and about the need to adjust one's dress. The world of daily banality (lavatories and fly-buttons) is one where the moments of possible social embarrassment (as when eating or making love) are indeed the moments of great vulnerability, and are monstrously continuous with murder. Then the three sets of parentheses, which occupy two-thirds of the sentence and which settle into stubborn procrastination (from six words to thirty-one and twenty-nine), dilate with a murderous impatience at the lord's delays, throbbing at once with a sharp pun on "wayted on": "(that had long wayted on him, and his Lordship had often told him that he would doe something for him, but did not, but still putt him off with delayes)." What could more dramatically realize the scene, its unfulfilled promises and its mounting tensions, than putting the reader off with delays? Yet all the while the sentence's plot is undisguised even within delay's swaddlings: "with whom he lived to his death, which was that a servant of his . . . stabbed him." Are the "points" (tags) both pointed toward and at odds with "stabbed him"? Are the breeches alive to such contrarieties as those in *Macbeth,* where a breach is stabbed between "breach" and "breeched"?

> Here lay *Duncan,*
> His Silver skinne, lac'd with his Golden Blood,
> And his gash'd Stabs, look'd like a Breach in Nature,
> For Ruines wastfull entrance; there the Murtherers,
> Steep'd in the Colours of their Trade; their Daggers
> Unmannerly breech'd with gore.
>
> (2.3)

Is Aubrey's prose instinct with something of Shakespeare's genius, or am I imagining all this, transubstantiating clumsiness to felicity? There were those who thought Aubrey a maggotty-headed credulous fellow, and it is possible that his especial attraction is for those of us who are maggotty-headed credulous fellows.

Few have suspected Clarendon of being maggotty-headed or credulous, but his prose too, for all the differences between its high equanimity and Aubrey's down-to-earth astonishments, must make any reader who exercises his imagination wonder whether he is imagining things. Consider the following death sentence about the Earl of Holland's anger at the Earl of Strafford:

> The first could never forget or forgive a sharp sudden saying of his, (for I cannot call it counsel or advice,) when there had been some difference a few years before between his lordship and the lord Weston, in the managing whereof the earl of Holland was confined to his house, "that the King should do well to cut off his head:" which had been aggravated (if such an injury were capable of aggravation) by a succession of discountenances mutually performed between them to that time.[3]

What flashes out so directly here is the direct speech of that saying, "that the King should do well to cut off his head," a phrase all the more cutting and lethal because of the silky, understated suavity of "should do well" as against the edged and stated indubitability of "cut off his head." We are not told at once or suddenly what the "sharp sudden saying" was, or why "sharp" will prove glintingly the word; and something of the same frightening imperturbability attaches to the word "injury," ensconced within those parentheses that play as important a part within Clarendon's prose as within Aubrey's. For although it is questionable whether there could as a remark be anything more injurious than that quoted, the effect of the word "injury"—as a summing-up of this particular saying—is, first, to sound chillingly flat, and, second, to set disconcertingly before us the fact that, though it might not at first seem possible to inflict a graver injury than cutting off the head, they were at the time all too capable of aggravating even this injury. Hanging, drawing, and quartering, for a start. Then again, what are we to make of "discountenances," with its woundedness at the slights of incivility? Is the word given a greater gravity, aggravated, a different face put on it, by the succession "sharp . . . cut off his head . . . injury . . . discountenances," which speaks of a succession of discountenances?

Clarendon's intelligence, though not simply greater than Aubrey's, is so much more deliberative than his, so much more weighed, pondered, and concerned explicitly with what should be credited, as to make it likely that his prose should be credited with these germane provocations. "The style was not answerable to the provocation": this may sometimes have been true between King and Parliament, but it is not true of their historian. Clarendon's prose, like all great prose, is alive in its tissue, alive, since his subject is civil war, with sadness and reproof at everything that ruptures the tissue and that puts asunder those whom God hath joined: the English people, joined by courtesy not only of the English land but of the English language. So that an apparently innocuous word like "succession" not only intimates that we should be alive to the succession of words within such a sentence but also—through its political commitment—asks us to be pained by those successions within the words that realize a nocuous severance. Clarendon writes with his greatest somber acuteness when the tissue of his prose has to acknowledge a civil war; has to acknowledge, within the very words that constitute its successive life, those misguided energies that cut off life or that cut off one English life from another.

Cut, or dissolve. Clarendon gives salience to the word "dissolution" in the conviction that it was the ill-judged dissolutions of Parliament that led to the dissolution of the kingdom.[4]

And here I cannot but let myself loose to say, that no man can shew me a source from whence these waters of bitterness we now taste have more probably flowed, than from this unseasonable, unskilful, and precipitate dissolution of Parliaments. (1, 6)

"Dissolution" is fed by the confluence of "loose," "source," "waters," "flowed," and "precipitate"; and the bitterness that we taste not only in the political diagnosis but also in the words themselves has as its source this tragic apprehension: that the self-same process, the sequence of words which recalls a flow of events, and which gives depth to the word "dissolution," is a death-dealing sequence. The word "unseasonable," which is crucial to Clarendon's sense of things and of the sadness of things, precipitates later in this sentence the words "at those sad seasons."

The continuities that are constitutional and a matter of legality and succession are at one with those that constitute a language, and the depth of Clarendon's dismay (not despair) at what he contemplates is felt in how the continuities of his own prose are so often obliged to incarnate discontinuity.

> And therefore one day sir Arthur Haslerigge (who, as was said before, was used by that party, like the dove out of the ark, to try what footing there was) preferred a bill "for the settling the militia of the kingdom, both by sea and land, in such persons as they should nominate;" with all those powers and jurisdictions which have been since granted to the earl of Essex or sir Thomas Fairfax by land, or to the earl of Warwick by sea. (3, 244)

The biblical dove was innocent and peaceful in its enterprise; the acute wresting of Genesis both diagnoses (the more trenchantly because in passing), and at the same time preserves antisepsis by lodging the witticism within the parenthesis. For this dove is as cunning as a serpent (is a decoy dove), and is in collusion with hawks. The political realities are, first, that the flood, the blood-dimmed tide, has yet to be loosed, rather than being blessedly over; and second, that the footing in question is not the ancient mountain but the modern militia by sea and land. Such are the elements of Clarendon's prose.

The sense of profound travesty is active in Clarendon's lucid perception of collusion, of—for instance—the perfect fit with which man's imperfection can fashion its travesties of what ought to be the case. A civil war is particularly cursed with this fittingness, a monstrous match of breach and observance, as in the vicious circle of honor rooted in dishonor:

> And as this breach of the articles was very notorious and inexcusable, so it was made the rise, foundation, and excuse for barbarous injustice of the same kind throughout the greatest part of the war; insomuch as the King's soldiers afterwards, when it was their part to be precise in the observations of agreements, mutinously remembered the violation at Reading, and thereupon exercised the same license; and from thence, either side having somewhat to object to the other, that requisite honesty and justice of observing conditions was mutually, as it were by agreement, for a long time after violated. (7, 37)

Only a great writer, more in sorrow than in anger though in anger, could have effected so pained a movement, first, from the "inexcusable" to the "excuse," and then (a heartfelt shaking of the head) from "the observations of agreements" to the laconically exact "as it were by agreement." The true agreements within the prose devote themselves to the doomed falsity of collusive agreement.

What agrees, or what adheres, is bitterly at odds with the ways in which things are at odds:

> So aguish and fantastical a thing is the conscience of men who have once departed from the rule of conscience, in hope to be permitted to adhere to it again upon a less pressing occasion. (11, 249)

The aguish and fantastical conscience is perfectly caught in what is at once the perseverance and the perversity of the move from "departed" to "adhere" to "less pressing." "*More* pressing" would after all have made more sense in terms of adherence. It is the imaginative ingenuity of ingratitude that is sadly acknowledged within a prose to which we feel gratitude for its lacerated equanimity.

> A second act of the same day, and the only way they took to return their thanks and acknowledgment to the Queen for her intercession and mediation in the passing those bills, was the opening a letter they intercepted which was directed to her majesty herself. (4, 308)

Clarendon is writing about two other kinds of writing: parliamentary bills and a letter. Each, like all writing, is a "mediation," and a letter might be thought particularly suited to the "return" of "thanks." The mediations of this prose are vibrantly indignant at the interception, the profound discourtesy; and the word "intercepted" is given its tone of a just rebuke, of effrontery confronted, by its tingling proximity to and distance from the word "intercession." The Earl of Essex

> died without being sensible of sickness, in a time when he might have been able to have undone much of the mischieve he had formerly wrought; to which he had great inclinations; and had indignation enough for the indignities himself had received from the ingrateful Parliament. (10, 80)

Clarendon's sound-effects are sound; not jinglings but tinglings. He is repeatedly though diversely drawn to such collocations as "intercession"/"intercepted," or "inclinations"/"indignation"/"indignities"/"ingrateful." On some occasions, the likeness of sound may intimate a hope (or a fear) that essential likeness may yet win the day, resolving the antagonisms within language (of which too much may be made). But on other occasions, the unlikeness of sound may suggest that a very small breach may yet be unbridgable and may grievously be prised open further by the divisive. The way in which words, like fellow-countrymen, may so easily run with or run against each other: this is caught, with the simplicity of genius within a complicated elucidation, when Clarendon sets *con-* with and against *contra-*. So near and yet so far.

> For in religion he [Falkland] thought to carefull and to curious an enquiry could not be made, amongst those whose purity was not questioned, and whose authority was constantly and confidently urged, by men who were furthest from beinge of on minde amongst themselves, and for the mutuall supporte of ther severall opinions, in which they most contradicted each other; and in all those contraversyes, he had so dispassioned a consideration, such a candor in his nature, and so profounde a charity in his conscience, that in those pointes in which he was in his owne judgement most cleere, he never thought the worse, or in any degree declined the familiarity of those who were of another minde.[5]

The aspiration that we should be of one mind has to contemplate the large fact (which daunts smaller men than Falkland in his charity and magnanimity) to which the small prefixes *con-* and *contra-* bear witness: that not only were there "those who were of another mind" but there were those "who were furthest from being of one mind amongst themselves."

Trust and truth must do their best to pinion treachery, but they must not feel confident that they will succeed. Unlike Wilmot, Goring would

> without hesitation have broken any trust, or done any act of treachery, to have satisfied an ordinary passion or appetite; and, in truth, wanted nothing but industry (for he had wit and courage and understanding and ambition, uncontrolled by any fear of God or man) to have been as eminent and successful in the highest attempt in wickedness of any man in the age he lived in or before. (8, 169)

"In truth" he was false: within a world so bent upon destruction and self-destruction, it is all too likely that words will turn upon themselves and undo themselves. Fortunately it will sometimes be folly that undoes itself, here where any word may be hoist with its own petard.

> And such as were brought in and delivered to the officers, declared such an averseness to the work to which they were designed, and such a peremptory resolution not to fight, that they only increased their numbers, not their strength, and ran away upon the first opportunity. (7, 203)

The words themselves run away upon the first opportunity from their agreed meanings: "resolution," which should mean firmness and unyielding temper, turns tail and becomes the firm decision not to stand firm ("resolution not to fight"), just as the army's "strength," which in a proper parlance would mean its numbers, finds itself cut off: "they only increased their numbers, not their strength."

The continuities within the prose once more set themselves to advertise and to advise ("that he had advertised the first, and advised the last, to take the same course" [2, 104]), to make real the discontinuities and hostilities that they contemplate. These exact effects impinge within a prose that does not allow itself to settle into a routine or into any one angle of junction, but which—vigilant through 360 degrees—spins round to catch every tangent of sound and sense. For want of a word, or for want of the ability to distinguish one word from another, a kingdom may be lost.

And it is not here unseasonable, (how merry soever it may seem to be,) as an instance of the incogitancy and inadvertency of those kind of votes and transactions, to remember, that, the first resolution of the power of the militia being grounded upon a supposition of an imminent necessity, the ordinance first sent up from the Commons to the Lords for the execution of the militia expressed an *eminent* necessity; whereupon some lords, who understood the difference of the words, and that an *eminent* necessity might be supplied by the ordinary provision which possibly an *imminent* necessity might not safely attend, desired a conference with the Commons for the amendment; which, I remember, was at last with great difficulty consented to, many (who, I presume, are not yet grown up to conceive the difference) supposing it an unnecessary contention for a word, and so yielding to them for saving of time rather than for the moment of the thing. (5, 151)

It is no unnecessary contention for a word that sets in balance or in imbalance such characteristic Clarendon turns as these, evincing—as Clarendon said of Falkland—"the wit and weight of all he said":

But by the King's interposition, and indeed imposition. (2, 58)

But this was rather modestly insinuated than insisted upon. (2, 71)

the only persons excepted from pardon and exempted from the benefit of that oblivion. (4, 43)

purely to perfecte his conversion by the conversation of those who had the greatest name.[6]

would distress, if not destroy, his whole army. (7, 204)

L. C. Knights, to whom many of us feel special gratitude for having joined Matthew Arnold in bringing home, not to historians but to students of English literature, how great a writer Clarendon is: even Knights underrates the extent to which the movement of Clarendon's prose has its own economy of balance.[7] With some writers, you might at small cost drop a short parenthetical bit. But there is a high price to be paid when Knights abbreviates the beginning of Clarendon's sketch of Attorney-General Noy.

The first, upon the great fame of his ability and learning, (and very able and learned he was,) was by great industry and importunity from Court persuaded to accept that place for which all other men laboured, (being the best for profit that profession is capable of,) and so he suffered himself to be made the King's Attorney-general. (2, 157)

Knights effects a false economy by dropping the second parenthesis, "(being the best for profit that profession is capable of)." This is unprofitable, because it removes, first, the characteristically telling antithesis of the two parentheses: the honest admission of Noy's abilities— "(and very able and learned he was)"—against the admission that the opportunities for the dishonest or the self-serving were strong within the office—"(being the best for profit)." Second, the excision removes the alert prefix and its magnetism: "for profit that profession," which is not only taut in itself but is tautened against the play of "industry and importunity." Third, it removes the word "capable," which might seem relatively unimportant but which gathers so much around it, as in that other parenthesis, "(if such an injury were capable of aggravation)." Most of Clarendon's capabilities are exerted upon what men are capable of, what can and cannot be effected. Clarendon raises political history to the art of the possible. He is drawn therefore, naturally and unobsessively, to the suffix -ible or -able. Within a mere four pages in Knight's excellent excerpting, the eye falls on these:

Mr Jermin, who still valued himself upon the impossible faculty to please all and displease none. (7, 189)

a weak judgment, and a little vanity, and as much of pride, will hurry a man into as unwarrantable and as violent attempts as the greatest and most unlimited and insatiable ambition will do. (6, 402)

very few men of so great parts are, upon all occasions, more counsellable than he . . . nor is he uninclinable in his nature to such an entire communication in all things which he conceives to be difficult. (4, 128)

And the temper and composition of his mind was so admirable, that he was always more pleased and delighted that he had advanced so far, which he imputed to his virtue and conduct, than broken or dejected that his success was not answerable, which he still charged upon second causes, for which he could not be accountable. (9, 126)

So that to remove that parenthesis, "(being the best for profit that profession is capable of)," is to "save" ten words that ought to be saved.

This sketch of Noy itself ends:

In a word, he was an unanswerable instance how necessary a good education and knowledge of men is to make a wise man, at least a man fit for business. (1, 157)

"Unanswerable": in a word, and this is the right word for Clarendon's succinct sentencing. Often when he is moved to this calm decisive introduction of his climax, the word in question then incorporates his valued suffix. There is wit in moving from "In a word" to "unanswerable," of all words. There is authority in moving from "in a word" to "despicable" ("In a word, he became the most despicable to all men" [6, 403]). Supremely, in the end, in the penultimate paragraph of the great work, at the Restoration, there is a high gratitude with a high modesty in the movement from "In a word" to the word "unexpressible":

> On Monday he went to Rochester, and the next day, being the 29th of May and his birthday, he entered London, all the ways from Dover thither being so full of people and exclamations as if the whole kingdom had been gathered. About or above Greenwitch the Lord Mayor and aldermen met him, with all those protestations of joy which can hardly be imagined; and the concourse so great that the King rode in a crowd from the bridge to Temple Bar. All the companies of the city stood in order on both sides, giving loud thanks for his majesty's presence. And he no sooner came to Whitehall but the two Houses of Parliament solemnly cast themselves at his feet, with all the vows of affection and fidelity to the world's end. In a word, the joy was so unexpressible and so universal, that his majesty said smilingly to some about him, that he doubted [feared] it had been his own fault that he had been absent so long, for he saw nobody that did not protest he had ever wished for this return. (16, 246)

There is ground for gratitude, at last, in that succession of *all*'s: "all the ways," "all those protestations," "all the companies," "all the vows."[8] Then the conclusion of this great paragraph takes up the earlier awe of "all those protestations of joy which can hardly be imagined"; takes it up, goes beyond it, and "in a word" finds the perfect word, the one that admits the insufficiency of words especially at such a moment: "In a word, the joy was so unexpressible." At which, with a true balance of alternate tones, the sentence moves at once from the unexpressible to something that was ne'er so well expressed: the King's salty, salutary expression of benign wit, that he feared "it had been his own fault that he had been absent so long, for he saw nobody that did not protest he had ever wished for his return." The King, unlike some of those who welcome him, does not protest too much.

The art of the possible is one that has to acknowledge both what proves impossible even to art, the unexpressible, and what proves impossible even to prosperous politics. Even the miracles of God have their sacred limits, as the penultimate sentence of the entire history shortly insists:

> Yet did the merciful hand of God in one month bind up all these wounds, and even made the scars as undiscernible as in respect of their deepness was possible. (16, 247)

One reason why Clarendon's style is answerable, in both senses, to the provocations of the civil war is that, in this civil war, fighting was continuous with writing. More than usual force attaches here to such a phrase as "the authors of a civil war"; to "paper combat" and "paper skirmishes"; to "sovereignty of language" and "that new license of words"; to the wrestling of words like "law" and "liberty," "words of precious esteem in their just signification"; and to the sturdy old phrases with which Clarendon opposes the new "hard words": "in plain terms," and "in plain English." Charles Whibley said of Clarendon:

> He did not set the persons of his drama against any background, natural or artificial. His world has not houses, nor courts, nor fields. The personages of his drama seem to move hither and thither, in vast, vacant spaces.[9]

But whatever he may or may not have seen, Clarendon always heard the persons of his drama against the background of—or rather, as brought into this breathing world by—the English language, and filling like air every cubic inch of his vast unvacant space.

Fills it, some have thought, a shade too full. Matthew Arnold, who honored Clarendon for honoring Falkland, was careful not to be excessive in his praise:

> Clarendon's style is here a little excessive, a little Asiatic. And perhaps a something Asiatic is not wholly absent, either, from that famous passage,—the best known, probably, in all the *History of the Rebellion*,—that famous passage which describes Lord Falkland's longing for peace.
>
> > Sitting among his friends, often, after a deep silence and frequent sighs, he would with a shrill and sad accent ingeminate the word *Peace, Peace;* and would passionately profess that the very agony of the war, and the view of the calamities and desolation the kingdom did and must endure, took his sleep from him, and would shortly break his heart.
>
> Clarendon's touch, where in his memoirs he speaks of Falkland, is simpler than in the *History*. But we will not carp at this great writer and faithful friend. Falkland's life was an uneventful one, and but a few points in it are known to us. To Clarendon he owes it that each of those points is a picture.[10]

But it is better to carp if the alternative is to condescend. The passage of Clarendon, indeed the best known in the *History*, is supremely well judged. The strong sighing repetition of *Peace, Peace* finds both strength and sadness in its assonance with "deep" and "sleep" ("Silence, you troubl'd waves, and thou Deep, peace" [*Paradise Lost*, 7.216]); the singular word— "the word *Peace, Peace*," instead of the word*s*, exactly captures what it is to double the one word; and, linguistically unique in the passage, "ingeminate" is a double touch of genius. It was a much less unusual word in Clarendon's day than in Arnold's, and a fortiori than in ours; and in Clarendon it is informed by much of its current life, so that it can stand as an unaffected and (*pace* Arnold—*pace, pace*) unexcessive, albeit striking, complement to the profound simplicity of *Peace, Peace*.

Ingeminate: 1. to utter (a sound) twice or oftener; to repeat, reiterate (a word, statement, etc.), usually for the purpose of being emphatic or impressive . . . (Freq. in 17th c.; now chiefly used in echoes of quot. 1647 [Clarendon]. (OED)

It is important not to hold against Clarendon his very success in having so imprinted his greatness forever upon, and via, the word; there is some happy irony in those later "echoes" of him, since ingemination is itself an echoing, and one of the OED instances before Clarendon is from Sandy's translation of Ovid, where it is Echo itself who "yet ingeminates."

Falkland (and hence Clarendon) is himself echoing or ingeminating. "They have healed also the hurt of the daughter of my people slightly, saying, Peace, peace; when there is no peace." The verse of Jeremiah (6 : 14) is itself, moreover, repeated verbatim, ingeminated (as 8 : 11), and it is the double fact—that there may be no healing of the hurt of his people, and that the completion of the cadence remains unspoken but all too acknowledged ("saying peace, peace; when there is no peace")—which gives such heartbreaking depth to the sad accents of Falkland and of Clarendon.

We should accept it as evidence of Clarendon's strength that journalists have been incited to artificial ingemination:

> 1887, *Murray's Magazine:* "Thus our Canon ingeminates peace." With a pun on *cannon,* presumably;

> 1892, *Pall Mall Gazette:* "Here comes Mr. Balfour with his olive branch, ingeminating peace." Like the dove out of the ark, to try what footing there was.

For one of the things that we might ask of our great writers is their giving occasion for happy wit, such as that recorded by Horace Walpole, Walpole who elsewhere wrote of Clarendon: "His majesty and eloquence, his power of painting characters, his knowledge of his subject, rank him in the first class of writers—yet he has both great and little faults. . . . Perhaps even his favourite character of Lord Falkland takes too considerable a share in the history":[11]

> T'other night at Brooks' the conversation turned on Lord Falkland; Fitzpatrick said he was a very weak man and owed his fame to Lord Clarendon's partiality. Charles Fox was sitting in a deep reverie, with his knife in his hand. "There," continued Fitzpatrick, "I might describe Charles meditating on the ruin of his country, ingeminating the words, Peace! Peace! and ready to plunge the knife in his own bosom."—"Yes," rejoined Hare in the same ironic dolorous tone, "and he would have done so, but happening to look on the handle of the knife, he saw it was silver, and put it in his pocket."[12]

How different (and not just because the dolorous tone is here ironic) is "ingeminating the words Peace! Peace!" from "the word *Peace, Peace.*" Yet it is not just the ingeminating peace, peace, but that "deep" reverie that shows how deeply Clarendon's words etch themselves, even for those light-fingered and light-hearted wags who merely pocket the silver sentence.

To repeat a cry—Peace, Peace (no exclamation marks in Clarendon, not incidentally, any more than in Jeremiah)—may be both to acknowledge a fact and to resist it. Geoffrey Hill has drawn attention to the "stubborn reiterative outcry" in the poems of John Crowe Ransom and has remarked that "the particular significance of the reiterated cry" may be "in its power to transform pure spontaneous reflex into an act of will."[13] Then again, "ingeminate" is happily suited to the unhappy fact of civil war, the deep kinship of twinship at war with itself. Moreover, the word had often figured within the evocation of the savior, the prince of peace who came not to bring peace but a sword. The OED cites such instances from 1616, 1637, and 1658: "This ingeminated zeal of Christ for his people's unity and love." Likewise the ingeminated zeal of Falkland for his people's unity and love, at a time of disunity and hate ingeminating the word *Peace, Peace*. The OED's "for the purpose of being emphatic or impressive" sadly sells short the possibilities and the actualities of such a repetition.

"In a word": and there was one word that incarnated Clarendon's zeal for unity and love. *Composition* is the word—"The temper and composition of his mind was so admirable"—and is so at one with his temper as to move naturally into "was" not "were." Almost all of the senses given in the OED could be illustrated from Clarendon, and many are at the heart of his lifelong endeavor.

> OED 3. The putting [of things] into proper position, order, or relation to other things.
>
> 6b. The due arrangement of words into sentences, and of sentences into periods; the art of constructing sentences and of writing prose or verse.
>
> 7. The composing of anything for oral delivery, or to be read; the practice or art of literary production.
>
> 11. The composing or settling (of differences etc.).
>
> 12. The settling of a debt, liability, or claim by some mutual arrangement.
>
> 16b. Mental constitution, or constitution of mind and body in combination; the combination of personal qualities that make any one what he is.
>
> 17. Artistic manner, style; the mode or style in which words or sentences are put together.
>
> 22. A mutual agreement or arrangement between two parties, a contract.

23. An agreement for the settlement of political differences; a treaty etc. (b) A mutual agreement for cessation of hostilities, a truce; an agreement for submission or surrender on particular terms.

24. An agreement or arrangement involving surrender or sacrifice of some kind on one side or on both; a compromise.

25. An agreement by which a creditor accepts a certain proportion of a debt, in satisfaction, for an insolvent debtor. "The fines paid by Royalists under the Commonwealth were called *Compositions of Delinquents.*"

That which makes up an individual or a society, a sentence or a style or a work of art; that which makes up terms, treaties, settlements, and compromises: nature, art, and society meet in the word, and it is the word for which Clarendon reserves the highest praise and for which he himself deserves the highest praise:

He was a person of so rare a composition by nature and by art, (for nature alone could never have reached to it,) that he was so far from being ever dismayed upon any misfortune, (and greater variety of misfortunes never befell any man,) that he quickly recollected himself so vigorously, that he did really believe his condition to be improved by that ill accident, and that he had an opportunity thereby to gain a new stock of reputation and honour. (10, 13)

Just such a stock of reputation and honor as Clarendon himself gained.

In her moving and challenging book on history and the novel, *The Story-Teller Retrieves the Past,* Mary Lascelles has said:

Though civil war is the most tragic of all conflicts yet it allows the belief that something might be said on either side. There can be no two thoughts about an invading army; about King and Parliament there may be—afterwards; seldom at the time.[14]

Seldom, not never, since there may be a person—someone who retrieves the present and, thereby, centuries later retrieves the past—of so rare a composition by nature and by art.

Notes

1. W. H. Auden, "In Defence of Gossip," *The Listener* 8 (22 December 1937).

2. *Aubrey's Brief Lives,* ed. Oliver Dick (London: Secker and Warburg, 1949), 85–86.

3. Quotations from Clarendon's *History of the Rebellion* are from the edition by W. Dunn Macray (Oxford: At the Clarendon Press, 1888), 6 vols. (2, 101). I have followed the usual convention of giving references in the form book, paragraph.

4. See B. H. G. Wormald, *Clarendon: Politics, Historiography and Religion* (Cambridge: Cambridge University Press, 1964), 104.

5. Clarendon, *Life,* quoted from D. Nichol Smith, ed., *Characters from the Histories and Memoirs of the Seventeenth Century* (Oxford: Clarendon Press, 1920), 93–94.

6. Clarendon, *Life,* in Nichol Smith, *Characters,* 175.

7. L. C. Knights, "Reflections on Clarendon's *History of the Rebellion,*" Scrutiny 15 (1948); rpt. in *Further Explorations* (London: Chatto and Windus, 1965).

8. These *all*'s contrast with the poignant reiteration of "all" in the account of the captivity of Charles I (11, 157).

9. Charles Whibley, *Political Portraits* (London: Macmillan, 1917), 60.

10. Matthew Arnold, "Falkland" (1877) in *Mixed Essays* (1879). Arnold changed the balance and spirit of Clarendon's passage for the worse by beginning at "Sitting"; Clarendon had said:

> When there was any overture or hope of peace he would be more erect and vigorous, and exceedingly solicitous to press any thing which he thought might promote it; and sitting amongst his friends, often, after a deep silence and frequent sighs, would, with a shrill and sad accent, ingeminate the word *Peace, Peace.* (7, 233)

For an exact and penetrating account of some important reservations about Clarendon's style, see George Watson, "The Reader in Clarendon's *History of the Rebellion,*" *RES,* n.s., 25 (1974): 396–409.

11. Horace Walpole, *A Catalogue of the Royal and Noble Authors of England* (1758).

12. Horace Walpole to William Mason, 7 February 1782: *The Yale Edition of Horace Walpole's Correspondence,* ed. W. S. Lewis, 29 (New Haven: Yale University Press, 1955), 179.

13. Geoffrey Hill, "What Devil Has Got into John Ransom?", Judith E. Wilson Lecture on Poetry, Cambridge, February 1980.

14. Mary Lascelles, *The Storyteller Retrieves the Past* (Oxford: Clarendon Press, 1980), 61–62.

5

The Barbinade and the She-Tragedy: On John Banks's *The Unhappy Favourite*

David Wykes

The matter of Elizabeth and Essex has for over three centuries fueled a great deal of popular romantic fiction and biography. The occasions, however, on which the story may be said to have achieved "literary" status are few. Perhaps the object of great magnitude in a dim English galaxy is John Banks's *The Unhappy Favourite, or the Earl of Essex, a Tragedy,* first acted in 1681 and printed in 1682, a play that still has standing in the history of seventeenth- and eighteenth-century drama, though one may prophesy with some confidence that it will never again get a professional performance. The play was reprinted in photo-offset facsimile, with scholarly and critical apparatus, by T. M. H. Blair in 1939. Calling it "a good, representative Restoration play," Blair made on its behalf two claims to distinction. "It was the first dramatic treatment of the Elizabeth-and-Essex theme in English, and it set the stage for the she-tragedy, a new type of drama destined to be known as John Banks's original contribution to the theater."[1] These claims are seconded by more recent students. James Sutherland speaks well of Banks in his volume of the *Oxford History of English Literature*[2] and has recently included *The Unhappy Favourite* in an anthology of Restoration tragedies.[3] Eric Rothstein and Robert D. Hume have given Banks serious though—quite properly—not reverent attention.[4] Banks is literature, just about.

In 1691 Gerard Langbaine, perhaps in the exercise of "his unamiable proclivity for detecting and recording plagiarisms,"[5] informed the world that Banks's play was "founded on a Novel called, The Secret History of the most renowned Queen *Elizabeth* and the Earl of *Essex,* printed in 12°. Lond. 1680."[6] Blair examines the relationship of source and play in his edition, but nothing much has been done on this aspect of *The Unhappy Favourite* since 1939. Progress in enumerative bibliography since then has con-

siderably enlarged what is known about this "secret history," and I shall
retail that accession of knowledge here.

I intend also to place *The Secret History* in the context of the French
nouvelle historique, to genre to which it in fact belongs, and in so doing, to
open certain new vistas on Banks's play. The publishing history of the
novel, both in France and England, is diverting and instructive, especially
for what it suggests about the audience for that prose fiction of the seventeenth and eighteenth centuries which does not display the "formal realism" endorsed by the Whig history of the novel that our own age has
canonized.[7] *The Secret History* is literature too, emitting light of its own and
not solely the faint glow reflected from the play based upon it.

⁊⁊⁊⁊⁊⁊⁊⁊

Banks's use of subjects from English history coincides with what it would
be fatuous to call his "major phase"; it is rather the type of play, the "historical she-tragedy," that gives him his place in the reference books. Rothstein
sees the motive for this choice of topic in Banks's search for probability.
"The near and the probable, he felt, were in direct proportion, and English
history therefore guaranteed him a measure of 'Nature.' "[8] Sutherland as-
signs a similar motive. "Dealing with the actual, Banks was encouraged to
avoid the implausible and the extravagant; the English theme had at once a
sobering and an inspiring influence on his mind."[9] It is a paradoxical truth,
however, that Banks was ultimately indebted for his "English theme" to an
anonymous French author, for *The Secret History of the Most renowned Queen
Elizabeth and the Earl of Essex* is a translation of *Le Comte d'Essex. Histoire
Angloise,* published in Paris in 1678.

The British Museum Catalogue has stated this fact for some time.[10] The
only other acknowledgment I have found of a relationship between *The
Secret History* and *Le Comte d'Essex* comes in Georges Ascoli's *La Grande-
Brétagne devant l'Opinion Française au XVIIᵉ Siècle.* After discussing La Cal-
prenède's tragedy of 1638, *Le Comte d'Essex,* Ascoli turns to the year 1678,
which quite justifies his claim that "c'est surtout aux tardives amours d'-
Elisabeth pour le comte d'Essex que notre littérature s'est attachée." In
January of that year, Thomas Corneille's *Le Comte d'Essex* was performed,
followed in February by the abbé Claude Boyer's tragedy of the same title.
Both were printed later that year.

> Pour profiter de la vogue qu'un tel succès assurait à cette histoire, le
> libraire Barbin s'empressa de prendre, le 1ᵉʳ mai 1678, un privilège pour
> un *Comte d'Essex, histoire anglaise.* Le volume sortit de ses presses, le 6 juin,
> avec une feuille de titre faussement datée de 1677, pour qu'on ne le
> soupçonnât point de plagier la tragédie.

The novel is indeed independent of the tragedy, but Ascoli then attributes
it to another source. "C'était la traduction d'un livre anglais, ancien de
vingt-cinq ans et souvent réédité."[11]

This error seems to indicate that the supposed English original of about 1650 had not been examined by Ascoli, for it is in fact a species of ghost that plays a small role in this story, but one that has been very distracting.

I surmise that Ascoli was relying on either the British Museum's *Catalogue of Printed Books, 1881–1900*[12] or on Sir Sidney Lee's biography of Essex in the *Dictionary of National Biography*.[13] In discussing the Essex literature, Lee wrote: "About 1650 was published a 'History of the most renowned Queen Elizabeth and her great Favourite, the Earl of Essex. In Two Parts. A Romance." This work, "printed by and for W. O.: London," is a chapbook of twenty-four pages and in the British Museum 1881–1900 *Catalogue* it is given the hypothetical date of 1650 and placed first in the list of editions. I assume that Lee did not know of the French original and simply accepted the hypothetical date in the catalogue. Ascoli, accepting the date, assumed that it must be the original *Le Comte d'Essex*. In the 1960 edition of the British Museum *Catalogue, Le Comte d'Essex* is identified as the original, and the date of the chapbook has been changed to "[1700?]."[14] The British Museum's copy of *Le Comte d'Essex* is stamped 14 Ap 96.

The text of the W. O. Chapbook is based on that of *The Secret History* but is much abbreviated and rewritten (see n. 44).

⁂⁂⁂⁂⁂⁂⁂

The *libraire* whose name appears on the title page of *Le Comte d'Essex* was Claude Barbin, one of those publishers, like the Englishman Jacob Tonson, who may be said to have played "un véritable rôle littéraire."[15] Barbin was active as a *libraire-imprimeur* between 1660 and 1698 (the year of his death), having his place of business for most of that time at various locations around the Sainte-Chapelle. Alone and (more rarely) in partnership, Barbin issued works of most of the great writers of the "grand siècle" in France: La Rochefoucauld, La Fontaine, Molière, Racine, Boileau, and Perrault. Molière mentions Barbin in *Les Femmes Savantes,* and Boileau places the combat in *Le Lutrin* before the shop "où, sans cesse, étalant bons et méchants écrits,/Barbin vend aux passans des auteurs à tout prix."[16]

But, as Boileau's phrase about "bons et méchants écrits" may indicate, Barbin's reputation bore another facet that Longchamp opposes to "le côté honnête et sérieux de [sa] production."

> Claude Barbin semble avoir été le seul libraire du grand siècle qui se soit occupé, avec quelque réussite, du genre léger, un peu trop libre parfois, de facéties et de littérature finement galante et sans obscénité, qui fut l'une des plus saillantes caractéristiques des XVIIe et XVIIIe siècles en France.[17]

The splendid bibliography of Maurice Lever reveals that Barbin was by no means the only *libraire* to specialize in this "genre leste," but it amply documents his eminence in the field.[18] More than ninety titles in Lever's list, ranging in size from works in several volumes to others brief enough to be called pamphlets, bear Barbin's name, usually as sole and first publisher, though he sometimes produced new editions of novels first published by others. In 1678, the year of *Le Comte d'Essex,* he brought out nine other prose fictions listed by Lever, including *La Princesse de Clèves.*

The "livrets et pamphlets galants" that obviously made a large contribution to the success of Barbin's business became known as *barbinades.*[19] *Le Comte d'Essex* is one such work that attracted the attention of an English bookseller whose reputation in some respects strikingly parallels that of Barbin: Richard "Novel" Bentley.[20]

ટ*ટ*ટ*ટ*ટ*ટ*ટ*ટ*

When *Le Comte d'Essex* appeared in English translation in 1680, the title page announced that its author was the ubiquitous and highly productive "Person of Quality" and that it was printed for "Will with the Wisp, at the Sign of the Moon in the Ecliptick," the place Cologne. The title of the work underwent considerable change. *Le Comte d'Essex. Histoire Angloise* is replaced by *The Secret History of the Most Renowned Q. Elizabeth and the E. of Essex,* and the French version's subtitles, such as *Histoire de la Reyne Elizabeth* (1.18) become in the English version *The Earl of Essex or, the Amours of Queen Elizabeth.* The book had the duodecimo format so strongly associated at that time with novels and was provided with an engraved frontispiece, which deserves some attention since it chimes with the details of the title page to indicate that the preliminaries, like the format, were aspects of salesmanship.[21]

The engraving depicts a paved terrace, with a balustrade in the middle ground and trees behind. To the left, a man in a Roman armor is seated in profile, his right hand raised, the fingers spread. At his feet kneels a woman, her right arm round his shoulders, her left hand over his left thigh in a gesture that had well-established erotic significance.[22] To the right, behind the balustrade, a black boy observes the couple. On a pedestal behind the couple to the left is a large cartouche, surmounted by a crown and surrounded by a wreath, and bearing the words "The E. of Essex and, Q. Elizebeth novell."[23] This frontispiece was obviously considered important to the book's commercial viability, since almost all the numerous subsequent editions faithfully attempt to reproduce it, albeit often in crude woodcut. (The crudity, in fact, is sometimes more than technical. In several versions of the work, which I take to be piracies, the neckline of the woman's dress has dropped to expose the breasts completely, thus adding an unmistakable emphasis to the fairly refined erotic gestures of the hands.) The sum effect of frontispiece and title page together is to imply a degree of eroticism or even salaciousness that the text actually and resolutely denies.

"Will with the Wisp, at the Sign of the Moon in the Ecliptick" is, of course, a bookseller-publisher whose very name proclaims his fictitiousness. But this attribution, clearly deriving from publishing practices on the Continent, is not designed to protect a publisher from the attentions of an efficient censorship. Proof of that is to be found at the end of the text of this first edition where, on the last pages of the last gathering, appears a catalogue of "Books printed for R. Bentley and M. Magnes," which includes, among the novels in twelves, "The Earl of Essex, and Queen Elizabeth; A Novel, in two Parts." The partnership of Bentley and Mary Magnes of Russel Street, Covent Garden, wanted it to be known that *The Secret History* was their property.[24] Besides the catalogue advertisement, they had entered the book in the *Term Catalogue* of the Stationers' Company.[25] The imprimatur of the Licenser of the Press, Sir Roger L'Estrange, does not appear, presumably since that would have spoiled the effect of title page and frontispiece, but by making themselves so easily traceable, Bentley and Magnes indicated that they had no fear of the censor.

The fictitious preliminaries, therefore, may be considered at one with the fiction of the tale itself. Bentley was providing for the novel the type of preliminary matter that had become associated with *nouvelles* printed in French in the Low Countries, especially Holland. In place of the well-known Barbin, whose productions conformed to the system of *privilèges* and censorship in Paris, appears an imprint that would unmistakably have signaled to a late seventeenth-century bookbuyer that the work had come from a press in liberal, Protestant Holland, with the implication that it would not have received a *privilège* had one been applied for in France.

Nouvelles, whether *galantes, historiques, amoureuses, curieuses, instructives, véritables,* or combinations thereof, were a staple of French publishing in the late seventeenth century. Hundreds were published in France and many beyond the borders. The extraterritorial examples sometimes offer to inspection no characteristics distinguishing them from those published within France, but in many cases there are differences. Royal personages, if safely insulated by time and nationality, were suitable topics in France, but *privilèges* could not be expected for fiction handling contemporary royal figures, or works treating revered figures from French history with disrespect. Any *nouvelle* that could earn the epithet *licentieuse* or—worse—*ordurière* would be possible only for a publisher outside France. The imprints of such books generally did not give the real identity of the publisher and rarely the true place of origin. The imprints communicated primarily their own fictitiousness. Cologne as a place of origin, for example, generally indicated "not Cologne, but probably Holland." Fictitious publishers became famous.

Les libelles, les satires, les romans d'un genre hasardé, ne se montraient que sous des noms supposés. Parfois, on mettait en avant des villes imaginaires . . . , mais Cologne était d'un très-grand usage; c'était le séjour supposé de l'infatigable Pierre Marteau, qui ne s'éteignit qu'à une épo-

que assez avancée du dix-huitième siècle; c'était là que travaillait aussi
son gendre Adrien Lenclume, beaucoup moins actif d'ailleurs.[26]

In England, however, fictitious imprints were great rarities. One encounters the occasional "Margery Mar-Prelat" or "Martin Marpope" but nothing
comparable to the Continental situation. Bentley's experiments with such
fictions were slight but interesting. "Will with the Wisp, at the Sign of the
Moon in the Ecliptick" appeared on one other book, *The Secret History of the
Duke of Alançon and Q. Elizabeth,* 1691 (Wing S2341), clearly an attempt to
follow up on the success of the earlier *Secret History.*[27] When he reissued
Gabriel de Brémond's *Hattige, or the Amours of the King of Tamaran* in 1680,[28]
the same year as *The Secret History,* it bore the imprint of "Simon the African, Amsterdam." Apparently, Bentley had decided to borrow "Simon the
African" to broaden his experiment, but after 1691 he seems to have made
no further attempts. Yet the fictitious imprint of the translation of *Le Comte
d'Essex* was obviously an important feature in the eyes of its subsequent
publishers since, like the frontispiece, it was reproduced again and again.
(One edition compounds the fiction: "Printed for The Man in the Moon;
and Will o'th'Wisp, in the Ecliptic" [Wing S2342A].)

   Le Comte d'Essex had been published in France within the boundaries of a
system that ensured its conformity to certain standards of respectability.
(The *méchanceté* of the *barbinades* was very relative.) In bringing out the
English version, Bentley had tried—apparently with some success—to suggest that it belonged to the alternative society of the French *nouvelle* in the
seventeenth century, the extraterritorial tradition of fictitious imprints and
enticing secrecy. In adapting it for the stage, John Banks put *The Secret
History* through a more far-reaching process of transformation that demonstrates the wide differences in expectations of the reading public for novels
in England and those of the audience for tragedy in the theater.

                              ❧❧❧❧❧❧❧❧

   The translation into English of *Le Comte d'Essex* is essentially complete,
skillful, and shows few errors. It takes only the slightest of the liberties
common in translations of the period, though there is present the general
expansion in the number of words that normally occurs in translation.
Were there any doubt as to the direction of the translation (from French to
English or from English to French?) a collation would establish the French
as unmistakably the original. Certain words in the French text (*Wermonster,
Wesmester, Soubtantonne, Hasvarde, Plemuht*), which one might guess to be
evidence of the French printer's struggle with his manuscript's use of un-
familiar names, emerge confidently in the English text (*Westminster, South-
ampton, Howard, Plymouth*). The English translator has occasionally
functioned as an editor, clarifying matters misunderstood by the French

author. On the continental pattern, for instance, the French original gives
the son of the "Comte de Rutland" the identical title. Although prepared
when the original specifies "le jeune Comte" to translate "the young Earl,"
the English version is otherwise careful to translate "le Comte de Rutland,"
when the son is meant, as "the young Gentleman" or "the Earl of Rutland's
son." When Elizabeth gives Essex the ring that could save his life, the
French version explains that the giving of such a ring "est la derniere, & la
plus forte marque de la faveur des Rois d'Angleterre" (1.106). The English
omits this imaginary custom altogether.

The English translator, therefore, served the original well, and what was
given in Bentley's edition of 1680 was stylistically as true a reflection of *Le
Comte d'Essex* as could have been hoped for according to standards more
exacting than those of the late seventeenth century.

T. M. H. Blair gives a detailed summary of the plot of *The Secret History* in
his edition (36–49), emphasizing the changes Banks made in adapting it for
the stage. The most striking change, however, more pervasive than any
detail of structure, is simply the difference in idiom between the French
original (faithfully, albeit inadequately, shadowed by its English version)
and the idiom of Banks's play. The French style, only lightly figurative,
nevertheless makes few concessions to informality. Throughout it is
homogeneous, a feature reinforced by the uniformity of all the encounters
in the novel. The work consists, in fact, of a series of affecting interviews
between the principal characters. In several cases the interview is essentially
a monologue in the presence of a confidant, and the vital complication of
plot is supplied by assigning the role of confidant to the Countess of
Nottingham, whose passion for Essex has been spurned by him, and who in
consequence secretly hates and wishes to destroy him. Nottingham forms
with Cecil (who is in love with her) an alliance of hatred toward Essex. Thus
Queen Elizabeth reveals the state of her feelings for Essex to Nottingham,
and later the Countess of Rutland, secretly married to Essex, relates her
history likewise to Nottingham. Essex in the Tower asks Nottingham to
bear to the Queen the ring that will save his life, thus assuring that it will
never reach her. Nottingham and Cecil, the vengeful parties, are given little
dialogue, so the greater part of this short novel (of about eighteen
thousand words) consists of lovers' tales and complaints, very uniform in
style.

Here is a passage from the first speech of Elizabeth.

Je contribuois ainsi à cultiver cette foiblesse, qui m'avoit fait murmurer
tant de fois. Plus le Comte d'Essex s'avançoit dans les charges, & plus il
s'aprochoit de ma personne. Tout conspiroit à me trahir; ces regards qui
me paroissoient tendres, sa complaisance, son respect, & ma tendresse,
qui donnoit des interpretations favorables à la moindre de ses actions.
(1.30–31)

In English, this becomes:

> Thus did I Cherish and Indulge the Weakness I had so long struggled with, and condemn'd My Self for. The higher he grew in Office, the nearer he was to My Person. His Complaisance, his Respect, his Looks (which to Me appear'd all Kind and Languishing) and especially My Affection, which had Tenderness enough, to give a favourable Construction to the least of his Actions, conspir'd to Betray Me. (13–14)

The translation here expands a little more than I judge to be customary in this work, but it will be seen that the doubling of elements ("struggled with and condemned myself for" for "m'avait fait murmurer") simply increases the stylistic balance of the French. Likewise the periodic structure that the translator has supplied is very much in the stylistic spirit of the original, contributing to a prose that presents emotion formalized, suspended under the analytic scrutiny of the speaker herself. These narratives are truly "histories," studied accounts of past events. Within the narratives, moments of extreme passion appear to break through the glaze of style, only to be reabsorbed immediately. Essex seems to the Queen to be on the point of declaring his love to her.

> Je porterois peut-estre mes souhaits trop loin, interrompit le Comte avec un peu d'émotion. Souhaitez hardiment, adjoutay-je, je vous aime, & si je rougis en vous l'avoüant, ce n'est ny de honte, ny de repentir. L'effort est grande pour une personne de mon humeur qui vous a veu, soûpirer pour une autre; pendant qu'elle méprisoit des Roys pour vous seul, & qu'elle eut voulu vous sacrifier davantage. (1. 100–101)

The English faithfully reproduces this style (39), as it does throughout, but Banks had no use for it. He completely avoided any reliance on the texture of his source, as juxtapositon of one of Elizabeth's soliloquies will demonstrate.

> Why stands my jealous and tormented soul
> A spy to listen, and divulge the treasons
> Spoke against Essex?—O you mighty powers!
> Protectors of the fame of England's queen,
> Let me know it for a thousand worlds;
> 'Tis dangerous.—But yet it will discover,
> And I feel something whispering to my reason,
> That says it is.—O blotted be the name
> Forever from my thoughts! If it be so
> And I am stung with thy almighty dart,
> I'll die, but I will tear thee from my heart,
> Shake off this hideous vapour from my soul,
> This haughty Earl, the prince of my control;
> Banish this traitor to his queen's repose,
> And blast him with the malice of his foes:

Were there no other way this guilt to prove,
'Tis treason to infect the throne with love.[29]

The formal features of this speech, its nature as soliloquy, its blank-verse-becoming-rhyme, are not in themselves reasons sufficient to account for the divergence of styles. To understand that, we must consider a contrast in genres and traditions.

꒰ꂚ꒰ꂚ꒰ꂚ꒰ꂚ꒰ꂚ꒰ꂚ

Le Comte d'Essex is a *nouvelle historique,* and although it is unwise to attach much importance to the genre labels that *nouvellistes* gave to their works, some generalizations can be safely ventured; Antoine Adam's, for instance:

> Souvent, dans ces fades récits, les révolutions et les guerres, réputées inexplicables, se trouvaient soudain éclâirées par une passion inavouée du prince, par une jalousie, par un désir de vengeance.
>   C'étaient alors des "histoires secrètes."[30]

Essex's was a political rebellion, but the *nouvelle* reveals that he was "in reality" the rather helpless victim of circumstances that originated in Elizabeth's passion for him, his rejection of Nottingham, and his marriage to Rutland. His rebellion here is the invention of his enemies, but they make their charges stick.

To the fact that its principal characters are themselves persons of historic importance can be attributed much of the attraction that the novel held for Banks. He would have found unusable the form of the *nouvelle historique* that, by the force of one illustrious example, has become the genre's justification. This is the love story of persons who may bear historical names but who have no political or public dimension in the tale, although the events are set against a historical background, more or less carefully researched. If Banks had considered adapting *La Princesse de Clèves* (published by Barbin in 1678, and by Bentley in translation in 1679), he would have found it unsuitable, not because of its highly novelistic dependence on the analysis of emotions, but because those emotions had no political implications whatever. No throne shakes because Madame de Clèves loves the Duc de Nemours. Banks makes love his subject, but to be suitable for his dramatic skills it had to be love with political meaning. The *Princesse de Clèves* is private history against the background of a court; what Banks needed was the secret history of public persons.[31]

In his prototype she-tragedy, Banks was modifying a tradition rather than inventing a new type of play. He takes the play of political intrigue in history, whose roots run back into pre-Elizabethan drama, and makes concealed love a motive working against the openly avowed concerns of politics. This concealed interest of Elizabeth gives rise to a structural feature of the play that has always struck its readers: the importance of the queen's asides. Very frequently, a speech of hers consists of two parts, one aside and one spoken out. The aside, of course, reveals her feelings, notably her pity for Essex, while the other element gives voice to the Queen's "official" and political opinions. The effect of schizophrenia, no doubt enormously taxing for the technique of the actress playing the role, must be credited with much of the play's popularity. Banks had, almost literally, inserted a sentimental element into a well-established genre where sentimentality usually took only the form of patriotic display.[32]

To study *The Secret History* and *Le Comte d'Essex* as the source of *The Unhappy Favourite* means facing a paradox. Can a "source" supply so little and still be worthy of the name? From *The Secret History* Banks took the hatred of Nottingham for Essex and the affair with Cecil (whom, to avoid confusion with his famous father, he called Burleigh, supplying too, since the French author was ignorant of it or chose to ignore it, the piquant details of Burleigh's distorted physique, "This rocky, dismal form of thine"). He took, too, the intrigue of the ring, though that particular myth was in print, both in England and France, much earlier. Banks supplied large amounts of historical information from sources indicated by Blair, including the famous box on the ear that Elizabeth administers in act 3.[33] Banks ignored altogether the Countess of Rutland's narrative of her secret marriage to Essex, which covers twenty-seven pages of part 2 of *The Secret History*, except inasmuch as he makes Rutland an important character in his play. The public and political elements, of great extent in Banks's work, are minimized to the utmost in the French text, and the particular styles of the French narrative and of its English version, as we have seen, were quite inimical to Banks's dramatic idiom. Is it fact that Banks was indebted to *The Secret History* for little of real importance? Is his debt to Camden, for example, really greater?

The truth is, I believe, that Banks's debt to the tradition of the French *nouvelle historique* was great and singular. In putting on stage characters of historical dignity whose dealings with each other have a "secret history" of amorous intrigue, Banks had contributed to the opening of a seam that was to be mined eagerly and widely, to such an extent, indeed, that this way of reading history has become a staple of modern culture, especially in its popular manifestations (the Hollywood historical "epic," for instance) and in some highbrow ones (the Elizabeth and Essex story was a natural for *bel canto* opera).[34] Banks is obviously not the sole fountain of an attitude so enormously influential, but in going to the continental tradition of "secret history" and employing it with notable success, he helped bring into the English literary tradition a romantic and sentimental attitude that has reproduced enormously.[35] "We are perpetually moralists, but geometricians only by chance." Let "amoureux" stand in place of "moralists," add a dressing of clichés (Cleopatra's nose, *cherchez la femme*), and there appears a powerful modern platitude. *The Secret History* itself was popular, both in its French and English versions, and Banks's play stayed in the repertory for much of the eighteenth century.

That popularity, however, is a datum pointing to no conclusion. *The Secret History* lacks the circumstantial, formal realism that would make a place for it in the rise of the novel. Its wide dissemination in the eighteenth century helps define a readership, yet that readership seems to have no role in literary history, apart from its contribution to the rise of "sentimentality." *Le Comte d'Essex*, though no champion, has bloodlines that touch those of *La Princesse de Clèves* (republished in England throughout the eighteenth century), but Ian Watt has said that French fiction from Madame de Lafayette to Laclos "stands outside the main tradition of the novel" and is "too stylish to be authentic."[36] The tendency to find "democratic," "bourgeois," or "common denominator" explanations for the deeds of the great has real importance for political attitudes in the eighteenth century, as Robert Darnton has shown,[37] but the English forms of this particular mental development are elusive, particularly since there was no revolution to set scholars hunting for "intellectual origins." A lot of people read these books for a long time, and we can only begin to guess why.

The textual histories of *Le Comte d'Essex*, *The Secret History*, and *The Unhappy Favourite* are lengthy and involved. I have not been able to present them in full here. What follows, therefore, is a tentative summary, lacking empirical thoroughness.

Le Comte d'Essex reappeared several times in French after its initial publication in 1678. Ascoli records new editions (Paris and Augsbourg) in 1689,[38] but these do not appear in Lever. An anthology of *nouvelles*, *Histoires Tragiques et Galantes* (published first, according to Ascoli, in 1710; I have consulted a 1715 version) included the work with the significantly modified subtitle *Histoire secrète d'Elisabeth reine d'Angleterre* (Paris: Pierre Witte).[39]

Banks's *The Unhappy Favourite*, acted in 1681, was entered in the *Term Catalogues* in November 1681 by Bentley, and a quarto edition was published by him and Mary Magnes in 1682 (Wing B663). At the end of the play text appears "A Catalogue of some Plays" published by Bentley and Magnes, which includes "Novels printed this year, 1680," which in turn includes "The Secret History of the Earl of *Essex* and Queen *Elizabeth*." Blair, who included the catalogue in his photo-offset reproduction, nowhere remarks on this. Banks had thus turned into a play, published by Bentley, a novel published by Bentley about two years earlier.

This relationship of texts seems initially to support speculation about the personal relationship of Bentley and Banks. Blair says (66): "Bentley was apparently a good friend of Banks" and quotes the dedication to *The Innocent Usurper*, dated 1693. "Here Banks speaks of him as 'a very good Patron' who has never been 'close-fisted to a good Poet': A good poet is always 'freely welcome to your Table too . . . you are a Mecaenus, and such I will stile you.'"

This is misleading. In that dedication, Banks is in fact quoting the opinion of "no mean Author, who before me, made you a Present of his best Comedy [Banks refers to Otway and his *The Soldier's Fortune,* 1681], with this Encomium, that you were a very good Patron. You never were closefisted to a good Poet, and your Generosity was always suitable to the Merit of the Author and his Book, and he is freely welcome to your Table too; if so, you are a Mecaenas, and such I will stile you."[40] This seems to indicate that Banks was hoping for a personal relationship that did not exist between Bentley and himself in 1693, despite the fact that Bentley had been his "stationer" for about ten years. In light of this, speculations about Bentley's personal role in Banks's literary development seem useless.

The Unhappy Favourite went through four editions in the seventeenth century and was performed frequently on the eighteenth-century stage. The popularity of the Essex theme led to a number of exploitations and adaptations of Banks's work.[41]

The *Secret History* proved very popular, too. Bentley republished it and included it in his well-known twelve-volume collection, *Modern Novels,* in 1692. After Bentley's death in 1697, Richard Wellington, who seems to have taken over properties of Bentley, brought out editions of *The Secret History* and included it in his *Collection of Novels* in 1699. I believe there were at least two pirated editions, undated but probably in the seventeenth century.[42] The British Museum Catalogue lists eight English editions spread over the eighteenth century. There was a Dublin edition in 1725, and one appeared in Rutland, Vermont, in 1799. The work was translated into German (1731, republished 1743) and back into French in 1787.[43]

Perhaps the most interesting descendent of *Le Comte d'Essex,* particularly for its implications regarding the popularity and accessibility of the work, is the transformation into a chapbook (Wing H2173) by "W. O.," presumably William Onley. Plomer states that Onley was active between 1697 and 1709,[44] so his intervention in the textual transmission of *The Secret History* must have occurred about twenty years after Bentley's first edition. The choice of chapbook format (which did not employ, it should be noted, the catchpenny frontispiece and fictitious preliminaries of Bentley's version and of other editions) and the fact that there are several chapbook editions seem to indicate an unexpectedly wide public for a relatively refined and sentimental—though robust—"secret history."[45]

⁂

Reading as a late nineteenth-century historian, Sidney Lee declared in the *Dictionary of National Biography* that the translation of *Le Comte d'Essex,* which has been called here *The Secret History,* "abounds in glaring historical errors and is quite worthless as an historical authority."[46] As Lee defined history, that was quite true. But if history includes the odd currents of popular myth and popular taste, then it is no longer defensible to describe this *histoire secrète* as "valueless." And if the biographical history presented in Bellini's *Roberto Devereux,* last descendent of *Le Comte d'Essex,* seems risible now, it reveals at the same time a way of thinking about personality in history that the late twentieth century has not outgrown but merely displaced.

NOTES

1. Thomas Marshall Howe Blair, ed., *The Unhappy Favourite or the Earl of Essex,* by John Banks (New York: Columbia University Press, 1939), vii. Subsequent references to this work appear in the text.

2. James Sutherland, *English Literature of the Late Seventeenth Century* (Oxford: Clarendon Press, 1969), 76–79.

3. James Sutherland, ed., *Restoration Tragedies* (London: Oxford University Press, 1977).

4. Eric Rothstein, *Restoration Tragedy: Form and the Process of Change* (Madison: University of Wisconsin Press, 1967), 96–99; Robert D. Hume, *The Development of English Drama in the Late Seventeenth Century* (Oxford: Clarendon Press, 1976), 217–18, 351.

5. Sutherland, *English Literature,* 542.

6. Gerard Langbaine, *Account of the English Dramatick Poets* (Oxford, 1691; rpt. New York: Burt Franklin, 1969), 9. I owe my own introduction to Banks to Dick Hoefnagel and am grateful to him for much assistance with the project.

7. Ian Watt, *The Rise of the Novel* (Berkeley: University of California Press, 1957).

8. Rothstein, *Restoration Tragedy,* 98.

9. Sutherland, *English Literature,* 76.

10. *General Catalogue of Printed Books, Photolithographic Edition to 1955* (London: W. Clowes, 1960), p. 51, col. 1068; p. 60, col. 765.

11. Georges Ascoli, *La Grande-Brétagne devant l'opinion française au XVIIe siècle* (Paris: Gamber, 1930), 1:245–47. Ascoli's mention of an edition of *Le Comte d'Essex* dated 1677 coincides with other references. Gervais E. Reed's *Claude Barbin: Libraire de Paris sous la règne de Louis XIV* (Geneva: Droz, 1974), 103, explains the date 1677 as "une faute typographique." The British Museum copy I have used is dated 1678, and the only copy located by Lever in his bibliography is also dated 1678 (see n. 18). The frequency of references to a copy dated 1677 in the Bibliotheque Nationale (Y^{2}23549 is the call number always cited) suggests that this is a copy that has escaped Lever's attention, unlikely though that must be.

12. (Rpt. Ann Arbor: Edwards, 1946), 13 (DEV): col. 164; 15 (ELI): col. 254.

13. *Dictionary of National Biography, s.v.* "Devereux, Robert."

14. Charlotte E. Morgan's *The Rise of the Novel of Manners: A Study of English Prose Fiction between 1600 and 1740* (New York: Columbia University Press, 1911) accepts the date 1650 for the chapbook, states that it was "reprinted" in 1680 as *The Secret History,* and declares that it was "Translated from the French of Devereux," thus somehow attributing the family name of Essex to the author of this fiction (172; see also 56). Dr. Morgan thus became the first scholar to identify *The Secret History* as a translation from the French.

15.The terms *publisher* and *publish* are, of course, anachronisms when speaking of the late seventeenth century. To do without them, however, is mighty inconvenient. I have therefore used the words in seventeenth-century contexts but not, I hope, so as to mislead the reader.

16. F. Longchamp, "Un libraire du XVIIe siècle: Claude Barbin," *Le bibliographe moderne* 17 (1914–15): 10–39.

17. Ibid., 30.

18. Maurice Lever, *La fiction narrative en prose au XVIIe siècle: Répertoire bibliographique du genre romanesque en France, 1600–1700* (Paris: Éditions du Centre National de la Recherche Scientifique, 1976).

19. Longchamp, "Claude Barbin," 31. Reed is unable to confirm the provenance Longchamp gives for the name (*Claude Barbin*, 67).

20. Henry R. Plomer, *A Dictionary of Printers and Booksellers . . . 1668 to 1725* (Oxford: Bibliographical Society, 1922), 31–32: "The well-known publisher of novels, plays, and romances, hence referred to by Dunton as 'novel' Bentley."

21. I have consulted and quote from the copy in the Yale University Library, reproduced on microfilm in the series *English Books, 1641–1700* (University Microfilms), reel 293.

22. Convention had established that certain arrangements of arms and legs in works of art had sexual meaning. Maynard Mack in *The Garden and the City* (Toronto: University of Toronto Press, 1969) reproduces (pl. 36, p. 133) an engraving called "Solomon in His Glory" that depicts George II dallying with Madame Walmoden. The king's leg is raised over the lady's, "a motif used in sixteenth- and seventeenth-century paintings to symbolize sexual possession." Mack refers to the article of Leo Steinberg, "Michael-Angelo's Florentine Pieta: The Missing Leg," *Art Bulletin* 50 (1968): 343–53, which gives the history of the motif. In the frontispiece to *The Secret History*, the man's feet are firmly on the ground, but the positions of the woman's hands, one over the man's thigh, the other around his shoulders, are strikingly similar to those of the woman's hands in "Solomon in His Glory." (The *décolletage* is reminiscent, too.) Steinberg's illustrations include several in which the hands in these positions accompany the slung leg motif. The arrangement in the plate from *The Secret History* suggests that the woman's passion is rejected by the man.

23. The costumes and poses of the figures in this engraving strongly suggest arrangements found elsewhere in seventeenth-century art. Were one to guess at the subject of the engraving without knowing where it is found, the most likely suggestion would be Dido and Aeneas. A painting by Guido Reni in Kassel provides an interesting analogy. Aeneas at the left is in classical armor, Dido, holding his hand, pleads with him in the center, and at the right a woman (perhaps Dido's sister) observes the couple; her position and function are filled by the black boy in the engraving. In Reni's picture the characters are standing and are depicted only at half-length (C. Garboli and E. Bacceshi, *L'opera completa di Guido Reni* [Milan: Rissoli, 1971], 103–104). I am grateful to Linda Krause for pointing me to Guido Reni.

24. For most of his career, Bentley was in partnership with members of the Magnes family. He began as junior partner to James Magnes, but by 1680 was clearly the dominant partner, James Magnes having died and been succeeded by his widow, Mary. Mary was succeeded in partnership with Bentley by S. Magnes.

25. Edward Arber, *A Transcript of the Registers of the Company of Stationers of London 1554–1640* (London: privately printed, 1875–77), 1:417.

26. Pierre Corneille Blessebois, *Le lion d'Angélie* (Paris, 1862), xxii–xxiii. Blessebois' *nouvelle*, first published in 1676 ("Cologne"), bore the imprint of the fictitious S. L'Africain (Lever, *La fiction narrative*, 180).

27. To judge by the first sentence quoted in Lever (*La fiction narrative*, 145) (Wing S2341) is a translation of *Le duc d'Alençon* by an anonymous author, published in Paris by F. Du Chemin, 1680.

28. The first English edition of this had appeared in 1676, "for R. Bentley."

29. Sutherland, *Restoration Tragedies*, 224 (act 3, lines 173–89).

30. Antoine Adam, *La fin de l'école classique, 1680–1715*, vol. 5 of *Histoire de la littérature française au XVIIe siècle* (Paris: Domat, 1956), 314. The definition of the *histoire secrète* as one of the forms of the *nouvelle histoire* is not without controversial variations. I use the term in the sense given by Adam, and well explained by Charles Mish: "the notion that all history depends

solely on the sexual propensities of great men (and women), whose doings constitute the world of power. All statecraft, all wars, all history depends ultimately upon the 'amorous intrigues' of the rulers of mankind and their coteries" ("English Short Fiction of the Seventeenth Century," *Studies in Short Fiction* 6 [1969)]: 289, n. 104). Since *The Secret History of . . . Elizabeth . . . and . . . Essex* has to make some obeisance to nonamorous motives (Essex's dealings with Tyrone, for example, lead to his arrest), it may be called less than "pure" secret history, but all is done that may be to play down politics in favor of love. Other critics use the term *secret history* to refer to accounts of historical events in which only the names have been changed to protect the author. *Crypto-history* might be better.

31. However one evaluates Nathaniel Lee's adaptation, *The Princess of Cleve* (acted before 1682; published 1689), whether as a "masterpiece" (Robert D. Hume) or as "a rotting dung-heap" (Allardyce Nicoll), one is unlikely to disagree that Lee forced the work to serve ends very remote from those of Madame de Lafayette. Yet Lee's version is as far from Banksian she-tragedy as it is from the French original. See Thomas B. Stroup and Arthur L. Cooke, eds., *The Works of Nathaniel Lee* (New Brunswick, N.J.: Scarecrow Press, 1955), 2 : 147–227.

Banks's employment of sources from French literature follows with striking closeness the major development in French prose fiction in the latter half of the seventeenth century. For *The Rival Kings* (1677) he had used La Calprenède's romance *Cassandre* which, between 1642 and 1645, appeared in five parts, amounting to more than fifty-five hundred pages (Lever, *La fiction narrative*, 98). For *Cyrus the Great* (written before 1681 but not published until 1696) he drew on Mme. de Scudéry's *Artamène, ou Le Grand Cyrus*, which appeared in ten volumes, beginning in 1649. The fifth edition of 1656 had more than seventy-five hundred pages (ibid., 73–76). But for *The Unhappy Favourite* his source was a *nouvelle* of 330 tiny pages, about 120 in its various English versions. Banks's sources bear witness to "the decline of the heroic-epic novel" that was apparent in France in the 1670s. "As early as 1671 Sorel remarked on the growing favor enjoyed by the 'nouvelles' and 'histoires scandaleuses.'" By 1683 Du Plaisir could state: "Les petites histoires on entièrement détruit les grands Romans" (Moses Ratner, *Theory and Criticism of the Novel in France from L'Astrée to 1750* [n.p.: 1938], 39). Banks was, in this matter at least, a close follower of fashion.

32. Though patriotic display does occur in the plan. The "Armada ensemble" (act 1, lines 218–90) is a good example (Sutherland, *Restoration Tragedies*, 199–201).

33. Blair, *The Unhappy Favourite*, 44.

34. Donizetti's *Roberto Devereux* is based on a French play of 1829 that apparently derives from the first Essex play of all, Antonio Coello's *El Conde de Sex*, first performed in 1633 (ed. Donald E. Schmiedel [Madrid: Playor, 1973]). Herbert Weinstock, however, cites as another source drawn on by Camarano, Donizetti's librettist, Jacques Le Scène des Maison's *Histoire secrète des amours d'Elisabeth d'Angleterre et du comte d'Essex*. This was published in 1787, if it is the same as the *Histoire d'Elizabeth et du comte d'Essex, tirée de l'anglois*, attributed to Le Scène des Maisons in the British Museum Catalogue. I have not been able to examine this, but by its title it seems to be a retranslation back into French of *The Secret History* (Herbert Weinstock, *Donizetti* [New York: Pantheon, 1963], 353).

35. Charles Mish is the only literary historian I know to give proper weight to the influence of French fiction in England in the period from 1660 to 1700. "By first translating and then imitating French models, English fiction was to take its first firm steps in the direction that leads to the modern novel" ("English Short Fiction," 280–81). Mish's judicious survey is an essential component of Restoration literary history.

36. Watt, *Rise of the Novel*, 30.

37. Robert Darnton, "Trade in the Taboo: The Life of a Clandestine Book Dealer in Prerevolutionary France," in Paul J. Korshin, ed., *The Widening Circle: Essays on the Circulation of Literature in Eighteenth-Century Europe* (Philadelphia: University of Pennsylvania Press, 1976), 62–63.

38. Ascoli, *La Grande-Brétagne*, 2 : 285.

39. René Godenne states that this anthology went into "Autres ed.: 1731–1756" (*Histoire de la nouvelle française aux XVIIe et XVIIIe siècles* [Geneva: Droz, 1970], 139).

40. University Microfilms, reel 51.

41. Listed by Blair, *The Unhappy Favourite*, 123–27.

42. One of these is Wing S2342A.

43. See n. 33.

44. Plomer, *Dictionary of Printers*, 224.

45. In his consideration of the source of Banks's tragedy, Blair had some ado to explain the Countess of Rutland's use of the word "Revenge" when explaining to the Queen what Essex sought in traveling outside her dominions (42). R. M. Lumiansky pointed out that Blair was the victim of textual corruption ("A Note on Blair's Edition of The Unhappy Favourite," *MLN* 56 [1941]: 280–82). The copy of *The Secret History* Blair consulted reads "Revenge," but an Onley chapbook version that Lumiansky consulted in the Harvard Library reads "Refuge" at that point. (And "Refuge" is the reading of the first edition, following the French.) Lumiansky perceived, too, that the chapbook's title page corresponded with that cited by Lee in the *Dictionary of National Biography* as of the "1650" edition. Lumiansky then made the intelligent guess that, since both Banks's play and the chapbook omit the Countess of Rutland's narrative of her secret marriage to Essex, perhaps Banks's source was in fact the chapbook version. This, however, for the reasons given above, is not possible. Nor does it seem likely that the Onley chapbook was influenced in the omission by the form of Banks's play. The type in the Harvard copy of the chapbook gets progressively smaller from first page to last. The printer was perhaps experiencing difficulty in getting all his copy in, which may be why Rutland's narrative was cut.

46. *Dictionary of National Biography*, s.v. "Devereux, Robert."

6

Fatal Marriages? Restoration Plays Embedded in Eighteenth-Century Novels

Susan Staves

The eighteenth-century novel seems to have suffered from a peculiar form of repetition compulsion. Again and again these novels invoke representations of action in Restoration drama, juxtaposing Restoration stage representations against the representations of later eighteenth-century life that presumably are their primary task. Richardson's Lovelace, before he rapes Clarissa, decides to take her to the theater to see Otway's *Venice Preserved*, confiding to Belford, "it were worth while to carry her to the play of *Venice Preserved*, were it but to show her, that there have been, and may be, much deeper distresses than she can possibly know."[1] Fielding's Sophia sits quietly in Lady Bellaston's house reading Southerne's *Fatal Marriage* until, when she reads of "poor distrest Isabella" disposing of her wedding ring, Sophia drops the book and lets "a Shower of Tears" run "down into her Bosom."[2] At this juncture, Lord Fellamar appears, bent upon the rape of Sophia. Goldsmith's Parson Primrose, looking for his seduced daughter Olivia, pauses to watch strolling players perform Rowe's *Fair Penitent*, only to discover his lost son George about to make his dramatic debut.[3] Examples could be multiplied almost endlessly.[4] But why should such Restoration plays be so embedded in eighteenth-century novels?

First, there is the common sense explanation. People in the eighteenth century actually did spend considerable time attending plays, reading plays, and writing and talking about characters in plays. If the novel is to represent the real life of its contemporaries, it must undertake to represent these activities. Richardson or Fielding can hardly show us their characters changing flat tires, filling out income tax forms, or going to the movies. In the leisure-class circles that dominate the representations of eighteenth-century fiction, the entertainment provided by plays had a realistic importance that rivaled that of gambling, a not entirely unrelated activity significantly called "play."

That characters spend their time being entertained by plays, however, is also part of the romance element in eighteenth-century fiction, part of the representation of what was thought desirable, what was considered ideal.[5] Gentlemen in the eighteenth century also spent time haggling over the price of fencing, deciding whether or not to put in turnips, drawing up or having drawn up for them mortgages and other instruments of private and commercial debt, and so on, and ladies—though there is less evidence of this—spent time deciding what to have for dinner or whether to fire the cook; but such humdrum activities are not much represented. In fiction people are not usually seen working on providing basic material necessities or earning money, or even worrying much about investing, increasing, or preserving their capital. Instead, they spend money. What leisure-class people desired was not work but money to spend, at a minimum, the "competences" about which Edward Copeland has recently written a good essay.[6] Impecunious novelist after impecunious novelist writes not of dodging creditors or of making do with less heat or cheaper food, writes not of the old Grub Street as George Gissing later wrote of the New, but of parties at cards, excursions to Vauxhall or Bath, balls, masquerades, buying gowns or hoods, and, of course, going to the theater. Indeed, the ladies and gentlemen of the eighteenth century were fortunate that the Renaissance and Restoration had bequeathed to them such a rich stock of amusing plays, for they proved relatively inept at making their own.

More crucially, the embedding of Restoration play-texts in the eighteenth-century novels reveals an appropriation by bourgeois women of sentiments and entitlements that had formerly been the property of aristocratic men. This appropriation takes two forms, both of which would have seemed bizarre from an older perspective. In one form, bourgeois women in later novels appropriate to themselves and their own circumstances the words, sentiments, and feelings expressed by the protagonists of earlier drama, establishing an identification with them. Sometimes these identifications constitute claims to heroic stature and significance. Sometimes the words of the earlier drama allow later hearers, speakers, or readers to possess intensities and kinds of feeling which the polite world stipulated they could not own more directly. In the second form of appropriation, bourgeois women treat the older elite drama as an object that they can not only possess, but, reversing the older hierarchies of class and gender, one that they are empowered to censor and criticize. Their criticism is not a simple rejection of earlier drama; instead, it transforms the earlier drama into an object that they can possess and alter, an object over which they can proclaim their superiority. Both class and gender are at issue: some of the shock of these appropriations is provoked by the transfer from the aristocracy to the middling sorts of people, some by the transfer from male to female; but the most intense shock results when class and gender change simultaneously.

The first form of appropriation, identification, is the simpler. A typical dedication to a Restoration play suggests that a playwright who belongs to the lesser gentry (to be kind about it) has produced a work intended to amuse and honor an aristocrat and his world. In the eighteenth century, middle-class women could become the consumers of texts originally produced for aristocratic men. Within novels, women frequently appropriate the sentiments expressed by heroic and tragic heroes to themselves and their own circumstances. Alan McKillop, for instance, noticed that Clarissa speaks lines from the Dryden and Lee *Oedipus* ("To you, great gods! I make my last appeal"), applying them to her own situation. McKillop observed, "it may seem superfluous . . . that the sober tenacity and self-confidence of the middle-class girl should be elevated to the stoical pride of the tragic heroine."[7] But far from being superfluous, the quotation of Oedipus's exit speech after Tiresias's warnings, like the use of *Venice Preserved,* is a way to confer upon Clarissa and her circumstances the dignity and high seriousness of tragedy, to claim for her the entitlement to sympathy and serious consideration previously limited to kings and noblemen. Lovelace's earlier claim that the protagonists of Otway's drama experience "much deeper distress" than Clarissa could "possibly know" is ultimately disproved by the text of Richardson's novel.

Sarah Fielding's *David Simple* provides a similar example of this first form of appropriation. In that novel Lady Know-all and Lady True-wit are distinguished from some other ladies with literary interests by their fondness for Dryden's *Don Sebastian.* One day at a performance they are particularly moved by the scene in the fourth act between Don Sebastian and Dorax, the scene Dryden himself singled out for special praise. They identify themselves and their own friendship with that of these heroes: "I observed them more than the Play," says one of the other literary ladies, "to see in what manner they behaved: And what do you think they did? Why truly, all the time the Two Friends were quarrelling, they sat, indeed, with great Attention, altho' they were quite calm; but the Moment they were reconciled, and embraced each other, they both [the ladies] burst into a Flood of Tears, which they seemed unable to restrain."[8]

Both in fiction and in life Restoration plays also proved useful devices for introducing into eighteenth-century polite discourse subjects and intensities of feeling otherwise tabooed by the codes of eighteenth-century manners. A good example of a particular Restoration play's being used to allow the articulation of feelings otherwise taboo and hence to create a shared consciousness of those feelings is found in Charlotte Lennox's *Life of Harriot Stuart* where the characters relieve the boredom of the crossing to America by a dramatic reading of Otway's *Orphan.* The hero reads Castalio while the eponymous heroine, supposedly at the command of her mother, reads the women's parts, the chief woman's part being Monimia's. Lovemaking of an intensity and directness otherwise impermissible proceeds in public in the form of a dramatic reading. Afterwards, Harriot reports:

I received the general thanks of our hearers, for having so exquisitely touched the tender distress of Monimia. Dumont, without regarding the compliments that were paid to him, was wholly employed in lavishing praises on me. "Never," said he, (in a kind of transport) "have I heard a voice so harmonious as Miss Harriot's; yet the graces of her utterance, inimitable as they are, merits our admiration less than her judgment, by which she gave so exactly the true sense and spirit of the poet." "It must be confessed also," interrupted Mrs. Villars, (who was willing to spare me the confusion of replying to this compliment) "that Dumont has succeeded very happily in expressing the passion of Castalio."[9]

Otway is also used to overcome eighteenth-century inhibitions in Richard Graves's *Eugenius; or, Anecdotes of the golden vale*. Graves's Flora, an unspoiled Welsh girl, is discovered reading *The Orphan* and attempts to conceal the book. Eugenius takes the book from her; it opens "of itself" (presumably from repeated opening to that page rather than from the magic of a *sortes Otwayiana*) "and this passage was marked with a pencil":

> It was not kind
> To leave me like a turtle here alone,
> To droop and mourn the absence of my mate.
> When thou art from me, every place is desart,
> And I, methinks, am savage and forlorn.[10]

Flora blushes and claims the playbook belongs to a maid. As a heroine of 1785, she is debarred by the codes of female decorum from complaining that Eugenius has left her alone and debarred from articulating her love and grief. Otway does it for her.

This first form of appropriation of Restoration drama asserts identity between Restoration characters and those of the eighteenth century; both are seen to be capable of similar experiences and feelings, both entitled to be taken seriously. The more complex second form of appropriation, ultimately involving criticism, depends initially on the conversion of Restoration plays into objects constitutive of eighteenth-century polite culture. Restoration drama could be possessed by eighteenth-century people who bought tickets to see performances or bought play-texts to read. That drama was becoming less oriented toward performance and increasingly conceptualized as part of a printed literary canon, in fact, made Restoration plays available even to an audience that could not or would not visit the London theaters.[11] One way eighteenth-century people established their sensibility and gentility was by showing familiarity with Dryden, Congreve, Otway, Rowe, and their contemporaries. Such people were not only supposed to know the texts but also to have opinions about them, opinions that in turn were thought to reveal intelligence, morality, and sensibility—or their lack. Clarissa, who has already read *Venice Preserved* before she goes to see it, derives some satisfaction from observing that even the "hard-hearted" Lovelace appears "very sensibly touched with some of the most affecting scenes," and, at Anna Howe's request, has herself composed a "little book . . . upon the principal acting plays."[12] Fielding's Amelia's good taste is signaled when, left alone one evening while Booth is out gambling away more of their money, she frugally denies herself wine and her children tarts, instead settling down to read "one of the excellent Farquhar's comedies."[13] The husband in Mary Wollstonecraft's *Maria* engages in conversation consisting of "exaggerated tales of money obtained by lucky hits," but Maria distinguishes herself by preferring "literary society" and the theaters that are "a never-failing source of amusement":

> My delighted eye followed Mrs. Siddons, when, with dignified delicacy, she played Calista; and I involuntarily repeated after her, in the same tone, with a long-drawn sigh:

> "Hearts like our's were pair'd—not match'd."

The tedious husband demonstrates his worthlessness by silencing Maria's account of these theatrical pleasures with "sullen taciturnity."[14] Spending money on playbooks and theater tickets and taking time to formulate opinions about the earlier drama was a form of eighteenth-century conspicuous consumption and a way to mark gentility.

Given such possibilities of possessing Restoration drama, however, eighteenth-century people and characters were by no means content merely to appreciate it or merely to take pleasure in considering themselves the possessors of plays originally written for the Earl of Mulgrave or the Earl of Dorset. The second form of appropriation goes beyond possession to criticism. It is exemplified at its most outrageous in the second part of *Pamela*. There Richardson's former serving girl, now Mrs. B., undertakes to make Lady Davers the present of "a little book" containing all her observations on the plays she has seen during her first winter in town. She has prepared for this task by making marginal notes in the printed playbooks she has bought—"by referring to which," Pamela writes, "I shall be able to state what my thoughts were at the time of seeing them pretty nearly with the same advantage, as if I had written them at my return from each."[15] Richardson does actually give his readers the benefit of Pamela's critiques of Dryden's *Virgil; The Distressed Mother,* Philips's play based on Racine's *Andromache;* and Steele's *Tender Husband.* All of these works have distinct faults according to Pamela. Here is a cultural revolution worthy of Madame Mao! The agricultural laborers and menial servants have come in from the countryside to declare the errors of the elite. What is significant is not only the content of the critique but also the fact that Pamela considers herself entitled to judge the works of Dryden or Steele and that Richardson clearly supports this sense of entitlement.[16]

Eighteenth-century criticism of Restoration drama included not only the

Pamela as critic

sort of commentary Pamela offers, but also censorship. As is well known, Restoration plays, particularly the comedies, were thought to require expurgation to fit them for the consumption of later audiences.[17] The power of these plays to introduce otherwise tabooed thoughts and feelings is, in fact, acknowledged by such expurgations and by the distinctions felt between reading excerpts from plays in private; reading entire plays in private; reading entire plays aloud dividing the parts among friends; and, finally, performing them for money in public—each of these activities constituting a level on a continuum from distanced and private awareness of the play to intimate and public involvement with it. Depending on the content of a particular play, characters who will participate in one of these activities may balk at the next more public one. Scholars have discovered that Richardson seems to have preferred to take his Restoration drama in the diluted form of quotations to be found in the "Collection of Thoughts" in Edward Bysshe's *Poet's Handbook.*[18] Long before the evangelical disapproval of theatricals evident in *Mansfield Park,* eighteenth-century people and characters evince a very strong sense that to utter the words of love or rage is, in a serious sense, to perform an act of love or revenge. To perform means not simply to use one's voice and body as artistic media to represent a text but, literally, to act out, to do the acts of love or hate, acts that are themselves tabooed. Merely to be seen attentively reading about an emotion marks the reader as possessing that emotion. Thus, in the examples quoted above from Lennox's *Life of Harriot Stuart* and Graves's *Eugenius* Harriot blushes as she reads the part of Monimia aloud and Flora blushes to be discovered silently reading Monimia's complaint. Even in its expurgated form, Congreve's *Love for Love* proves "so extremely indelicate" that Burney's Evelina cannot watch it in Lord Orville's company without being put "out of countenance."[19] A further rejection of the thoughts and feelings of Restoration drama is evident in the many examples of later novelists marking their villains or otherwise dangerous or unworthy characters by attributing to them a taste for the earlier drama as, most memorably, Richardson makes Dryden Lovelace's favorite poet and decorates his correspondence with quotations from heroic drama.[20]

This critique of Restoration drama masks a deeper struggle over cultural definitions of reality. The so-called excesses of Restoration drama were declared beyond the pale on the grounds that people do not scream, wail, sigh, stamp their feet, tear their hair, act like lust-driven animals, think often of sex, or make lewd remarks—although of course people are capable of doing all these things, and are at least as capable of doing them as of sitting quietly in drawing rooms, never raising their voices or laughing aloud, at every instant preserving the demeanor of a Sir Charles Grandison. The range of feeling and action in Restoration drama was stigmatized as "extravagant," while the restrictions on feeling and action in the polite world of eighteenth-century discourse were denominated "ordinary" and "real." The eighteenth century attempted to decree that the intensities and horrors of earlier tragedy were merely unrealities and absurdities. Thus, amidst a panoply of direct references to Dryden's *Rival Ladies, Conquest of Granada,* and *Cleomenes,* Fielding kills off the ranting characters in *The Tragedy of Tragedies,* including the King who declaims a mock-epic simile while killing himself. Belford in *Clarissa* attacks Rowe's *Fair Penitent,* complaining of earlier dramatists generally, "our poets hardly know how to create a distress without horror, murder, and suicide; and must shock your soul to bring tears to your eyes."[21] The eighteenth-century critique of Restoration drama is in part an attempt to enforce the banishment of ranting and raving ("I'll rave; I'll rant; I'll rise; I'll rush; I'll roar," says Grizzle in *The Tragedy of Tragedies*), of horror, murder, and suicide, and also of the conscious and articulated awareness of sexuality.[22] What goes on in Dryden, Wycherley, Otway, and even Rowe will from henceforth be rejected as unnatural and unreal. The debate is over how reality will be defined.

The repetitions of Restoration drama embedded in eighteenth-century fiction thus aggressively assert an identity between the worlds of the earlier aristocracy and the eighteenth-century bourgeoisie; simultaneously, they claim a superiority for the bourgeois world, the formerly low and vulgar world, which now shows its power over the aristocratic world of the earlier drama by criticizing and censoring it. This is, of course, contradictory. The eighteenth-century bourgeois world cannot simultaneously be the same as and better than the earlier aristocratic world. But the contradiction was a necessary one: the bourgeois world needed to dignify itself by apropriating the prestige that previously belonged to the aristocratic world and it also needed to define itself by asserting differences. Richardson's use of Restoration drama in *Clarissa* fully exploits the contradictions. Clarissa is elevated by her citations from earlier tragedy and heroic drama; Lovelace too is dignified to a certain extent by his dramatic tastes and quotations, but they are also used to underline his immorality. Merely to have ignored Restoration drama, as of course some moralists and a good number of pious and virtuous people recommended, would have been a weaker response to the challenge it represented. At the very least, it was necessary to engage in criticism trying to disentangle its supposed virtues (fire, warmth, genius, strong passion, wit, sparkle, spirit) from its supposed vices (rant, fustian, extravagance, grossness, licentiousness, indelicacy, immorality).[23] Yet to dissociate the virtues from the vices in order to have the virtues alone proved impossible. The reformed drama of the eighteenth-century was almost universally acknowledged even by contemporaries to be a weaker drama. The strongest bourgeois responses to Restoration drama acknowledged its power, dared the frisson of confrontation, and, finally, incorporated its texts into new novelistic texts with new meanings.

So far I have made this marriage of Restoration drama and eighteenth-century fiction sound at least like a marriage of convenience, if not actually a happy marriage. Beyond their important but rather blank usefulness in the sheer filling of time, Restoration plays became objects of literary culture satisfyingly capable of being possessed by nonaristocratic people, who could, like Pamela, purchase playbooks upon which they could inscribe whatever reflections they pleased. Yet neither the bourgeois appropriation nor the female appropriation of Restoration drama could effect a perfect union. And, I suggest, there is a sense in which the embedding of Restoration plays in eighteenth-century fiction may have represented, for women at least, not such a happy marriage but, to borrow Southerne's title, a fatal one.

In relation to women, especially, playgoing and playreading were activities both enthusiastically praised and strenuously condemned. To love the theater as Wollstonecraft's Maria did could be to show oneself a woman of taste and sensibility. Some gentlemen in novels fall in love with girls who betray their susceptibility to feeling with a flood of tears at a tragedy, as Charles Beverley does in *Maple Vale, or the History of Miss Sidney* when Miss Fancourt sobs aloud while watching Mrs. Siddons.[24] The consumption of plays might also increase the value of a wife by making her able to provide more amusement for her husband. *Letters Addressed to Young Married Women,* for instance, urges them to keep this possibility in view: "If a [wife] reads a new work, a poem, or a play, it must be to form her taste, that she may be able to entertain the man she loves."[25]

On the other hand, love of plays, playgoing, and playacting were frequently said to be particularly dangerous for women. Rakes like Lovelace were sure that the theater was an ideal scene of seduction. In Garrick's *A Peep behind the Curtain; or, the New Rehearsal,* Lady Fuz is so entranced by the theatrical wonders of a rehearsal that she fails to notice her own daughter's elopement.[26] For women to consume plays without strictly subordinating the process to the end of making themselves more desirable to men might be to risk the contamination of romantic desires doomed to frustration by existing realities. The satire and moralizing consistently directed at women devotees of romance, whether in the form of French prose romances or English dramatic verse, insist on their unreality and warn that expectations derived from them lead only to misery. Jane Barker in *A Patch-work Screen for the Ladies* depicts a girl who reads so many plays and romances that she thinks herself a heroine and marries her footman, convinced he is a prince in disguise.[27] Such an apparently commonsensical view is echoed in our own day by Lawrence Stone when he remarks, "Among the upper classes, the demand for romantic love and sexual fulfilment was stimulated—especially among women—by the reading of romances and love stories, which created exaggerated expectations of marital felicity which were very often frustrated."[28]

Yet, as I have said, attacks on the alleged extravagances and unrealities of romance mask a deeper struggle over the cultural definitions of reality—

and this struggle includes the cultural definitions of "woman" and "woman's experience." Clarissa is a true fair penitent, Belford and Richardson insist; Rowe's Calista a false penitent and actually not a woman. Women, Belford declares, do not feel lust and rage, and since Calista expresses both, it follows that she can be neither a real woman nor a proper object of pity: "Calista is a desiring luscious wench, and her penitence is nothing else but rage, insolence, and scorn. Her passions are all storm and tumult; nothing of the finer passions of the sex, which, if naturally drawn, will distinguish themselves from the masculine passions by a softness that will even shine through rage and despair."[29] In a subtler way, Fielding's invocation of *The Fatal Marriage* in *Tom Jones,* while used in part to illustrate Sophia's sensibility, also functions to deny the possibility that a tragedy like Isabella's can be part of Sophia's experience. Fielding marks Lord Fellamar's attempt at rape as less than a real threat by casting it in the "artificial" high style of tragedy, labeling his words "Bombast," omitting some of them as merely part of "another and a longer Speech of the same Sort," and, finally, interrupting him with the more "realistic" low language of Squire Western ("Where is she? D-m me, I'll unkennel her this Instant").[30] In Southerne's drama a good woman can be guilty of adultery; in Fielding's novel a good woman cannot be raped.

One possible response to warnings about the dangers of romance, extravagance, and high expectations would be simply to abandon them. In Steele's *Tender Husband,* Barsheba Tipkin, the spinster aunt of romance-addicted Biddy Tipkin, thinks this would be a good idea. Biddy heads her list of heroic lovers with Philocles from Dryden's *Secret Love.* Her aunt urges the burning of such books and the replacement of reading by the exercise of "writing out receipts for broths, possets, caudles, and surfeit-waters, as became a good country gentlewoman":

> *Aunt.* Oh dear, oh dear, Biddy! Pray, good dear, learn to act and speak like the rest of the world. Come, come, you shall marry your cousin and live comfortably.
> *Biddy.* Live comfortably! What kind of life is that? . . . Pray, aunt, learn to raise your ideas. What is, I wonder, to live comfortably?
> *Aunt.* To live comfortably is to live with prudence and frugality, as we do on Lombard Street.[31]

Such an utter descent into female ordinariness, however, is not really recommmended by eighteenth-century fiction.

At the other extreme, the tension between extravagance and ordinariness might be resolved by renouncing ordinariness and using romance as a critique of the current realities. This is a potentially revolutionary position and the one that appealed to Mary Wollstonecraft. In *Maria* Mr. Venables taunts his wife by ironically complimenting her "very pretty . . . theatrical flourishes," addressing her as "fair Roxana," as though she were a heroine in Lee's *Rival Queens,* and unironically demands she "stoop" from her "altitudes" to remember she is "acting a part in real life." Maria resists his attempts to define real life for her and observes, hostilely, that "romantic" was merely "the indiscriminate epithet" Venables "gave to every mode of conduct or thinking superior to his own."[32]

The dominant culture of the eighteenth century, however, preferred neither of these extremes and attempted to compromise, to mediate the contradictions. Discussing the settlements of Biddy Tipkin's marriage, her banker guardian and Sir Harry Gubbin agree to reduce her allotment of pin money—"that foundation of wives' rebellion and husbands' cuckoldom"—and to specify the uses to which the reduced sum shall be put: "we'll put in the names of several female utensils, as needles, knitting needles, tape, . . . playbooks, with other toys of that nature."[33] Plays will be allowed in so far as they amuse idle women, keep them from complaining of boredom, make them in turn more amusing to their husbands, and provide an opportunity for identification in fantasy with intensities of feeling and kinds of awareness that it is agreed will otherwise not exist in life. Heroines in fiction will be allowed to establish their entitlement to special consideration by memorizing verses from Otway or Rowe and formulating opinions about them. But they can indulge in identification with witty or pathetic protagonists only so long as they agree to dissociate themselves from full participation in the dramatic worlds by articulating the sort of moralistic criticism Pamela attempts, to take warning from the fates meted out to the protagonists of she-tragedy, and, perhaps, most important of all, so long as they agree to renounce what are stigmatized as dramatic excesses and to discover true romance in their very own husbands.

Again and again women who are satirized as deluded by extravagant, romantic expectations are forced to renounce their extravagances and, at the very moment they do so, made to discover that romance has been present in the ordinary men who have been there all along and in ordinary life. Lady Fanshaw in Elizabeth Griffith's *Platonic Wife* begins by lamenting, "I almost wish I had never learned my letters; for the delicate and refined sentiments, which books have inspired me with, have only served to disgust me with almost all mankind." Her husband refuses to act the romantic lover, refuses to whine and sigh, but does concoct a scheme to lower her expectations. The scheme succeeds and Lady Fanshaw exclaims, "For what illusions have I strayed from real happiness, which I am now convinced is only to be found in the calm indulgences of rational affections." Also as a consequence of her conduct during her test, however, her formerly unromantic husband becomes romantic, acknowledging that a successful completion of the test will mean that she "will be something more than woman; and adoration, late her claim, will then become her due."[34]

The work of Eliza Haywood also aptly illustrates these contradictions. Haywood was the author of numerous romances and of books of advice concerning marriage, though her own marriage led to an early separation.

In the books of advice she warns women against "the imprudence of indulging too flattering expectations in Marriage" and insists it "would be ridiculous" in a husband "to entertain his wife with those romantic hyperboles which he found necessary to address her with as a mistress."[35] Yet she recommends the theater as "innocent and improving" for wives and her advice is punctuated with romantic stories (supposedly true) and quotations from Restoration drama. Wives are warned not to rail at unfaithful husbands, but unfaithful husbands are warned that even forgiving wives, courted again, "may say with Statyra in the Tragedy":

> Oh! I shall find Roxana in your arms,
> And taste her kisses left upon your Lips;
> Her curst embraces have defil'd your body:
> Nor shall I find the wonted sweetness there,
> But artificial scents, and aking odours.[36]

In this same supposedly nonfictional advice book, one husband, not very realistically called Corydon, cools toward his loving wife. Left alone, she dissolves into tears when reading Belvidera's speech complaining of Jaffeir's unkindness. This "excellent wife" dies of grief and the husband repents when it is "too late to make atonement."[37] Romance, ostensibly rejected at the front door, comes in by the back.

For women in plays and fiction, to renounce romance, to renounce claims of high entitlement, is magically to gain romance and adoration. This is the bargain the heroine of an eighteenth-century sentimental novel like *Amelia* strikes. The difficulty is that women have to renounce all claim to deference and consideration as matters of right, and such free gifts were much more apt to be bestowed in novels than in life. Eighteenth-century fiction claimed to be more realistic than seventeenth-century romance, but women who supposed that by imitating the discipline and renunciation of Pamela, Amelia, or Evelina they would earn the same rewards were vulnerable to disappointments more bitter than any that faced Biddy Tipkin. Few husbands whose wives displayed total sympathy, self-abnegation, and devotion were likely to embrace them rapturously repeating Jaffeir's "Woman, lovely woman" speech, as does one husband supposedly known to Eliza Haywood.[38] It is in this sense that the appropriation of Restoration drama by eighteenth-century fiction could constitute, for leisure-class women at least, a fatal marriage.

NOTES

1. Samuel Richardson, *Clarissa; or, the History of a Young Lady* (London: Everyman's Library, 1932), 2:342.

2. Henry Fielding, *Tom Jones*, ed. Sheridan Baker (New York: Norton, 1973), bk. 15, chap. 5, p. 610.

3. *Collected Works of Oliver Goldsmith*, ed. Arthur Friedman (Oxford: Clarendon Press, 1966), 4:105.

4. A convenient source of such examples is Robert Gale Noyes, *The Neglected Muse: Restoration and Eighteenth-Century Tragedy in the Novel (1740–1780)* (Providence, R.I.: Brown University Press, 1958). Noyes was especially interested in the novels as sources of eighteenth-century theater history and drama criticism.

5. I understand the eighteenth-century novel to involve a more or less constant tension between realism and romance. Eighteenth-century novelists attempted to develop a critique of earlier romance, partly by representing characters, actions, circumstances, and sentiments that had not been represented in romance. Also important, however, was their need to overcome the lack of structure and meaning a perfected realism would have entailed by resorting to romance for plots and ways of representing the ideal, indeed, using the novel to represent life as contemporaries wished it to be as well as to represent life as they supposed it actually was. Cf. Susan Staves, "Don Quixote in Eighteenth-Century England," *Comparative Literature* 24 (1972): 193–215; "*Evelina:* or, Female Difficulties," *MP* (1976): 380–81; "Studies in Eighteenth-Century Fiction, 1979," *PQ* (1980): 472–73.

6. Edward Copeland, "What's a Competence? Jane Austen, Her Sister Novelists, and the 5%s," *MLS* 9 (1979): 161–68. On spending money on leisure, see, J. H. Plumb, *The Commercialisation of Leisure in Eighteenth-Century England* (Reading: University of Reading, 1973).

7. Alan Dugald McKillop, *Samuel Richardson: Printer and Novelist* (Chapel Hill: University of North Carolina Press, 1936), 153. Cf. *The Spectator,* ed. Donald F. Bond (Oxford: Clarendon Press, 1965), 1:172, for quotation of this speech and Addison's comments. Cf. also Helen Sard Hughes, "Characterization in Clarissa Harlowe," *JEGP* 13 (1914): 110–23.

8. Sarah Fielding, *The Adventures of David Simple,* ed. Malcolm Kelsall (London: Oxford University Press, 1969), 84.

9. Charlotte Lennox, *The Life of Harriot Stuart. Written by Herself* (London 1751), 1:14. Readers and spectators were urged in didactic writing to take warning from the sufferings of characters in tragedy; and sometimes in fiction characters who themselves cannot act on feelings without losing entirely the narrower sympathies of the later novel's audience can substitute contemplation of the actions of characters in the earlier drama. Thus, in *The Memoirs of Lady Woodford* Fanny Osgood goes to see *Jane Shore* and feels Jane's "exquisite distress the more strongly, by considering that I might have been in the same dangerous situation by living with the man whom I loved. The performance of this play made me shudder to think of what had passed relating to my self." Quoted from Noyes, *Neglected Muse,* 111.

10. Richard Graves, *Eugenius: or, Anecdotes of the golden vale: an embellished narrative of real facts* (London, 1785), 2:51. Cf. *Spectator,* ed. Bond, 2:436, where the same speech is quoted to a lady who supposedly requests a "Dissertation upon the Absence of Lovers."

11. Cf. Peter Holland, *The Ornament of Action: Text and Performance in Restoration Comedy* (Cambridge: Cambridge University Press, 1979), 99–137. This is not, of course, to deny that acting and spectacle were crucial elements of eighteenth-century drama or that there were provincial performances of Restoration plays in the eighteenth century. From a neo-Marxist perspective, such an "assimilation of drama to literature" must be "an ideologically significant appropriation." See Terry Eagleton, *Criticism and Ideology: A Study in Marxist Literary Theory* (London: New Left Books, 1976), 46.

12. Richardson, *Clarissa,* 2:372.

13. Henry Fielding, *Amelia* (London: Everyman's Library, 1930), 2:194.

14. Mary Wollstonecraft, *Maria; or, the Wrongs of Woman* (New York: Norton, 1975), 92–93.

15. Samuel Richardson, *Pamela* (London: Everyman's Library, 1914), 2:262–63.

16. Richardson frequently expressed his sense that great learning served few purposes. See Jocelyn Harris, "Learning and Genius in *Sir Charles Grandison,*" *SEC* 4 (1979): 167–91.

17. See, for example, Emmett L. Avery, "*The Country Wife* in the Eighteenth Century,"

Research Studies of the State College of Washington 10 (1942): 142–58; Emmett L. Avery, *Congreve's Plays on the Eighteenth Century Stage* (New York: Modern Language Association, 1951), 161–70; Aline MacKenzie Taylor, *Next to Shakespeare: Otway's Venice Preserv'd and The Orphan and Their History on the London Stage* (Durham, N.C.: Duke University Press, 1950), 271–83; Kalman A. Burnim, *David Garrick, Director* (1961; Carbondale: Southern Illinois University Press, 1973), 174–79.

18. A Dwight Culler, "Edward Bysshe and the Poet's Handbook," *PMLA* 63 (1948): 858–85.

19. Fanny Burney, *Evelina; or, the History of a Young Lady's Entrance into the World* (New York: Norton, 1965), 67.

20. This aspect of Lovelace's character has been much commented upon. A wonderful if sometimes provoking essay by John Traugott, "Clarissa's Richardson," is throughout sensitive to the relations between Lovelace and the absolutism of both heroic tragedy and cynical comedy, "only opposite sides of the same coin." Traugott observes, "In every way Richardson tries to domesticate the absolutism of the Restoration, preserving its high drama but bringing it down at the same time to household words." *English Literature in the Age of Disguise*, ed. Maximillian E. Novak (Berkeley and Los Angeles: University of California Press, 1977), 157–208.

21. Richardson, *Clarissa*, 4:119.

22. Henry Fielding, *Tom Thumb and The Tragedy of Tragedies*, ed. L. J. Morrissey (Berkeley and Los Angeles: University of California Press, 1970), 62. The entire sentence reads:

> I'll swim through Seas; I'll ride upon the Clouds;
> I'll dig the Earth; I'll blow out ev'ry Fire;
> I'll rave; I'll rant, I'll rise; I'll rush; I'll roar;
> Fierce as the Man whom smiling Dolphins bore,
> From the Prosaick to Poetick Shore.

H. Scriblerus Secundus's note casts doubt on the existence of smiling dolphins.

23. The qualities listed in this sentence are all mentioned in Hugh Blair, *Lectures on Rhetoric and Belles Lettres*, ed. Harold F. Harding, (Carbondale: Southern Illinois University Press, 1965), 523–27, 541–50. Blair published in 1783 and I take this to be a conventional discussion.

24. Described, along with similar scenes from other novels, in J. M. S. Tompkins, *The Popular Novel in England, 1770–1800* (1932; reprint, Lincoln: University of Nebraska Press, 1961), 148–49.

25. *Letters Addressed to Young Married Women* (Philadelphia, 1796), 37.

26. Dane Farnsworth Smith and M. L. Lawhon, *Plays about the Theatre in England, 1737–1800; or, The Self-conscious Stage from Foote to Sheridan* (Lewisburg, Pa.: Bucknell University Press, 1979), 49.

27. Ruth Perry, *Women, Letters, and the Novel* (New York: AMS Press, 1980), 154.

28. Lawrence Stone, *The Family, Sex and Marriage in England: 1500–1800* (New York: Harper and Row, 1977), 396.

29. Richardson, *Clarissa*, 4:118.

30. Fielding, *Tom Jones*, 611–12.

31. Richard Steele, *The Tender Husband*, ed. Calhoun Winton (Lincoln: University of Nebraska Press, 1967), 29–30.

32. Wollstonecraft, *Maria*, 116.

33. Steele, *Tender Husband*, 19.

34. Elizabeth Griffith, *The Platonic Wife* (London, 1765), 10, 73, 61.

35. Eliza Haywood, *The Wife. By Mira* (London, 1756), 202, 205.

36. Eliza Haywood, *The Husband. In Answer to the Wife* (London, 1756), 238.

37. Haywood, *The Husband*, 250.

38. Haywood, *The Wife*, 237.

7

Sincerity, Delusion, and Character in the Fiction of Defoe and the "Sincerity Crisis" of His Time

Maximillian E. Novak

Few writers on Defoe have wasted much ink over the famous "Bangorian Controversy," even though the number of pamphlets that he devoted to it is impressive. The reason for this neglect is not hard to fathom; the pamphlet literature is extensive, and some aspects of the controversy turn entirely on personalities and the politics of religion in the reign of George I. But many of the events associated with the controversy were concerned with the question of sincerity, a question that has been a crucial part of modern literary debates over the reliability of Defoe's narrators. Sincerity even has some importance in defining the genre of Defoe's fictions. Spiritual autobiographies are, by definition, works in which the writers demonstrate their struggle toward a state of grace through a sincere confession of their sins. Picaresque fictions, on the other hand, often present a parodic version of spiritual autobiography in the form of a narrator whose lack of sincerity in relation to social forms carries over to a personal failure of insight into his motives. The picaro or picara tries to win the reader's sympathy with an apparent honesty, while, at the same time, attempting to draw the audience into the circle of trickery that lies at the very heart of the picaresque narrator's raison d'être. If we decide to classify *Robinson Crusoe* as a fictional spiritual autobiography, as G. A. Starr and J. Paul Hunter have suggested, and *Moll Flanders* as picaresque, a classification accepted by almost all writers on the picaresque, we are separating these two first-person narratives according to the sincerity of the narrators as they reveal their characters in the accounts of their lives.[1]

I want to suggest in this brief discussion that the Bangorian Controversy precipitated what might be called a "sincerity crisis" in the period between 1715 and 1724, a time span that included all of Defoe's major fiction, and that this crisis, merging as it did with events like the South Sea scandal, had an important influence on Defoe's treatment of human psychology, both on his development of completely sincere characters and on his creation of characters whose apparent sincerity is no guarantee of their moral righteousness in the eyes of the reader. This complex subject deserves a full monograph covering all aspects of the controversy and Defoe's part in it; here I will simply sketch some aspects of Defoe's involvement in the debate and suggest a few of the ways in which it influenced his fiction.

Lionel Trilling included *sincerity* among those words that "are best not talked about if they are to retain any force of meaning," but it was a crucial word and concept for the English Dissenters in the late seventeenth and early eighteenth centuries.[2] Their main argument for refusing to join the established church was based on the dictates of conscience, and to counter charges of hypocrisy the Dissenters professed their complete sincerity. The Bangorian Controversy gave the word some respect among low churchmen and from this base it spread throughout the eighteenth century to become omnipresent in tracts, poems, and novels.[3] But sincerity held little interest for philosophers who specialized in morality and ethics. Writers like Hutcheson and Wollaston were not interested in that highly differentiated sense of truth to be found in each heart. They wanted to speak of moral ideals that could be judged and evaluated.[4] Sincerity, like a number of other ideas that suffer by a history-of-ideas treatment, has only narrow dimensions. No wonder then, that Leon Guilhamet, in his suggestive study, *The Sincere Ideal,* tended to avoid discussing the intellectual history of sincerity during the eighteenth century in favor of analyzing its presence in individual poems. He relegated his concern with the novel to an appendix on Richardson and dismissed any discussion of sincerity in Defoe's fiction with the evasive comment, "The sincerity of Moll Flanders and Robinson Crusoe is a relevant question only within their respective fictional worlds."[5]

Benjamin Hoadly, Bishop of Bangor, shared more than a few ideas with Defoe. Hoadly's position on the succession was regarded as belonging to the branch of radical Whiggery in which Defoe had a long-standing membership, and an attack on him, in the form of a mocking letter from Thomas Hobbes in the underworld welcoming him to the club of seditious authors, has numerous parallels in the many attacks on Defoe.[6] For both Hoadly and Defoe, the successful transition of power after the death of Queen Anne should have put an end to party strife and to Jacobitism. Both regarded the uprising in Scotland during 1715 in favor of the Pretender as an enigma. It came after a brief period during which the High Church claimed once more to be in danger and seemed to be encouraging popular unrest. In his sermon on these events, *The Present Delusion of Many Protestants Consider'd,* Hoadly chose for his text 2 Thessalonians 2:2, "And for this Cause God shall send them strong delusion, that they should believe a lie." He expressed his belief that the obvious sincerity of the Jacobites could be explained by the powerful emotional force of ingratitude. Nothing short of this could explain how Jacobites could mistake evil for good and how conscience—that usually reliable agency—could become so confused.[7]

This sermon was followed by two that were far more startling. In *A Preservative against the Principles and Practices of the Nonjurors* (1716), Hoadly was responding to a work by the nonjuror George Hickes questioning the sincerity of the Anglican clergy, as well as to the widely publicized dying speeches of the Jacobite rebels taken prisoner in the course of crushing the uprising.[8] To their last moments they professed themselves justified in their revolt against George I. Hickes's volume also concluded with dying words—those of nonjuring clergymen who remained true to their beliefs until the end. Hoadly responded by upholding the right of a government to act for the safety of the whole by depriving of their offices bishops who would not swear allegiance and by denying that sincerity of belief at the end of life could be measured on earth, however much it might earn a place in heaven.

In March of the following year, Hoadly clarified his position by arguing in *The Nature of the Kingdom or Church of Christ* that in matters of religion no man may set himself up as a judge over the conscience of another. The real "Church of Christ" was composed of those who believed "sincerely." It was not to be found in any religious body on earth.[9] What such a doctrine meant to the Church of England is obvious. The Lower House of Convocation, in voting to expel the Bishop of Bangor, argued that his doctrines would mean "an End of all Church Authority," since all judgments would be left to the individual conscience, making "every Man, how illiterate and ignorant soever, his own sole Judge and Director upon Earth in the Affair of Religion."[10] George I prorogued the meeting, and it did not come together for more than a century.

If this dispute was ended by the "infallible artillery" of the monarch's power, the issues raised did not die so quickly. William Law suggested that by a little extension of Hoadly's doctrines, "sincere *Jews, Turks,* and *Deists,* are upon as good a Bottom, and as secure of the Favour of God, as the sincerest Christian." Law agreed that sincerity was an important component of true religious belief, but not at all sufficient. "A little Knowledge of human Nature," he wrote, "will teach us, that our Sincerity may be often charged with Guilt; not as if we were guilty because we are sincere; but because it may be our Fault that we are hearty and sincere in such or such ill-grounded Opinions." And turning the tables on Hoadly, he quoted the same scriptural passage used previously by the bishop: *"God may send them strong Delusion."* Sincerity, according to Law, might be reduced merely to a "private Persuasion"—to thinking that we are right.[11]

More violent in his attacks on Hoadly was Henry Stebbing, who could find no sign at all that Hoadly was restricting his idea of sincerity to Christians. Noting that Hoadly's argument was "as old at least as Mahomet," he reduced it to a simple formula by which equal sincerity on earth would receive an equal reward in heaven.[12] The Convocation had been correct in its condemnation, he argued, because Hoadly had shown no respect for the doctrines and authority of the church.[13]

Hoadly had his strong defenders, like Thomas Pyle and Daniel Whitby. Whitby tried to distinguish between the guilty person who "is conscious to himself" and guilty of a "presumptuous sin," and the good man who, following his conscience, acts with "a sincere, and honest, and true Intention to do the Will of God."[14] But in the end Whitby merely left things where he found them. A worldly church might well seem redundant when sincere belief was the only requirement for salvation. More effective and influential among Hoadly's defenders was John Balguy, who wrote under the name of Silvius. Like Defoe, Balguy identified himself with the "Lovers of Truth" and proceeded to defend Hoadly not only on metaphysical grounds but on those of the nature of civilized discourse.[15] Balguy enlarged the notion of sincerity to include a social and moral good, a stance of honesty, fairness, and open-mindedness. He adopted the position of *The Spectator* papers on the benefits of even-tempered discussion and made Hoadly's enemies seem oddly out of step with contemporary life.[16]

The Bangorian Controversy was not one of those religious disputes that involved only the clergy. Mist's *Weekly Journal*, one of Defoe's newspapers, reported in its issue of 6 July 1717 that the controversy between Hoadly and his chief antagonist, Andrew Snape, had "engrossed all Conversation for this last Week," even eclipsing the debates between the two Houses of Parliament on the trial of Robert Harley.[17] The story recounted Snape's accusations that Hoadly kept a former Jesuit, Pilloniere, as his secretary, that the sermon on sincerity as originally written was far more offensive. Snape named the Bishop of Carlisle as his source for this information. Carlisle, after stating publicly that he wished that his informant would come forward, named White Kennett, Dean of Petersborough, as his source. White Kennett denied everything. The question was, who was the liar and who was sincere? Mist's *Weekly Journal* of 13 July 1717 noted that "the Gall and Animosity, with which they treat one another, without respect to Religion, or the Character of Christian Bishops, encreases daily," and lamented the spectacle of "two Clergymen, two Christians . . . affirming a direct contrary to one another, and one of which is not possible to be true, both calling God to witness and pledging their eternal Salvation upon it" as something never before witnessed in the history of Britain.[18] What was certainly unusual was the use of the public newspapers for such a bitter dispute.

If the political implications of this controversy were ever in question, all doubts disappeared with the publication of the dying speech of a would-be Jacobite assassin of George I named James Shepheard. Dying men, after all, had nothing to gain, and the salvation of their souls to lose, by continuing in their sin. Hence the continuing fascination of such confessions. The ordinary of Newgate, Paul Lorrain, urged Shepheard to acknowledge and confess his sin. Instead, according to Lorrain, he stated, "I am satisfied I was in the right; adding, that he had not alter'd his Mind in the matter, nor ever would alter it; and That if it was in his Power, he would still kill him who we own for our King, or any Friend of his."[19] A paper printed surreptitiously and widely circulated in manuscript that purported to be discovered in Shepheard's pocket after his execution contained a "Hymn to the Holy and Undivided Trinity" and "A True Copy of a Prayer." But the most damaging document was an attack on George I for attempting to bring down the Church of England while pretending to be its defender. Such actions revealed the King's hypocrisy and could be classified as "a prime instance of his Bangorian Sincerity."[20]

For Shepheard or whoever wrote these pieces for him, "Bangorian Sincerity" meant claiming justification for any act on the basis of private conscience. It was the opposite of real sincerity. For Hoadly, sincere belief was a matter of private conscience. Only God could determine whether anyone was truly sincere; a few years later, Hoadly was to argue for an end to the Test Act on the grounds that the state could not set itself up as a judge of conscience. One might have thought that everyone would stop using the term *sincerity* after so much debate, but on the contrary, in this later controversy between Hoadly and Sherlock, each antagonist insisted on his complete sincerity, as if the only way of distinguishing between sincere belief and delusion were the vehemence with which sincerity was claimed. Yet it had become clear in the dispute between the Bishop of Carlisle and White Kennett that something like sincere delusion was possible. When, later in the century, Rousseau tried to explain the workings of unconscious desires, he did so precisely in terms of sincere delusions.[21] What a wonderful time for a novelist interested in exploring the workings of mind, conscience, and action in a series of very different characters!

Enter Defoe. Disputes of this kind amused and intrigued him. And he hardly needed prodding to interest himself in questions of conscience and sincerity. His pamphlet of 1703, *The Sincerity of the Dissenters Vindicated,* upheld sincerity of religious belief as the only reason for dissent from the established church,[22] and he was always ready to discuss conscience and sincerity whenever the Test Act and the Act against Occasional Conformity was at issue as it was in 1703, in 1714, and again in 1719 and 1720. Defoe was far from rigid in his attitude toward sincerity. Long before the Bangorian Controversy, he had decided that certain lies and half-truths might be justified by a good or sincere intention, and mingled with the rhetoric of honest confession in his apologia of 1715, *An Appeal to Honour and Justice Tho' It Be of His Worst Enemies,* were numerous evasions, silences, and interesting detours, all included with the sincere intention of saving his skin by making a counterattack against his enemies. I have no doubt that Defoe

considered himself an upright man, but his attraction to the Quakers during this period may suggest a retreat into a private religious faith. That his
fictional Quakers are always finding ways of squaring their consciences with
their self-interest shows that Defoe had not lost his sense of humor.

As I have suggested, Defoe's response to the events following the rebellion of 1715 was similar to Hoadly's. Throughout his writings, he held up
the reign of George I as a period of potential happiness for all, and, faced
with the spectacle of a section of the population trying to bring in the
Pretender, he began to contemplate the problem of self-deception more
carefully than ever before. In his *Remarks on the Speeches of William Paul
Clerk and John Hall of Otterburn* (1716), he addressed himself to the dying
speeches of two rebels executed on 13 July. In addition to denying the
authenticity of the speeches, Defoe argued against the Jacobites on both
political and religious grounds. The idea of a right of succession inherent
in the family of James II he found absurd. Disagreeing with Hoadly, Defoe
maintained that James had been removed from the throne because he was
a tyrant, not because he was a Catholic. But like Hoadly, he reserved his
harshest criticism for the Nonjurors and insisted that the established
church was subservient to the power of the state; and he maintained that
within the state, the individual conscience took primacy over any power
that the Church of England might want to exert.

Despite such general agreement with Hoadly, Defoe was a Dissenter and
something of a renegade Dissenter at that. A quarrel within the Church of
England could only inspire his sense of the absurd, and he quoted with
some approval the title of a pamphlet on the quarrel: *You Rogue, and You
Rogue; and Perhaps Both Rogues.*[23] He threw himself into the pamphlet war
with glee, writing a number of pamphlets in the persona of a Quaker.
Though he makes some criticism of Hoadly, Defoe's "Lover of Truth" tends
to agree with Daniel Whitby's defense of Hoadly's concept of sincerity.[24] In
his strongest attack on Hoadly's opponent Andrew Snape, Defoe writes in
the mask of those supposed masters of insincerity, the Jesuits, to advise
Pilloniere to transfer his allegiance to Snape, whom they consider one of
the true friends of their order.

With the Shepheard case Defoe's interest became fully aroused. In the
pamphlet *Some Reasons Why It Could Not Be expected the Government Wou'd
Permit the Speech or Paper of James Shepheard . . . to Be Printed* (dated by Moore
27 March 1718), Defoe defended the government's right to protect itself
against assassins like Shepheard and ridiculed Shepheard's claim to having
acted on religious principles. But there still remained the disturbing notion
of the sincerity of men in their last moments. In May Defoe attempted to
turn the tables on the Jacobites in *A Letter from Paris*, which purports to
show that in her last moments, the dying Queen of James II refused to
acknowledge her son, the Pretender. Defoe goes on to say that it was even
reported that she disowned him, confirming the rumors that he was never

truly her son. If the queen Dowager was delerious, she would be even more likely to tell the truth. And since "our Dying Hours are supposed to be the freest from Hypocrisy, and the Words spoken on our Death-beds have more of influence than at other times," her actions and the supposed confession must have been sincere.[25]

The *Letter from Paris* may have been a useful hoax, but Defoe really spoke his mind in a work that I have recently put forward as a candidate for the Defoe canon, *A Collection of Dying Speeches of All Those People Call'd Traytors, Executed in This Reign.* Published sometime during April 1718, the *Collection* has a preface in which Defoe throws doubt on the authenticity of most of these productions. He allows that some are genuine and confronts the issue of assassins representing different extremes of the political spectrum. "The Question," he writes, "is only, whether they have not on all Sides esteem'd the Quarrel as the Cause of God, whenever they are brought to Execution for it?"[26] For a solution to this question, Defoe refers the reader to the arguments of Benjamin Hoadly:

> I might enquire here into the natural Causes of this obstinate Spirit on all Sides, and might perhaps account very well for it from the Principles of the Bishop of *Bangor,* who tells us to be perswaded in the Mind of this or that Way being the Right, is, in Matters of Religion, a sufficient Authority, etc. Doubtless, whosoever embark'd in a Cause, at the hazard of his Life, is fully perswaded in his Mind that he is in the Right, otherwise he must be a very unaccountable Person that would embark at all. And being thus effectually perswaded, who can wonder that they espouse such openly dangerous Undertakings, and own them, and insist upon them even at the Place of Execution.[27]

The conclusions Defoe draws from Hoadly's sermons are far from the original intent of the argument, but Defoe was not the only party to the dispute who drew such conclusions.

Although Defoe focuses on those who felt justified by their religious principles to plot against the established government, he leaves little doubt that the real motives of those executed for treason were political. Indeed if Defoe had not disliked Swift so much, he might have quoted *A Tale of a Tub,* where Swift noted that "when a Man's Fancy gets *astride* on his Reason . . . the first Proselyte he makes is Himself."[28] Such a quotation reminds us that Defoe may not have needed the arguments of Hoadly to conclude that all judgment is essentially private and that every man and woman is capable of deluding him or herself about the righteousness of a course of action. With Swift such self-delusion was one of the more unpleasant characteristics of humanity. For Defoe and Hoadly it was an aspect of human psychology to be taken into account. Hoadly gave the idea a currency that Defoe was able to exploit, but when Defoe reminded Hoadly in *A Friendly Rebuke to One Parson Benjamin,* written in 1719, that since the Friends had long ago said that "every Man has a Supremacy within himself," Hoadly had just as well be quiet, he may have been expressing a certain irritation with the bishop's "discovery" of a psychology that was hardly new.[29]

The year 1719 brings us to *Robinson Crusoe,* but before glancing at the major fiction in the light of these religious controversies, it is worth demonstrating how they are reflected in two works of fiction published during 1718: *A Continuation of Letters Written by a Turkish Spy at Paris* and *The Memoirs of Major Alexander Ramkins.* Although nominally set in Paris between 1687 and 1693, the letters of Mohamet have some significance for Defoe's England and the disputes over sincerity and conscience. Mohamet remarks on the hypocrisy of the French in their religious practices. While showing the most ardent devotion in their public religious observances (what Defoe has his Turk call "the Mask of Devotion"), they engage in the most brutal kind of warfare against neighboring states.[30] Mohamet is indignant that in their worship they presume "to give him Thanks for the Devastation and Ruin of their Fellow Creatures, and for the Rapine and Destruction which Men, given up to the Furey of their Lust and Rage, shall execute in the World."[31] And in matters of religion the Christian world in general seems to be completely divided. "Every man," writes Mohamet, "sets up a Religion of his own, and walks in the light of his own Vision; thinking it his Duty to damn all the rest of Mankind to the Infernal Pit, who are not of his Opinion."[32] One of the texts on which Defoe's Turkish Spy moralizes is that which Hoadly used for his sermon on the Jacobite rebellion of 1715. He draws from the behavior of the Christian world the conclusion that Christ must indeed have been a "true Prophet," since his followers have been brought to "believe Lies, and be given up to strong Delusions."[33]

Major Ramkins is even more obviously connected with the Bangorian Controversy. Defoe set out to discredit French aid to James II and his son. A Catholic and a loyal follower of the Jacobite cause, Ramkins repeats over and over again his conviction that Louis XIV was guilty of "Insincerity."[34] The French king professed to be helping James II, but, like a true disciple of Richelieu, he followed what he conceived to have been the interest of his country and his court. Ramkins expresses his indignation at the broken promises, the abortive expeditions, and the lack of support when uprisings actually occurred. Louis XIV had the benefit of an army loyal to the family of James that could be used in battle or for keeping England in fear of invasion. Ramkins speaks sadly of the poverty of these men: "It was but a melancholy Sight to behold poor Men strolling upon the Road, not knowing which way to direct their Course, and begging Alms through those Towns in which a little before they had Triumph'd in Victory."[35] Ramkins is ready to abandon the allegiance of his entire life at the end of the novel. In so far as Jacobitism depends on the help of France, Ramkins concludes, it must be regarded not as a political belief but rather as "an uncurable Distemper."[36]

When traveling in England, Ramkins is robbed by a new breed of high-waymen, and with this incident Defoe introduces another line of thought into the work. After the robbery, Ramkins and his companion make their way to an inn where they are entertained by the keeper's account of what he considers to be a kind of profession. The new highwaymen are skilled at their trade and some of them are even younger sons of good families. Ramkins states that he is delighted by this account, but while it is amusing, it seems at first to be merely a digression. A little thought, however, suggests a parallel between the Jacobites and these men. The highwaymen go about their business as if they are engaged in an honorable profession. The dangers involved give it an aura of romance, and they do not question that theirs is as moral as many another more respectable profession. In the same way, those fighting for the Pretender think themselves engaged in an honorable cause, but are in reality no better than outlaws. Both groups wallow in self-delusion.

These two works reveal how profoundly the disputes that swirled around the Bishop of Bangor brought certain ideas crucial to Defoe's fiction to a state of malleability. Probably the most obvious influences were on the treatment of character, particularly in matters of individuality and identity. If the tendency of much literature of the eighteenth century was toward variation within defined character types, the implications of Hoadly's theory of sincerity were all in the direction of the private and eccentric vision. When Mohamet argues that every Christian seems to have his particular brand of faith, he both presents his private view of the world of Western Europe and makes a more or less true statement based on Hoadly's law of individual conscience. Shaped by their respective environments and moved by their hereditary proclivities, Defoe's narrators all represent exercises in eccentric characterization. Mohamet is continually attacking the hypocrisy of Christian society, but what are we to think of this representative of what Defoe considered a barbarous society and religion? And if Ramkins endears himself to us by his sincerity, how are we to regard this Jacobite Catholic who has fought against every political ideal that Defoe held sacred? In the issue for 22 August 1720 of his journal *The Commentator,* Defoe was to give a somewhat sympathetic portrait of a Jacobite on the verge of abandoning his rebellious cause as a mere "Bubble." But his features still betray traces of fanaticism: "There was in his Face some Lines," writes Defoe, "which to a discerning Eye, retain'd the Marks and Indications of Rage, Envy, Cruelty, Rebellion, and Treason, by which a true Jacobite was formerly so easy to be known."[37] Perhaps we should imagine Ramkins looking just so, but nothing in his narrative suggests anything of the kind.

I have no intention of tracing degrees of sincerity in all of Defoe's fictional characters, but it should be apparent that before turning to what we consider his major fiction Defoe experimented with two figures whose sincerity was overcast by a haze of doubtful political and religious opinions. As I suggested at the beginning of this essay, the tergiversations of Defoe's characters are better analyzed by other methods than an exploration of their sincerity, but in so far as degrees of sincerity would have constituted one of the categories occupying Defoe's mind at the time, we would be negligent to ignore it. For example, the confessions of Crusoe, H. F., and the Cavalier, despite some obvious concealments, appear to be honest enough. Others involve considerable difficulties. In many ways, Colonel Jack appears to be the most sincere and straightforward of Defoe's narrators, yet as David Blewett has recently suggested, most critics may have misread his quest after gentility. Defoe once promised to write a history of fools and fulfilled his obligation, at least in part, in *Mere Nature Delineated* (1726). Colonel Jack, for all his worldly success in America, has to rank high on Defoe's list of fools. His education is not one that teaches him to be completely insincere, but it does suggest that without some degree of deception the honest man cannot survive. No wonder Defoe was fond of quoting Rochester's lines,

> If with known cheats you'll play upon the square
> You'll be undone.[38]

Perhaps only on Crusoe's island, before the advent of Friday, is complete sincerity possible. For those living in society, concealment is a way of life. For Moll Flanders it pervades her language as well as her approach to society and to her fellow human beings. Although she conceals a good deal, Roxana may be the most honest of Defoe's narrators—the one who refuses to tell herself lies or suffer "strong delusions"—yet her complete sincerity may be an aspect of her despair. Since both her faith and true conversion are in doubt at the end of the novel, Defoe may have limited his trust in sincerity to a sincere profession of Christian faith at a given moment in time. He did not expect too much from humanity after the Fall.

The problem of identity is also crucial here. Ian Watt was unquestionably right to locate the problem for Defoe and his period in the formulations of John Locke, but we should be aware of how much the Bangorian Controversy turned on the point of inner conviction. And we should also remember that Defoe's fiction is contemporary with the Salter's Hall Controversy—a controversy that arose when a number of Dissenting congregations demanded that their ministers express a sincere belief in the Trinity. James Peirce, Defoe's friend and correspondent, and the Dissenting community at Defoe's Stoke Newington were intimately involved in that quarrel.[39] Is it any wonder that Crusoe, alone on his island, puts his emphasis on sincerity of belief rather than on doctrinal considerations?

In finding his faith, Crusoe comes to know himself and his errors in a way that no character in prose fiction before him had understood such

matters. The self he comes to know is no abstraction. When he lands on his
island, he carves his name and the date of his arrival. He comes to understand himself as well as he knows the goats, caves, and currents—the
realities—of his island. Rousseau was right about that.[40] His contact with the
reality of objects brings him to understand the workings of his mind and
soul, and from that knowledge he is able to achieve to a sincere faith in
God.

If the influence of the Bangorian Controversy on the first part of
Robinson Crusoe seems more implicit than explicit, that influence becomes
clear enough in *The Farther Adventures*. After arriving at his island and
receiving a full account of the events since his departure, Crusoe prepares
to depart once more, but he is approached by a Catholic priest who had
been a passenger on the ship that Crusoe's party had rescued on their
voyage. We have been introduced to the Priest as a person of "a serious
well-govern'd Mind,"[41] and to a certain extent Defoe uses *seriousness* and
sincerity interchangeably. But it is the "Sincerity" of the Priest that Defoe
underscores in the later section, after warning the reader:

> It is true, this Man was a *Roman,* and perhaps it may give Offence to some
> hereafter, if I leave any Thing extraordinary upon Record, of a Man,
> who before I begin, I must, (to set him out in just Colours) represent in
> Terms very much to his Disadvantage, in the Account of Protestants; as
> *first,* that he was a Papist; *secondly,* a popish Priest; and *thirdly,* a *French*
> Popish Priest. (3:13)

Having left no doubt in the mind of the reader that he was initially suspicious of the Priest, Defoe then shows him acting out of sincere faith and a
general goodness of heart in his wish to see that the inhabitants of the
island are properly married and in his willingness to stay on the island to
minister to the religious needs of the inhabitants.

The dialogue that follows is carried forward in a spirit of understanding
and sympathy. Interestingly enough, John Balguy, in his *Silvius's Letter to the
Reverend Dr. Sherlock* (1719), had also presented a dialogue between a Protestant and a Papist, and the respectful interchange of Balguy's figures is
remarkably similar to that of Crusoe and the Priest. If Balguy's Papist
comes off second in the debate, the Protestant never questions his claim to
"Sincerity." Defoe goes even further. His Priest agrees to stifle all the peculiarly Catholic aspects of his Christianity in deference to Crusoe's beliefs
and advances a generalized Christian faith free from dogma:

> That there is a God; and that this God having given us some stated
> general Rules for our Service and Obedience, we ought not willingly and
> knowingly offend him; either by neglecting to do what he has com-
> manded, or by doing what he has expressly forbidden: And let our
> different Religions be what they will, this general Principle is readily
> own'd by us all, That the Blessing of God does not ordinarily follow a

presumptuous sinning against his Command; and every good Christian
will be affectionately concern'd to prevent any that are under his Care,
living in a total Neglect of God and his Commands. It is not your Men
being Protestants, whatever my Opinion may be of such, that discharges
me from being concern'd for their Souls, and from endeavouring, if it
lies before me, that they should live in as little Distance from and Enmity
with their Maker, as possible. (3 : 18)

Such a viewpoint is not merely that advanced by the Bishop of Bangor and
his defenders, but it suggests that the Crusoe of *The Surprising Adventures*
who ruled peacefully over a kingdom populated by Protestant, Catholic,
and pagan was already a convert to such doctrines.

Crusoe introduces this discourse with the Priest with some key suggestions about his sincerity. He tells how he is impressed by the Priest's understanding of God's ways when he makes an apposite application of the story
of Achan to the situation of the inhabitants of Crusoe's islands. "'I was
sensibly touch'd with his Discourse," says Crusoe, "and told him his Infer-
ence was so just, and the whole Design seem'd so *sincere* [my italics], and was
really so religious in its own Nature, that I was very sorry I had interrupted
him, and begg'd him to go on'" (3 : 17). The Priest than explains his desire
to marry the Englishmen to the women with whom they have been living in
what might be regarded as a marriage sanctified by the laws of nature.
Crusoe has been willing to accept such a situation, but the Priest, while
acknowledging the sincerity of Crusoe's feelings, questions the propriety of
the arrangement:

How, Sir, is God honour'd in this unlawful Liberty? And how shall a
Blessing succeed your Endeavours in this Place? *However good in themselves,* and *however sincere in your Design,* while these Men, who at present
are your Subjects, under your absolute Government and Dominion, are
allow'd by you to live in open Adultery? (3 : 20)

The premise of the dialogues between Crusoe and the Priest is that each
man is perfectly sincere in his faith.

This sincerity is even more apparent when the Priest volunteers to stay
on the island to convert the thirty-seven savages there to Christianity. Defoe's picture of the Priest draws a sharp distinction between Crusoe's lay
religion and the genuine fervor of a person who has dedicated his life to
religion:

I discover'd a kind of Rapture in his Face while he spoke this to me; his
Eyes sparkl'd like Fire, his Face glow'd, and his Colour came and went, as
if he had been falling into Fits; in a Word, he was fir'd with the Joy of
being embark'd in such a Work. I paus'd a considerable while before I
could tell what to say to him, for I was really surpriz'd to find a Man of
such Sincerity and Zeal, and carry'd out in his Zeal beyond the ordinary
Rate of Men, not of his Profession only, but even of any Profession
whatsoever. (3 : 26)

Crusoe questions him "seriously," and as I have stated previously, while Defoe seems to use *serious* and *sincere* synonymously, he may have considered the latter a stronger word. The *Serious Reflections of Robinson Crusoe* are sincere enough in the usual sense of that word, and Crusoe lays claim to "sincere" intentions in writing, but his general emotional state is far less intense than that of the Priest.[42]

The final comment on the Priest's "Sincerity" comes after he has told Crusoe that he would be happy enough if all the savages of America could be turned into Protestants rather than that their souls should be lost in their heathen state. Crusoe approves wholeheartedly:

> I was astonish'd at the Sincerity and Temper of this truly pious Papist, as much as I was oppress'd by the Power of his Reasoning; and it presently occurr'd to my Thoughts, that if such a Temper was universal, we might be all Catholick Christians, whatever Church or particular Profession we join'd to, or join'd in; that a Spirit of Charity would soon work us all up into right Principles; and in a Word, as he thought that the like Charity would make us all Catholicks, so I told him I believ'd, had all the Members of his Church the like Moderation, they would soon be all Protestants. And there we left that Part, for we never disputed at all. (3 : 42)

This passages breathes the spirit of Hoadly and Balguy, and the use of the term "Moderation," so annoying to the High Church, proclaims the triumph of Low Church and Dissenting attitudes toward toleration.[43] Crusoe remarks to the Priest that his doctrines would bring him to the attention of the Inquisition were he in Spain or Italy, but the Priest merely remarks that he never considered persecution very Christian.

Although Crusoe's dialogue with the Priest represents the most programmatic evidence for the existence of traces of the Bangorian Controversy in *Robinson Crusoe,* it may be seen as an important influence on the general spirit of humanity that permeates the work. In his isolation, Crusoe longs for any human being who might relieve his loneliness. When he comes upon the single footprint in the sand, however, his strongest reaction, after the initial questioning and curiosity, is an overwhelming fear of the presence of another human being. Following his discovery that cannibals have been coming to his island, Crusoe's fear is mixed with hatred and a desire for revenge. But after realizing how unwise such an action would be, he also comes to the conclusion that they have not harmed him in any way, that their terrifying feasts, however disgusting to him, are a part of their ordinary lives, and that a comparison between their behavior and that of the armies of supposedly civilized European nations would not reveal any very great difference in degree of barbarism. Crusoe may insist that Friday abandon his cannibal ways, but he accepts him—takes him to his heart—as a fellow human being.

The High Flyers of the Church of England, in Defoe's mind, had always acted in an opposite spirit. Long before *Robinson Crusoe* Defoe had parodied the manner of Sacheverell in calling for a crusade against the Dissenters. The High Churchman of *The Shortest Way with the Dissenters* lacked all moderation and was ready to start a persecution of the Dissenters, to massacre their leaders in the expectation of forcing their followers into the church. Defoe saw the attack on the principles of Benjamin Hoadly and his defenders in much the same light. Once more, all moderation had been cast aside in an effort to crush the humane and ecumenical principles of the Low Church. Henry Stebbing had violated all rules of polite discourse in his attack on a fellow churchman and fellow human being, and Crusoe's discovery of his religious faith and his approach to the cannibals are reminders that both a spiritual and temporal life may be lived better without the savagery and inhumanity of High Church politics.[44]

I would not want to extend this reading too far, and as I suggested earlier, the debate over sincerity in the Bangorian Controversy produced results that were far more complex than any I have suggested. No other character in Defoe's fiction has such a direct relationship with the question of sincerity as Crusoe. Even H. F. in *A Journal of the Plague Year* is more problematical. He is sincere enough, but one of the lessons of the Bangorian Controversy appeared to be that most people are sincere enough. H. F. believes that he remains in London because he has a strong impulse— perhaps a direct message—to remain, but his motivation for wandering the streets and observing the plague seems to be little more than the "Curiosity" to which he ascribes his actions over and over again. Now H. F.'s curiosity may involve a little more than the fascination for scenes of death and sickness that appears in the Gothic novel at the end of the century, but it hardly seems a spiritual quest. Thus his encounter with Robert the Waterman is especially significant. Not only is Robert a completely sincere person, as shown by the simplicity of his language and the openness of his emotions, but he remains in the city because he must help his sick wife, Rachel, and their children. It is after Robert expresses his faith in God's mercy that H. F. comes to recognize the doubtfulness of his reasons for remaining in the city:

> And here my Heart smote me, suggesting how much better this poor man's Foundation was on which he stayed in the Danger than mine; that he had nowhere to fly, that he had a family to bind him to attendance, which I had not; and mine was mere Presumption, his a true Dependance, and a Courage resting on God; and yet that he used all possible caution for his Safety.[45]

Defoe always seems to confront a *degree* of sincerity with the real thing.

But for Defoe the real thrust of the discussions that grew out of the Bangorian Controversy involved the apparent sincerity of almost anyone committed to a cause, however bad that cause might be. The thief or pirate might plead the sincerity of his personal feelings as an excuse for his crimes, and after the South Sea Bubble burst, the newspapers were filled with accounts of thieves who revealed high principles of honesty.[46] And the directors of the South Sea Company made honesty more relative than it had been before. These men had been intimately connected with the governing forces of the land, and despite the punishments handed out to a few, most Englishmen had the sense that the real criminals had escaped. If Defoe makes his pirates feel that they are more honest and sincere than such men, there was a famous criminal case in which a man proposing a murder was to suggest that such behavior was hardly worse than the morality practiced by the directors.[47]

The possibilities in such material were enormous, and in *Moll Flanders, Colonel Jack,* and *Roxana,* Defoe exploited sincere confessions with all the doubts and ambiguities that surrounded the idea of sincerity at the time. He was writing for an audience that was suspicious of claims about sincerity and that obviously relished the spectacle of having a number of clergymen assert their complete honesty in a situation that guaranteed that one or more of them were lying. Real events may have prepared the ground for Defoe's exploitation of his own versions of spiritual autobiography, fictional memoir, and picaresque adventure. I began this essay by suggesting that the question of sincerity may have had an influence on genre. One of the conclusions that may be drawn from this investigation is that the discovery of a "new" notion of sincerity tended to undercut stereotyped characterization in favor of a realistic assessment of personality. *Robinson Crusoe* was unquestionably influenced by the form of spiritual autobiography; but Defoe's novel, with its simplistic and highly formalized treatment of the progress of the soul toward spiritual enlightenment, is anything but an ordinary example of this genre. *Moll Flanders* may allow the reader considerable distance from the narrator in the manner of the picaresque, but there are times when we are asked to, and indeed do, sympathize with Moll's situation. And Defoe deepened the usually externalized memoir form by filtering experience through the mind of the narrator.

Defoe had written fictions before the Bangorian Controversy, and some of these had employed a narrator claiming complete honesty and sincerity. He probably didn't need an Anglican clergyman to help him with either his theology or his politics, and however strongly he may have defended Hoadly there were also times when he seemed annoyed that Hoadly was claiming so much attention. But as much as Defoe expressed thoughts on sincerity before Hoadly's controversial sermons, those ruminations did not lead him in the direction of truly great fiction. He always had a command of vivid narrative and realistic description. But it was the Bangorian Controversy and the debate over sincerity that turned Defoe toward a type of fiction that fused a vivid presentation of a real world of things, people, and events with a focus on the inner life.

NOTES

1. See G. A. Starr, *Defoe and Spiritual Biography* (Princeton: Princeton University Press, 1965), 74–125, and J. Paul Hunter, *The Reluctant Pilgrim* (Baltimore: Johns Hopkins University Press, 1966), 76–92.

2. Lionel Trilling, *Sincerity and Authenticity* (Cambridge, Mass.: Harvard University Press, 1974), 120.

3. Probably the most famous example is in Gray's *Elegy* where, in the epitaph, we are told of the rustic poet, *"Large was his bounty, and his soul sincere,"* but sincerity is an omnipresent theme in the literature of the period. In a work like Elizabeth Inchbald's *Nature and Art*, published in 1796, sincerity becomes the criterion for dividing good from bad. Sincerity is the "nature" that operates in those human beings whose lives have not been distorted by the "art" of contemporary, civilized life.

4. However vague Wollaston's appeal to "Truth" may seem, he held it up as a clear and determinable standard of morality. Hutcheson tried to reduce ethics to a mathematical formula. See William Wollaston, *The Religion of Nature Delineated* (London, 1722); and Francis Hutcheson, *An Inquiry Concerning the Original of our Ideas of Virtue or Moral Good,* in *British Moralists,* ed. L. A. Selby-Bigge (Oxford, 1897), 1:108–16.

5. Leon Guilhamet, *The Sincere Ideal* (Toronto: University of Toronto Press, 1974), 287.

6. Cf. *Advice from the Shades Below. Or, A Letter from Thomas Hobbes of Malmesbury to his Brother B—n H—dly* (London, 1710), 6–8, and the picture of Defoe entering the underworld in "A Dream," *Read's Weekly Journal,* 1 November 1718, 1206–7.

7. See Hoadly, *The Present Delusion of Many Protestants Consider'd,* 4th ed. (London, 1716), 21–27.

8. See George Hickes, *The Constitution of the Catholic Church, and the Nature and Consequences of Schism* (London, 1716), especially 95–96.

9. Hoadly, *Works* (London, 1773), 2:404–9.

10. *A Report of the Committee of the Lower House of Convocation Appointed to Draw up a Representation concerning the Bishop of Bangor's Preservative,* 3d ed. (London, 1717), 8. For a defense of this judgment, see William Hendley, *An Appeal to the Consciences and Common Sense of the Christian Laity* (London, 1717), 18–21.

11. Law, *Three Letters to the Bishop of Bangor,* 9th ed. (London, 1753), 8.

12. Law, *A Reply to the Bishop of Bangor's Answer,* 2d ed. (London, 1717). 212. See also Stebbing, *An Appeal to the Word of God for the Terms of Christian Salvation* (London, 1720), xv.

13. Stebbing, *The True Meaning & Consequences of a Position of the Right Reverend the Lord Bishop of Bangor* (London, 1719), 36–66.

14. Whitby, *A Defense of the Propositions Contain'd in the Lord Bishop of Bangor's Sermon* (London, 1718), 26.

15. Balguy, *Silvius's Defence of a Dialogue between a Papist and a Protestant in Answer to the Rev^d. Mr. Stebbing* (London, 1720), 11. Cf. Daniel Defoe, *A Reply to the Remarks upon the Lord Bishop of Bangor's Treatment of the Clergy and Convocation* (London, 1717), 14–20.

16. Balguy, *Silvius's Defence,* 21–28.

17. *Weekly Journal: or Saturday's Post,* no. 30, 6 July 1717.

18. For examples of some of the collections made from the materials of the dispute, see *A Collection of Papers Scatter'd Lately about the Town,* 2d ed. (London, 1717), 1–36; and *A Muster Roll of the Bishop of Bangor's Seconds* (London, 1720), A4, p. 27.

19. Paul Lorrain, *A Dialogue between P. Lorena and James Shepheard* (n.p., n.d.), folio half-sheet in the Bodleian Library (Ms. Rawl. D. 383).

20. James Shepheard, *Last Speech* (n.p., n.d.), folio half-sheet in the Bodleian Library (Ms. Rawl. D. 383).

21. Jean-Jacques Rousseau, *Les Reveries du promeneur solitaire,* ed. Jacques Voisine (Paris: Garnier-Flammarion, 1964), 81–91.

22. Daniel Defoe, *The Sincerity of the Dissenters Vindicated* (London, 1703), particularly p. 16 where, after outlining the differences between the Dissenters and the followers of the Church of England, he repeated his claim to complete sincerity and added, "And with the same Sincerity, I protest I wish I could conform wholly to the Church."

23. *Weekly Journal*, no. 31, 13 July 1717.

24. See "A Lover of Truth" [i.e., Daniel Defoe], *Observations on the Bishop's Answer to Dr. Snape* (London, 1717), 20–28.

25. Daniel Defoe, *Letter from Paris* (London, 1718), 6.

26. Daniel Defoe, *Collection of Dying Speeches* (London, 1718), 14. For a discussion of the reasons for ascribing this work to Defoe, see my article, "Defoe's Authorship of *A Collection of Dying Speeches* (1718)," *PQ* 61 (1982): 92–97.

27. Defoe, *Collection of Dying Speeches*, 14.

28. Jonathan Swift, *A Tale of a Tub*, ed. A. C. Guthkelch and D. Nichol Smith, 2d ed. (Oxford: Clarendon Press, 1958), 171.

29. *A Friendly Rebuke* (London, 1719), 18. Defoe had already argued in *The Sincerity of the Dissenters Vindicated*, 4, that while he did not question the sincerity of those practicing occasional conformity with the Church of England, he was forced to conclude that their consciences, however clear they might seem, were wrongly informed.

30. Daniel Defoe, *A Continuation of Letters of a Turkish Spy* (London, 1718), 9:135.

31. Ibid., 9:29.

32. Ibid., 9:21.

33. Ibid., 9:20.

34. Daniel Defoe, *The Memoirs of Major Alexander Ramkins* (London, 1718), 60–61: "But in the midst of all the Disasters I met with, nothing affected me with a more sensible Grief than the Thoughts of Lewis the XIVth's Insincerity, for though it only rid my Mind in the Nature of a Scruple or first Impression, yet I found it grew daily upon me, and often in the height of my Diversions it lay upon my Stomach like an indigested Meal." See also pp. 23, 84, 108, 139, 145, and 174.

35. Ibid., 140.

36. Ibid., 157.

37. *Commentator*, no. 57. This essay is devoted to a discussion of the decline of the Jacobites, depicting them as aging and disillusioned romantics in politics.

38. John Wilmot, Earl of Rochester, "A Satyr against Reason and Mankind," in *The Complete Poems*, ed. David Vieth (New Haven: Yale University Press, 1968), 100. See also David Blewett, *Defoe's Art of Fiction* (Toronto: University of Toronto Press, 1979), 93–115.

39. For Peirce's contact with Defoe, see Defoe's *Letters*, ed. George Healey (Oxford: Clarendon Press, 1955), 116. See also Michael R. Watts, *The Dissenters* (Oxford: Clarendon Press, 1978), 1:381.

40. Jean-Jacques Rousseau, *Emile*, trans. Barbara Foxley (London: Dent, 1911), 147–58.

41. Defoe, *The Farther Adventures of Robinson Crusoe*, in *The Shakespeare Head Edition of the Novels and Selected Writings of Daniel Defoe* (Oxford: Basil Blackwell, 1927), 2:130. Subsequent references to this work will be included within parentheses in my text.

42. See Defoe's *Serious Reflections*, in *Romances and Narratives of Daniel Defoe*, ed. George Aitken (London: Dent, 1895), 3:ix. Lionel Trilling's discussion of F. R. Leavis's use of *serious* and its relation to sincerity, though mainly concerned with literary criticism, has some relevance for Defoe's tendency to find distinctions between these two terms.

43. For a discussion of the High Church's dislike of *moderation*, see Robert M. Adams, "The Mood of the Church and a *Tale of a Tub*," in *England in the Restoration and Early Eighteenth Century*, ed. H. T. Swedenberg (Berkeley and Los Angeles: University of California Press, 1972), 76–93.

44. John Balguy wrote, "It scandalizes the Minds of well-meaning People, and gives the enemies of our Faith a lamentable occasion of Derision and Reproach." That Defoe devotes a

section of *Serious Reflections of Robinson Crusoe* to the benefits of "Conversation" as a means of rounding off the rough edges of personality is highly significant. Defoe had already written a tract in which a Moslem, writing to a friend in his native country, had gloated over the disarray that the Bangorian Controversy had created among the Christians of England. See John Balguy, *Silvius's Letter to the Reverend Dr. Sherlock* (London, 1719), 26; and Daniel Defoe, *The Conduct of Christians Made the Sport of Infidels* (London, 1717), especially 7–14.

45. *A Journal of the Plague Year,* ed. Louis Landa (London: Oxford University Press, 1969), 108. In his study of Wordsworth, David Perkins argues that a belief in the value of sincerity often leads to a distrust of all but the most simplified type of language. Defoe, who frequently lamented the failure of language to communicate directly enough, reduces Robert's language to a very simple level and gains for him a kind of dignity similar to that which Wordsworth attained for his shepherds and farmers. See Perkins, *Wordsworth and the Poetry of Sincerity* (Cambridge, Mass.: Harvard University Press, 1964), 5–23.

46. See for example *Mist's Weekly Journal,* no. 158, 9 December 1721, in which one thief promises to restore what he has stolen if the South Sea stocks rise and another says that he is robbing only to stave off starvation.

47. Anon., *The Tryal and Condemnation of Arundel Coke* (London, 1722), 15.

8

Swift's Self-Portraits in Verse

Timothy Keegan

> . . . whoever should form his opinion of the age from
> [Pope's and Swift's] representation, would suppose
> them to have lived amidst ignorance and barbarity,
> unable to find among their contemporaries either vir-
> tue or intelligence, and persecuted by those who
> could not understand them.
> —Samuel Johnson, *Life of Pope*[1]

When, in his public literary works, Swift explicitly writes about himself as a public figure, his aim is always self-justification. He may treat with mock self-deprecation his foibles as a public man, but even these foibles—his unusual freedom with persons of high station, his innocence of guile amidst the court—he means to redound to his credit. Even admissions to private faults are self-congratulatory. When the poet confesses to envy early in the *Verses on the Death of Dr. Swift*, the failing he finds in himself is, as he insists, universal; but his willingness to acknowledge the failing shows his good nature, his emotional security, his exceptional self-honesty. In an age not distinguished for confessional poetry, Swift's literary presentations of his own public career are meant, unremarkably, always to justify that career.

Swift's essential strategies of self-justification are similarly unremarkable. When he wishes to suggest traits that his readers may find implausible, he turns to fiction, insinuation, and self-deprecating irony, which often delight and persuade. But sometimes, when he wishes to defend actions that he feels are creditable but perversely brushed aside or misconstrued by enemies, he resorts to hyperbole, a tone of wounded innocence, and heavy insistence. The result of the last method is usually bad poetry—bad neither because the historian can discover distortions or exaggerations in Swift's view of his own character, nor because what Swift says is occasionally misleading, but because what he says is unconvincing, because the poet's heated tone and wounded pride cannot be reconciled with the amiability or indifference to opinion that he portrays in himself. In poems about himself, Swift often proclaimed his virtues clumsily but insinuated them skillfully. In poems such as *The Author Upon Himself* and *Verses on the Death of Dr. Swift,* artistic failure results not from the falsity of Swift's self-portraits to external fact but from his failure to make the poetic character dramatically engaging within the poem itself. In dealing with such poems or passages, it is the nature of the artistic failure with which criticism ought to begin.

Indeed, the *themes* of those of Swift's literary self-portraits that have produced disgust and disbelief do not differ much from the themes of those that have charmed and delighted. Swift's expressed ideals of public and private conduct are remarkably consistent. Even the self-portraits written in Swift's old age, for instance, reveal the profound influence of the example of his earliest employer, Sir William Temple, who saw himself as a disinterested public servant insufficiently valued or rewarded for his services to his country, a man of "patience, temperence, and deeds of peace," who had at last retired from public employments that, under Charles II, would inevitably have tarnished a man of his principles.[2] To the end, Swift imitated this posture of disinterested virtue; he viewed himself as a patriot who, like Temple and like the nonjuring Archbishop Sancroft, had chosen the high road and sacrificed the emoluments that his abilities would have brought to a man of weaker virtue. Swift adopted toward his own ministerial friends the manner that Temple had adopted toward Charles: "I have resolved never to ask anything, otherwise than by serving him well."

Swift also embraced fully Temple's emphasis on private character. He viewed the admirable public man as typically straightforward, practical, of sound common sense and reliable honesty. Such a man is motivated not by ambition but patriotism; high office to him represents deprivation of the more civilized life that he prefers. Rather than accommodate himself to the sordid realities of statecraft, he will withdraw, his virtue and good name intact, to pursue a life of genteel retirement and civilized pleasures. Temple, the very type of the gentlemanly man of letters, epitomized such retirement.

An embodiment of these same ideals was to be found in the poetry of Horace. As Reuben Brower has indicated, "for the small yet influential class that created what we call eighteenth-century civilization, Horace was a kind of 'culture hero.' . . . The Augustans saw in Horace's poetry a concentrated image of a life and a civilization to which they more or less consciously aspired."[3] Horace, Temple, Pope, and Swift all imagined themselves members of a tiny fraternity of civilized men in an age of almost unexampled moral, intellectual, and political corruption. All prided themselves on patriotism and on principled retreat from the wicked world of public affairs. In poems about himself, Swift not only appealed to these Horatian ideals but emulated the qualities of irony, urbanity, gentle self-deprecation, and staunchness in friendship that inform the poems of Horace. Self-identification as one of an especially virtuous fraternity of civilized men who stood out as an ornament in a corrupt age was at the very core of this ideal.

Swift's idealization of such civilized friendship is at the heart of the first of his Horatian autobiographical poems, an imitation of Horace's *Epistle* 1.7, published in October of 1713.[4] The poet tells of his gradual transformation from sleek, genial, unassuming parson to harried, poor, shabby dean. Because of his amiability, wit, and integrity, he is taken into a prime minister's friendship. He allows himself to hope for a canonry at Westminster, but his exalted friend pooh-poohs so humble a benefice as unworthy of his merits. He must instead be made an Irish dean, and Swift cannot but accept. Then, in debt from the cost of "Patents, instalments, adjurations,/ First-fruits and Tenths, and chapter-treats," he arrives, miserable and bedraggled, at the great man's door, only to be chided for his close-fistedness:

> Why sure you won't appear in Town
> In that old wig and rusty gown!
> I doubt your heart is set on pelf
> So much, that you neglect your self.
>
> (123–26)

The ostensible point of the poem is that Lord Oxford, who is responsible for Swift's plight, ought to relieve his financial distress. And Swift in fact felt that his installation expenses had been promised by the ministry; the poem was meant to remind Oxford of the obligation.

But what animates the poem is Swift's celebration of his intimacy with Oxford. Swift focuses the poem on Oxford's friendship, suggesting that it is an exception to his lordship's normal reserve and hence a mark of Swift's charm. Yet his tone also implies that this sort of alliance is natural between two civilized men. To avoid seeming boastful, Swift employs ironic self-deprecation, making himself a butt, suggesting that Oxford left him worse off than he found him. But the emphasis remains solidly on the intimacy of parson and statesman; for all its drawbacks, the deanery of St. Patrick's is a mark of the great man's esteem for Swift. Through his bantering complaints, therefore, the poet invites sympathy for his treatment by Oxford, yet proudly shows how easy he feels with England's first minister.

The character of himself that Swift presents here conforms to the patterns of self-justification which we have observed. He is a man of simple, steadfast virtue and saving good humor, unambitious but inevitably drawn into the precincts of power because of his abilities. Because of his modesty, his virtues are insufficiently appreciated and rewarded, but his good humor prevails in the face of unmerited misfortune. Beyond the petty vexations of the world of affairs, the poem suggests, is a more enduring reality dependent on intellect and virtue and character. However much events and position may pull them apart, Swift and Oxford remain bound together through their common qualities of character. In the view of the poem, each of them emerges as above the illusions of pride and of power. The reader is permitted to view at close range the deep intimacy of two extraordinarily appealing men, and it is this privileged view of an ideal friendship that lends the poem its charm.

In a second Horatian self-portrait written in the following year, an imitation of Horace's *Satire* 2.6 ("Hoc erat in votis"), Swift again presents two versions of himself: the hapless butt of circumstance, a victim of his own virtues; and the speaker who shows his good nature by the breezy detachment with which he makes himself a butt. Adopting a favorite Horatian rhetorical ethos, the poem begins as a paean to civilized retirement.

Swift again means to complain of financial distress. But again it is the deft self-portraiture that gives the poem life; the poet's character is embodied in his emotional balance. Though his public role consists of thankless vexation, he retains his good humor and retires decently to the civilized country life that he prefers. His conduct is ennobled and his involvement in public affairs made clean by the nature of his friendship with Oxford. What is suggested in the earlier poem is here reaffirmed: that the poet's relation to the lord attains to a classical ideal of friendship and is no mercenary alliance of wily minister and ambitious priest. Swift's simple characterization of this relationship is meant to be taken not as literal truth, but as an indication that honest and creditable motives lie at the foundation of his public conduct.

The appeal of the two poems rests almost entirely on Swift's success in creating a charming version of his own character. The character accepts his own misfortunes with such grace that the reader's sympathy is easily secured. The geniality that Swift claims as his distinguishing characteristic is perfectly embodied in the easy, gently self-deprecating verses:

> Harley, the Nation's great support,
> Returning home one day from Court
> . . . .
> Observ'd a parson near Whitehall
> Cheapning old authors on a stall.
> The priest was pretty well in case,
> And shew'd some humour in his face;
> Look'd with an easie, careless mein,
> A perfect stranger to the spleen;
> Of size that might a pulpit fill,
> But more inclining to sit still.
>
> (1–2, 5–12)

Although Swift portrayed his own character with considerable grace in these two Horatian self-portraits, he was also capable of clumsy self-justification in verse. *The Author Upon Himself* (1714), another in the series of reflective poems that Swift wrote during the collapse of the Oxford ministry, is a rhetorical failure, largely because it reveals too openly anxieties that its author wishes to mask. Swift's method is to justify himself straightforwardly; and although the poem contains powerful lines conveying his indignation, it suffers—as do all of Swift's straightforward apologias—from heavy-handed boasting.

Swift again portrays himself as a man of integrity who gains the ministers' trust through his unusual personal appeal; his favor arouses the malicious jealousy of others, who succeed in misrepresenting him to the Queen as an ambitious, dangerous, irreligious priest. Though threatened by vindictive hatred, Swift, confident of his blamelessness, scorns to exert himself in his own protection and is preserved only by the efforts of his friends. Only when his own efforts to reconcile Oxford and Bolingbroke fail, when he has done all that he can do to save the ministry (and therefore, in his view, to serve the nation), does he retire. The poem thus contrasts Swift's refusal to retire for the sake of his safety with his willingness to retire when he can do nothing more to serve his country. Once again, the selfless public man, the victim of his own virtues, is placed at the center of attention.

But the speaker's tone reveals trepidation and bitterness. Because the emotional turmoil implied by the tone does not conform to the poet's claim of courageous composure in the face of unmerited censure, the anxious self-justification subverts the intended impression of detached indignation. The poem suffers not only from a loss of tonal control but also from strategic miscalculation, for, unwisely, Swift seeks simultaneously to flog his enemies and to display the mildness of his disposition.

The poet, speaking in the third person, essays a lofty impartiality—a tone he was to attempt again in the final portion of *Verses on the Death of Dr. Swift*. But his poise fails him, and he often sounds merely boastful:

> At Windsor S[wift] no sooner could appear,
> But, St. John comes and whispers in his ear;
> The waiters stand in ranks; the yeomen cry,
> *Make room;* as if a duke were passing by.

> (33-36)

Instead of mocking himself, Swift heatedly proclaims his blamelessness and hurls invectives at his enemies. He reiterates the familiar themes of the Horatian poems, but they are here subverted by bombastic rhetoric, for instance in his account of the consequences of having published *The Windsor Prophecy* and *The Publick Spirit of the Whigs:*

> Now [Madame Coningsmark] her vengeance vows
> On S[wift]'s reproaches for her [murder'd spouse;]
> From her red locks her mouth with venom fills:
> And thence into the royal ear instills.

> The Qu[een] incens'd, his services forgot,
> Leaves him a victim to the vengeful Scot;
> Now through the Realm a proclamation spread,
> To fix a price on his devoted head.
> While innocent, he scorns ignoble flight;
> His watchful friends preserve him by a sleight.
>
> (53–62)

The speaker of the passage—who is talking about himself—claims lofty disdain for his enemies but conveys resentment, alarm, bitterness. One assumes that the effect was not deliberate.

If *The Author Upon Himself* fails as attractive self-portraiture, it nevertheless does achieve another kind of rhetorical success. Swift was no mean practitioner of invective. We may expect that when he wishes to express indignation and scorn, his expression will be powerful. His delight in political partisanship, which he disclaims or makes light of in the Horatian self-portraits, here energizes his verses.

In the best passages, his expression perfectly suits his meaning, his tone is adroitly modulated, his pentameters are balanced and resonant:

> Now Finch alarms the Lords; he hears for certain,
> This dang'rous priest is got behind the curtain:
> Finch, fam'd for tedious elocution, proves
> That S[wift] oils many a spring which Harley moves.
>
> (37–40)

The words "he hears for certain" and "proves" impugn the Earl of Nottingham's reliability with droll sarcasm. The headlong pace of the first couplet, the word "alarms" in the first line, and the exaggerated air of intrigue in the second line, all suggest his lordship's vapid excitability. The conciseness and liquidity of the final line are nicely counterpoised to the hobbled rhythm of the third line and, implicitly, to the ponderousness of the Earl's oratory in Parliament—which consists not of eloquence but of mere "elocution." The denunciation of Nottingham is sure-handed, and a few other passages impart a similarly memorable impression of concise power.

The same passage also helps to illustrate Swift's divided purpose, however. The final line implies that Swift *does* oil many a spring which Harley moves, and the bold implication can only add to the pointed contempt for Nottingham. Swift's effect here is subtle. He seeks simultaneously to parade his influence—to taunt his enemies by proclaiming his importance to the ministry—and to mock his enemies for fearing his influence. Here, and in the poem as a whole, Swift again tries to have things both ways—as he had in the two Horatian poems, simultaneously boasting of intimacy with the exalted and eliciting sympathy for his neglect by his powerful friends.

The terms of self-justification of his earlier self-portraits also animate

Swift's best-known poem about himself, *Verses on the Death of Dr. Swift* (1731). The poem is ostensibly a meditation on a maxim of La Rochefoucauld, in the form of a fantasy about Swift's death. Those who survive the Dean will, by their reactions to his death, demonstrate the truth of the maxim,

> "In all distresses of our friends
> "We first consult our private ends."
>
> (7–8)

The first 300 lines of the poem follow the programme that the poet has announced. The final 200 lines, however, comprise a straightforward justification of Swift's entire public career.

The early examples of La Rochefoucauld's maxim in action are calculated to engage the reader's sympathy; Swift's tone is intimate and candid, his attitude familiar and confiding:

> In Pope, I cannot read a line,
> But with a sigh, I wish it mine:
> When he can in one couplet fix
> More sense than I can do in six:
> It gives me such a jealous fit,
> I cry, pox take him, and his wit.
>
> (47–52)

Here we meet again the essential strategy of Swift's earlier self-portraits: a reversal of roles, described with rueful self-deprecation. Swift courts sympathy by suggesting that he is the good-natured victim of circumstances that, in themselves, do him no discredit.

The impression of intimacy and candor in this section thoroughly eclipses the self-blame. Swift exploits the reader's fascination at hearing a famous man talk casually about his famous associates. The reader, who is supposed already to have assented to his own participation in the common human failing of vanity, hears the reassuring voice of a great man confiding the ways in which he too is vain.

But the poet then turns the charge of vanity back against the world. Swift, who has so far confessed to relatively harmless vanities, now begins his apologia, portraying himself as the unoffending victim of the vanity of others. He imagines how his friends, his enemies, and the world at large will react to his death. The mimicry, the poised versification, and the psychological acuity of this section (lines 47–298) are widely admired. Less often remarked, however, is the degree to which these passages court sympathy for the poet as a victim of neglect and mistreatment, a man whose best qualities are viewed with suspicion and turned against him.

The world reacts to the demise of great men with malicious, petty speculation and essential indifference; this datum, with which Swift had once bludgeoned the Duke of Marlborough in a *Satirical Elegy,* is here a source of more ambiguous emotions. The poet's tone suggests that he takes this inevitable fate in good humor; the details of the narrative, however, reveal that indifferent friends and spiteful enemies, not the innocent poet, are ruled by vapid or trivial-minded self-indulgence. Swift's generous bequests to the public, for instance—despite the fact that the public had done nothing for him—are made excuses for spiteful fault-finding and impertinent suspicion:

> "What has he left? And who's his heir?
> "I know no more than what the news is,
> "'Tis all bequeath'd to publick uses.
> "To publick use! A perfect whim!
> "What has the publick done for him!
> "Mere envy, avarice, and pride!
> "He gave it all:—But first he dy'd.
> "And had the Dean in all the Nation,
> "No worthy friend, no poor relation?
> "So ready to do strangers good,
> "Forgetting his own flesh and blood?"
>
> (154–64)

The poet thus praises his own generosity, and courts sympathy for the ways in which the credit of his good works is denied to him.

The nature of the distinction between Swift's vanity and the vanity of the world at whose hands he suffers thus begins to come clear. Swift's admissions to vanity show him to be appealingly human; the vanity of others is fundamentally mean-spirited or self-absorbed. His vanity is founded on a generous estimation of the gifts of others, theirs on indifference to or perverse denial of the merits of even conspicuously admirable character (i.e., Swift's). His vanity entails honest recognition of his own faults and limitations, theirs smug self-satisfaction and blindness to their own failings. It is the innocent and undeservedly neglected Swift who is throughout the poem the victim of the darker strain of vanity.

The most famous passage of the poem, the card-table chatter of Swift's "female friends," embodies the problematic mixture of generosity of spirit and veiled resentment that pervades the poem's early portions. The tone of the passage has always suggested a liberating, emotionally composed confrontation with the poet's own insignificance in the scheme of things. But, although the tone reminds us of Swift's raillery, the passage does not end up as a compliment to the inconsiderate friends. Rather, it remains to the end a complaint that Swift's friends do not value him as they ought.

The *Verses,* therefore, which begin as a charmingly self-deprecating fantasy, are transformed, even before the controversial encomium that ends the poem, into an exercise in point-by-point portraiture of Swift as unoffending victim. The crucial argument for the straightforwardness of the encomium, in which many critics have strained to discover irony, is that in it Swift rides all of his favorite hobby-horses; he in fact begins to ride them much earlier.

Swift finally shifts the scene of action to a year after his death, when he "no more is mist,/Than if he never did exist" (lines 247–48), and he speculates about the fate that his literary works will meet. They will, he says, be forgotten and ignorantly denigrated, driven out of the market by just the sort of rubbish that he has spent his entire life opposing: birthday odes for the King by Colley Cibber; Whig propaganda; unorthodox religious tracts by latitudinarian and free-thinking bishops. Many of these complaints are supported by cantankerous footnotes.

Swift then proceeds to the encomium upon his public career. The narrative and dramatic context of the encomium has been much discussed and much misunderstood.[5] The poet has stipulated that he is now generally forgotten; he has just finished cataloguing opinions about himself that immediately follow his death, opinions composed of the malice of enemies, the indifference of the small-minded to genuine merit, and the ignorance of the general public of his accomplishments and standards. He is now concerned to suggest what an unbiased view of his character would be. It is surprising that this passage has been regarded as suggesting in some dark way a special bias on the part of the speaker of the encomium:

> Suppose me dead; and then suppose
> A club assembled at the *Rose;*
> Where from discourse of this and that,
> I grow the subject of their chat;
> And, while they toss my name about,
> With favour some, and some without;
> One quite indiff'rent in the cause,
> My character impartial draws.
>
> (299–306)

Swift creates a climate in which the dust of initial reaction to his death has settled. He stresses that his name comes up casually, that opinion about him is divided and offhand, and that the speaker is "indiff'rent" and "impartial"—that is, not controlled by the envy, self-interest, or aimless malice that the poem has been depicting. The "impartial" speaker will reveal what has generally been forgotten about Swift; he will provide a catalogue of the features of Swift's life that the world's vanity or indifference has eclipsed.

Not surprisingly, this catalogue includes the public accomplishments and private qualities of character that Swift had often complained were misunderstood, perversely denied, or misrepresented by his enemies to the world at large. Also unsurprisingly, it includes his uncontested achievements: his satires; his role as Irish nationalist, especially his activities as M. B., Drapier. The praise of Swift is everywhere generous; when the

speaker touches on Swift's most neuralgic concerns—his patriotic motives
for public service, his steadiness during the collapse of the Oxford ministry,
his suffering at the hands of unrelenting enemies—the praise becomes
fulsome and bombastic.

The fulsomeness of the self-praise has disturbed readers ever since Swift
first showed the poem to a few friends. Also, some of the encomium's
claims struck Swift's friends as embarrassingly self-serving because not
true.[6] Swift had made all of these claims elsewhere, usually in letters, but
they create a very different impression strung together in the encomium;
they sound like a programmatic distortion of his own character.

One example will illustrate the sort of difficulty that Swift's method
creates for his readers. The very first couplet of the encomium makes an
assertion that seems far-fetched:

> "The Dean, if we believe report,
> "Was never ill-received at Court."
>
> (307–8)

Of these lines, Arthur Scouten and Robert Hume write sarcastically: "Of
course not—everyone knew that the author of *A Tale of a Tub* and *The
Windsor Prophecy*, in 'exile' after 1714, had always been a particular pet of
each succeeding monarch."[7] The comment is typical of recent treatment of
the encomium. By treating the assertion as *obviously* false, Scouten and
Hume generate two exclusive alternatives: that Swift was clumsily lying; or
that he was manipulating obvious falsehoods for some subtle purpose.

But the truth is that Swift believed his explicit claim, which is not that he
had ever been cherished by any English monarch but that he had *been well-
received at Court*. In fact, Swift had never been received by Queen Anne at
all. But he had been a prominent figure at her court and had boasted of his
prominence (for instance, as we have seen in *The Author Upon Himself,* a
poem that *attacks* the Queen). During Oxford's ministry Swift had often
visited the court, where his special friends formed a distinguished group—
Oxford, Bolingbroke, Lady Masham, Dr. Arbuthnot. The comments he
made at the time indicate his feelings about the figure he cut: "I am so
proud I make all the lords come to me"; "The Court serves me for a
coffeehouse"; "I was at Court at noon, and saw fifty acquaintance I had not
met this long time: that is the advantage of a Court, and I fancy I am better
known than any man that goes there."[8] There are elements of self-
deception in these statements, of course—of the same sort that we find in
the encomium.

In 1727, after George's accession, Swift *was* received by George and
Caroline; he had also been received several times by Caroline when she was
Princess of Wales. What he stressed about these meetings when he later
spoke of them was that he had been *well-received:* "It is six years last spring

since I first went to visit my friends in England, after the Queen's death. Her present Majesty heard of my arrival, and sent at least nine times to command my attendance. . . . At last I went, and she received me very graciously"; "When I took my leave of her Highness, on coming hither [Ireland], she was very gracious"; "I went to kiss their new Majesties hands, and was particularly distinguished by the Q—n."[9] If we believe Swift's own "report," therefore, the claim he makes in the couplet is perfectly accurate.

To readers familiar only with the outlines of Swift's biography, however, such claims understandably have the effect of obvious lies or distortions. But unlike Pope, who complained that the "latter part" of the *Verses* was "too vain in some respects, & in one or two particulars, not true,"[10] some modern readers have found themselves unable to believe that a poem which commences with gently self-deprecating irony could degenerate into long stretches of ham-handed boasting. There has arisen a movement, therefore, to show that the entire encomium is an instance of sustained irony. The *explanations* of such irony have generally relied on far more subtle notions of poetic unity than Swift's poems customarily exemplify. The *evidence* of such irony has chiefly been the historical inaccuracy of some of Swift's claims about himself.[11]

But it has now been established beyond cavil that Swift had made elsewhere, in contexts where there seems no possibility of irony, virtually all of the claims he makes about himself in the encomium.[12] What Swift has done is to end a poem that begins as a meditation on vanity and self-interest with a straightforward catalogue of his own real but forgotten accomplishments, picturing himself as an especially virtuous man in a corrupt age, as a victim of the world's vain and self-interested reluctance to appreciate and reward such virtues and accomplishments. The biographical details are offered as literal truth. The terms of justification are those to which Swift had time and again insistently appealed.

Critics who believe the encomium to be ironic have not been oblivious to the fact that Swift dwells on accomplishments of which he was genuinely and justifiably proud. But they have been hard put to resolve the difficulty that this creates for an ironic reading of the encomium. The preferred course has been to eschew explanations of Swift's *individual* claims as ironic (other than to insist that they are ironic) and to focus instead on the structural function of the encomium as a whole within the poem as a whole. Is it possible, they ask, that a poem which begins as a meditation on vanity could end as an indulgence of it? Deciding that it is not, they conclude that the fundamental point of the excessive self-praise must be meant to lie in its excessiveness; most argue that the fulsome self-praise must be meant *in general* as one more cautionary example of vanity.

But no explanation that seeks both to have the irony and to avoid its implications—by saying that Swift meant not to deny his accomplishments but to display vanity by overpraising them—can account for the impossible list of "ironic" claims. How does one overpraise oneself for being an incorruptible public servant? And if one does so, must not the implication be either that one was in fact corrupted, or that incorruptibility is not such an outstanding accomplishment in a public man? The same difficulty appears throughout the encomium. If Swift overpraises himself as Drapier, is he implying that he was not a champion of liberty? Or that leading his country in opposition to English tyranny was not a fine achievement?

Even had Swift meant to show that in the prospect of history (or of eternity) his worldly accomplishments were ephemeral things, he would hardly have opened his most sensitive wounds merely for this purpose. Furthermore, strategy would demand that for such a purpose Swift magnify the individual accomplishments through mock-humility, not undercut them through hyperbole; there is not much point in demonstrating, after all, that accomplishments which are dubious on their face will seem, in the prospect of history, more tenuous still.

I do not mean to suggest, of course, that the encomium is artistically or rhetorically successful. Rather, I suggest that it exemplifies the same artistic failures that are common to Swift's other straightforward self-justifications in verse. The speaker's lament for the fall of the Oxford ministry and the death of Queen Anne, for instance, illustrates at once the most and least successful qualities of Swift's rhetoric in the encomium:

> "With horror, grief, despair the Dean
> "Beheld the dire destructive scene:
> "His friends in exile, or the Tower,
> "Himself within the frown of power;
> "Pursu'd by base envenom'd pens,
> "Far to the land of slaves and fens;
> "A servile race in folly nurs'd,
> "Who truckle most, when treated worst."
>
> (391–98)

The opening six lines, which convey the same heated resentment and depict the same trammeled and long-suffering innocence that we have observed in *The Author Upon Himself,* puncture the speaker's objectivity. The epic allusions are so out of proportion to the subject that the elevated tone is exploded; hyperbole creates bathos. The final, powerfully concise couplet, however, is characteristic of Swift at his best. It expresses pithily the fierce sentiments that animate "A Modest Proposal" and some of the finest passages of the *Drapier's Letters.*

The same tonal discordancy that plagues *The Author Upon Himself* may be discovered throughout the encomium, for example in the following:

> "In exile with a steady heart,
> "He spent his life's declining part;
> "Where folly, pride, and faction sway,
> "Remote from St. John, Pope, and Gay."
>
> (431–34)

Few, perhaps, will be persuaded of the straightforwardness of the first line, which surely professes an outright falsehood, merely by the fact that the succeeding three lines repeat complaints that had filled Swift's letters sometimes to the point of tedium. But a look at the artistry of the quatrain confounds the notion that Swift's "ironies," identifiable by their glaring falseness to life, are marked by a bombastic tone. Surely, the tonal disharmony here arises from the fact that the final three lines, which are indisputably straightforward, subvert, by their bombastic, self-pitying tone, the explicit claim to composure made in the first. Surely one does not need to go outside the passage itself to realize that a man does not, in the act of lamenting that he has been compelled to spend his "declining" years in a land of "folly, pride, and faction," convey very convincingly the notion that he endures these circumstances with a "steady heart." But those who see the encomium as systematically undercut by ironical bombast must explain why the false claim of the first line is unmarked by bombast, while the claim which Swift poses bombastically in the rest of the quatrain is one that we know he believed true.

Indeed, among the encomium's most hyperbolic passages are those that seem least likely to be ironic, those, for example, that describe not the poet's virtue but the wickedness of others, such as the Irish gentry:

> "Biennial squires, to market brought;
> "Who sell their souls and votes for naught;
> "The Nation stript go joyful back,
> "To rob the Church, their tennants rack."
>
> (445–48)

If Swift's method in the encomium is ironic self-praise, we must wonder why he sounds equally hyperbolic when reasserting his most deeply settled and widely known antipathies.[13]

The closing passage of the encomium is understated and tonally subdued in comparison to what has come before. The poem concludes with a lofty comment on Swift's benefactions to Ireland. But just before this, the poet offers a view of the private side of his character:

> "He knew an hundred pleasant stories,
> "With all the turns of Whigs and Tories:
> "Was cheerful to his dying day,
> "And friends would let him have his way."
>
> (475–78)

These may seem curious details for Swift to intrude at such a strategic point, only six lines before the end of the poem; but they help to set precisely the tone that makes the conclusion more affecting than any earlier part of the encomium. After all the discussion of controversy, of political achievements and disappointments, of the sordid and pressing evils that pervade a chaotic world, the homely details help to create a more elegiac mood, a sense that beyond all the crises and clashes in the realm of public affairs is an equally important but more intimate reality. The character of himself that Swift presents here is simply an older version of the parson whose personality attracted Oxford's attention in the Horatian self-portaits, who "shew'd some humour in his face," was "a perfect stranger to the spleen," and who "went where he pleas'd, said what he thought." The justification of Swift's public career rests finally on his estimable qualities of character. The example of his life, he suggests, is valuable to posterity because his public achievements were, fundamentally, expressions of private virtue.

The most substantial achievement of the successful self-portraits is the appealing impression that Swift creates of his own personality. When Swift tries to defend specific conduct by resort to factual argument, on the other hand, he sometimes achieves great concision and aphoristic power; but he sometimes spoils his intended effect by giving an impression of a personality at odds with the character he specifically claims.

Although critics have been bothered by lapses from truth in Swift's autobiographical poems, therefore, it is not truth but plausibility that has determined the poet's success. When Swift handles biographical details straightforwardly, we sometimes receive an impression of deceit; when he creates fictions about himself or treats the details of his life ironically, we usually receive an impression of honesty.

In Swift's self-portraits an increase in art produces an increase in nature as well. That is, Swift's ironical self-portraits both portray and embody the essential elements of his character more successfully than do his straightforward self-justifications, which, by contrast, give us the clearer picture of the poet's temperamental weaknesses. There are two reasons why this should be so.

First, many of the characteristics that most distinguish Swift perfectly fit the rhetoric and metric of his ironical self-portraits. His "droll sobriety" (in William Cowper's phrase), his playfulness, his geniality, his awareness of the capriciousness of fate, his delight in mimicry—all are features suited to an ironic treatment of self; they shine best in the rapid colloquialisms of his octosyllabic verse.

Second, by allowing him to distance himself from his own character, the fictional portraits lead Swift to create an ideal self and thus to reveal his moral commitments more fully than he does in straightforward defenses of his conduct. This ideal self embodies also temperamental traits that he admired and, to a very large degree, possessed. The graceful hints to Oxford about financial troubles enact the very charm that the poet portrays himself as having; the humor and tact of these poems confirm the good nature that Swift claims for himself within the poems.

Swift's poetry, as Maurice Johnson observed, sometimes creates a remarkably strong sense of biographical presence.[14] In the successful self-portraits, the character with whom we feel in contact is not so much the man of public accomplishment as the more intimate Swift. Swift's anxiety, indignation, and vanity are certainly no less real than his ideals; but they are less central to the character which we value both in his life and his literature. The brilliant expressive effects with which Swift charms his reader are crucial to his portrayal of this character. But no less crucial to our sense of both the public and private Swift are the ideals of conduct and character that animated, in prose and verse, the moralist and champion of political liberty. On these ideals Swift finally rested all his self-justifications. Hence, the concluding lines of *Verses on the Death of Dr. Swift,* which are meant to cap a summary of the poet's finest achievements, emphasize not particular public accomplishments, but rather his compassion, his amiability, and his generosity.

NOTES

1. *Lives of the English Poets,* ed. G. B. Hill (Oxford: Clarendon Press, 1905), 3:212.

2. Quoted in Irvin Ehrenpreis, *Swift: The Man, His Works, and the Age,* vol. 1 (Cambridge, Mass.: Harvard University Press, 1962), 104. My account of Temple's influence upon Swift is drawn from vol. 1, pt. 2.

3. Reuben A. Brower, *Alexander Pope: The Poetry of Allusion* (London: Oxford University Press, 1959), 163, 176.

4. All quotations of Swift's poetry are from *The Poems of Jonathan Swift,* ed. Harold Williams, 2d ed. (Oxford: Clarendon Press, 1958).

5. See Edward W. Said, "Swift's Tory Anarchy," *ECS* 3 (1969): 64; Arthur H. Scouten and Robert D. Hume, "Pope and Swift: Text and Interpretation of Swift's Verses on his Death," *PQ* 52 (1973): 224–25; Peter J. Schakel, "The Politics of Opposition in 'Verses on the Death of Dr. Swift,'" *MLQ* 35 (1974): 254; David M. Vieth, "The Mystery of Personal Identity: Swift's Verses on his Own Death," in *The Author in His Work: Essays on a Problem in Criticism,* ed. L. L. Martz and P. M. Spacks (New Haven: Yale University Press, 1978), 253.

6. See James Woolley, "Autobiography in Swift's Verses on His Death," in *Contemporary Studies of Swift's Poetry,* ed. J. I. Fischer and D. Mell, Jr. (Newark: University of Delaware Press, 1981), 112.

7. Scouten and Hume, "Pope and Swift," 225.

8. *Journal to Stella,* ed. Harold Williams (Oxford: Clarendon Press, 1948), 322, 522, 421.

9. Swift to Lady Elizabeth Germain, 8 January 1732–33, *The Correspondence of Jonathan Swift,* ed. Harold Williams (Oxford: Clarendon Press, 1963–65), 4:98, 99.

10. Pope to the Earl of Orrery, 25 September 1738, *The Correspondence of Alexander Pope,* ed. George Sherburn (Oxford: Clarendon Press, 1956), 4:130.

11. For the view that the encomium in *Verses on the Death of Dr. Swift* is ironic, see Barry Slepian, "The Ironic Intention of Swift's Verses on His Own Death," *RES,* n.s., 14 (1963): 249–56. For the continuing debate, see Edward Rosenheim, review of Slepian in *PQ* 43 (1964): 392; Marshall Waingrow, *"Verses on the Death of Dr. Swift," SEL* 5 (1965): 513–18; Ronald Paulson, *The Fictions of Satire* (Baltimore: Johns Hopkins University Press, 1967), 189–91; Said, "Swift's Tory Anarchy"; John Irwin Fischer, "How to Die: *Verses on the Death of Dr. Swift," RES* 21 (1970): 422–41; Donald Mell, Jr., "Elegiac Design and Satiric Intention in *Verses on the Death of Dr. Swift," Concerning Poetry* 6 (1973): 15–24; Hugo Reichard, "The Self-Praise Abounding in

Swift's *Verses,*" *Texas Studies in Literature* 18 (1973): 105–12; Scouten and Hume, "Pope and Swift"; Robert W. Uphaus, "Swift's 'whole character': The Delany Poems and 'Verses on the Death of Dr. Swift,'" *MLQ* 34 (1973): 406–16; Irvin Ehrenpreis, *Literary Meaning and Augustan Values* (Charlottesville: University Press of Virginia, 1974), 33–37; Peter J. Schakel, "The Politics of Opposition"; Nora Crow Jaffe, *The Poet Swift* (Hanover, N.H.: University Press of New England, 1977), 14–19; Louise K. Barnett, "Fictive Self-Portraiture in Swift's Poetry," in Fischer and Mell, eds., *Contemporary Studies,* 101–11; James Woolley, "Swift's Verses as Autobiography"; Ricardo Quintana, *Two Augustans: Locke, Swift* (Madison: University of Wisconsin Press, 1978), 111–13; David M. Vieth, "The Mystery of Personal Idenity"; C. J. Rawson, "'I the Lofty Stile Decline': Self-apology and the 'Heroick Strain' in Some of Swift's Poems," in *The English Hero, 1660–1800,* ed. Robert Folkenflik (Newark: University of Delaware Press, 1982), 79–115.

   12. See especially Waingrow, Paulson, Uphaus, Ehrenpreis, and Woolley. Further examples of straightforward statements by Swift that duplicate supposedly ironic statements in the poem are easily discovered. For Swift's insistence that he "sought for no man's aid" (line 238), see *Journal to Stella,* 660–63; for his claim that he "left the Court in meer despair" (374), see Swift to Oxford, 3 July 1714 (*Correspondence of Jonathan Swift,* 2:44–45); for Swift's claims of literary originality, see the Apology to *A Tale of a Tub,* ed. A. C. Guthkelch and D. Nichol Smith, 2d ed. (Oxford: Clarendon Press, 1958), 3–21, and the Advertisement to the second volume of Faulkner's edition of Swift's works, reprinted in *The Prose Writings of Jonathan Swift,* ed. Herbert Davis (Oxford: Basil Blackwell, 1939–68), 13:184; for Swift's claims of habitual cheerfulness and amiability, see his *Correspondence,* 1:154; 2:429; and the *Journal to Stella,* 560, 661.

   Even the two most "obviously" ironical lines in the encomium are probably not ironic. Swift's supposed allusion to Sir John Denham's elegy for Abraham Cowley (line 318: "But what he writ was all his own") was first noticed in 1905 by George Birkbeck Hill (*Johnson's Lives of the English Poets,* 3:66, n. 2), and, even if Swift remembered the featureless line from Denham's mediocre poem, it must be doubted that he expected anyone less curious than George Birkbeck Hill to remember it with him. The second supposed irony—for Swift, a clumsy one indeed—the claim, made just after personal attacks by name on no less than thirteen individuals, that "He lash'd the vice but spar'd the name" (line 460), is easily dissolved upon application to a dictionary. A commonplace contemporary meaning of the verb *to spare* (OED) was: "To refrain from denouncing or exposing *in strong terms;* to deal gently or *leniently* with" (emphasis added). It was in this sense, for instance, that Swift used the word when he advised his friend Thomas Sheridan to "observe with care/Whom to be hard on, whom to spare" ("To Mr. Delany," lines 99–100). The perfectly conventional gist of the passage as a whole is that Swift's satires are lenient by comparison to those of other writers—because he attacks remediable vices only and excoriates only those who have earned the abuse.

   13. A great deal has been made of the encomium's hyperbole and bombast by critics who write as if these features were alien to Swift's ordinary poetic style. Slepian, for instance, suggests that the "amazing total of . . . superlatives" such as "*every*" and "*all*—perhaps the key word of the poem" (254) indicates irony. But what are we to think when we compare the passage I have just quoted from Swift's *Verses* to the following lines on Ireland from the notebook Swift kept at Holyhead?

> Remove me from this land of slaves
> Where all are fools, and all are knaves
> Where every knave and fool is bought
> Yet kindly sells himself for naught.

(Poems, 421)

   The word *all,* by the way, is used by Swift in poems more often than *by, that, as, is, then, this, not, if, or,* or *an;* he used only fifteen words—such as *the, and, a, I,* and *for*—more often. (See *A

Concordance to the Poems of Jonathan Swift, ed. Michael Shinagel [Ithaca: Cornell University Press, 1972], 945.)

Scouten and Hume, following Slepian, proffer the remarkable claim that the sort of "overblown rhetoric" to be found in the encomium "is alien to [Swift's] style and can be found only in his juvenalia and his parodies" (226–27). In fact, few poems by Swift, especially among those written in the 1730s, are wholly free of "overblown rhetoric."

14. Maurice Johnson, "Swift's Poetry Reconsidered," in *English Writers of the Eighteenth Century,* ed. John H. Middendorf (New York: Columbia University Press, 1971), 239.

9

Insects, Vermin, and Horses: *Gulliver's Travels* and Virgil's *Georgics*

Margaret Anne Doody

> I would fain be at the Beginning of my Willows grow-
> ing. . . . The Cherry trees by the River side my Heart
> is sett upon.
>
> > Swift to Stella, 26 March 1712[1]

> God . . . hath placed Things in a State of Imperfec-
> tion, on purpose to stir up human Industry; without
> which Life would stagnate . . . : *Curis acuens mortalia
> corda.*
>
> > Swift, "On Imperfections in Nature"[2]

Any student of Augustan literature soon becomes aware that the *Georgics* is an accustomed point of reference, a favorite book with both writers and readers, and a familiar source of allusion. The essential reason for the work's popularity in England in the late seventeenth and early eighteenth centuries most probably lies in the concern expressed in the *Georgics* with renovating a land torn by a grievous civil war—a concern intimately related to English experience after the 1640s. The *Georgics* spoke to fears and hopes. In the high Renaissance, Virgil's second great work seemed only an interesting preparation for the *Aeneid;* Scaliger, for instance, says surpris-ingly little about the poem. Addison, in his "Essay on Virgil's Georgics" (1697), remarked

> There has been abundance of Criticism spent on Virgil's *Pastorals* and
> *Aeneids,* but the *Georgics* are a subject which none of the Critics have
> sufficiently taken into their consideration; most of them passing it over in
> silence, or casting it under the same head with the *Pastoral;* a division by
> no means proper.[3]

The *Eclogues,* which belonged to an important and elegant genre going
back to Theocritus and forward to Renaissance Italian poets, supplied a
model of great importance to Spenser, for instance. There is no Spenserian
equivalent of the *Georgics.* But in the later seventeenth century the *Georgics*
becomes, certainly in English eyes, a major work in its own right, supplying
an alternative to epic style and subject in its celebration of the arts of peace.

A succession of translators from Ogilby in his big translation of Virgil's
Works (1654) to Trapp (1731) made Virgil accessible to the general reader.
The most influential translator of Virgil is, of course, Dryden, whose *Works
of Virgil* first appeared in 1695. Dryden's version of the *Georgics* (prefaced
in the 1697 and later editions by Addison's critical essay) is an important
poem in itself. The work of translation and poetic imitation of the *Georgics*
continued through the eighteenth century, at least until the version by
Joseph Warton (1753); the influence of the translations can be felt in the
poems of Cowper and Keats. It was, however, Dryden's version that was to
be most important, familiarizing readers not competent to read the Latin
verse with Virgil's rural world and with his themes and images, and thus
equipping such readers to understand allusions (direct or indirect) to Virgil's *Georgics.*

The period that reflects the greatest familiarity with Virgil's four-book
poem, and the most delighted play with it as a strong source of reference,
seems to be the period from Pope to Thomson. Allusions to the *Georgics*
abound in Pope's work, from *Windsor Forest* and *The Rape of the Lock* to the
Dunciad. Gay's *Trivia* (1716) is a mock-Georgic poem, while his *Rural Sports*
(1714) is a more straightforward (if not entirely serious) experiment with
Virgilian country matters. *Rural Sports* influenced Thomson's extensive imitation of Georgic effects, and even supplied phrases in *The Seasons.* Since
Dryden had naturalized Virgil, writers could play on ideas and phrases
suggested by the translator as well as by the original. Swift's own "Description of a City Shower" (1710) plays with the description of the storm and of
weather signs in *Georgics* I—both in the original poem and in Dryden's
version. Swift, like Gay in the later *Trivia,* creates comic effects in a manner
that cannot be termed mock-heroic, but can properly be called mock-
Georgic.

As well as possessing a lively appreciation of the vivid beauty and attractive detail of Virgil's great rural poem, Augustan writers were conscious of
the social and political implications of the *Georgics.* They were particularly
fond of *Georgics* IV with its description of the bees. Here Virgil offers a
mode of examining human life by use of a comic analogy that is not as
simple as an Aesopian fable and that both makes a strong appeal to the
realities of human society and points up the paradoxes in society and
nature. Swift in *The Battle of the Books* appears to be indebted to Virgil in his
substitution of the bee for Seneca's ant in his own Fable of the Spider and
the Bee; idea and treatment seem to carry Virgilian echoes: see, for exam-

ple, *Georgics* IV, "tantus amor florum et generandi gloria mellis" ("so deep is their love of flowers and their glory in begetting honey," line 205, and passim), and "aut inuisa Mineruae/laxos in foribus suspendit aranea cassis" ("or the spider, hateful to Minerva, hangs in the doorway her loose-woven nets," lines 246–47).[4] Mandeville in *The Fable of the Bees* (1714) elaborates and points out something that already exists in the *Georgics,* the relationship between animal (or insect) behavior and human social activity. Mandeville's own poem, the foundation of his treatise, is a mock-Georgic piece, a verse fable referring to *Georgics* IV. Throughout this period (from Pope to Thomson) Virgil's moral comments and his expressive and lively images are generally popular. Virgil's statements (and his ways of making them) on the differences between luxury and simplicity, war and peace, good and bad government, are taken up, overtly imitated with allusive variation, by a number of writers. Thomson has his own version of the "O fortunatos nimium" sequence of *Georgics* II, into which he, like Virgil, works his disapprobation of greed and war:

> Let others brave the flood in quest of gain,
> And beat for joyless months the gloomy wave.
> Let such as deem it glory to destroy
> Rush into blood, the sack of cities seek—
> Unpierced, exulting in the widow's wail
> . . . .
> and those of fairer front,
> But equal inhumanity, in courts,
> Delusive pomp, and dark cabals delight.[5]

Thomson would be disappointed if the reader did not recognize his version of *Georgics* II, lines 495–512. Dryden's version of the passage is certainly present here too, whether Thomson means us to know it or not.

Since the *Georgics* is such a significant work during Swift's period, figuring prominently in contemporary discussions of man, nature, and society, it is not foolish to ask whether Swift may not (if only briefly) be considered in this Virgilian connection. Certainly the author who wrote "A City Shower" and who penned the stern and moving quotation *"Curis acuens mortalia corda"* in "Thoughts on Various Subjects" did know the *Georgics.* And Swift, like other writers of his time, lived alternately in town and country, remembering even in London the willow trees and cherries of Laracor. The landowner's or landholder's concern with crops and the planting of trees naturally touched his private life, as it did that of so many other gentlemen of his time, rendering the Virgilian interests congenial to normal experience. If we admit that the *Georgics* must have been one of the many literary works furnishing Swift's imagination, it might well be worth while to examine *Gulliver's Travels* in the light of the *Georgics.* That the educated reader, Swift's "ideal" reader (such as John Gay), knew the *Georg-*

ics too is well worth bearing in mind. Certain images, activities, and ideas in Swift's story would have had for his contemporaries an accepted frame of reference upon which the author could partially rely (that this frame of reference is now less accessible to most modern readers is an accident of cultural history).

I am not claiming that *Gulliver's Travels* constitutes a Swiftian *Georgics* (though crazier things have been said about books). Neither do I claim that this particular reading will startlingly subvert all previous notions of Swift's book. Rather, what I am offering, speculatively, is a reading that may enable us to see one strand of a complex work and to recover the resonances of certain ideas and images whose conscious (or half-conscious) associations could help to establish meaning by unostentatiously governing the attentive reader's responses to Swift's tale. Swift certainly did not write his satiric *Travels* with a copy of Virgil in front of him, but the modern critic must painfully present an array of detail in order to trace something which was once the very stuff of thought. Works that in the past flourished in the minds of men as green and living presences have to be restored to our twentieth-century minds before an argument about particular design and effects can even begin. In the case of the exploration of Swift's *Gulliver* and Virgil we should remind ourselves not only of Virgil's great poem but also of Dryden's translation, that source of thematic power and exemplary phrase for so many writers of Swift's time.

It is traditionally agreed that the *Georgics* was written with a genuine didactic intention. Deep and multifarious as the work is in many ways, the author does what he overtly pretends to be doing, encouraging men, after the pain of civil war, to take up the cultivation of the land. The work is not merely a farmer's handbook, but it is that. One of the striking things about the poem is the amount of attention given to the details of doing work. Ordinary simple facts and objects, efforts and achievements in mundane things, have never been more beautifully presented. Book I, which deals with agriculture, contrasts the Golden Age with the life of toil that men must now endure. Book II, on viticulture and arboriculture, describes the happiness that man may achieve here and now; the worthy peasant, the wise landowner, the philosopher-poet can achieve a life not of careless ease but of hard-won stability arising from rational and emotional exertion. Book III, on animal husbandry, emphasizes the beautiful if irrational power of sexuality in the animal creation and in men, and the terrifying forces of pain and death to which all creatures are subject. This most violent of the poem's books describes various aspects of the violent in nature; it includes the well-known description of the Scythians in their forbidding icy land and it ends with the famous description of the cattle-plague.[6] Book IV, by contrast, begins on a light and happy note, as the reader is called upon to enjoy the serio-comic description of the bees (in lines that were partly to inspire the opening of *The Rape of the Lock:* "admiranda tibi leuium spectacula rerum/. . . dicam./in tenui labor; at tenuis non gloria," 3–6). The bees are comic, absurd in their tiny belligerence, but they are admirable because, like human beings, they work to produce their golden store. Labor and laborers can be swept away, as Aristaeus' swarm is suddenly blighted, but the Orpheus myth is here introduced with a (tenuous and complex) hope of regeneration and rebirth; another swarm is born and work begins anew for bees and bee-keeper, that is, for animal creation and for human beings.

Before proceeding to a comparison of the *Georgics* and *Gulliver's Travels* (or before entertaining the notion that such a comparison is possible), we ought to do more than nudge memory with such an outline. It is necessary to focus attention more closely on some major themes in Virgil's *Georgics*, and on some of Virgil's images and techniques. We ought also to become accustomed to the spirit and language of the translators, so that we recognize not only Virgil himself but also Virgil in his English dress. *Work* is certainly a theme in Virgil—and those who generalize too glibly about "the Protestant work-ethic" (as if no one before Luther set a value on human labor) should consider the high place a Roman could give to work. Once there was no work, no property, no pain attached to getting food. But the Golden Age is in Virgil's poem subordinated to the tougher world of the later age, and seen only in disappearance. The Golden Age is no longer; Jove put an end to it:

> The Sire of Gods and Men, with hard Decrees
> Forbids our Plenty to be bought with Ease:
> And wills that Mortal Men, inur'd to toil,
> Shou'd exercise, with pains, the grudging Soil.
> Himself invented first the shining Share,
> And whetted Humane Industry by Care.
>
> (Dryden, I. 183–88)[7]

Curis acuens mortalia corda: and sharpened ("is sharpening"—the word is a present participle) mortal minds (spirits, hearts—*corda*) with trouble, anxiety, occupation, and preoccupation. The whole of the great poem makes us feel the stimulation of the mind in common things, the sharpening of the heart to activity and response. Throughout *Georgics* I there is a strong sense of the painful effort of survival; the harvest is one of the greatest human achievements, and the most essential. This industry is not only human but "humane" (in the modern sense). Agriculture is, however, an "Iron war" (Dryden's phrase happily sums up the effect of an accumulation of Virgilian metaphors). Nature herself threatens man's hopes, not only with poor ground and bad weather but with plant-disease and weeds. Vermin threaten the crops in the fields and even on the very threshing floor:

> For sundry Foes the Rural Realm surround:
> The Field Mouse builds her Garner under ground;

For gather'd Grain the blind laborious Mole,
In winding Mazes works her hidden Hole.
In hollow Caverns Vermine make abode,
The hissing Serpent, and the swelling Toad:
The corn-devouring Weezel here abides,
And the wise Ant her wintry Store provides.

(I. 264–71)

In this passage I am using Dryden's translation of 1697, which has "Weezel" for 1659's "Weevel." There seems to have been some dubiety in the minds of the translators about *Georgics* I. 184–86:

atque plurima terrae
monstra ferunt; populatque ingentem farris aceruum
curculio atque inopi metuens formica senectae.

Thomas May in 1628 translates *curculio* correctly as "weevil"; the word itself seems nicely descriptive of a little curly being, like the larva. But Ogilby translates the line as "Thence Weesels plunder mighty hoords of Corn."[8] Dryden had "Weevel" but changed back to "Weezel." And even later there is the same confusion: Trapp has "Weevil," but Joseph Warton writes "The weasel heaps consumes."[9] The persistent introduction of the weasel might have been influenced by Columella's description of the threshing floor: "Nam ea res a populatione murum formecarumque frumenta defendit," the ant's companion in destruction associated with a small furry animal. Which is the "monster"—Weevil or Weasel? In any case, Virgil's lines describe the monstrosity of small hidden creatures, and their depredations, while at the same time endowing these pests sympathetically with their own lives and intentions, not noxious to themselves. It is in such descriptions of animated nature, rather than in his more conventional evocations of natural beauty, that Virgil excels. His whole poem is populated by animals, birds, insects—secondary characters in relation to man who yet live their own independent lives with a homely beauty, like the birds who rejoice after the storm in book I, or the solitary raven stalking the sands before the rain in the lovely comic line: "et sola in sicca secum spatiatur harena." The constant presence of other lives than ours gives to man's rural existence its truth to varied reality, a deep consciousness of life that makes for sanity. But the creatures are no mere ornaments for our own observation, nor are they all necessarily contributors to human ease.

Virgil never makes human life on the land too easy. Human beings are only too willing to forsake attention to the life-giving work for any folly—for ease, for ambition. The famous passage toward the end of book II, "O fortunatos nimium sua si bona norint," does not merely celebrate the happiness of innocent rural life; it is also an attack on the sophisticated objects of desire that seduce men from the truth. The happy man "unmov'd, the Bribes of Courts can see;/Their glitt'ring Baits and purple Slavery" (II. 704–5). Dryden gives a neat turn to Virgil's phrasing, heightening a satiric effect certainly present in Virgil by referring to contemporary English political life in the list of activities with which the happy rural man has nothing to do:

> The Senate's mad Decrees he never saw;
> Nor heard, at bawling Bars, corrupted Law.
> Some to the Seas, and some to Camps resort,
> And some with Impudence invade the Court.
> In foreign Countries others seek Renown,
> With Wars and Taxes others waste their own.
> . . . .
> Some Patriot Fools to pop'lar Praise aspire,
> Or Publick Speeches, which worse Fools admire.
> While from both Benches, with redoubl'd Sounds,
> Th' Applause of Lords and Commoners abounds.
> Some through Ambition, or thro' Thirst of Gold,
> Have slain their Brothers, or their Country sold:
> And leaving their sweet Homes, in Exile run
> To Lands that lye beneath another Sun.
>
> (II. 718–37)

Sophisticated social life is not only corrupt and sterile but mad. The energies that should be spent in fighting the good war with nature, in providing the food needed by all mankind, are perverted into destructiveness. The achievement of what is desired comes inevitably to mean the ruin, not the succor, of fellow human beings; the later phases of the insanity mean murder, war, and imperialism. Some ambitious warmonger will destroy a town, putting it and its household gods to the sword, in order that he may drink from a gemmed goblet and sleep on a Tyrian bed, an ostentatious model of conspicuous consumption and false achievement: "hic petit excidiis urbem miserosque penatis,/ut gemma bibat et Sarrano dormiat ostro" (505–6). It all costs too much. Virgil, nearly as much as Swift himself, seems in the *Georgics* to have deep-rooted objections to conquests and systems. Human survival depends on escaping dehumanizing madness. The true well-being of the state as community rests on life-giving cultivation, not on death-dealing war. Corn is the true wealth. Hard continual endeavor is required to maintain human life. Virgil says civilization is like a rower going against the current; if he rests on his oars, he is swept backwards (I. 199–203). The true heroism of mankind is found in those who assume the willing discipline of labor in winning bread and wine from the stubborn land. Human nature is most vile in its "monstrous Crimes," of which war is ugliest, and most admirable in the tough but creative struggle with nature. That struggle is—though neither easily nor glamorously— rewarded, and rewarded not only with the life-giving food. The paradoxical and animated relationship with nature evokes man's truest self.

In *Gulliver's Travels* as in the *Georgics* we notice a constant attention to the cultivation of the land and to food. The practice of agriculture and husbandry here too provides a basic point of reference, a standard by which other activities can be judged. In *Gulliver's Travels* such straight Georgic elements are not obtrusive even when visible. They are apparently subordinate to the satire even though they supply major meanings, whereas in the *Georgics* the satiric elements are subordinate to the description of rural works and days, even though unobtrusive but recurrent satire supplies emphasis and direction. Yet, just as the *Georgics* would not be itself without the social criticism and the satire, so *Gulliver's Travels* would not be itself without the georgic affirmations. Moreover, *Gulliver's Travels* is related to the *Georgics* not only in certain affirmations but also in subtle touches of play. Swift seems to be playing some of his favorite games with Virgil's tropes and *topoi*, extending or reversing them, or making literal and permanent what was originally temporary or metaphorical. The *Georgics* provides one (though not the only) congenial source of material for Swift's imaginative logic.

To begin this Georgic reading of Swift's book at the beginning: in book I we are introduced to Lilliput, a tiny community of insect-like creatures, a society full of a comic sense of its own importance and unaware of its miniature status. Virgil had described such a community, in mock-heroic manner:

> Embattl'd Squadrons and advent'rous Kings:
> A mighty Pomp, tho' made of little Things.
> Their Arms, their Arts, their Manners I disclose,
> And how they War, and whence the People rose.
>
> (IV. 4–7)

As Addison succinctly remarks,

> Virgil seems no where so well pleased as when he had got among his Bees
> . . . and ennobles the actions of so trivial a Creature with metaphors
> drawn from the most important concerns of mankind. . . . In short, the
> last Georgic . . . very well showed what the poet could do . . . by his
> describing the mock-grandeur of an Insect with so good a grace.[10]

Virgil's bees make war and follow a warlike king:

> With ease distinguish'd is the Regal Race,
> One Monarch wears an honest open Face;
> Shap'd to his Size, and Godlike to behold,
> His Royal Body shines with specks of Gold,
> And ruddy Skales; for Empire he design'd
> Is better born, and of a Nobler Kind.
>
> (IV. 137–42)

Dryden shows less approbation of absolute monarchy than does Virgil (whose comedy is also not without satiric point). Dryden adds an extra modern satiric touch in translating book IV lines 215–26 as "They crowd his Levees" (IV. 316), and he makes a political pun: "their high-flying Arbitrary Kings" (IV. 162).

The description of the Lilliputian Emperor (a sufficiently "high-flying Arbitrary King") is very like Virgil's mock-heroic rendition of the Bee King, godlike, majestic, and ornate—but absurd:

> He is taller by almost the Breadth of my Nail, than any of his Court; which alone is enough to strike an Awe into the Beholders. His Features are strong and masculine . . . and his Deportment majestick. . . . His Dress was very plain . . . but he had on his Head a light Helmet of Gold, adorned with Jewels, and a Plume on the Crest.[11]

Every reader of *Gulliver's Travels* recalls the shrill bellicosity of the Lilliputians. They have engaged in civil war and are waging fierce war with Blefescu. Virgil's bees are also factious ("The Vulgar in divided Factions jar;/And murm'ring Sounds proclaim the Civil War"), and they too engage in impressive wars (between two swarms):

> The shocking Squadrons meet in mortal Fight
> Headlong they fall from high, and wounded wound,
> And heaps of slaughter'd Souldiers bite the Ground.
> . . . .
> With mighty Souls in narrow Bodies prest,
> They challenge, and encounter Breast to Breast;
> So fix'd on Fame, unknowing how to fly.
>
> (IV. 115–26)

But all this bluster of glory, this shocking war, can easily be ended by a human being:

> Yet all those dreadful deeds, this deadly fray,
> A cast of scatter'd Dust will soon alay.
>
> (130–31)

Gulliver is, as he often feels, living among insects. The Lilliputian peacetime occupations resemble those of the bees: they live according to civil law, they have division of labor, they are extremely patriotic, and they are monarchists and courtiers.

Swift comes very close to Virgil's effects, or rather retains them, and the mock-heroic style, while reversing the process. Swift is not comparing insects to men, but men to insects. Yet Virgil too makes us feel the fragility and absurdity of much human society through his description of the bees. Considering the Virgilian tradition, it is not surprising that Swift, imagining Gulliver's first experience in a wonderful country that disturbingly images his own, should hit upon the miniature commonwealth with its laws, polity, government, and wars all solemnly conducted by an insectlike race. Swift enjoys describing, in the words of Addison (which Swift could hardly help knowing), "the mock-grandeur of an Insect with so good a grace."

Yet the Lilliputians remain insistently human, and, both like bees and like the better human societies, they understand work. They are able to feed Gulliver. They have become sophisticated; their court is a source of bribes, "glitt'ring Baits, and Purple Slavery," their law is corrupt, and they pursue foreign wars. Their community has evidently degenerated, like Virgil's Rome and Dryden's England, but both in Lilliput and in Blefescu the arts of peace are sufficiently practiced for the citizens to have a prospect of survival. Gulliver, when he takes with him the miniature cattle, the hay, and the corn, shows, however ridiculously, that he has not lost contact with nature, with georgic cares. He has a tenuous hold on the proper human priorities, as do Lilliput and Blefescu, those imperfect societies.

In book II we are introduced to the least corrupted of the human societies Gulliver discovers in his travels. We discover this place by seeing, with the hero, a prospect of country "fully cultivated" with enormous fields of grass, "kept for Hay . . . above twenty Foot high," and then by making our way through a field of grain. We struggle through the forest of barley with the vulnerable Gulliver, who is now in the position of one of the vermin threatening cultivation—which is what the reapers first think he is. The illustration at the beginning of book II in the French translation (*Voyages de Gulliver*, 1727) perfectly captures this comic georgic moment; the giant reapers are so enormous and facially expressive, and their grain so important and impressive that Gulliver (whose expression can't really be seen) is at first glance a minor detail, a little thing near the ground (see figure 1).[12]

The first Brobdingnagians we encounter are laborers and a farmer. These georgic figures are not in the least idealized, but their work establishes the idea that Brobdingnagian life rests upon the proper basis. That admirable personage, the King of Brobdingnag, like the good Caesar evoked and created by Virgil's poem, hates war, fraud, and rapine. He understands the importance of agriculture and encourages it. His famous dictum,

> that whoever could make two Ears of Corn, or two Blades of Grass to grow upon a Spot of Ground where only one grew before; would deserve better of Mankind, and do more essential Service to his Country, than the whole race of Politicians put together, (GT II, 135–36)

is exactly in the spirit of *Georgics* I. In the first scenes after his arrival, Gulliver is thought to be a *splacknuck,* an animal like a weasel; the laborer who first picks him up does so

> with the Caution of one who endeavors to lay hold on a small dangerous Animal in such a Manner that it shall not be able either to scratch or to bite him; as I my self have sometimes done with a *Weasel* in *England*. (GT II, 87)

Figure 1

At first sight of Gulliver everyone thinks he is a *splacknuck*—that is, he is like the "Corn devouring Weezel" which so frequently (if mistakenly) appears in translations of Virgil by Swift's contemporaries. Gulliver first thinks of the giants as "Monsters," but to them he is one of the monsters that the earth brings forth ("atque plurima terrae/monstra ferunt"). He is monstrous philosophically in being *"Relplum Scalcath"* (*lusus naturae*: 104), but he is also "monstrous" in being, like the creatures in Virgil's list of pests, noxious to the works of man. Gulliver is apparently one of the creatures that threaten Brobdingnagian labor and are inimical to the vital harvest of the corn.

Yet the more kindly or better educated among the Brobdingnagians are enlightened and Virgilian enough to accept and enjoy the variety of animal life in the world and to take pleasure in a miniature domesticity that parallels that of man. This Virgilian attitude itself poses problems for Gulliver, who is indignant at the King's laughing speech:

> he observed, how contemptible a Thing was human Grandeur, which could be mimicked by such diminutive Insects as I: And yet, said he, I dare engage, those Creatures have their Titles . . . they contrive little Nests and Burrows, that they call Houses and Cities . . . they love, they fight, they dispute, they cheat, they betray. (GT II, 107)

Virgil intermittently gives us the animal's-eye view, the animal feelings about things, in his rendering of the vital life—so like the human—going on around the human one; he introduces human concepts and phrases into descriptions of animal activites, amusing us with what Addison calls "mock-grandeur," while making the animals (including birds and insects) vivid and attractive, if not necessarily lovely:

> The Frogs renew the Croaks of their loquacious Race . . .
>
> (I. 521)
>
> Then, thrice the Ravens rend the liquid air,
> And croaking Notes proclaim the settled fair.
> Then, round their Airy Palaces they fly . . .
>
> (I. 557–59)
>
> Or Wasps infest the Camp with loud Alarms,
> And mix in Battel with unequal Arms.
>
> (IV. 358–59)

Swift extends and recreates the Virgilian effects to comic and ironic purpose, giving Gulliver the animal's-eye (or pest's-eye) view of things, even while the diminutive Englishman insists indignantly that he ought not to be seen as merely *like* the human beings. Gulliver has, however, to meet frogs and birds and wasps at their own, and not at the human level, and in his peculiar case alone the mock-heroic attributions of grandeur and fearfulness to their existence and activities becomes realistic. Swift has played one of his favorite games with Virgilian tropes, ironically turning the metaphorical into the literal.

Throughout book II Gulliver encounters small animals—vermin and pests—at close quarters. The destructive energy of predators and vermin is felt throughout "A Voyage to Brobdingnag." The King's famous unanswerable condemnation of the bulk of mankind as "little odious Vermin" (132) is the more crushing because in the background there are cornfields and other fruits of the earth that must be preserved from pests. In Virgil also there is a comparison, implicit rather than explicit, between the aspects of nature that threaten man's sustenance and human life-threatening destructiveness. In the Golden Age man lived in peaceful sustaining relationship with the food-giving earth; that was before there were blights and pests, and before there was war: "necdum etiam audierant inflari classica, necdum/impositos duris crepitare includibus ensis" (II. 538–40). Dryden stresses the point in his translation by adding a word: "E're sounding Hammers forg'd th' *inhumane* Sword" (II. 788; emphasis mine). He achieves a similar effect in his amplified rendering of Georgics I, lines 505–8:

> Where Fraud and Rapine, Right and Wrong confound; ⎫
> Where impious Arms from ev'ry part resound,   ⎬
> And monstrous Crimes in ev'ry Shape are crown'd. ⎭
> The peaceful Peasant to the Wars is prest;
> The Fields lye fallow in inglorious Rest.
> The Plain no Pasture to the Flock affords,
> The crooked Scythes are streightned into Swords.
>
> (I. 678–84)

(The effect of Virgil's "et curuae rigidum falces conflantur in ensem" is heightened in a modern European translation like Dryden's by inevitable and ironic echoes of Isaiah 2:4 and 40:4; the paradox present in Virgil—of the "crooked" (good) being "streightned" (bad)—is the more striking as we see an inhumane and *ungodly* subversion.)

In book II of *Gulliver's Travels* the brutality of war is starkly examined. We see the psychological basis of bellicosity in the individual, in Gulliver's aggressive desire to reestablish himself by offering the secret of gunpowder; in compensation for his personal weakness he relishes descriptions of the new weapon's lethal potency. We all remember the king's horrified reaction:

> He was amazed how so impotent and groveling an Insect as I (these were his Expressions) could entertain such inhuman ideas. (134)

There is a comedy in the language here—how can an *insect* be other than *inhuman*? The condemnation sums up everything that is noxious, hurtful to crops and to human life in a manner essentially mean, whether such violence to human survival and dignity is committed on a large or small scale.

The Brobdingnagians are humane. They live in no Golden Age of Saturn; they are fallen (if gigantic) mankind. But they know (certainly the King knows) how much effort is needed to keep from being drawn backwards and downwards by the strong current of degeneration. Their past history has given them warning. They too have been "troubled with the same Disease, to which the whole Race of Mankind is Subject"; social and political divisions "have more than once occasioned Civil Wars" (138). In a famous passage at the end of *Georgics* I, Virgil describes the battle of Pharsalia with wonder and pity, pointing out in striking combinations of images that war is both awesome and futile. In such cruel waste of time the race degenerates, so that men of his era will seem remote antique giants to men of future ages. The only other long-term result will be the discovery of unnecessary sad souvenirs left to encumber the good earth:

> just Heav'n thought good
> To fatten twice those Fields with *Roman* Blood,
> Then, after length of Time, the lab'ring Swains,
> Who turn the Turfs of those unhappy Plains,
> Shall rusty Piles from the plough'd Furrows take,
> And over empty Helmets pass the Rake.
> Amaz'd at Antick Titles on the Stones,
> And mighty Relicks of Gygantick Bones.
>
> (I. 660–67)

The Brobdingnagians, like the Romans (but more impressively) giants in their time, also believe that

> it was very reasonable to think, not only that the Species of Men were originally much larger, but also that there must have been Giants in former Ages; which, as it is asserted by History and Tradition, so it hath been confirmed by huge Bones and Sculls casually dug up in several Parts of the Kingdom, far exceeding the common dwindled Race of Man in our Days. (GT II, 137)

How did those "Bones and Sculls" come to be in a spot where they could be "casually dug up"? The implication, in a passage closely associated with the account of the country's recent civil wars, is that these bones are the relics of the Brobdingnagians' ancient or prehistoric civil wars. The modern Brobdingnagians are now determined, as Virgil hoped his Romans would be, to put an end to this pattern of destruction and to embrace the life-affirming arts of peace.

If book II presents a georgic community, good though touched with human imperfection, book III, "A Voyage to Laputa," presents a society insanely anti-georgic. The Laputians have forsaken proper agriculture in the carelessness of oppression and in the deliberate conceit of their minds. Balnibarbi is a waste land:

> neither did I observe any Expectation either of Corn or Grass, although the Soil appeared to be excellent. . . . I never knew a Soil so unhappily cultivated, Houses so ill contrived and so ruinous, or a People whose

Countenances and Habit expressed so much Misery and Want. (GT III, 175)

Grass (for cattle), corn (for bread), the very things that we see first in the Brobdingnagian landscape, are the foundation of truly civilized life. All culture depends on agriculture. The central image is repeated: "except in some very few Places, I could not discover one Ear of Corn, or Blade of Grass." The Lord Munodi, a happy exception among the Laputians, is a landowner in the Virgilian (and ideal English) style. His estate manifests the three basic forms of farming dealt with at realistic and symbolic length in the first three books of the *Georgics*—agriculture, viticulture, husbandry:

> we came into a most beautiful Country; Farmers Houses at small Distances, neatly built, with Fields enclosed, containing Vineyards, Corngrounds and Meadows. Neither do I remember to have seen a more delightful Prospect. (GT III, 175–76)

But according to Laputian standards, Munodi is not successful at all. Degeneration seems to have won, as the landowners of this country assiduously cultivate ruin and abuse the land that offers to support them. Munodi's position is a parody of the position of the happy man in Virgil, who gathers the fruits of the earth heedless of the madness of the world (II. 490–502). According to Virgil, this happy man is not disturbed by the envy of the rich or pity of the poor.[13] But Munodi is disturbed, as he can see poverty all about him that he is not allowed to relieve; nor can he himself remain free from "The Senate's mad Decrees." Swift seems to be arguing with Virgil by pointing out that virtuous solitude is not possible once things get bad enough. Society can exert great pressures; Munodi is about to give in and destroy his estate by "modern Usage" (176). Happiness will not be permitted.

In Virgil's poem, the passage about the good landowner appears in a section describing various forms of happiness. One of the means of mental pleasure is a knowledge of the operations of nature. The poet wishes to learn, under the tutelage of the muse, about the wonders of nature, to be another Lucretius:

> Give me the Ways of wandring Stars to know:
> The Depths of Heav'n above, and Earth below.
> Teach me the various Labours of the Moon,
> And whence proceed th' Eclipses of the Sun.
>
> (II. 676–79)

These lines might be the prayer of the Laputians; this Virgilian passage was often quoted in defence of the New Science. Yet in Virgil, too, the curiosity of energetic worldly men is criticized: "solicitant alii remis freta caeca, ruuntque/in ferrum, penetrant aulas et limina regum" ("others vex with

oars unknown seas, dash upon the sand, or press into courts and the
portals of kings," lines 504–5). The activities censured, described in words
suggesting blind furious motion, arise from greed that carries the mind
beyond the point where happiness can be recognized. Gulliver himself is
one of those who have vexed unknown seas and pressed into the courts of
kings (to his cost) because of his "insatiable Desire of seeing foreign Countries" (I, 80). Desires should be satiable. The Laputians are anti-sensual, but
they are insatiable. Theirs is a land of cupidity. As an example of reckless
cupidity which the good man shuns, Virgil cites the man who is willing to
ruin a city and its wretched homes for his own ends (II. 505–6). The
Laputian aristocracy are quite willing to ruin cities on the mainland, if it
can be done to advantage and without danger. Their mental activity and
moral habits lead to nightmare, and when they think on the ways of wandering stars they are insane. In Virgil's poem, most particularly in book II
with its discussion of happiness, speculative thought is not divorced from
harmonious and sensed relationship with nature. Intellectual and practical
pleasures united yield psychological satisfaction:

> Happy the Man, who, studying Nature's Laws,
> Thro' known Effects can trace the secret Cause.
> His Mind possessing, in a quiet state,
> Fearless of Fortune, and resign'd to Fate.
> And happy too is he, who decks the Bow'rs
> Of Sylvans, and adores the Rural Pow'rs.
>
> (II. 698–703)

The happy man is not obsessed, and limitations are recognized. The poet
realizes that his prayer to the muse might not be answerable, that he might
be incapable of reaching the lofty heights:

> But if the colder Blood
> About my Heart forbid me to approach
> So near to Nature; may the rural Fields,
> And Streams, which murm'ring glide along the Vales,
> Delight me: Groves, and Rivers may I love,
> Obscure, inglorious.
>
> (Trapp, II. 586–91)[14]

A rejection of obsessive egotism is enacted in the poem. Virgil drops grace-
fully back into the middle state, accepts limitation, and enjoys what the
world around him has to offer. This is exactly what the Laputians are
incapable of doing. In the course of *Georgics* II Virgil's humility has acquired profound meaning; nowhere else in literature is there poetry so
truly down to earth, nowhere else is the practical interest and sensual
pleasure of feeling the soil in one's hands so vividly conveyed (e.g., II. 249–
50). Down-to-earth is exactly what the floating and vertiginous rulers of

Laputa are not, and they are no more capable of tasting and feeling the soil (the neglected good soil that Gulliver sorrowfully admires) than they are of kissing their children, as Virgil's happy farmer does at the end of *Georgics* II. As rulers, the Laputians are at one with the bad rulers and oppressors satirically described in Virgilian passages contiguous to the descriptions of felicity; they have created their own "insanum forum" and have agitated "discordia fratres." Although they fear death by collision with the sun, the Laputians have forgotten that they are mortal men, that it is mortal hearts that Jove sharpens by the need to take thought. The visit to the Struldbruggs, and Gulliver's absurd flight into imagined everlasting survival shows the dangers of forgetting that mortality: *cura acuens mortalia corda.* Mortality means a common responsibility for common sustenance, and mortal men—even in Swift—have the pleasures appropriate to their state. The Laputians have not only forgotten that there are things they ought to do and things that they ought not to do; they have also forgotten all the pleasures of the earth:

> Oh, that we were at Laracor this fine day! the willows begin to peep, and the quicks to bud. My dream's out: I was a-dreamed last night that I eat ripe cherries.—[13]

> rura mihi et rigui placeant in uallibus amnes,
> flumina amem siluasque inglorius. . . .
> > o qui me gelidis conuallibus Haemi
> sistat, et ingenti ramorum protegat umbra!
>
> > > > (II. 485–89)

Since the reader of *Gulliver's Travels* has observed the Laputians' mad hostility to nature, he is prepared—in fact, over-ready—to accept a simple direct relationship with the soil and its plants as an absolute good. In book IV, "A Voyage to the Houyhnhnms," the reader is at first reassured by the rough, plain wholesomeness of the land in which he finds himself: "There was great Plenty of Grass, and several Fields of Oats" (223). The contrast with Laputa and Balnibarbi is cheerful; here, we feel, is proper cultivation without artifice or false doctrine. That Gulliver's arrival here as in book II is associated with fields and grain seems a good sign. This country also seems to be a land where husbandry is practiced; the beaten road bears "many Tracks of human Feet, and some of Cows, but most of Horses." The first "Animals in a Field" that Gulliver sees are the disagreeable creatures for which he has at that point no name; Gulliver is afraid to strike one, lest the inhabitants be offended "that I had killed or maimed any of their Cattle" (223, 224). The first horse that Gulliver sees is found where one would expect to find a horse—in a field.

This seems to be a land whose inhabitants practice simple agriculture and animal husbandry. So it is—even when we find out that it is the Houyhnhnms who are in control.

> They milk their Cows, reap their Oats, and do all the Work which re-
> quires Hands. . . . With Tools made of . . . Flints, they . . . cut their Hay,
> and reap their Oats, which there groweth naturally in several Fields: The
> *Yahoos* draw home the Sheaves in Carriages, and the Servants tread them
> in certain covered Hutts, to get out the Grain, which is kept in Stores.
> (274)

The agriculture is of the simplest kind; unlike ourselves, or Virgil's Roman
farmers, the Houyhnhnms do not need to plant seeds or tend the crops,
and their manner of threshing is clumsy and primitive. The Houyhnhnms
are far more expert in animal husbandry than in agriculture. They keep
cows and have domesticated the Yahoos, which are housed in a kennel or
stable. In the past, when the Yahoos became too numerous, the
Houyhnhnms destroyed the adults but kept a few of the young:

> every *Houyhnhnm* kept two young Ones in a Kennel, and brought them to
> such a Degree of Tameness, as an Animal so savage by Nature can be
> capable of acquiring; using them for Draught and Carriage. (271)

The Houyhnhnms need only two of the three basic types of domestic
beasts: cows for food (milk only), and Yahoos for "Draught and Carriage"
(in place of our horses). They have no need for sheep as they don't wear
clothes. They now regret that "the Inhabitants taking a Fancy to use the
Service of the *Yahoos,* had very imprudently neglected to cultivate the Breed
of Asses" (272). The General Assembly of the Houyhnhnms is almost entirely taken up with questions of animal husbandry. Gulliver's master, taking up an idea offered by Gulliver, proposes that the Yahoos be castrated;
the eventual extinction of the noxious species would be ensured, and
meanwhile Yahoos would be rendered "tractable and fitter for Use." In the
interval between the operation on the Yahoos and that species' disappearance, the Houyhnhnms "should be *exhorted* to cultivate the Breed of Asses,
which, as they are in all respects more valuable Brutes; so they have this
Advantage, to be fit for Service at five years old" (273). It crosses the
reader's mind, though the idea doesn't seem to have occurred to the
Houyhnhnms, that the proximity of he-asses could at times be dangerous
to the Houyhnhnm mares—the result could be a few mules.

Although such a disgusting idea as the production of a mule could not
enter Houyhnhnm views of the nature of things, the Houyhnhnms are
devout students of animal breeding. They practice animal husbandry, so-
berly and thoroughly, upon themselves. The Houyhnhnms treat themselves as objects, as a breed. Every reader remembers the Houyhnhnms'
treatment of mating:

> In their Marriages they are exactly careful to chuse such Colours as
> will not make any disagreeable Mixture in the Breed. *Strength* is chiefly
> valued in the Male, and *Comeliness* in the Female; not upon the account of

Love, but to preserve the Race from degenerating. . . . The young Couple meet and are joined, merely because it is the Determination of their Parents and Friends. (268–69)

It has already been explained to Gulliver that inferior types are not allowed to interbreed with the better stock:

> He made me observe, that among the *Houyhnhnms,* the *White,* the *Sorrel,* and the *Iron-grey,* were not so exactly shaped as the *Bay,* the *Dapple-grey,* and the *Black;* nor born with equal Talents of Mind . . . and therefore continued always in the Condition of Servants, without ever aspiring to match out of their own Race. (256)

Swift's horses' color bar is derived from book III of Virgil's *Georgics* (lines 81–83):

> honesti
> spadices glaucique, color deterrimus albis
> et giluo.

Ogilby translates that sentence,

> White, Sorril, worst; Bay, or bright Gray is best,

while Dryden amplifies the lines in his version:

> Brawny his Chest, and deep, his Colour gray;　⎫
> For Beauty dappled, or the brightest Bay:　　⎬
> Faint White and Dun will scarce the rearing pay,⎭
>   (III. 127–29)

and Trapp, later, has

> His Chest with swelling knots
> Luxuriant; (Best for Colour is the Bay,
> And Dappled; Worst, the Sorrel, and the White:). . . .
>   (Trapp, III. 105–7)[16]

Swift's passage can be seen as an amusing collation of all possible meanings given by commentators and translators to that passage in Virgil and is in itself a free translation, expanded by Swift's own joke. Swift includes "Black" among the superior colors, so the Houyhnhnms' concepts of color and race are in most perfect opposition to the prejudices of Europeans. In this land white skins are thought the worst ("deterrimus albis") and red-brown and black skins are signs of superior intelligence and other characteristics of higher races. The mock-solemn account of the Houyhnhnms' care in breeding conceals a satiric point based on a play upon Virgil.

If any of Swift's educated contemporaries had been asked "What striking piece of literature deals with animal husbandry and devotes particular attention to the breeding of horses?" the inevitable answer would have been "The third book of Virgil's *Georgics*." Once one has read the *Georgics* with attention and delight, it is almost impossible not to feel some recollection of book III hovering about one's response to the fourth book of *Gulliver's Travels,* creating comic and ironic contrast. For that book of Virgil's poem which deals with animal husbandry is also preeminently a poem of passion and of suffering—the qualities so emphatically removed from the Houyhnhnms' condition.

The first part of *Georgics* III is a celebration of sensual life in its description of the physical—and particularly sexual—activities of animals, especially of domestic beasts. Virgil's depictions of the animals' lives among themselves, the activities they enter into without reference to man (until the humans interfere and redirect or restrain their energies) are very appealing. We see an animal life going on in its own right, the animals slightly humanized but not caring about us, going about their own concerns. Virgil makes the beasts attractive without sentimentality, and comic without vulgarity. Even Dryden nearly topples into the cartoon comic, as in his description of the bull pining for the cow (see Dryden, III. 329–38, a very free version of Virgil III. 212–18). But something has to be done to render the effects of, for instance, the cow's attractions, with her "dulcebris inlecebris": "sweet charms"? "soft enticements"?—in any case an unexpected phrase to apply to a cow. The effects of *amor* in cows and bulls take up nearly as much of Virgil's attention as its influence on horses and mares. In the fourth book of *Gulliver's Travels* cows are mentioned frequently. One might ask whether the cows kept by the Houyhnhnms, and the bulls—there *must* be bulls—do not embarrass the Houyhnhnms and keep the Yahoos somewhat in countenance? Such a question might occur to anyone who has lived in the country (as Swift had) whether or not he knew a line of Virgil, but the reader of *Georgics* III will remember the passion of cattle and the great simile of the wave, which presents the bull's triumphant plunge. That simile presents sexual energy as part of nature's beautiful power, like the sea, and immediately precedes the passage that universalizes what has hitherto been particular to cattle, and offers the aphorism known to schoolboys for centuries:

> omne adeo genus in terris hominumque fararumque
> et genus aequorum, pecudes pictaeque uolucres
> in furias ignemque ruunt; amor omnibus idem.
>
> (III. 242–44)

> Thus every Creature, and of every Kind,
> The secret Joys of sweet Coition find:
> Not only Man's Imperial Race; but they
> That wing the liquid Air, or swim the Sea,

Or haunt the Desart, rush into the flame:
For Love is Lord of all; and is in all the same.

(III. 375–80)

Virgil makes us observe the effect of passion in various animals, wild and tame, including ourselves; we see it at work in Lion, Bear, Tiger, Stallion, Boar, Man, Lynx, and so on. Finally—as a climax, for here it is most power-ful—we observe the violence of love in Mare:

scilicet ante omnis furor est insignis equarum;
et mentem Venus ipsa dedit . . .
. . . .
illas ducit amor trans Gargara transque sonantem
Ascanium; superant montis et flumina tranant.

(III. 266–70)

But far above the rest, the furious Mare,
Barr'd from the Male, is frantick with Despair.
. . . .
For Love they force through Thickets of the Wood,
They climb the steepy Hills, and stem the Flood.

(III. 419–27)

Sex is—strangely, because of the constant negation of its importance, power, or beauty—as much a subject of book IV of *Gulliver's Travels* as it is of *Georgics* III. Swift's book IV continues and amplifies Virgil's techniques of making us see animals living their own lives without concern for man (though in both cases they are, after all, watched by a human observer). But Swift provides a comic refutation and reversal of Virgil, for it is precisely here, in the animals' own land, that "amor" is *not* "omnibus idem." The Yahoos possess the familiar "furor," but the Houyhnhnms are distinct from the rest of creation. It is an especially comic paradox that we should be presented with an unimpassioned *horse*. Traditionally, the horse has been associated with strength and impulse—and with war, too, in the Bible and in Virgil. But the horse has also been traditionally—and in Virgil very vividly and unallegorically—associated with sexual passion. Sexual *furor* is attributed by Virgil to the male of the human as of the equine species. The effect on man is presented in a short version of the story of Leander:

What did the *Youth*, when Love's unerring Dart
Transfixt his Liver; and inflam'd his heart?
Alone, by night, his watry way he took;
About him, and above, the Billows broke.

(III. 403–6)

In the memorable scene of the female Yahoo's assault on Gulliver we have a comic reversal of the Leander story. The young female is "inflam'd by Desire" ("Magnum cui uersat in ossibus ignem/durus amor," says Virgil of

Leander) and "came running with all Speed, and leaped into the Water" (266–67). The female of *this* species, like the mare, and also like the rash swimmer of the Hellespont, attempts to "stem the Flood" to get at the object of desire. In Virgil, the human male and the female horse are implicitly compared by being associated with the same images; the phrase "calor redit ossibus" used of the mare (line 272) echoes the phrases used shortly before about Leander (lines 258–59). Well-known images of passion and the picture of the inflamed lover leaping into the water to come at the beloved are adapted here by Swift for a comic scene which he might expect the reader to appreciate as a humorous allusion. The Yahoo's actions are what we might expect in a man, or in a female *horse*. Gulliver, not at all willing to play the male Hero to this odd female Leander, delicately shrinks from the attack. The ambiguity of his reactions is increased, and the scene's comedy heightened, if we recall the traditions with which Swift is playing. We might remember too the good connotations of passion in Virgil and the enthusiasm with which the first part of book III of the *Georgics* was treated, not only by late seventeenth-century translators but also by illustrators. The large engraved plate by Cleyn and Lambert representing the *amor omnibus idem* passages adorned both Ogilby's and Dryden's folio translations (see figure 2).[17] Many readers in Swift's generation and later would have come upon this picture in their first reading of the *Georgics* and would have associated it with any piece dealing with animal sexuality. It is a delightful representation of the loves of the beasts—and it stands for everything the Houyhnhnms do not have. Passion can have good connotations, and in Virgil there is virtue as well as absurdity in the idea of plunging in.

Houyhnhnms never plunge into anything spontaneously. Houyhnhnm colts are educated, trained, *forced* to take exercise:

> The Houyhnhnms train up their Youth . . . by exercising them in running Races up and down steep Hills . . . and when they are all in a Sweat, they are ordered to leap over Head and Ears into a Pond or a River. (269)

In Virgil, the high-bred colt does not have to be *ordered* to do these things; you can tell he is a fine horse by observing what he does of his own accord:

> His motions easy; prancing in his Gate.
> The first to lead the way, to tempt the flood;
> To pass the Bridge unknown, nor fear the trembling Wood.
> (III. 122–24)

"His beginnings must be in rashness; a Noble Fault."[18] The Houyhnhnms altogether lack what we would call "spirit"; they are anti-horse as much as anti-human.

Sex and death, two overwhelming forces, the sources of desire and fear, are tidied away by the non-sensual Houyhnhnms; they are mortal, but they

Pascitur in magna Sil:
Illi alternantes multa
Vulneribus crebris: lavit
Versaque in obnixos
Cum gemitu, reboant sil:
Philippo Warwick Armigero.

va formosa juvenca:
vi prælia miscent
ater corpora sanguis,
vrgentur cornua vasto
væque et magnus Olympus.
Tabula merito votiva.

Figure 2

have no fear of death, no experience of untimely death or sickness. Reading book IV of *Gulliver's Travels* is like reading *Georgics* turned upside down.
Virgil's book of the animals is devoted to the life of the flesh, to sex and
death. After the rage of love in the first part, the last section of the poem
deals with death and with the unmerited pain of sickness. After discussing
various natural diseases of animals, the poet gives a lengthy and horrifying
description of a great cattle murrain, a universal plague that fell upon the
dumb creation "From the vicious Air and sickly Skies" (III. 721; "morbo
coeli," line 478). Virgil arouses pity and terror in his account of the suffering of individual representative animals:

> The Victor Horse, forgetful of his Food,
> The Palm renounces, and abhors the Flood.
> . . . .
> But in Time's process, when his pains encrease,
> He rouls his mournful Eyes, he deeply groans
> With patient sobbing, and with manly Moans.
> He heaves for Breath: which, from his Lungs supply'd,
> And fetch'd from far, distends his lab'ring side.
>
> (III. 747–57)

The "pineing Steer" shrinks and droops in the slow process of dying:

> Now what avails his well-deserving Toyl
> To turn the Glebe; or smooth the rugged Soyl!
> And yet he never supt in solemn State,
> Nor undigested Feasts did urge his Fate;
> Nor Day, to Night, luxuriously did joyn;
> Nor surfeited on rich *Campanian* wine.
> Simple his Beverage; homely was his Food,
> The wholesom Herbage, and the running Flood;
> No dreadful Dreams awak'd him with affright;
> His Pains by Day, secur'd his Rest by Night.
>
> (III. 784–93)

Virgil explicitly says that this mortal disease, with all its attendant pain, is
not attributable, as some human diseases are, to luxury. He has brilliantly
captured the sensation of indignant sorrow we feel when we watch the
suffering of innocent animals. It is ironic that the simple, wholesome "natural" existence does not save the animals from Nature herself, nor can such
an existence be counted upon as insurance for man. The life of the flesh
involves susceptibility to inexplicable and undeserved pain, disease, and
death.

  In the section on the great murrain Virgil says that when the cattle were
stricken human beings were forced to undertake the work of domestic
beasts. Men became their own draught animals, with straining necks pull-
ing the creaking wagons uphill:

montisque per altos
contenta ceruice trahunt stridentia plaustra. . . .

(III. 535–36)

The picture by Cleyn and Hollar illustrating both Ogilby's and Dryden's translations captures the paradoxes of misery presented by Virgil: the sacrifice dying at the altar before the priest can strike, the strong horse vanquished, fierce and tame animals together sharing weakness and misery. The foreground of the picture is taken up by dying animals; the human figures, subordinate but individualized, are the astonished priest and the sad peasant who unyokes the steer so it can die in peace, as its mate has already died. But in the very top and center of the picture, though in the background, are men drawing a hay cart, unindividualized figures nearly naked and straining at their extraordinary labor. It takes four humans to do the work of one or two animals (see figure 3.)[19] Here surely is an intimation of the Yahoos, those draft beasts. In Virgil's work, this degeneration from the human position results from a poisoned world. The general economy of life is subverted and activities become paradoxical because of universal ruin; the disintegration of human life and pride is associated with animal misery. Human beings take the place of animals because the animals collapse. In Swift's book, there is an extended play with Virgil's image and a reversal of the context. Human beings in Houyhnhnmland "draw home the Sheaves in Carriages" (274) not because the animals (the horses) are sick unto death, but because they are well. The Houyhnhnms are in full life and pride, and the "unnatural" reversal happens not in a poisoned environment but in one of unheard-of wholesomeness. Houyhnhnms never get sick.

The Houyhnhnms are not susceptible to disease or illness of any kind; their stallions are not called upon to exhibit fortitude, to endure "With patient sobbing, and with manly Moans," still less to know the pitch of pain that leads Virgil's horse to suicidal cannibalism: "Recruited into Rage, he grinds his Teeth/In his own Flesh, and feeds approaching Death" (III. 766–67). The Houyhnhnm master could understand none of this, "that Nature, who worketh all things to Perfection, should suffer any Pains to breed in our Bodies, he thought impossible" (253). Nobody gets ill save Yahoos, who create sickness in themselves. So impressively is the horses' and Gulliver's certainty conveyed that the European reader nods assent. If only we lived a healthy life, we would never become ill or diseased. This is a salutary reaction. Much of our sickness could be prevented by temperance—as Virgil's satiric touches about high living in human society point up. But the final point of Virgil's irony is that even a life of exercise, vegetarian diet, abstinence from wine, and freedom from mental stress— an ideal that the poet ironically suggests can best be discovered in the life of a domesticated animal—affords no protection against suffering. The

F. Clcyn inu.   W. Hollar fecit.

Sæpe in honore Deum   medio ſtans hoſtia ad aram
Lanea dum nivea cir-   cundatur inſula vitta,
Inter cunctantes cecidit   moribunda miniſtras,

Philippo Egerton Armigero   Tabula merito votiua.

Figure 3

Houyhnhnms are, after all, *incredibly* successful in escaping the ills that flesh is heir to. Our reaction of rueful approval is based on a partial and even a wishful delusion. Nature herself produces "vicious Air, and sickly Skies." Disease is a part of life, something that men may bear with fortitude and that animals must innocently bear. If we take the Nature that man knows—the Nature Virgil is talking about—to be the Nature the Houyhnhnms know, we are deluded.

Houyhnhnmland is a parody of the earth in the Golden Age:

> ante Iouem nulli subigebant arua coloni:
> . . . .
> . . . ipsaque tellus
> omnia liberius nullo poscente ferebat. . . .
>
>   (I. 125–28)
>
> E're this, no Peasant vex'd the peaceful Ground;
> . . . .
> But all was common, and the fruitful Earth
> Was free to give her unexacted Birth. . . .
>
>   (I. 191–96)

Nature in Houyhnhnmland seems, as far as the horses are concerned, Saturnian; the earth belongs to some realm "ante Iouem" and gives her goods freely with no vexing of the ground. The crop reaped by the Houyhnhnms "groweth naturally in several Fields." The oats require no ploughing, sowing, or tilling. Houyhnhnm houses are made of "a Kind of Tree, which at Forty Years old loosens in the Root, and falls with the first Storm" (274). The horses do not have to plan their crops or watch out for weather signs, mildew, or pests. They do not have to plant, graft, or even cut down their trees. (Of course the Houyhnhnms have no need for grape vines, so there are none, and there is no viticulture.) Everything is provided—but frugally provided. There is no splendid fruit, no honey on the leaves, no field of *golden* wheat. This nature is dully bounteous, not lavish; everything is rough and utilitarian. This pre-Jove—and pre-Jovial—world seems comically Saturnian in the other sense, Saturnine. The Golden Age of the Houyhnhnms' existence is a Golden Age turned grey.

The Houyhnhnms' (parodic) Golden Age life is not suited to man and not suited to Gulliver. Food for Gulliver is not readily available (as critics have noted, one of the many signs that he is neither Houyhnhnm nor Yahoo); he keeps resorting to the traditional human arts, which, even at their simplest, are different from the Houyhnhnms' limited activities. When he is, to use Homer's expressive phrase "far from men who eat bread," Gulliver makes bread by winnowing and grinding the oats, and baking bread from the meal. He varies his diet (he is never quite a vegetarian):

I sometimes made a shift to catch a Rabbet, or Bird, by Springes made of
Yahoos Hairs; and I often gathered wholesome Herbs, which I boiled, or
eat as Salades with my Bread; and now and then, for a Rarity, I made a
little Butter, and drank the Whey. (232)

He makes rush mats, ticking, clothes, furniture (the two chairs indicating
that his rejection of the human race is incomplete). He searches out a food
that Houyhnhnms and Yahoos don't bother with: "I often got Honey out of
hollow Trees, which I mingled with Water, or eat it with my Bread" (276)
("aerii mellis caelestia dona": IV. 1) He keeps his knife, that bequest of the
Iron Age. It is his own activities that make Houyhnhnmland a place in
which he can survive, and only because he can survive can he persuade
himself that this is the perfect place. The Golden Age of Houyhnhnmland
depends, for Gulliver, on his wits and labor. Like Virgil's farmers, he
creates the Golden Age through work. His life is full of little georgic arts.

> The Sire of Gods and Men, with hard Decrees,
> Forbids our Plenty to be bought with Ease:
> . . . .
> Himself invented first the shining Share,
> And whetted Humane Industry by Care:
> Himself did Handy-Crafts and Arts ordain;
> Nor suffer'd Sloath to rust his active Reign.
> . . . .
> Then first on Seas the hollow'd Alder swam;
> Then Sailors quarter'd Heav'n, and found a Name
> For ev'ry fix'd and ev'ry wandering Star:
> . . . .
> Then Toils for Beasts, and Lime for Birds were found
> . . . .
> And casting Nets were spread in shallow Brooks,
> Drags in the Deep, and Baits were hung on Hooks.
> Then Saws were tooth'd, and sounding Axes made;
> (For Wedges first did yielding Wood invade.)
> And various Arts in order did succeed,
> (What cannot endless Labour urg'd by need?)
>   (I. 183–218; cf. Virgil, I. 121–46)

Most utopias, and certainly Houyhnhnmland, exemplify rusty sloth, inhuman stagnation. Houyhnhnm life has a somber durable inaction; it is a
life passed in "torpore graui ueterno," in stupefying lethargy.

God hath placed Things in a State of Imperfection on purpose to stir up
human Industry; without which Life would stagnate. *Curis acuens mortalia
corda.*

So Swift wrote in his short passage "On Imperfections in Nature," after
listing various evils, including disease and hostile climate.
It would be a mistake to overemphasize the Virgilian strain in Swift's

thought, but there is a definite georgic strain in *Gulliver's Travels,* and Swift plays continuously with the *Georgics.* A discussion of *Gulliver's Travels* in the light of the *Georgics* seems too optimistic a reading of Swift (not comprehending the dark side, the rage) only if we forget the elements of rage and horror in Virgil's poem. The reassurance of the *Georgics* is, after all, hard-won; there is a full consciousness of imperfection and misery and of the violent absurdities and cruelty of human behavior, especially in war. Virgil constantly refers to the tendency of human affairs and activities to slip into chaos. Because these elements are there in Virgil's poem, the *Georgics* could provide inspiration for *Gulliver's Travels.* There is in Virgil and Swift also a shared realism about common everyday things, which have their own interest and attractiveness and set up a contrast to the ugly splendors of wealth and battle. Neither writer takes a complacent view of life, even at its best: *curis acuens mortalia corda.* Always there is the "labor . . . improbus et duris urgens in rebus egestas." The hard work must be carried on, to make two ears of corn grow where one grew before—or to ensure that no Wood's pence are circulated where too many were before.

NOTES

1. Swift, *Journal to Stella,* ed. Harold Williams, vols. 15 and 16 of *The Prose Writings of Jonathan Swift* (Oxford: Basil Blackwell, 1974), 2:525.

2. Swift, "Thoughts on Various Subjects," *Prose Writings,* 4:245.

3. Joseph Addison, "An Essay on Virgil's Georgics," in *The Miscellaneous Works of Joseph Addison,* ed. A. C. Guthkelch (London: G. Bell and Sons, 1914), 2:3–4. Guthkelch's text is taken from the 1721 edition of Addison's *Works,* but the variations from the 1697 version (the first) are very slight, affecting only spelling and punctuation.

4. All quotations from Virgil's *Georgics* are taken from *P. Vergilii Maronis Opera,* ed. R. A. B. Mynors (Oxford: Clarendon Press, 1976).

5. James Thomson, *Autumn,* lines 1278–96, in *"The Seasons" and "The Castle of Indolence,"* ed. James Sambrook (Oxford: Clarendon Press, 1972), 123–24.

6. The description of the Scythians afforded Pope the basis for some favorite lines of his own—"Lo! where *Maeotis* sleeps" (*Dunciad* III. 87–88)—and was adapted by many eighteenth-century poets, including Thomson and Cowper. The description of the cattle plague was praised by Scaliger in his relatively brief comments on the *Georgics.* Addison praises both the winter piece and the plague description: "The Scythian winter-piece appears so very cold and bleak to the eye, that a man can scarce look at it without shivering. The Murrain at the end has all the expressiveness that words can give" ("Essay on Virgil's Georgics," 10).

7. Quotations from Dryden's translation of the *Georgics* are taken from *The Poems of John Dryden,* ed. James Kinsley (Oxford: Clarendon Press, 1970), 2. This text is based on the 1697 edition, collated with others.

8. John Ogilby, *The Works of Publius Virgilius Maro. Translated, adorn'd with Sculpture, and illustrated with Annotations* (London: Printed by Thomas Warren for the Author, 1654), 70. For May's translation, see *Virgil's Georgicks Englished, by Tho: May Esq.* (London: Thomas Walkley, 1628):

> There Toades, and many earth-bred Monsters ly:
> There little Weevils heapes of corne destroy,
> And frugall Ants, that toyle for times to come.

(10)

9. Joseph Trapp, *The Works of Virgil: Translation into English Blank Verse. With Large Explanatory Notes, and Critical Observations* (London: J. Brotherton et al., 1731), 1 : 107 (bk. I, lines 238–40).

For Warton, see *The Works of Virgil, in Latin and English. The Aeneid Translated by the Rev. Mr. Christopher Pitt, The Eclogues and Georgics, with Notes on the Whole, by the Rev. Mr. Joseph Warton* (London: R. Dodsley, 1753). "The weasel heaps consumes, or prudent ant/Provides her copious stores, 'gainst age or want" (1 : 185, lines 216–17).

10. Addison, "Essay on the Georgics," 10–11.

11. *Gulliver's Travels*, ed. Herbert Davis, vol. 11 of *Prose Writings*, bk. 1, p. 30. All quotations from Swift's book, hereafter cited as GT, are from this edition.

12. Illustration by unnamed artist and engraver, in book 2 of *Voyages de Gulliver* (trans. by l'Abbé Desfontaines) (Paris: Gabriel Martin, Hyppolite-Louis Guerin, 1727), 1; facing p. 88. For the same scene in *Gulliver's Travels*, see bk. II, pp. 85–87.

13. See *Georgics* II. 498–99; Trapp comments:

This seems to be no great Commendation of the Person he is describing. 'Tis said to be spoken *Stoically:* but I rather take it Thus: He pitys not the Poor, because in the Country there are none so Poor as to be the Objects of Pity; Nature supplying all Necessarys. Poverty, strictly such, is only in Cities. (Trapp, *Virgil,* 1 : 65)

Trapp's comment does not allay the suspicion of callousness or complacency. Munodi is not allowed to supply any "Necessarys," nor is nature.

14. Trapp, *Virgil,* 1 : 164–65 (*Georgics* II. 586–91). Trapp's translation is here clearer and better than Dryden's.

15. Swift, *Journal to Stella,* 1 : 220 (19 March 1711).

16. See Ogilby, *The Works of Publius Virgilius Maro,* 118; Trapp, *Virgil,* 1 : 177. Thomas May has:

> Let his colour be
> Bright bay or grey; white proves not commonly
> Nor flesh-colour,
>
> (77)

while Joseph Warton translates the lines as follows:

> Of colours chuse the dapple or the grey,
> For white and dun a dastard race betray.
> (*Georgics* III. 116–17, p. 289)

John Martyn in his edition (with prose translation in margin) of *P. Virgilii Maronis Georgicorum* (London: R. Reily, 1741), translates (adjectivally), "the best colour is a bright bay, and beautifyl grey; the worst is white and dun," and supplies a lengthy and detailed note about the color-words *spadix* and *glaucus* (279–84).

17. Picture taken from Ogilby's great folio *Virgil* of 1654, facing p. 123; F. Cleyn invt. P. Lombart Sculpsit. The same plate is to be found in Dryden's folio *Virgil,* facing p. 106.

18. Dryden, "To the Right Honourable Philip, Earl of Chesterfield," Dedication of the *Georgics,* 914–15. Dryden is complimenting Chesterfield with an implicit reference to Seneca's second Epistle, cited thus by Ogilby in a side-note:

We shall onely insert an observation which Seneca long since made upon this place: *Whilst our Virgil* (saies he) *does one thing, he intends another, for in this description he hath painted out a Valiant Man: Certainly, were I to draw the Picture of a gallant Person, I could not doe it in better Colours.* (Ogilby, *Virgil,* 118)

That Virgil's verses on (in Ogilby's words) "a generous and well bred Horse" could describe the noblest man was an established critical truism.

19. Picture from Ogilby's *Virgil* (1654), facing p. 135; F. Cleyn invt. W. Hollar fecit. The plate can be found in Dryden's *Virgil* (1697), facing p. 117.

10

Jonathan Richardson's *Morning Thoughts*

Roger Lonsdale

The various achievements of Jonathan Richardson the Elder may seem to have received their due in the last two decades. Proper attention has been paid to his claim to be the leading English portrait painter between Kneller and Reynolds, and in particular to his numerous depictions of his friend Alexander Pope. Of equal interest has been Richardson's idealistic attempt to provide an Augustan theory of painting in a series of books published between 1715 and 1722, which impressed Johnson and influenced Reynolds, and his later biographical and critical work (in partnership with his son) on Milton, whom he passionately admired both as a man and a poet.[1]

Satisfaction with this situation has to be qualified in certain respects. Writers on aesthetic theory often quote Richardson from the convenient editions of his *Works* published in 1773 and 1792, which were in fact carefully "corrected," with some extensive omissions, by his son. If the essence of Richardson's aesthetic theory survived in the *Works,* Jonathan the Younger succeeded in taming his father's idiosyncratic style and other "singularities" (as, according to Horace Walpole, they struck early readers), and did not hesitate to remove long passages of fervent and highly individual speculation on philosophical and religious subjects that, in context, can impart an interesting instability to Richardson's neoclassical assumptions.[2] It is also striking that so little is known about Richardson. It is possible, of course, that there is not much to be known, that the essence of his energetic and successful career is contained in the lists of his portraits and the titles of his publications. Born in the mid-1660s, apprenticed to the painter John Riley, Richardson eventually married his niece and heiress and was well established as a portrait painter by the early decades of the eighteenth century. His friendship with Pope, based on an apparently genuine mutual regard between two contrasting personalities, dates from about 1721. Most of his familiar drawings of the poet were made in the 1730s. He did not retire from his profession until 1740 and died in 1745 at the age of about eighty. His characteristics as a painter are competence, sobriety, and good sense with, it is always implied, a lack of real imagination. His numerous self-portraits convey a similar impression of solid, even stolid, integrity, sturdy self-confidence, and lack of mystery.

There is an element of mystery, however, about the posthumous publication of a book by Richardson. W. K. Wimsatt, in the fullest biographical account of the painter yet published, had to cite from Lowndes's *Bibliographer's Manual* (1864) the title of *Morning Thoughts: Or Poetical Meditations, Moral, Divine and Miscellaneous. Together with several other Poems On Various Subjects. By the late Jonathan Richardson, Esq.* (1776).[3] With one exception, all other writers on Richardson appear to have ignored the book. Its rarity, given that it was published by James Dodsley, is hard to explain: it is in neither the British Library nor the Bodleian, and, in the United States, there is a copy only at Harvard.

Jonathan Richardson the Younger (1694–1771) had evidently prepared various editions of his father's and his own works for publication, apparently content that this should be posthumous. The plan may well have been carried out by one Gregson, grandson of the painter, who presumably inherited the family papers.[4] Richardson's *Works* appeared in 1773; *Morning Thoughts* and his son's *Richardsoniana* in 1776. Further volumes of the two last works were promised but did not appear. John Duncombe, whose father had been a friend of the painter and who had access to the poetry in the 1750s, may also have been involved. It is notable that *Morning Thoughts* was sympathetically received only in quarters where Duncombe had some influence. John Langhorne in the *Monthly Review* in 1776 was patronizing, the *London Magazine* politely noncommittal, and the *Critical Review* ignored the book. In the *Gentleman's Magazine,* where Duncombe was in charge of reviews, *Morning Thoughts* was at least discussed at some length. A few years later a poem by Richardson appeared in John Nichols's *Select Collection of Poems,* with a note praising "the truly original colouring of his poetical sketches" by "D", obviously Duncombe, whom Nichols thanked for his assistance at the beginning of the volume.[5]

Such efforts were unavailing. Poetry that had been pronounced pious, incorrect, and old-fashioned must have found few readers, and plans for further volumes were abandoned. *Morning Thoughts* did, however, make an impression in an unexpected quarter. In the first edition of his *Anecdotes of Painting,* Horace Walpole referred unenthusiastically to the mediocre verses that Richardson had occasionally included in his early prose works. By 1780 he had read *Morning Thoughts* and found it "not much to the honour of his muse, but exceedingly to that of his piety and amiable heart." Walpole elaborated this impression in a passage added to the *Anecdotes* two years later:

> in general the poetry is very careless and indifferent—Yet such a picture of a good mind, serene in conscious innocence, is scarcely to be found. It

is impossible not to love the author, or not to wish to be as sincerely and intentionally virtuous. The book is perhaps more capable of inspiring emulation of goodness than any professed book of devotion.[6]

Such forceful testimony appears to have excited no interest. *Morning Thoughts* seems, in fact, not to have been discussed until 1974, when Leon Guilhamet devoted ten pages to it in the course of a study of "sincerity" in eighteenth-century poetry. His response was similar to Walpole's: *Morning Thoughts,* while negligible as poetry, is remarkable for its period as a kind of spiritual diary in which poetry is used for unusually subjective purposes, some of the verse conveying "deep personal emotion." With the perspective of a literary historian, Guilhamet saw Richardson in this aspect as an "incompetent . . . revolutionary."[7] His short and interesting discussion seems, however, unaware of the rarity of the volume or of its biographical implications.

A detailed description of its contents is therefore justified. *Morning Thoughts* is divided into two main sections. Part 1 (pp. 8–162) contains a sequence of 113 poems, written between 15 September 1732 and 9 November 1736, ending with a translation of the Ugolino episode from Dante's *Inferno,* which had been previously published in 1719.[8] Part 2 (pp. 163–308) contains a series of 127 poems dated between 17 February 1704 and 12 May 1735; most (108) were written between 1729 and 1735. A final section (pp. 309–59) contains material in both verse and prose about Richardson's travels on horseback (including a journey to Bath) in the summer of 1731. The poems published in 1776 were only "a part of a much larger number intended for publication" (p. xv), but there is no explanation of the principles of selection. No poem later than 1736 is included, although his son had quoted a poem from the manuscript "Morning Thoughts," dated 9 August 1741, in his edition of his father's *Works,* confirming that his versifying had continued well into his seventies.[9]

It is not clear who was responsible for the arrangement of the poems. They are prefaced by remarks by Richardson himself (probably written about 1740) and by further remarks by his son, who also annotated the poems sporadically. Most of the poems are precisely dated, sometimes by the hour. Richardson himself may well have left the poems in chronological order, but he seems consciously to have started writing a new kind of poem in September 1732, the "Morning Thoughts" proper, most of which were composed literally in the dawn. His son may have decided to extract this fairly distinct sequence as part 1 and to place in part 2 any earlier poems, together with others on humorous, trivial, domestic, or otherwise problematic subjects. As a result, part 2 gives a rather more uniformly pious and contented impression than would be the case if the poems were in a single chronological order.

Questions of the literary interest of Richardson's verse can be deferred temporarily. In view of W. K. Wimsatt's statement that "Pope's letters to Richardson are our main source of information about Richardson's later career, nearly all that rescues his personality and domestic life from oblivion,"[10] the survival of at least part of this very personal verse diary must be of interest. In addition to what they reveal about his personality, the poems, together with his son's commentary, add to our knowledge of Richardson's sparsely documented career.

To begin at the beginning: all reference works give 1665 as the date of Richardson's birth, without day or month. George Vertue, from whom Walpole seems to have derived the year, was noticeably uncertain about the matter, twice recording vaguely that Richardson was born "about 1665" and elsewhere that he died in 1745 "an? Aetat. 80."[11] In a poem dated 16 June 1729 Richardson unambiguously stated his age as sixty-two, and his son annotated accordingly: "He was born the 12th of January, 1667" (MT, 209).[12] Unfortunately this does not quite settle the matter. Consistent about the day and month, the younger Richardson elsewhere wavered about the year, at one point giving it as 1666 (MT, 42). If this could be explained as 1666/67 Old Style, the younger Richardson disconcertingly annotates his father's poem of 21 August 1732 with the statement that "he was now 67 years old" and to another of 22 December 1733 adds the note "Aet. 68" (MT, 47, 257). The authority of the elder Richardson's own statement surely deserves to prevail. It is consistent with a note made by Vertue, probably deriving from the painter himself, that he became a pupil of John Riley at the age of about twenty and spent four years with him until Riley's death in 1691.[13] If Richardson was about twenty in 1687, the most likely year of his birth is 1667.

Passing through Chelsea in the summer of 1731, Richardson paid affectionate tribute to his former master John Riley (MT, 319). It was through Riley, an early Milton enthusiast, that he had come across the battered 1674 edition of *Paradise Lost* that made such an impression on him.[14] Yet all had not been entirely harmonious. The younger Richardson gives two examples of how his father "ran the risk of all his fortune for conscience-sake":

> Once with Mr. Riley, his master in his profession, and on whose favour (at that early time very much unsettled and precarious, for he had been in a manner obtruded upon him by his brother, Mr. Thomas Riley,) were all his hopes and dependence, refusing to second him in a lie, by which he exposed him to the resentment of a man of the first quality. . . .[15]

The second example of Richardson's scrupulous conscience came a decade or so later,

> in his "great religious scruples," in which he abandoned his profession itself, on a doubt concerning the lawfulness of it, when he had a most beloved wife, and a dear family coming on, and that profession his darling study! (MT, 307–8)

The two earliest poems by Richardson to have survived, the first dated 17 February 1703–4, concern his "most threatening perplexities" and "religious scruples," which, according to his son, "gave him so much terror" and produced "a most calamitous lowness of spirits for two or three years." Such anxieties led him to give up painting for several months, until Archbishop Tenison of Canterbury and other eminent divines set his mind at rest (MT, 155, 163–67, 308).

There is other evidence of a depressive tendency in his youth. After seeing the tragedy *Oedipus* when eighteen or nineteen, Richardson had suffered a violent asthmatic attack,

> which affected him so, that he was obliged to have a lodging at Highgate, to be in the air; and here, after two or three days, from his lowness of spirits doubtless, he fancied he had received a violent tap on the shoulder, when no one was by; which alarmed him to such a degree, as a hint and fore-runner of death, that it was some months before he could get clear of this fright, as he had a strong and lively imagination, and was, in his early youth, much more than afterwards, of a melancholy turn. (MT, 291)

Beneath the apparently calm, pious surface of Richardson's life, there was evidently some turmoil, and there are signs in the later poetry that anxiety about religious questions stayed with him to the end of his life. What can at times verge on a deistical suspicion of organized religion[16] had a counterpart in the strongly anti-authoritarian views that surface unpredictably in his poetry. There are, for example, stern lines in one of his verse journals in the summer of 1731 on passing by Hampton Court, that deplore the "foul luxury," flattery, insincerity, and slavishness of the court (MT, 318). On his journey to Bath in the following month, the ruins of Newbury Castle provoked a further outburst against tyranny and arbitrary power, Richardson allying himself with the "honest people" and preferring death to being "a beggar and a slave" or "the tool/Of a proud rascal, or a high-born fool" (MT, 323–24). He approved of Bath: its society had the politeness of a court without the concomitant insolence, pride, meanness, and slavery (MT, 350). A poem of 1734, "Shunning Courts," proudly asserts that he is "a free-born *Briton*," seeking no preferment or, worst of all, "A bribe, a pension, constitution's curse" (MT, 281–82). Commenting on this aversion to "the slavery of court dependence," the younger Richardson added that his father twice declined to be King's Painter, "though powerfully invited." He was compelled, however, to paint the King and also the Prince of Wales, who "came home to sit to him."[17]

Such attitudes may be unexpected in one whose profession must have depended on the patronage of the upper classes. It is consistent, however, with Richardson's intense admiration of Milton. In 1734 he would demand from his reader respect for Milton's sincerity and integrity, not agreement with his political and religious views.[18] On the evidence of *Morning Thoughts* he must have found Milton's anti-authoritarianism more directly sympathetic than might otherwise have been suspected. Whatever his views, by relentless industry—a matter on which he reflected frequently in his verse in later years—Richardson was highly successful professionally, and in other ways. "An Answer to the Calculators," a fable written in May 1720, commends caution to those carried away by South Sea speculation. A note by his son reveals that, by following his own prudent rules, the painter himself emerged with a profit of £2000 at a time when most of his friends had lost heavily (MT, 171–72).

At about this period, when he was also producing the theoretical treatises on painting for which he is now best remembered, Richardson became friendly with Pope. Information in *Morning Thoughts* clarifies some uncertainties in recent Pope scholarship. George Sherburn dated a letter of condolence from Pope to Richardson on the death of his wife 20 January [1724/25], relying on a statement by John Nichols that she died aged fifty-one on her birthday in 1725.[19] Sherburn conceded that the year could have been 1725/26, as turns out to have been the case. Richardson's series of poems on his wife's death begins on 18 January 1725/26, two days before the date of Pope's letter (MT, 174). A later poem (MT, 178) reveals that she became ill at the theater during Handel's *Rodelinda,* first performed on 13 February 1725, which confirms that Pope's letter could not have been written in January 1725. *Rodelinda* was performed at the King's Theatre four times in January 1726, and it was probably on 11 January that Mrs. Richardson was taken ill.[20]

The younger Richardson's account of Pope's habits of translating Homer may relate to a slightly earlier period but appears to have come directly from the poet himself:

> Mr. Pope had the happy talent, on having translated two hundred lines of Homer in bed, (which was his usual way, having the little correct edition of Wetstenius always behind his pillow, and a candle burning,) to remember them all, so as to write them down after he was up, as if from a copy before him; sometimes after a whole day's interval, spent in business or pleasure, just the same; of which he gave us several proofs. (MT, 118)[21]

On 23 June 1728 the elder Richardson wrote "An Epigram on Pope's Dunciad—To Him" (MT, 181). He had "lik'd the wit, but thought it too severe" when the satire had appeared in the previous month, but now he felt that its abusive reception had only proved the truth of Pope's accusations. More significant are his lines "*Sent to* Mr. Pope, *when his* Essay on Man *was first published*" (MT, 262–63). Pope's letter of thanks for these verses confirms that the Richardsons were in on the secret of the publication from an early stage. Pope also explained that his desire for anonymity prevented his making any immediate use of the poem, although he eventually included it in the prefatory matter to the *Essay on Man* in volume 2 of his *Works* (1739). Richardson dated his lines 17 March 1733. Sherburn's text of Pope's letter, based on a conflation published by Pope and an untraced manuscript published by Roscoe in 1824, is dated 2 November 1732, which is clearly incorrect.[22]

A brief anecdote about Pope recorded by the younger Richardson describes a visit from the poet in September 1731, when his father was in Bath:

> Mr. Pope, one day, when he came to see me, while my father was gone this journey, and we were considering one of the small works of St. Evremond, asked me, "How I liked that way of writing, where prose and poetry were mixed together?" I said, 'I liked it well, for that sort of offhand, occasional productions.' "Why, (said he) I have had thoughts of turning out some sketches I have by me, of various accidents and reflections, in this manner." My dear father was actually doing the same thing at this very time. (MT, 359)

This refers to his father's account, in alternate verse and prose, of his return journey from Bath. Nothing further seems to be known of Pope's rather vague scheme.

Richardson's journal of his travels in the summer of 1731 reveals that, still grieving for his wife five years after her death and well into his sixties, he was not impervious to female charms. At Henley he had a vivid dream of being married to an attractive young bride, at Bath was both shocked and fascinated by the sight of female bathing, and at an inn near Newbury the attractions of the landlady left him pondering the possibility of a second marriage (MT, 313, 340–46, 355). At the back of his mind was no doubt his recent friendship with a Mrs. Catherine Knapp. Wimsatt noted a number of drawings of Mrs. Knapp by Richardson from the period 1731–33, in one of which the artist depicts himself looking out from close behind her. Rejecting the speculation of a former owner of the drawing that the lady was Richardson's second wife, Wimsatt suggested that such pencil portraits merely commemorated "the solace of a close friendship," perfectly in accord with his "romantic, even sentimental, though orderly and cautious character."[23] Richardson's "romantic" attachment to Mrs. Knapp is indeed confirmed by a series of poems in *Morning Thoughts* from the same years as the drawings. Their varying tones, by turn sprightly and sentimental, differ markedly from those of his introspective poems and express an ardent enough admiration for Mrs. Knapp to oblige his son to offer repeated explanations of the relationship. She was the friend and companion of a Mrs. Drake of Sharloes in Buckinghamshire, with whom Richardson stayed in October 1731; "a fine woman, had been a very fine one; now a little in the vale of life; sensible withal, and discreet"; "a lady of family and fortune,

and fine qualifications," for whom Richardson had "an extraordinary esteem and regard." His numerous gallant or sentimental poems to or about
her were, however, "only the amusement and overflow of a lively imagination . . . and she, who was a very ingenious woman, not young, (at least five
and forty!) understood them as such" (MT, 242, 251, 265).

The poems themselves suggest that the elderly widower was rather more
emotionally involved than was Mrs. Knapp, and there is little about her
after 1733. This ardent friendship does help to clarify a matter not entirely
to Richardson's credit as hitherto understood. Wimsatt prints a verse inscription from the back of a pencil self-portrait dated 12 April 1732, which
depicts Richardson wearing a laurel wreath. These lines appear to claim
with ludicrous complacency that he has no less a claim to the laurel than the
greatest of ancient and modern poets. Morris Brownell also cites the poem
as evidence of Richardson's literary aspirations:

> Yes Pope, yes Milton I am Bayes'd you see.
> But Why—go ask my Oracle, not Me:
> Shee, not Severe is Beautyfull, & Wise,
> Shee Thus Commanded me, & Thus it is.
> May You enjoy your plentitude of Fame!
> While Shee with Smiles embellishes my Name
> I ask not Your Applause, nor Censure Fear,
> I am Pope, Milton, Virgil, Homer Here.
>   12 April 1732 JR[24]

These lines, clumsy as Richardson's inscriptions on his drawings usually
are, read quite differently if, as seems certain, they were addressed to Mrs.
Knapp, the "Oracle" who has "Commanded" a laureated self-portrait. It
was her friendship (not his own literary or artistic merits) that made him
feel "I am Pope, Milton, Virgil, Homer Here."

Most of the surviving poems in *Morning Thoughts* were written between
1729 and 1736, and, apart from the insight they give into Richardson's
mind, they contain much scattered information about his working habits.
He himself described the poems as written in the hours "taken from those
the generality of the world give to sleep" (MT, 1–2). His son explained in
more detail that his father habitually wrote between 4 or 5 A.M. and 8 A.M.
In summer, when the light was favorable, painting occupied him from 9
A.M. till 8 P.M., often with four or five different sitters, although he also
walked or rode during the day. He then worked again "in his chamber-
chair, often 'till midnight." Even in winter he would rise by 6 A.M. and light
his own fire and candles from a rushlight: "These hours he used to call 'his
own.'" Sometimes he wrote in bed in the dark, although the results might
be illegible (MT, 19, 118, 256–57, 286).

Richardson had evidently been an obsessively hard worker throughout
his life. What changed in September 1732, with the poems he called

"Morning Thoughts," was that his habitual early rising itself became the background if not the subject of his verses. He had written earlier verse descriptions of the rising sun, but he now began to write a consciously different kind of poem, in which he is literally awaiting or witnessing the dawn. The descriptive features of the poems are predictable and inevitably repetitive, but the interplay between his mental state and the features of the weather, season, and landscape he observes is often effective, as he paces the terrace of his house in Queen's Square, Bloomsbury, expectantly awaiting the reappearance of God's providential light, taking as the starting point of his verses stars, moon, frost, mist, rising sun, or at other times using his bed and desk, even his nightcap or the calls of the watchman, as imagery. Some poems were written late at night. All are usually dated precisely, sometimes by the hour: "On my terrace, before sun-rising," "Walking on my terrace near midnight," "10–11 at night," "Begun and finished half an hour after seven" (MT, 26, 49, 50, 140, 308).

Richardson's habitual early rising and obsessive writing were evidently well known to Pope. Writing to the painter in 1738 Pope explained that his letter would be delivered "soon after Sunrise, for that is an Hour to find You & the Lark, awake & singing." A few months before his death and eighteen months before Richardson's, Pope complained that he had been sleeping badly, adding, "If you did so, you, at your Age wou'd make Verses."[25]

As a close friend of Pope and a fervent admirer of Milton, Richardson can have had few illusions about his poetic powers. Annotating a couplet in a poem written in 1734,

> Unmusical the cuckow's note is heard;
> By *Philomel*'s the woods and sprays are chear'd,

his son took it to be a compliment to Pope, who saw several of Richardson's poems "with great satisfaction, and desired to see many more; but my father was hardly prevailed on to shew them to any but me. My father had often called himself the cuckow, and Mr. Pope the nightingale" (MT, 56). In another poem from the same year, Richardson again compared himself unfavorably with Pope:

> *To Mr. Pope, who said "I had made more verses than he."*
>
> I make more rhymes than you, you say.
> No doubt I do, and well I may:
> You them create; I'd have you know,
> With me spontaneously they grow.
> Your's ven'son are; but I, a glutton,
> Must fill my belly with my mutton.

(MT, 275)

Yet Richardson had written verses throughout his life, had included them in his treatises on painting, and in some ways took this activity very seriously. In 1734 he declared, "I have from my Infancy Lov'd and Practic'd Painting and Poetry; One I Possess'd as a Wife, the Other I Kept Privately, and shall Continue to do So whilst I Live." At the end of his biography of Milton, he stated mysteriously, "I have indeed no further Design upon the Publick, (Unless perhaps Somthing may come to them after Men shall *see my Face no more*)."[26] He may well have been referring to his numerous poems, in the preface to which he explained that they represented for him "a kind of additional life, more advantageous to myself (and, in some measure, I hope to others) than all the rest would have been without it. Indeed this hath spread a warmth and beaminess over that, which else would have been a sort of barren wintry soil." He aspired "to no finished poetry, no nice correction," comparing his verses hopefully to "sketches in drawing," which could have "an ease and spirit" lacking in the works of "accuracy and labour." Alternatively, "I call these, *Thoughts*, not poems; consider them accordingly; or as in verse what *familiar letters* are in prose, where the natural flow of the soul hath a beauty and force which the most studied orations frequently want" (MT, 2–4). The comparison with the spirit and freedom of the spontaneous sketch, which could outweigh defects of "Incorrectness," was not casual. This had been a frequent topic in his works on painting,[27] and it recurs in the poems themselves:

MY MANNER IN WRITING.

If I am told what some have done,
How wine dropp'd verses one by one;
How *Virgil*, and how *Horace*, taught
The muse to drudge a single thought,
My answer is; if I must sing,
My lyre must use its native string;
And if velocity of sense
I feel, such sounds must come from thence,
As that velocity allows,
In all my swift successive nows.
But greatest masters often fetch
More glory from a rapid sketch,
Than from the most completing toil,
And charge of colours, cloth, and oil.

Sept. 29, 1735.

(MT, 125–26)

Some lines addressed to his son in 1728 show him attempting just this sort of spontaneity:

Little sketch of my own joy in fine weather and country.

Grass, hay, a stream, variety of trees,
Blue sky, and clouds, hot sun, and cooling breeze,
Leaves rustling, murm'ring water, and the airs
Of birds, a mind delighted, free from cares.
If lovely were the season and the place,
My son was with me, who most lovely was.

Near Hendon, June 16, 1728.

The four first lines were written on the spot in my pocket-book. (MT, 180)

Elsewhere Richardson justified his versifying in a variety of ways. In 1729 he defended it somewhat ambiguously as a pleasing escape from the strenuous and frustrating search for truth that is the duty of the rational man (MT, 189–93, 222). The formula adopted in the "Morning Thoughts" proper after September 1732 has a more confident purpose: his artless poems were, if nothing else, "well-meant labours" offered as a "glad sacrifice" to God (MT, 83–84, 142–43, 156–57). Perhaps, as his son suggested, the "morning orisons" of Adam and Eve in *Paradise Lost,* book 5, were a conscious model (MT, 6–7). At other times Richardson stressed the importance of his introspective verses to the moral regulation of his own life. Even if they were never read by others, they were justified as an important exercise that prepared his mind for the coming day or enabled him to review its events at night. So he depicts himself, after a journey in August 1731, literally retiring to his study in the company of the muse to meditate on his thoughts and actions (MT, 152–53, 320–21).

Poetry also preserved something, however trivial, from the flux of thought and swift passage of time that Richardson felt acutely. The depiction of his soul's lineaments might eventually teach sincerity and virtue to others, but it was a means also of giving form and substance to restless and evanescent consciousness:

Alone, as oft I am, ('tis my delight)
I think, and think, and what I think, I write.
The naked thought, an unsubstantial shade,
Embody'd thus, a living creature's made;
It else had wander'd in the air; at most
It had to all but to myself been lost;
Perhaps had by myself forgotten been;
Not so, substantial now, 'tis felt, 'tis seen. . . .

(MT, 62)

Writing at hours when other poets might understandably find inspiration elusive, Richardson was never short of material. In lines quoted above, he

had contrasted himself as a "spontaneous" writer with Pope the genuine
"creator," and he seems genuinely to have believed that there was something involuntary or passive about his versifying. The dawn of each new
day brought a flood of thought, of spontaneous devotion:

> I know not how, but my obsequious muse
> Uncall'd attends, and not, as others use,
> Oft sleeps, requires some stimulation strong,
> And oft with step compell'd scarce moves along;
> Soon as my life returns, and op'ning eyes
> Survey new light, devotion's thoughts arise.
>
> (MT, 119)

Six months later, in March 1736, he returned to the theme of his poetic
visitations:

> As when experienc'd troops, without command,
> In order'd bright array or move, or stand;
> My Morning Thoughts themselves forthwith dispose,
> Words take their number'd place, disdaining prose,
> My earliest language! like another me,
> Another voice explaining what I see.
>
> (MT, 144)

Given this passive role, and with so much always to be thought and
written, it is not surprising that Richardson was relatively indifferent to the
"correctness" that could come only with careful revision. As acts of pious
devotion, as a means of inspecting and fortifying his own conscience, as the
results of involuntary visitations, his poems are essentially, and for the
period remarkably, private, with no immediate audience in mind, except in
the case of the small number explicitly addressed to Pope, Mrs. Knapp, his
son, and one or two other friends. Who if anyone, apart from Pope and his
son, ever read or heard the remainder is uncertain. What is clear is that the
possibility of posthumous publication did begin to occur to him. Three
poems written in April 1736 express the hope that his poems, however
humble, might delight, instruct, or move others after his death, a purpose
for which he was evidently, if diffidently, bequeathing them to his son (MT,
152–57).

The younger Richardson did, as we know, eventually edit a selection of
the poems,[28] offering them as "the genuine and lively transcript" of his
father's mind, an "exact picture (from life, every stroke of it) of a truly
happy man," and later referring to *Morning Thoughts* as "this glorious series
of a daily philosophical and poetical history of his mind" (MT, 5–7, 258). He
may, however, ultimately have lacked conviction about whether he would
really be serving his father's reputation by publishing the poems, even

when he had decked them out with numerous classical parallels in languages of which he had to admit his father was ignorant. And, indeed, it appears that the posthumous volume has so far brought material or spiritual benefit to virtually no one.

Whatever the poetic merits of *Morning Thoughts,* it remains in many ways a remarkable document, as, in his son's words, "the genuine and lively transcript" of the inner life behind the firm, apparently self-confident features that gaze out from so many self-portraits. And as Walpole was later to write, "such a picture of a good mind, serene in conscious innocence, is scarcely to be found. It is impossible not to love the author." The poems are highly subjective and, since most of those which have survived were written in his sixties, their most frequent subject is naturally the onset of old age. The younger Richardson's decision (if his it was) to place first the sequence of "Morning Thoughts" proper (beginning in September 1732) guaranteed a series of poems which, however personal, are more contentedly pious than those in part 2. They are poems of praise and gratitude to God for the providential dawning of each new day, or celebrations of his own inner contentment and integrity, in contrast to the vagaries of weather and season, darkness, mist, and frost. (Significantly, a poem that inverts this pattern, contrasting inner melancholy with the happiness of nature was held back to part 2, MT, 257–58.)

A reading of all the poems in chronological order, however inconvenient an exercise, reveals a less complacent picture. In 1729, the first year from which a substantial number (forty-six) of poems survives, Richardson was brooding repeatedly on the meaning of his long and laborious career, at times in a mood of some disillusionment. He was also instructing himself, at first tentatively, later less cautiously, to enjoy life while he could, to make "art my mistress, not my wife" (MT, 201). He recognized old age in his contemporaries with a shock:

MY OWN OLD AGE.

Whatever other people say,
I find no symptoms of decay;
The hand, the eye, the fancy strong,
As I have known them all along.
But a contemporary face,
Which is no longer what it was,
Diminish'd strength, and shoulders bending,
And all to dissolution tending
Open my partial eyes to see
That thus, alas! it is with me.

May 17, 1729.

(MT, 197)

An acute awareness of impermanence and ephemerality can enter the poetry, as he senses time's flowing relentlessly away. If former cares and griefs have lost their potency, the possibility of love has faded also, so that only "angelic pleasures" seem to remain. Yet the pursuit of truth itself is arduous and frustrating, and at times a sense of potential universal chaos and absurdity threatens the simple piety to which Richardson aspires. Increasingly, however, conscious integrity and self-reliance in the pursuit of truth, or trust in providential guidance in the darkness that surrounds human life, sustain him:

God, light; we in dark futurity.

From darkness, and from dreams I come,
Some pleasant, undelighting some,
I come to re-salute the day,
To light, to truth—I dare not say.
The sun comes rolling on apace;
As nature shows a gloomy face,
For fog surrounds, insults the hills,
The sky and all the valley fills,
So still my way in darkness lies,
In cheats, and in uncertainties;
Through waves of a tumultuous flood,
Through brambles of a pathless wood;
Shall the next minute's point produce
Enjoyment real, or abuse,
Pleasure, or sorrow, who can tell?
Life's vigour, or the dismal bell?
Before us lies the desert dark,
Not one illuminating spark;
We noises hear, but nothing see,
All, all a blank non-entity;
Yet on we go, and on we must—
But Providence may safely trust.
In vain pretenders have been try'd,
The cloud, the pillar is our guide.

Oct. 21, 1734.

(MT, 84)

Some of these preoccupations, it should be admitted, had already appeared in Richardson's prose, though often in passages omitted by his son from the *Works* in 1773: the sturdy independence of authority, a heightened awareness of the human mind and will as being at the mercy of a flux of sense impressions, the instability or isolation of human identity, the necessary but frustrating search for truth.[29] It may also be conceded that Richardson could write more forcefully and vividly in prose than in his verse, in which the verbal interest and metrical accomplishment are usually

modest and the syntax at times clumsy. One recalls, for example, the image
he uses to praise the flashes of eloquence in Milton's prose, even "in his
most Furious Disputes"—" 'tis seen even There; as I once saw the Sunbeams
Wreathing amongst the Flames and Smoak and Horror of a House on
Fire"—or his description in the same work of the obscurity of incompetent
poetry as "a Sort of Moon-Light Prospect over a Landscape at Best not
Beautiful."[30]

The few who have ever read *Morning Thoughts,* from the original review-
ers and Walpole to Guilhamet, all agree that its poetic merit is negligible. If
the cumulative impression of reading the book can be a striking and even
moving one, as some of its few readers have also testified, the explanation
may have to be found in its biographical interest or in Richardson's rather
lame historical role, as seen by Guilhamet, of incompetently anticipating
the subjectivism that developed later in the century. The only literary virtues one might claim for Richardson must appear negative: the unusual
freedom of his verse from the conventional diction and pretentious gestures of contemporary poetry, the absence of which disarmingly reflects the
writer's own simplicity, integrity, and, to some degree, individuality. There
is at times more vigor and freshness in his verse than such a characterization might suggest:

> 'Tis not the gawdy stream of rosy flame
>   Decking the azure of the lofty sky,
> Nor all the beauties, early autumn's claim,
>   Nor what the taste delights, or what the eye:
>
> No such are now. Clouds rolling on the wind,
>   Darkness and wet, above and on the ground;
> And yet 'tis spring, 'tis summer, in my mind,
>   Within, the warbling nightingale is found. . . .
>
> (MT, 110)

If still more is to be claimed, it may when the poems are closest to the
spontaneous visitations Richardson himself spoke of and when they are
least consciously "created." The difference is apparent in the series of
poems he wrote after his wife's death in January 1726. If the first brief
poem is touching, it is no doubt for biographical reasons, now that we know
that she had died six days earlier and can understand the homely reference
in the last line to his habit of working till midnight, which, as his son
commented, has "an affecting propriety":

ON MY LATE DEAR WIFE

> Adieu, dear life! here I am left alone,
> The world is strangely chang'd since thou art gone.

Compose thyself to rest, all will be well;
I'll come to bed "as fast as possible."

Jan. 18, 1725–6.

(MT, 174)

The following poem, intended as an inscription for an early drawing of his wife made before their marriage, begins with tender simplicity:

My early crayon drew this virgin face;
Though love assisted, 'tis not what her's was;
Correcter features her's, and far more grace!
Then dawn'd a summer's day; its setting sun
Is dropp'd, and quiet night is hast'ning on . . .

but relapses into pious banality ("There's a good and ill in ev'ry scene of life," MT, 174–75). The third poem is fervent but relatively conventional in its trust in Providence and acceptance that his wife would not have wished him to be melancholy (MT, 175–76).

The next two poems, both based on dreams, are a very different matter:

Slumb'ring, disturb'd, appear'd the well-known face,
Lovely, engaging, as she ever was;
I kiss'd and caught the phantom in my arms,
I knew it such, but such a shade hath charms!
Devout, I thank'd kind heaven, that, with a wife,
Had brighten'd up my choicest years of life;
But now, alas! 'tis thus!—she sigh'd—poor heart!
A melancholy phantom as thou art,
From thee more happiness I thus receive,
Than all the living woman-kind can give.
    This, as I was about to say,
    But scrupling, is my heart yet free?
    It is, as on our wedding day,
    For she was all the sex to me.
I wak'd, and found it was a shade indeed,
She and her future sighs, or smiles, were fled;
I now am sighing in my widow'd bed.

Really dreamed, July 14–15, 1726.

(MT, 176–77)

I know not where, but gloomy was the place,
Methought I saw a gloomy phantom pass;
'Twas she, the much-lov'd form! nor spoke, nor stay'd,
No motion of her eyes, or hand, or head,
But, gliding on, I lost her in the shade.
All solemn was, no argument of love
Appear'd her inward sentiment to prove;

Confus'd and griev'd, I stood; then spoke my heart,
Who could have thought such lovers thus would part!

> *Dreamed, Sept.* 10–11.
> *Written, Sept.* 16, 1726.

                                                        (MT, 177)

To suggest that such haunting of the bereaved partner anticipates Hardy
might do no service to Richardson's more modest talents. Yet the immediacy of the experiences movingly survives its transmission through some
awkward syntax. A month later, as if in an attempt to put her ghost to rest,
Richardson wrote a short poem about the performance of *Rodelinda* at
which "Poor *Puddy*" had been taken ill and had gone home to die, while he
unwittingly remained in his seat elsewhere in the theater:

> Poor *Puddy* help'd to fill the crowded house,
> When *Rodelinda* and her noble spouse,
> In notes angelic, took a sad farewell,
> And the orchestra rang the funeral knell.
> Here rose my love, and said a long adieu,
> For we, alas! must now be parted too.
> Homeward she went, but on that spot of ground,
> Made for delight, nor joy, nor ease, she found.
> Unknowing she was gone, well-pleas'd sat I;
> But she, poor heart! was gone—was gone—to die!

> *Oct.* 18, 1726.

                                                        (MT, 178)

Two years after her death, the haunting dream returned. There is no
place in conventional literary history of the Augustan age for verse of such
simple directness and unself-conscious emotion. Since, so long forgotten, it
is not well equipped to compete with the familiar, dominant tones of the
period, whether urbane, acrimonious, elegant, or sublime, it is no doubt
too much to hope that a place will now readily be found:

ON MY DREAMING OF MY WIFE.

> As wak'd from sleep, methought I heard the voice
> Of one that mourn'd, I listen'd to the noise;
> I look'd, and quickly found it was my dear,
> Dead as she was, I little thought her there.
> I question'd her with tenderness, while she
> Sigh'd only, but would else still silent be;
> I wak'd indeed; the lovely mourner's gone,
> She sighs no more, 'tis I that sigh alone.

> Musing on her, I slept again, but where
> I went I know not, but I found her there;

Her lovely eyes she kindly fix'd on me,
"Let *Miser* not be *nangry* then," said she,
A language love had taught, and love alone
Could teach, we prattled as we oft had done;
But she, I know not how, was quickly gone.

With her imaginary presence blest,
My slumbers are emphatically rest;
I of my waking thoughts can little boast,
They always sadly tell me, she is lost.
Much of our happiness we always owe
To error, better to believe than know!
Return, delusion sweet, and oft return!
I joy, mistaken; undeceiv'd, I mourn;
But all my sighs and griefs are fully paid,
When I but see the shadow of her shade.

July 15, 1728.

(MT, 182–83)

NOTES

1. For Richardson as painter and theorist of painting, see W. K. Wimsatt, *The Portraits of Alexander Pope* (New Haven: Yale University Press, 1965), 73–89, 137–222; Lawrence Lipking, *The Ordering of the Arts in Eighteenth-Century England* (Princeton: Princeton University Press, 1970), 109–26; and Morris Brownell, *Alexander Pope and the Arts of Georgian England* (Oxford: Clarendon Press, 1978), 26–38. For Richardson and Milton, see John Kerslake, "The Richardsons and the Cult of Milton," *Burlington Magazine* 99 (1957): 23–24; Christopher Ricks, *Milton's Grand Style* (Oxford: Clarendon Press, 1963); and Peter M. Briggs, "The Jonathan Richardsons as Milton Critics," *Studies in Eighteenth-Century Culture* 9 (1979): 115–30.

2. For example, *The Connoisseur: An Essay on the whole Art of Criticism as it relates to Painting* (1719) lost all but a few sentences of its final section (pp. 204–20) in 1773; and sections from the *Discourse on the . . . Science of a Connoisseur* (1719), pp. 94–129 and 157–97, were omitted in 1773.

3. Wimsatt, *Portraits of Pope*, 80 n. 35.

4. George Sherburn, "New Anecdotes about Alexander Pope," *NQ* 203 (1958): 343–49.

5. William Duncombe edited Samuel Say's *Poems on Several Occasions* (1745), which includes two essays on "The Numbers of Paradise Lost" suggested by and addressed to Richardson. Duncombe also showed a poem by Richardson to Archbishop Herring in January 1754, having no doubt received it from his "friend," the younger Richardson (*Letters from the Late Archbishop Herring, to William Duncombe,* ed. John Duncombe [1777], 116–17, 143–44). For the reviews see *Gentleman's Magazine* 46 (1776): 371–74; *Monthly Review* 55 (1776): 233, 238; and *London Magazine* 45 (1776): 606. For John Duncombe, see John Nichols, *A Select Collection of Poems* (1780), 6:30 n., and *Literary Anecdotes of the Eighteenth Century* (1814), 8:277.

6. Horace Walpole, *Anecdotes of Painting in England* (1771; published 1780), 4:18; 2d ed. (1782), 4:36–37; and *Correspondence,* ed. W. S. Lewis et al., vol. 15 (New Haven: Yale University Press, 1952), 144.

7. Leon Guilhamet, *The Sincere Ideal* (Montreal: McGill-Queen's University Press, 1974), 151–61.

8. *A Discourse on the . . . Science of a Connoisseur* (1719), 26–35. Paget Toynbee, in *Dante in English Literature* (London: Methuen, 1909), 1:196–202, describes it as the first translation from Dante, produced avowedly as a translation, in English literature.

9. *The Works of Mr. Jonathan Richardson* (London, 1773), 115–16.

10. Wimsatt, *Portraits of Pope,* 138.

11. George Vertue, *Note Books,* vol. 3 (Oxford: Oxford University Press, for the Walpole Society, 1934), 57, 67, 125.

12. The copy of *Morning Thoughts* quoted is my own. References in the text are hereafter abbreviated as MT.

13. Vertue, *Note Books,* 3:23.

14. *Explanatory Notes and Remarks on Milton's Paradise Lost* (1734), cxviii, repeated in MT, 270–71.

15. According to Vertue (*Note Books,* 3:67), Riley's brother Thomas "lived with him & was a Painter. of no great use or consequence to his brother & died soon after him."

16. MT, 120–22, 188–89, 198–99, 220, 231–33. Guilhamet shrewdly points out that in a passage in praise of the Church of England in 1719 Richardson in effect praised it for *not* being a church (*Sincere Ideal,* 155–56).

17. The dates at which Richardson could have declined a court appointment appear to be in 1720, when his friend James Thornhill succeeded Thomas Highmore as Serjeant Painter and was knighted; in 1723, when Charles Jervas succeeded Kneller as Principal Painter to the King; and on Thornhill's death in 1734, the year in which Richardson wrote "Shunning Courts." His portrait of the Prince of Wales (1736) is in Warwick Castle. See Ellis Waterhouse, *Dictionary of British 18th Century Painters* (London: Antique Collectors' Club, 1981), 196, 310, 368.

18. Jonathan Richardson, Sr. and Jr., *Explanatory Notes and Remarks on Milton's Paradise Lost* (London, 1734), xxii.

19. Alexander Pope, *Correspondence,* ed. George Sherburn (Oxford: Clarendon Press, 1956), 2:284. The information in Nichols, *Literary Anecdotes,* 4:615n, must derive from MT, 175.

20. Emmett L. Avery, ed., *The London Stage 1660–1800: Part II, 1700–29* (Carbondale: Southern Illinois University Press, 1960), 2:848–50. According to the younger Richardson, his parents had been married thirty-three years, so were presumably married in 1692 or 1693. His assertion that Mrs. Richardson was born on Lord Mayor's Day and died on her birthday, aged fifty-one (MT, 175), is highly questionable. Lord Mayor's Day is traditionally in November. If she was taken ill on the evening of 11 January and died (of "a mortification in her bowels") early the following day without regaining consciousness (MT, 178), she would have died on her husband's birthday, which his son twice states was 12 January and which he must have confused with his mother's. She was probably born in November 1674 and died 12 January 1726. The niece and heiress of John Riley, her maiden name appears to have been Bray. Her first name is uncertain, but Richardson evidently called her "Puddy" (MT, 178, 316).

21. See Sherburn, "New Anecdotes," for similar anecdotes recorded by Richardson; and for a shorter account of Pope's habits, Joseph Spence, *Observations, Anecdotes and Characters of Books and Men,* ed. James M. Osborn (Oxford: Clarendon Press, 1966), 1:45, 85.

22. Pope, *Correspondence,* 3:326–27.

23. Wimsatt, *Portraits of Pope,* 139.

24. Wimsatt, *Portraits of Pope,* 157; Brownell, *Pope and the Arts of Georgian England,* 29.

25. Pope, *Correspondence,* 4:119, 484.

26. Richardson, *Explanatory Notes* (1734), clxxviii, clxxxi.

27. Richardson, *An Essay on the Theory of Painting* (1715), 140–43, 156; *The Connoisseur* (1719), 50, 132.

28. Probably in the 1760s, when he was editing his father's *Works,* according to a note dated 28 March 1763 (115).

29. "We have another kind of Property, and that is the Present time. We possess but one Single Point, the whole Circumference of Eternity belongs to Others. We talk of Years, we are Creatures but of a Day, a Moment! the Man I was Yesterday is now no more; If I live till to

Morrow, That Man is not yet born: What that *Self* shall be is utterly unknown; what Ideas, what Opinions, what Joys, what Griefs, nay what Body, all is yet hid in the Womb of Time; but This we are sure of, I shall not be the Same, the present Fabrick will be demolish'd for ever. What is past we know, but 'tis vanish'd as a Morning Dream; we are moving on; and every Step we take is a Step in the Dark." *A Discourse on the . . . Science of a Connoisseur* (1719), 178.

   30. *Explanatory Notes,* lxv, cxlv.

11

Sterne's Script: The Performing of *Tristram Shandy*

Peter Steele

With a nod and a shrug to Mr. Horace, I begin, not with Sterne himself but with one of his later affiliates—Saul Steinberg. Howard Nemerov has written, in "Metamorphoses, according to Steinberg,"

> These people, with their illegible diplomas,
> Their passports to a landscape full of languages,
> Carry their images on banners, or become
> Porters of pedestals bearing their own
> Statues, or hold up, with and against gravity,
> The unbalanced scrollwork of their signatures.
> Thumbprints somehow get to be sanderlings,
> And the cats keep on appearing, with an air
> Of looking at kings even as they claw
> Their way up the latticed cage of a graph,
> Balance with fish, confront photographers
> In family groups, or prowl music paper
> Behind the staves.
>   These in themselves, Master,
> Are a great teaching. But more than for these
> I am grateful for the lesson of the line,
> That wandering divider of the world,
> So casually able to do anything:
> The extended clothesline that will carry trains,
> For instance, or the lines of letters whose
> Interstices vary the planes between
> The far horizon and a very near nose.
> The enchanted line, defying gravity and death,
> Brings into being and destroys its world
> Of marvelous exceptions that prove rules,
> Where a hand is taken drawing its own hand,
> A man with a pen laboriously sketches
> Himself into existence; world of the lost

Characters amazed in their own images:
The woman elided with her rocking chair,
The person trapped behind his signature,
The man who has just crossed himself out.[1]

Harold Rosenberg, writing of Steinberg, remarks:

The theme of a world unfolding out of the artist's act of drawing is
reiterated in numerous ways, from the calligraphic landscape . . . in
which the horizon explodes into a flourish of penmanship, to drawings in
which objects are repeated upside down because a line indicates a body
of water in which they are reflected. To Steinberg the line of the horizon,
which marks the limit of the visible, is just another line that his pen can
manipulate as it sees fit. All things in Steinberg's pictures—scenes, people, cats, crocodiles—have their source in art. But art is not restricted to
pictures. Everything that exists has its source in art; that is, human invention. The skin on the fingertip is an organic product, but the fingerprint
is a device of society. It is a mark produced with ink for the purpose of
recording the identities of individuals and arranging them in files. The
fingerprint is art imposed on nature by society.[2]

There is a certain brio to each of these passages, a brio prompted by the
contemplation of the intellectual vivacity and the imaginative fertility of the
art with which they are concerned. Nemerov's poem is a salute, Rosenberg's paragraph an analysis: both, though, have some of the quality of the
laudatio, and the magisterial presence being praised is not only that of a
Steinberg, but that of the convivially witty intelligence wherever it is perceived in action. Both passages, too, direct us toward the *curiosity* of that
intelligence—its hungry, hunting character. Both imply ways in which new
avidities may be stirred in those who regard art's eager gesture of the mind.
Nemerov emulates Steinberg's metamorphoses, but also poses Steinberg's
stabilities: Rosenberg looks to both origin and culmination in the artist's
drawing, aware, as is Steinberg himself, of the suggestive ambiguity of the
word *drawing* itself. In each case, we find something of what Hopkins
sought for his poetry and displays everywhere in his prose reflections: "the
roll, the rise, the carol, the creation." And in each case we find traces of
perturbation and provocation—the instinct of those who will not allow
Prometheus to sit by his fireside and chat. In a fine line elsewhere,
Nemerov calls style "That fire that eats what it illuminates," which does
very well to indicate the conscious absorption, the fully witting analysis of a
Steinberg. It also points to a climactic quality in aspirant speech, and to a
combination of zest and rue, of elation and disputation, that one finds
pervasively in *Tristram Shandy.*

And so to my title. Like the book with which it is concerned, it is
equivocal, or at least polysemous. There need be no apology for this. Any
address to the master-work of this maestro of innuendo could be expected
to take just such a way. The *Oxford English Dictionary,* which might in its

fashioning have been dedicated to Tristram, but with which he would have made such little headway, gives us as ever some cues. Of *Script*, it says,

> Something written; a piece of writing. . . Handwriting, the characters used in handwriting (as distinguished from print). . . A kind of type devised to imitate the appearance of handwriting . . . used . . . of systems of shorthand which resemble longhand in general appearance and in the movements of the hand that are required. . . *Law:* The original or principal instrument, where there are part and counterpart. . . In theatrical parlance, short for MANUSCRIPT.

And of *Perform*,

> To carry through to completion; to complete, finish, perfect (an action, process, work, etc.). . . To grant, furnish, give, pay, that which is promised. . . To do, go through, or execute formally or solemnly (a duty, public function, ceremony, or rite; a piece of music, a play, etc.). . . To act, play (a part or character). . .

This swag of denotations, so easily imagined as furling within itself connotation upon connotation, may also be thought of as offering us a fabric to encompass *Tristram Shandy*.

"May" though, not "must." There is often not much future in etymological flirtation. If one does well to leave books to their fates, one may do even better to leave words to theirs. Yet it is a notorious fact that everywhere in *Tristram Shandy* the play of mind is a play of words. If the book's life, like my uncle Toby's, is put in jeopardy by words, words are also its only succor. To the great pleasure or displeasure of its readers, the traffic of words with one another is here not only (as in all literature) unremitting, but also overt. This is true to such an extent that the words can come to have the look of animated entities, now preying upon one another, now courting one another, now living in rather overwrought proximity to one another. To read Sterne is to be reminded sometimes of the Lucretian atoms, of Leibnitzian monads, even on occasion of Swift's sardonically conceived "Crowd of little Animals, but with Teeth and Claws extremely sharp . . . all Invention is formed by the Morsure of two or more of these Animals."[3] It is a hectic art, however domestic its ostensible occasions, an art of explicit writerly intervention, as Steinberg's is an art of explicit calligraphic intervention. The Steinberg who has said, "When I admire a scene in the country, I look for a signature in the lower right-hand corner," and that "My line wants to remind constantly that it's made of ink"; the Steinberg who, as John Hollander reports, has reflected that he always thought of the word *should* in connection with shoulders—this man has diplomatic relations with Sterne-land, where the words cannot point beyond themselves and be at peace, but must perform not only a function but themselves.[4]

To put it differently, reading Sterne is like following a voiceprint, whose fluctuations and oscillations betoken a weave of mind, and which holds the attention on precisely that weave, rather than on the message mediated by utterance. The hobby-horsical obsession with language in its courses characteristic of my father and my uncle Toby alike is no doubt an object of Sterne's laughter, but it is also an intense and stylized equivalent of Sterne's own bent. Just as there is an eerie reflexiveness in Steinberg's art—in the smug and suited man thinking, "Cogito, ergo Cartesius est," in the self-delineators and self-cancelers—so there is in Sterne's writing. And just as Steinberg's reflectiveness has little to do with conventional self-portraiture but is an instance of what he meant by saying that "drawing is a way of reasoning on paper,"[5] Sterne's reflectiveness has little to do with his allowing Tristram the autobiographical manner. It has to do rather with flicker and shimmer among the several rhetorics, major-seeming or minor-seeming, in *Tristram Shandy*. What William H. Gass claims generally for language as it moves toward poetry may be urged more particularly for Sterne's actions:

> As language moves toward poetry, it becomes increasingly concrete, denying the distinction between type and token, the sign and its significance, name and thing. It does not escape conventional syntax altogether, but the words may shift grammatical functions, some structures may be jettisoned, others employed in uncustomary ways, or wrenched out of their usual alignment. Terms redefine themselves, relegating what was once central to the periphery, making fresh essence out of ancient accidents, apples out of pies. Language furthermore abandons its traditional semantic capacities in favor of increasingly contextual interaction. The words respond to one another as actors, dancers, do, and thus their so-called object is not rendered or described but constructed.[6]

It was of course the late Sigurd Burckhardt who spoke most eloquently and exactly about the verbality of *Tristram Shandy;* and what he said of Toby one might say of Sterne: "the escape into the healing innocence of things is forbidden him; he is tied to language."[7] "Tied," though far from the whole story, is a vital part of it; the bond between Sterne and his language, the "word-set," one might call it, as we speak of a "mind-set," is such as to both constrain and steel him. It binds him, and it nerves him, to act out the paradox of human speech itself.

Almost at random, I find this:

> When this story is compared with the title-page,—Will not the gentle reader pity my father from his soul?—to see an orderly and well-disposed gentleman, who tho' singular,—yet inoffensive in his notions,—so played upon in them by cross purposes;——to look down upon the stage, and see him baffled and overthrown in all his little systems and wishes; to behold a train of events perpetually falling out against him, and in so critical and cruel a way, as if they had purposedly been plann'd and pointed aginst him, merely to insult his speculations.——In a word,

to behold such a one, in his old age, ill-fitted for troubles, ten times in a day suffering sorrow;—ten times in a day calling the child of his prayers TRISTRAM!——Melancholy dissyllable of sound! which, to his ears, was unison to *Nicompoop*, and every name vituperative under heaven.——By his ashes! I swear it,—if ever malignant spirit took pleasure, or busied itself in traversing the purposes of mortal man,—it must have been here;—and if it was not necessary I should be born before I was christened, I would this moment give the reader an account of it.[8]

No single rhetoric has supreme governance in this passage; several play upon one another. There are, first, the periods of high-toned, often homiletic lament echoing through it—the sort of thing that found a high point in Newman's *Apologia Pro Vita Sua*: "To consider the world in its length and breadth, its various history, the many races of men, their starts, their fortunes, their mutual alienation, their conflicts . . . all this is a vision to dizzy and appal; and inflicts upon the mind the sense of a profound mystery, which is absolutely beyond human solution."[9] The cadences, like the sentiments, had been in the mouths of many generations of homilists. This threnody on the death of the moral universe, this intonation of the vanity of human wishes, might be directed upon the race as a whole or upon any individual: it is a lament for the nonmakers. The sermon in *Tristram Shandy* is a reminder of Sterne's occasional engrossment in that highly stylized art-form, so adaptable either to direct attestation or to a designing address. It is also a reminder of the characteristic preacherly attention to a God-given human poise in men otherwise menaced by excesses and deprivations alike. Sterne, much exercised by mortality, is aware too of the constant likelihood that the life of human endeavor itself will gutter out. For all his customary briskness, he has many essays in the memento mori, as he calls to mind the embolism of futility that seems to be within us all the time. For all the comedy of circumstance in this paragraph, Sterne does mean, and care, that my father is the sport of fate. It hardly matters whether fate disports itself within him or without him. A quirk or my father's temperament or a pucker in the fabric of the world will do his business for him equally well.

But comedy, of course, there is. The young Auden used to give imitations of a preacher struggling with a speech defect; Tristram, keening over the death of all proportion in my father, has a streak of that rhetoric about him. Evelyn Waugh remarks in *A Little Learning* that a self-portrait of one of his ancestors shows him as both demure and dotty;[10] those coupled attributes of the uncoupled self might almost do for my father, making him stand toward self-possession as hobby-horse stands toward self. Tristram, modeling what is lamentable in my father's inconsequent fortunes, also models the good cheer that inexplicably comes over the hapless gazer—finds zest and rue, as I called them earlier. This is the *passion* of comedy, the buoyancy of sentiment. A friend of mine said once with analytical flair, "there's no use making things fool-proof; they just make better fools." That sparkling lugubriousness informs Sterne's paragraph.

The sparkle, though, comes not only from the ludicrous pursuits of my father, the manic assiduity of the "orderly and well-disposed gentleman" whose unkempt son is currently telling us in his unbridled work what his alienated father has produced. It comes also from the linguistic echoes and flickers in the passage, the shimmer in which Tristram's wordiness and worldliness plays over his father's wordiness and unworldliness. We may if we wish call it mock-lament, but on the understanding that mock-lament is no more a mockery of lament that mock-cream is a mockery of cream, or mock-epic of epic. It is a move made by the real mind prompted by vivid interests in a new direction, a novel dimension. The comedy is social, but epistemological, even ontological as well. The assonance and consonance of the paragraph help (as in the Newman passage) to make for propulsion in the sentences; but when, as here, they are intervened upon by the syntactical flurries in the first lines, they invoke the presence of such as Ancient Pistol—the simulacrum of a self. There is something gesticulant about, for instance, "In a word, to behold such a one, in his old age, ill-fitted for troubles, ten times in a day suffering sorrow,—ten times in a day calling the child of his prayers TRISTRAM!——Melancholy dissyllable of sound! which, to his ears, was unison to *Nicompoop,* and every name vituperative under heaven." One hears this as flourish, just as one sees it typographically as flourish. This need not dismiss it, of course, any more than the inescapable visual and verbal flourish of opera dismisses it: but it does place it. It is a very long way from naturalism, though it certainly insinuates that it is the nature of man to be excessive. It is not far from Nemerov's "enchanted line, denying gravity and death" which "brings into being and destroys its world/Of marvelous exceptions that prove rules." Comedy always cancels—not the dismays that go so far to induce it, but alternative representations of those dismays; it does this not by the securing of happy endings but by the carriage of the mind through what is not yet ended, and is perhaps unending. "When this story is compared with the title-page" would do suggestively not only for the little anecdote that Tristram has just "completed," nor only for the work as a whole, but for the story-ing and stammering of the paragraph itself, wherein we see Tristram to be his father's son indeed, ecstatic in his surrender to his own comic and humiliating predicament; just as we see this ex-homunculus looking with indulgent ruefulness at his mannikin father onstage.

Amidst the shifting rhetorical tides of such a work, a dictionary's decorum, its patient disposition of *script* and *perform,* enables one to keep a footing, but it can hardly be authoritative for one's procedures. *Tristram Shandy* begins with a wish and ends with applause for a botched story; both moves may remind us not only of the narrative resilience of the work as a whole but also of the overplus of intent everywhere evident in it. Henry James, at the conclusion of his preface to *Portrait of a Lady,* says, "There is really too much to say." James was concentrating on the suppositious plenitude of preliterary existence, whereas Sterne always talks by the book; yet Sterne might have said the same thing—meaning in his case that there is too much in the saying to be said about the saying, as in effect he has Tristram say many times. Unwilling to mystify, he is more unwilling still to deny those bents of the mind and the mind's utterance that tend to mystify us. Gaining that access to art which requires that we be more elated by lucidities than dismayed by opacities, he still looks on every page at his own art and finds, as in a candle, the darkness at the heart of the flame.

To change the metaphor, reading Sterne's writing is a matter of finding something Laocoon-like. The man is at grips with his own meanings, and thus he inevitably draws forth more and more of them. From one point of view, this is a late secularizing of the Metaphysicals' attempt to discern in the process of utterance a telling analogue of God's ubiquitous wording of the world—or, failing that, to effect a memorable lament for His vexing retirement from the scene, and a display of man's resolution, soldierly or cynical, to take over the role. The shades of Lancelot Andrewes and of the Earl of Rochester hover incongrously about Sterne as he plies his wit. From another point of view, we may see in *Tristram Shandy,* as in *A Sentimental Journey,* foreshadowings of that near-obsession with labyrinthine ways which has become a staple of modern literary exercise. Were Sterne ever a candidate for canonization—a sufficiently improbable notion—there would be no shortage of those offering themselves as *advocatus diaboli;* but Joyce and Borges would be there to beat them down. Either way, though, standing at some still point of the Sternean world, one would have to stress the impulse toward multiplication, polyvalence, and constellation. If, in simpleminded fashion, one were to divide writers into those who find meanings and let them be, and those who find meanings and let them go, there can be no doubt where Sterne would stand. The meanings he finds may be thought of as sociable with one another, but also in contest. Just as every modeled society except the utopian, and perhaps even that, precipitates the disparities in which thereupon it seeks parities, so *Tristram Shandy* constantly initiates forking paths of meaning in the hope that later convergences may occur after territory has been covered and gains thus been made. In philosophy, logic ramifies so as to codify; the quicksilver logic of *Tristram Shandy* goes into the thickets of linguistic potentiality in the confidence that command of and surrender to meaning will issue from the same complex gesture. It is a matter, one might say, of the eros of mind.

But "quicksilver" is only a phoneme away from "quacksalver"; and that may suggest why, quite apart from the sentimental mood-swings or the frequent sexual innuendo, Sterne has left so many of the great or the little Doctors sour-faced. His fast, volatile talk has led them to judge his script a forged or scrawled thing, his performance a factitious business. There is probably little or nothing that can be done about this. Sterne's domain, like his demeanor, is theatrical to the last, both in its ostentatious fascination with the finished gesture and in its expectation of interruptions. He is the actor-manager of the comedy of mind, in which intelligence makes other not only its objects but itself. To *perform*, as the dictionary hints, has to do with coming through to the final form of things or affairs; but it also has to do with *getting* through, making one's way, soldiering on. There are in a sense no leisurely performances—one goes fishing, does not perform fishing. To perform, whether as prima donna or as old trouper, is to be militant. And this is so because of the push of mind that wants both to match and to deviate. Hopkins, speaking of his instinct in the face of admired works, said that it was to "admire and do otherwise,"[11] and this is particularly true of the comic intelligence in its reflexivity. The code, script, or model of the world exists already in some sense, and in respect of this the would-be performer has a double intention: to replicate and to innovate. As the fingerprint is, in Rosenberg's words, "art imposed on nature by society," so the comic writer's fingering of his theme imposes upon the mind in its ordinary leisure an abrupt athleticism. The artist does not take the natural world away but takes it on, leading it into the countries of consciousness and undergoing metamorphoses in himself as he induces metamorphoses in it. The more witting comedy becomes, the more it has some of the hurt of thought, some of its ineluctable foreignness. *Tristram Shandy* may be very much in longhand so far as public events are concerned, but it is very much in shorthand so far as the mind's fortunes are concerned. One reason why one may sheer away from the book is that it enacts, over and above the abnormalities of society, the normalities of consciousness. One is alarmed to find that the "I" is, indeed, an other.

Alarm, though, was not Sterne's end. If we take his and Tristram's word that they are at war with the spleen, not indeed as the whole story, but as a good story, we will look the more sympathetically at the puppet-show of my father and the others in action. Robert Burton, to whose *Anatomy of Melancholy* Sterne is so slyly indebted, said that he never traveled but in map and card. My father, and those for whom he cares, are absolutely at a loss unless they have map and book near them to steady, and to stir, their cogitations. The dizzied reader, privy to their opinionated lives, sees them at their most accomplished as they gather round the *Tristrapaedia:*

> ——No,—I think I have advanced nothing, replied my father, making answer to a question which *Yorick* had taken the liberty to put to him,—I have advanced nothing in the *Tristrapaedia*, but what is as clear as any one proposition in *Euclid*.—Reach me, *Trim*, that book from off the scrutoir:——it has oft times been in my mind, continued my father, to have read it over both to you, *Yorick*, and to my brother *Toby*, and I think

it a little unfriendly in myself, in not having done it long ago:——shall we have a short chapter or two now,—and a chapter or two hereafter, as occasions serve; and so on, till we get through the whole? My uncle *Toby* and *Yorick* made the obeisance which was proper; and the corporal, though he was not included in the compliment, laid his hand upon his breast, and made his bow at the same time.——The company smiled. *Trim,* quoth my father, has paid the full price for staying out the *entertainment.*——He did not seem to relish the play, replied *Yorick.*——'Twas a Tom-fool-battle, an' please your reverence, of captain *Tripet's* and that other officer, making so many summersets, as they advanced;——the *French* come on capering now and then in that way,——but not quite so much.

My uncle *Toby* never felt the consciousness of his existence with more complacency than what the corporal's, and his own reflections, made him do at that moment;——he lighted his pipe,——*Yorick* drew his chair closer to the table,—*Trim* snuff'd the candle,—my father stir'd up the fire,—took up the book,—cough'd twice, and begun.[12]

Here, in little, we have much of what makes *Tristram Shandy*, the true *Tristrapaedia*, itself. There is my father's unquenchable ambition to instruct—he who, faced with his wife's refusal to ask a question, "had officiously told her above a thousand times which way it was,—but she always forgot." There is the companionable intent which nurtures that ambition, as it does Tristram's, for all his occasional tweakings and buffetings of the reader. There is the air of the narrative's emerging out of the unknown and falling back into it: Yorick's question is as irretrievable as the *Tristrapaedia's* "whole" is unattainable. There is the relish of ceremony and stagecraft, as the principal and the other actors are set in motion upon the boards of their little world. There is the recognition that all here is game, though deserving of all the gravity that mortal fools can muster. There is the matching of the mind's opaque eloquence with the body's lucid eloquence. Most teasingly, and most characteristically, there is the dialectic between the hubris of my father's claim to have "advanced nothing in the *Tristrapaedia*, but what is as clear as any one proposition in *Euclid*" and the quiet with which "My uncle *Toby* never felt the consciousness of his existence with more complacency than what the corporal's, and his own reflections, made him do at that moment." Yeats, in *Autobiographies,* remarks that "it is so many years before one can believe enough in what one feels even to know what the feeling is," asks, "Who does not distrust complete ideas?" and observes,

All empty souls tend to extreme opinion. It is only in those who have built up a rich world of memories and habits of thought that extreme opinions affront the sense of probability. Propositions, for instance, which set all the truth upon one side can only enter rich minds to dislocate and strain, if they can enter at all, and sooner or later the mind expels them by instinct.[13]

These are Sternean sentiments, though Sterne lends himself to them with more unalloyed jubilation than Yeats commonly managed. For Sterne, as for Yeats, they could all serve to indicate *Hodos Chameliontos,* the Way of the Chamelion, as any description of Steinberg must eventually talk about the Way of the Metamorphoses. For Sterne, too, as my father's and my uncle Toby's demeanor reminds us, there would be both parable and comedy in the Indian tradition that Brahma, deciding to write down his teachings, and needing to devise a script for the purpose, took his patterns mainly from the seams in the human skull. The god, apparently, was an ironist. It is not hard to think of Sterne as one of his votaries.

Notes

1. Howard Nemerov, *The Collected Poems of Howard Nemerov* (Chicago: University of Chicago Press, 1977), 276.

2. Harold Rosenberg, *Saul Steinberg* (New York: Knopf, with the Whitney Museum of American Art, 1978), 19.

3. Jonathan Swift, *A Tale of a Tub, to which is added The Battel of the Books and the Mechanical Operation of the Spirit,* ed. A. C. Guthkelch and D. Nichol Smith, 2d ed. (Oxford: Clarendon Press, 1958), 277.

4. Steinberg, quoted in Rosenberg, *Saul Steinberg,* 11; John Hollander, introduction to Steinberg, *The Passport,* revised ed. (New York: Vintage, 1979).

5. Quoted in Rosenberg, *Saul Steinberg,* 30.

6. William H. Gass, *The World within the Word* (New York: Knopf, 1978), 303–4.

7. Sigurd Burckhardt, "*Tristram Shandy*'s Law of Gravity," in *Tristram Shandy,* ed. Howard Anderson (New York: Norton, 1980), 599.

8. Laurence Sterne, *The Life and Opinions of Tristram Shandy, Gentleman,* ed. Melvyn and Joan New (Gainesville: University Presses of Florida, 1978), 63–64.

9. John Henry Cardinal Newman, *Apologia Pro Vita Sua* (London: Longmans, Green, 1891), 241–42.

10. Evelyn Waugh, *A Little Learning* (London: Chapman and Hall, 1964), 13.

11. *The Letters of Gerard Manley Hopkins to Robert Bridges,* ed. Claude Colleer Abbott (London: Oxford University Press, 1935), 291.

12. *Tristram Shandy,* ed. New and New, 465.

13. W. B. Yeats, *Autobiographies* (London: Macmillan, 1955), 103, 480, 469.

Johnson's *Rasselas*: Limits of Wisdom, Limits of Art

Leopold Damrosch, Jr.

Johnson's *Rasselas* has always been curiously resistant to criticism: it is surprisingly hard to explain what it is and why. The consensus seems to be that it is neither a novel nor a satire, but a philosophical fable or apologue whose function is to communicate wisdom. So far, so good. But the relation between story and lesson is strangely oblique and disturbing, so much so indeed that formal accounts of *Rasselas* are invariably disappointing. It may be useful instead to try to think about Johnson himself, both in the work and behind or outside it, in the hope of understanding what it might mean to him.

Most interpreters agree that Johnson here is as usual the Wise Man, whether conveying his lessons directly by way of moral precept or indirectly by way of ironic narrative. It is unquestionable that *Rasselas* expresses some of its author's deepest preoccupations, made subtler but not less serious by the tone of detached irony.[1] But I should like to draw attention to the ways in which the wisdom of *Rasselas* is introspective and self-defeating, and to propose that the work represents a turning point in Johnson's thought, a farewell to his own dream that wisdom can be taught either by didactic essays or by instructive fictions. It is at once the crown of his great decade of moral writing in the 1750s and a profound reconsideration of the overt wisdom of the *Rambler.*

Emrys Jones has performed a valuable service in emphasizing the affinities of *Rasselas,* in whose conclusion nothing is concluded, with the dislocating meanderings of *Tristram Shandy*. But to concentrate on its formless form may run the risk of ignoring the elegance and control of its parts, and to turn Johnson into an existentialist novelist who achieves, as another critic puts it, "a purgation of sorrow in absurd comedy."[2] That might be true if *Rasselas* were a novel, but it is not. Whether or not one favors the term *apologue,* one must accept Sheldon Sacks's argument that this form neither explores relationships between plausible human beings (as in the novel), nor uses arbitrary characters and incidents to expose vice and folly in a world outside itself (as in satire), but, rather, furnishes fictional illustrations of moral truths. Potentially alarming events, like the death of the Stoic's daughter, are carefully controlled to deflect the reader from novelistic involvement, but on the other hand Rasselas and his companions are permitted a real though limited life of their own, and are not true vehicles of satire like Swift's Gulliver or Pope's interchangeable Theobald and Cibber.[3] Critics have often noticed the sentimental exaggeration and self-infatuation of Nekayah's grief at the loss of Pekuah, but the point is not so much to satirize Nekayah's behavior as to distance the reader from deep sympathy—such as he might feel if it were Rasselas who had vanished, or died—and to concentrate instead on the truths which the event permits Imlac to convey: the relative lightness of grief uncomplicated by guilt, the healing power of time. "Do not suffer life to stagnate; it will grow muddy for want of motion: commit yourself again to the current of the world."[4]

But if *Rasselas* is intended to communicate wisdom, it is nonetheless not easy to define its message. This is true whether one construes the lesson from the narrative as Sacks does—"Earthly happiness does not exist, but its absence does not result in unbearable misery in this world for the reasonably virtuous who, in addition, may turn their eyes with hope toward heaven"—or from the ironies which, as Sheridan Baker observes, tend to subvert the narrative: "the psychological irony of the mind itself, always wishing, always imagining happiness even in the midst of happiness, always, by its very nature, incapable of satisfaction."[5] Each of these formulations is accurate enough, but each treats *Rasselas* as a fable from which a moral is to be drawn. I see its exemplary qualities as looser and more relative, and its focus on the limitations both of wisdom and of art.

First of all, one should emphasize the narrow field of vision that *Rasselas* permits, in contrast, for instance, to *The Vanity of Human Wishes.* Even when they emerge from the Happy Valley and seek to involve themselves in life, the characters occupy a world without evil (though it admits of a controlled degree of suffering) and very nearly without sexuality. "How the world is to be peopled, returned Nekayah, is not my care, and needs not be yours" (chap. 28). By inspection of other people Nekayah is able to analyze the Johnsonian (and Richardsonian) theme of the "artifices and feuds" by which members of a family use and betray each other (chap. 26), but she and her brother have no contact with their own parents, discover a wise and generous surrogate father in Imlac, and, apart from an occasional theoretical dispute, are innocent of mutual hostility. Northrop Frye compares the Happy Valley to the unborn world of Blake's *Thel;*[6] emotionally none of the characters ever leaves it. Only through Pekuah do the prince and princess permit a servant to do their living for them: it is she who has a mildly romantic adventure and she who forms a genuine attachment to another person (having regarded astronomy with indifference when it was only a way of passing time in the desert, she embraces it eagerly when it is a way to the astronomer's heart).

And it is not simply that Rasselas and Nekayah resist, or are not permitted, emotional attachment. They behold life in general in far milder terms than one might expect from the Hobbesian vision of the sages in the Valley who "described all beyond the mountains as regions of calamity, where discord was always raging, and where man preyed upon man" (chap. 2), or from Imlac's metaphorical version of the same "waves of violence" and "rocks of treachery" (chap. 12). The prince and princess founder on no rocks. Occasionally they see others founder, but never with much vividness. "In a short time the second Bassa was deposed. The Sultan, that had advanced him, was murdered by the Janisaries, and his successor had other views and different favourites" (chap. 24). This tiny exemplum is not felt so deeply as the exemplary histories in *The Vanity of Human Wishes,* and the most serious threat to equanimity, the astronomer's madness, becomes the story of a successful cure.

This careful control suggests that Johnson is not attempting to tell the whole truth about human life. Nor, though he dwells on the theme, is he simply concerned with the endless and inevitable self-delusions of the mind. Rather he is concerned with the process of education in its largest sense, with the truth that wisdom, however profound, does not exist until experience has forced it upon each individual. "Even a proverb is no proverb to you," Keats said, "till your life has illustrated it."[7] The poet, according to Imlac, must "consider himself as presiding over the thoughts and manners of future generations; as a being superiour to time and place" (chap. 10). That is precisely the attitude struck by the Olympian narrator of *Rasselas,* who loves sententious aphorisms so much that he constantly compels the most unlikely characters to deliver them. "Misfortunes, answered the Arab, should always be expected" (chap. 38); a little later Pekuah pronounces firmly that "avarice is an uniform and tractable vice" (chap. 39). These and many other instances of wisdom are perfectly true. But the book suggests that wisdom, simply *as* wisdom, tends to exaggerate its own usefulness. Perhaps some hint of this ironic perspective is conveyed by the shapeliness of the style itself: "On one part were flocks and herds feeding in the pastures, on another all the beasts of chase frisking in the lawns; the spritely kid was bounding on the rocks, the subtle monkey frolicking in the trees, and the solemn elephant reposing in the shade" (chap. 1). There is something deliberately playful here: the confident balancing is certainly not mocked, but neither is it presented as an occasion for sober meditation.

Throughout the book sententious truth is constantly juxtaposed with human context. When Rasselas conjures up the fantasy of "an orphan virgin robbed of her little portion," he is impelled to dash off in pursuit of her "treacherous lover." The pursuit cannot be easy, since "fear naturally quickens the flight of guilt." But this fact, though entirely true, is entirely irrelevant. The lover cannot be caught because he does not exist; Rasselas "recollected himself, and smiled at his own useless impetuosity" (chap. 4). Or consider Rasselas's critique of the flying man's theory that it will be easy to float airborne at high altitudes. "I have been told, that respiration is difficult upon lofty mountains, yet from these precipices, though so high as to produce great tenuity of the air, it is very easy to fall: therefore I suspect, that from any height, where life can be supported, there may be danger of too quick descent." To this the artificer replies splendidly, "Nothing will ever be attempted, if all possible objections must be first overcome" (chap. 6). The reply, though foolish, is brave. And the man's bathetic fate is not at all the consequence of mistaken theory. He has carefully studied "the structure of all volant animals," and with an adequate source of power he might indeed fly, for Rasselas does not deny that bats and birds can fly. The test must be practice, not theory.

As the story proceeds, moral wisdom is subjected to similar criticism. Rasselas gives the sensual young men an admirable Johnsonian lecture on the need to prepare for their final end. "They stared a while in silence one upon another, and, at last, drove him away by a general chorus of continued laughter" (chap. 17). Their derision is wrong but inevitable. More important, Rasselas himself, though he has rebuked the short-sightedness of youth, will prove equally impervious to the lessons of age. It has been suggested that chapter 45, "They Discourse with an Old Man," is an extraneous survival from an earlier, gloomier conclusion of the book.[8] The episode does violate the apparent logic of the narrative. But that is exactly its point: not only that old age is inveterately querulous, as Rasselas and Nekayah conclude, but also that young people are incapable of imagining themselves old. "Imlac, who had no desire to see them depressed, smiled at the comforts which they could so readily procure to themselves, and remembered, that at the same age, he was equally confident of unmingled prosperity, and equally fertile of consolatory expedients. He forebore to force upon them unwelcome knowledge, which time itself would too soon impress" (chap. 45). The gentle, wise Imlac is very different from the various professional experts whose wisdom is shown to be a function of ego. "Example is always more efficacious than precept," he had said earlier (chap. 30), and direct personal experience is more efficacious than either.

The characters, then, behold and to some extent participate in the world, but can learn only when experience affects them directly, and then perhaps too late. Moreover, the distancing effect of apologue prevents the reader from feeling that he has vicariously lived through experience, as he might in a novel like *Clarissa*. Instead he is forced to contemplate the limitations of wisdom when it is *not* deduced from experience—the limitations, in fact, to which *Rasselas* is confined by its very refusal to turn into a novel. Johnson had spent ten years as a moral teacher, offering the world his deepest insights in literally hundreds of essays. One lesson of the *Rambler* was that the world was not particularly eager for such advice: "I am far from supposing, that the cessation of my performances will raise any inquiry, for I have never been much a favourite of the publick" (*Rambler*, 208). Seven years later Johnson begins *Rasselas* with an appeal couched almost in the formal order of the heroic couplet: "Ye who listen with credulity to the whispers of fancy, and pursue with eagerness the phantoms of hope; who expect that age will perform the promises of youth, and that the deficiencies of the present day will be supplied by the morrow; attend to the history of Rasselas prince of Abissinia." By the end of the book we may suspect that the narrator himself, Olympian though his wisdom may be, should be numbered among the audience he addresses in his fanciful hope that we can learn wisdom from a moralist rather than from life.

"It is not commonly observed," Johnson had written in *Rambler* 184, "how much, even of actions considered as particularly subject to choice, is to be attributed to accident, or some cause out of our own power, by whatever name it be distinguished." Yet it is also true, as he went on to say, that "nothing in reality is governed by chance, but that the universe is under the perpetual superintendence of him who created it." Determinism, whether Puritan or mechanist, frees the individual from choice by referring all his actions to some irresistible force. Johnson's voluntarism might seem to make choosing central, and the original title of *Rasselas* was to have been *The Choice of Life*, yet the narrative constantly drains significance from the act of choosing. E. R. Wasserman convincingly argues that *Rasselas* subverts or parodies traditional fictions in which characters are educated in making choices and rewarded for making the right ones.[9] Johnson sees choice as constant and inevitable, for "No man can, at the same time, fill his cup from the source and from the mouth of the Nile" (chap. 29). But no choice on earth can ever be truly final, and life itself is only "a state which we know to be transient and probatory" (chap. 47) in which we prepare ourselves for the only choice that matters, "the choice of eternity" (chap. 48).

The problem is not that choices are hard to make—on the contrary, one cannot help making them—but that one choice is never clearly preferable to another. So the tale ends by endorsing a simple commitment to movement without goal, a ruefully comic version of the torrent of fate in *The Vanity of Human Wishes*. "To be driven along the stream of life," Carey McIntosh says, "implies a commitment to life, to friendship, travel and talk, learning, variety; implies also an acceptance of 'continual flux' as a condition of existence."[10] Such a description reminds one very much of Johnson's own life, punctuated by unpredictable decisions but sustained by a steady current of friendship and intellectual inquiry. But there is also a somber side to Johnson's awareness that these satisfactions, because of their mutability, are poignantly incomplete. When the old man is asked for the fruits of a lifetime's experience he replies simply, "I rest against a tree, and consider, that in the same shade I once disputed upon the annual overflow of the Nile with a friend who is now silent in the grave" (chap. 45). And he dismisses the value of reputation—"I have neither mother to be delighted with the reputation of her son, nor wife to partake the honours of her husband"—exactly as Johnson dismissed his great *Dictionary* with "frigid tranquillity" because "most of those whom I wished to please have sunk into the grave, and success and miscarriage are empty sounds."[11]

In itself this is traditional Christian *contemptus mundi* in the Augustinian tradition: "That City, in which it has been promised that we shall reign, differs from this earthly city as widely as the sky from the earth, life eternal from temporal joy, substantial glory from empty praises, the society of angels from the society of men, the light of the Maker of the sun and moon from the light of the sun and moon."[12] But there is an important difference. Augustine believed that the whole of human history was a systematic enactment of God's plan, and writers of fiction, well into Johnson's lifetime, took it for granted that art should mirror that structure of meaning. The narrative voice of *Rasselas* might seem to have close affinities with that of *Tom Jones:* they share a taste for sententious wisdom mediated in an ironic style and for the playful juxtaposition of instructive incidents. But whereas *Tom Jones* glories in form, in a finely tuned coherence that exhibits its author's mastery and mirrors the mastery of the Creator, Johnson resolutely refuses to allow fable to embody form. The resemblances to *Tristram Shandy* are not accidental; despite his Augustan qualities, Johnson belongs to the later period that rests uneasily between the grand mythopoeic gestures of the Renaissance and of romanticism, a period—like our own—of profound doubt as to the power of imagination to master reality. For Johnson there can be no adequate "concord fictions" that reconcile us to our fate.[13]

When the New Critics were still gigantic it was common to accuse Johnson of not knowing the difference between art and life: his mimetic assumptions prevented him from appreciating the poem as heterocosm, literature as closed system, disinterested contemplation as preferable to interested moralizing. But nowadays, when we are more willing than the New Critics to admit the wish-fulfilling gratifications of art, one might almost reverse the judgment and say that Johnson insists on the gulf between art and life. Art is a kind of delusion, a substitute for reality and often an illicit improvement upon it.[14] It is notable that in modern theory, romance has increasingly gained stature as the model of fictive invention. If the work of art is indeed a self-reflexive heterocosm, that is because we prefer it, as Johnson would say, to "the bitterness of truth" (*Rasselas,* chap. 44). Imagination, according to Bergson, is "a defensive reaction of nature against the representation by intelligence of the inevitability of death."[15] Johnson will not allow that inevitability to be evaded. As he wrote in a bleak letter of consolation, "Whether to see life as it is will give us much consolation I know not, but the consolation which is drawn from truth, if any there be, is solid and durable, that which may be derived from errour must be like its original fallacious and fugitive."[16]

Romance is above all an evasion or conquest of death. Perdita is not lost as her name seems to suggest, and the statue of the dead Hermione warms miraculously into life. But here precisely is the difficulty in interpreting *Rasselas*. Its deepest theme is the primacy of lived experience, but the ironic distancing of the apologue forbids any actual dramatization of this theme, and the vehicle is therefore in constant opposition to its tenor. Frye shrewdly notes that *Rasselas* resembles romances of the type in which "the dreamer is, so to speak, a god in relation to his dreamed self: he created him but remains in the background watching."[17] Writing just at the moment of his mother's death, perhaps the most disturbing event in his entire emotional life, Johnson indulges in *Rasselas* the fantasy of being a spectator of life and of being spared its irrevocable sorrows. But he permits Imlac, in his tender remarks to the distraught Nekayah, to touch on the dreaded theme, and we know from his other writings how fearlessly he normally confronted it. "For sorrow there is no remedy provided by nature; it is often occasioned by accidents irreparable, and dwells upon objects that have lost or changed their existence; it requires what it cannot hope, that the laws of the universe should be repealed; that the dead should return, or the past should be recalled" (*Rambler* 47).

In its ironic anti-romance *Rasselas* has obvious affinities with *Candide*, that sustained parody or subversion of plot in which murdered characters keep returning inexplicably from the dead. But an even more interesting comparison can be made with Voltaire's other great fable *Zadig*, whose folk-tale conventions lead up to the wry revelation of the angel Jesrad. *If* an angel in disguise could conduct us through the bewildering flux of life, *then* we might see Providence at work. But the revelation remains playful and hypothetical, and elicits the same kind of faith that the reader might give to an eloquent fairy story. No doubt *Zadig* would have seemed frivolous to Johnson, since it plays fast and loose with the problem of belief. But he inhabits the same world as Voltaire: he does not attempt to ground the "choice of eternity" in doctrine or to demonstrate its results. It is enough to lead the reader to see the futility of sententious wisdom, even when genuinely wise, and to challenge him to enter the world of experience that no fiction can adequately represent. We await eternity, but in this life we cannot know it, as is obvious if one compares Addison's optimistic Vision of Mirzah in *Spectator* 159 with Johnson's much darker imitation in *Rambler*

102. Addison emphasizes the paradise that lies at the end of life's journey, Johnson the irresistible current that carries us onward through "so thick a mist, that the most perspicacious eye could see but a little way."

The ultimate lesson of *Rasselas,* then, is not an aphorism or argument or doctrine, but a recognition of the radical disjunction between fiction and truth, time and eternity. If on the one hand it refuses to be a concord fiction, on the other hand it also refuses to be an allegory pointing clearly beyond itself to some atemporal realm of value, the primal state of myth. Man is immersed in the stream of time and cannot fight free of it until he passes that bourne from which no traveler returns. But since Johnson's theme is that *we ourselves* must be immersed and that no fictional invention can substitute for immersion, he refuses to let his imaginary characters enter the world of experience; they remain a party of mild Houyhnhnms gazing at Cairo with great unblinking eyes.

In his own career Johnson continued to be a moralist, but there were no more *Ramblers* and no more works of fiction. Increasingly his best work was dependent on subtle interpretation of data external to itself: vexed points in Shakespeare's plays, life in the Highlands, the rich complex puzzles of human biography. It cannot be irrelevant, as W. J. Bate has pointed out, that the decade of the *Ramblers* and *Rasselas* issued in Johnson's most serious mental breakdown.[18] And the *Rambler* itself contains plenty of hints that imaginary fictions are its author's own deepest temptation. "Many impose upon the world, and many upon themselves, by an appearance of severe and exemplary diligence, when they, in reality, give themselves up to the luxury of fancy, please their minds with regulating the past, or planning out the future; place themselves at will in varied situations of happiness, and slumber away their days in voluntary visions" (*Rambler* 89). Or as Imlac says in diagnosing the astronomer's illness, "To indulge the power of fiction, and send imagination out upon the wing, is often the sport of those who delight too much in silent speculation" (*Rasselas,* chap. 44).

The solution must lie in an escape from fiction. Johnson concludes in *Rambler* 89 that our best hope rests in "that interchange of thoughts which is practised in free and easy conversation," and there is a sense in which Boswell's *Life of Johnson* contains the heart of his later experience. Edward Said has written of the way in which the formal "vocation" gave way to the less unified "career."[19] Johnson, by contrast with Milton or Gibbon or Wordsworth, is the very type of the writer whose works reflect a miscellaneous career rather than a coherent mission. He loves conversation as an art form because it calls for improvisation rather than structure, allows him to respond to real people instead of mental inventions, and authorizes a paradoxical intensification of form: Johnson's speech has more structure than that of other men, whereas his writing has less. No wonder he welcomed Boswell's collaboration. The great conversations, in which wisdom springs from immediate contexts and is communicated to living people, are among his most characteristic works.

But behind all the wisdom, as the old man insists at the end of *Rasselas*, is the radical isolation of human beings. "A thousand miseries make silent and invisible inroads on mankind, and the heart feels innumerable throbs, which never break into complaint. Perhaps, likewise, our pleasures are for the most part equally secret, and most are borne up by some private satisfaction, some internal consciousness, some latent hope, some peculiar prospect, which they never communicate, but reserve for solitary hours, and clandestine meditation" (*Rambler* 68). And if this is true, then the moralist must finally withdraw into himself, abjure preaching and fiction alike, and implore the reader to do for himself what no dead author, however great, can do for him. "I am Pontanus, beloved by the powers of literature, admired by men of worth, and dignified by the monarchs of the world. Thou knowest now who I am, or more properly who I was. For thee, stranger, I who am in darkness cannot know thee, but I intreat thee to know thyself" (*Rambler* 28). The author of *Rasselas* still speaks to us in the *Lives of the Poets* and in Boswell's *Life*, but he never wrote another *Rasselas*.

NOTES

1. See Irvin Ehrenpreis, "*Rasselas* and Some Meanings of Structure in Literary Criticism," *Novel* 14 (1981): 101–17.

2. Emrys Jones, "The Artistic Form of *Rasselas*," *RES*, n.s., 18 (1967): 387–401; Patrick O'Flaherty, "Dr. Johnson as Equivocator: The Meaning of *Rasselas*," *MLQ* 31 (1970): 195–208.

3. Sheldon Sacks, *Fiction and the Shape of Belief* (Berkeley and Los Angeles: University of California Press, 1967), chap. 1. His approach is anticipated by Gwin J. Kolb, "The Structure of *Rasselas*," *PMLA* 66 (1951): 698–717.

4. All quotations are from Samuel Johnson, *The History of Rasselas, Prince of Abissinia*, ed. Geoffrey Tillotson and Brian Jenkins (London: Oxford University Press, 1971); here, from chap. 35.

5. Sacks, *Fiction*, 55; Sheridan Baker, "*Rasselas:* Psychological Irony and Romance," *PQ* 45 (1966): 250–51.

6. Northrop Frye, *Anatomy of Criticism* (Princeton: Princeton University Press, 1957), 200.

7. Letter to George and Georgiana Keats, 14 February–3 May 1819.

8. See Mary Lascelles, "*Rasselas:* A Rejoinder," *RES*, n.s., 21 (1970): 52.

9. Earl Wasserman, "Johnson's *Rasselas:* Implicit Contexts," *JEGP* 74 (1975): 1–25.

10. Carey McIntosh, *The Choice of Life: Samuel Johnson and the World of Fiction* (New Haven: Yale University Press, 1973), 198.

11. Preface to the *Dictionary*, final sentence.

12. Augustine, *The City of God*, trans. Henry Bettenson (Harmondsworth: Penguin Books: 1972), 206.

13. Frank Kermode's phrase, in *The Sense of an Ending: Studies in the Theory of Fiction* (London: Oxford University Press, 1967), 59.

14. See the passages discussed in Leopold Damrosch, Jr., *The Uses of Johnson's Criticism* (Charlottesville: University Press of Virginia, 1976), 137.

15. Henri Bergson, *Les deux sources de la morale et de la religion* (Paris: F. Alcan, 1932), 137.

16. To Bennet Langton, 21 September 1758, in *The Letters of Samuel Johnson*, ed. R. W. Chapman (Oxford: Clarendon Press, 1952), 1:111.

17. Northrop Frye, *The Secular Scripture: A Study of the Structure of Romance* (Cambridge, Mass.: Harvard University Press, 1976), 106–7.

18. Walter Jackson Bate, *The Achievement of Samuel Johnson* (New York: Oxford University Press, 1961), 151.

19. Edward Said, *Beginnings: Intention and Method* (Baltimore: Johns Hopkins University Press, 1975), 227.

13

Johnsonian Prospectuses and Proposals

J. D. Fleeman

One difficulty facing the publisher of a new book is the estimation of the potential sale of the work. Beginning in the seventeenth century this problem was partly resolved by advertising the work in advance and by inviting subscriptions. The subscriptions helped in deciding on the size of the edition and contributed toward the cost of production. Preliminary announcements in the form of *Proposals* for publication by subscription appeared as printed sheets advertising the intended title, setting forth the conditions of purchase and the price, and usually bearing some kind of notice designed to attract the interest of potential buyers. The conditions often favored the subscriber with a slightly reduced price, usually in two installments: generally one half on subscribing, the second on receipt of the finished work.

Further safeguards for an uncertain investment could be secured by publishing the work in parts, either weekly or over some longer period. Publication by subscription is frequently associated with part publication, and several of the works announced in Johnson's Proposals were so published.

It was perhaps inevitable that some undertakers should see in the raising of subscriptions a ready means of defrauding the public. Sir John Hawkins described the practice of the unhappy Samuel Boyse:

> The miseries of confinement did not teach him discretion: he was released, but his wants were little abated, and he made use of the most disgraceful arts to excite charity: he sometimes raised subscriptions for non-existent poems, and sometimes employed his wife to give out that he was dying.[1]

It was, no doubt, his suspicion of this kind of behavior that so outraged the Earl of Bristol in 1737.[2]

Publication by subscription was a common procedure for minor writers whose names could not assure sales, but whose work might nevertheless catch the current taste. Of all those whose careers began in Grub Street Samuel Johnson is perhaps the best known, and he was no exception in offering some of his works to the public in this manner; and not only his own works, but since he was a professional writer, those of other writers too.

The terms *proposal* and *prospectus* are not always distinguished, but it seems that proposals were those publications which specifically invited subscriptions while offering terms and conditions of publication, whereas prospectus is more of a generic term for the whole range of announcements of intended publications. In the following list are several items that do not invite subscriptions and that should be regarded as prospectuses (nos. 10, 14, 21, 24, and 28). The remainder are proposals, though since some are not yet known to survive their exact nature remains uncertain.

This list attempts to bring together the available information on prospectuses and proposals with which Johnson may have been concerned. Many have been well known since his own day, and certainly since 1791, for Boswell made great efforts to track down Johnsonian ephemera:

> What an expense, Sir, do you put us to in buying books, to which you have written Prefaces or Dedications.[3]

Two of the following items derive directly from Boswell himself (nos. 27 and 29), and later bibliographers have added to the total. The fullest list hitherto published was compiled by the late Albert Ehrman and Graham Pollard in their Roxburghe Club book, *The Distribution of Books by Catalogue* (1965).[4]

Notes

1. Sir John Hawkins, *The Life of Samuel Johnson*, 2d ed. (London, 1787), 160.
2. See item no. 2 in the List of prospectuses and proposals.
3. *Boswell's Life of Johnson*, ed. G. B. Hill, rev. L. F. Powell (Oxford: Clarendon Press, 1934–64), 2:224–25. Hereafter cited as *Life*.
4. Privately printed for the Roxburghe Club, 196–97. Descriptions have been kept short, and details of the conditions offered to subscribers have been abbreviated and formalized. Each item is dated when the original carries a date, but when the date is extracted from newspapers or other sources it is enclosed in brackets. In the record of copies, the holdings of libraries and collections in the United States precedes those recorded in Britain. The following abbreviated references have been used throughout.

Courtney	W. P. Courtney, *A Bibliography of Samuel Johnson* (Oxford: Clarendon Press, 1915; reissued 1925).
GM	*The Gentleman's Magazine*, London, 1731 to date.
Hazen	A. T. Hazen, *Johnson's Prefaces and Dedications* (New Haven: Yale University Press, 1937).

Letters   R. W. Chapman, ed., *The Letters of Samuel Johnson* (Oxford: Clarendon Press, 1952), 3 vols.
Rothschild   *The Rothschild Catalogue* (Cambridge: privately printed, 1954), 2 vols.
Sledd & Kolb J. H. Sledd and G. J. Kolb, *Dr. Johnson's Dictionary* (Chicago: University of Chicago Press, 1955).
Supp.   R. W. Chapman and A. T. Hazen, "A Supplement to Courtney," *Oxford Bibliographical Society Proceedings* 5 (1939).
Tinker   *The Tinker Library*, comp. R. F. Metzdorf (New Haven: Yale University Library, 1959).
Wiles   R. M. Wiles, *Serial Publication in England before 1750* (Cambridge: Cambridge University Press, 1957).

LOCATION SYMBOLS

Symbols for American libraries are those of the National Union Catalogue of the Library of Congress; for British libraries symbols have been invented on similar principles.

AAH   Arthur A. Houghton, Esq.
ANLW   National Library of Wales, Aberystwyth
BM   British Museum
BmP   Birmingham Reference Library
BSB   Basil S. Barlow, Esq.
CLU-C   William Andrews Clark Memorial Library, Los Angeles
CPc   Pembroke College, Cambridge
CSmH   Huntington Library
CTc   Trinity College, Cambridge
CTc(R)   Rothschild Collection
CtY   Yale University
CU   Cambridge University Library
DFo   Folger Shakespeare Library
DLC   Library of Congress
DmD   Durham University
ENLS   National Library of Scotland, Edinburgh
GM   Mitchell Library, Glasgow
GU   Glasgow University
HBM   H. Bradley Martin, Esq.
HWL   Herman W. Liebert, Esq.
Hyde   Hyde Collection, New Jersey
ICN   Newberry Library, Chicago
ICU   University of Chicago
IU   University of Illinois
LU(S)   Sterling Collection, London University
LVA   Victoria and Albert Museum
MB   Boston Public Library

MC   Central Library, Manchester
MCh   Chetham's Library, Manchester
MH   Harvard University
MiU   University of Michigan
MU   Manchester University
NCU   University of North Carolina
NdNC   Newcastle-upon-Tyne Public Library
NIBQU   Queen's University, Belfast
NjP   Princeton University
NPM   Pierpont Morgan Library
NRo   University of Rochester
O   Bodleian Library, Oxford
O(JJ)   John Johnson Collection, Bodleian Library
OASc   All Souls' College, Oxford
OPc   Pembroke College, Oxford
OWc   Worcester College, Oxford
PHi   Historical Society of Pennsylvania
PPRF   Rosenbach Foundation, Philadelphia
AGR   Arthur G. Rippey, Esq.
RHT   Robert H. Taylor, Esq.
SSL   William Salt Library, Stafford
TxU   University of Texas
ViU   University of Virginia
YM   York Minster
YwLB   Brotherton Library, Leeds University

JOHNSONIAN PROSPECTUSES AND PROPOSALS

1. The Latin Poems of Politian   [5 August 1734]

   Angeli Politiani Poemata Latina, quibus, Notas cum historia Latinae poeseos, a Petrarchae aevo ad Politiani tempora deducta, et vita Politiani fusius quam antehac enarrata, addidit SAM. JOHNSON.

   30 sheets 8°; 2*s.* − 6*d.* + 2*s.* − 6*d.*

   The work was never published.

   Hawkins, 26–27; *Life,* 1:89–90.

   Dated from an entry in Johnson's *Annales:* "Augusti 5to 1734. Conditiones edendi Politiani Poemata emisi."

   No copy known.

2. Henry Hervey's Collection of Poems   [October 1737]

   "You could not be more surprized and offended than I was at your brother Harry's beggarly project of printing by subscription his collection of poems, the very first notice of which I received from his brother Charles, to whom he sent a large bundle of proposals and signed receipts for him to dispose of, which I no sooner saw then I expressed that just indignation at which so mean and mercenary a scheme deserved . . . that . . . an immediate stop might be putt to it before it became more publick" (Lord Bristol to Lord Hervey, 17 October 1737, *Letter Books of John Hervey, First Earl of Bristol* [Suffolk Green Books, 1894], 2:1044).

   The work was never published, but two quarto volumes of Henry Hervey's compositions in MS are in the Record Office at Bury St. Edmunds. In his will he bequeathed "To John Crawley of co.Beds., Esq; my MS book of Miscellaneous Poems bound in red Turkey leather" (A. L. Reade, *Johnsonian Gleanings* [London: Privately printed, 1928], 5:246); and a similar volume is described in the catalogue of the sale of the library of Sir Henry Bunbury at Sotheby's 2 July 1896, lot 152: "MS Hervey Aston. Several Original Compositions in Prose and Verse 1746. MS neatly written, red morocco inlaid in blue, gilt, &c. inscribed round monogram in centre 'The gift of Henry Aston to Emily Bunbury.'"

Johnson came up to London in March 1737 and renewed his old friendship with Hervey (*Life,* 1:106, 532). His contribution to these proposals is conjectural.

No copy known.

3. Sarpi's *History of the Council of Trent*   11 October 1738

Proposals for Printing the History of the Council of Trent, Translated from the Italian of Father Paul Sarpi; With the Author's Life, and Notes Theological, Historical and Critical, from the French Edition of Dr Le Courayer; To which are added Observations on the History and Notes. By S. Johnson . . . Subscriptions are taken in by Mr. Dodsley in Pall-Mall, Mr. Rivington in St Paul's Church-yard, by E. Cave at St. John's Gate, and the Translator.

4° π², pp. *1* Title and Conditions, *2* blank, with receipt form at foot, *3–4* Specimen.

200 sheets, 2 vols. 4°: 10*s.* − 6*d.* + 10*s.* − 6*d.* vol. I, + 15*s.* vol. II; or 18*s.* per vol. 2*d.* abated for each sheet less than 200; Large Paper in 3 vols. £3 − 3*s.*

The work was never published, but Johnson's *Life of Sarpi* appeared in *GM* 7 (November 1738): 581–83.

Courtney 9; *Life,* 1:135; J.A.V. Chapple in *Bulletin of the John Rylands Library* 45 (1963): 340–69.

Copy: MU (Spec. Coll. 824.63/q.D.25).

4. Robert James's *Medicinal Dictionary*   24 June 1741

Proposals for Printing a Medicinal Dictionary; Designed as a Body of Physic and Surgery. Both with Regard to Theory and Practice. Compiled from the Best Writers Ancient and Modern: with Useful Observations. Illustrated with Copper Plates. By R. James, M.D. To be printed according to the following Conditions By the Society of Booksellers for Promoting Learning . . . Gentlemen . . . are desired to subscribe their Names (or to send Orders so to do) in a Book kept for that Purpose by James Crokatt, at the said Society's Office, near St. Bride's Church in Fleetstreet; or to T. Osborn, Bookseller in Gray's Inn, Holborn.

2° π², pp. *1* Title, *2* Conditions (dated "June 24. 1741"), *3–4* Johnson's *A General Account of the Work.* press-figure 3 on p. *2.*

About 400 sheets, 2 vols 2°; 5 sheets per fortnight, 1*s.*

The *Dictionary* was published in parts and in 3 folio vols., 1743–45. It was composed of 825½ sheets with 49 plates.

The Proposals were also printed on the blue paper wrappers of the individual parts of the *Dictionary* itself. The collation is the same as for the separate editions, but the conditions on some numbers bear the date "June 3. 1742" and Crokatt's address is given as "at the Black Horse, near St. Bride's."

> *Copies:* BM (777.1.1 (54), O (Rawl.J.4° .6.194–95, two copies of the second leaf only, pp. 3–4.) Blue-paper wrappers: O (Vet A.4.b.20*).

5. *Catalogue* of the Harleian Library   1 November 1742

Proposals for Printing, by Subscription, the Two First Volumes of Bibliotheca Harleiana: or, a Catalogue of the Library of the Late Earl of Oxford. Purchased by Thomas Osborne, Bookseller, in Gray's Inn.

2° π², pp. *1* Title, Conditions and receipt form, *2–3* Johnson's *An Account of the Harleian Library*, *4* Osborne's advertisements.

8° 30 sheets per vol.; 10*s.*, or 5*s.* + 5*s.*

The Catalogue was published altogether in 4 vols. 8°, 1743–44, with a fifth volume listing Osborne's old stock and some remainders from the first part, for this was a sale catalogue. Volumes 1–2 were issued in parts with five sheets in each part, price 1*s.* (*GM* 12 [November 1742]: 608), were published together on 1st March 1743, and were composed of 37¼ and 31½ sheets respectively.

Courtney 13; *Life,* 1 : 153; *Supp.* 125; *Hazen* 43; *Rothschild* 1220; *Wiles* 330.

A slightly different version of the proposals was published in the *London Evening Post,* 4 December 1742; the proposals and Johnson's *Account* were reprinted in *GM* 12 [December 1742]: 636–39, with an apology for a delay in publication, and in vol. 1 of the catalogue. A facsimile with notes by R. W. Chapman was published at the Clarendon Press in 1926.

> *Copies:* CtY (IIm.J637.742p), Hyde (ex R.H. Isham—H.L. Carlebach); CTc(R), MCh (Halliwell-Phillipps, 858), O (Antiq. b.E.1742/1).

6. The *Harleian Miscellany*   30 December 1743

Proposals for Printing, by Subscription, the Harleian Miscellany: or, a Collection of Scarce, Curious, and Entertaining Tracts and Pamphlets Found in the late Earl of Oxford's Library. Interspersed with Historical, Political, and Critical Notes. . . . Proposals at large, with an Account of this Undertaking, may be had of all Booksellers both in Town and Country; and of Jacob Robinson, Publisher, on Ludgate-Hill, where Subscriptions are taken in.

(a) 4° π², pp. *1* Title and Conditions, *2–3* Johnson's *An Account of this Undertaking, 4* blank.

6 sheets 1*s.* each Saturday. "they who think the Design worthy of their Encouragement, . . . favour the Proprietor Thomas Osborne, of Gray's Inn, Bookseller, with their Names, and Places of Abode. The first Number will be published on Saturday the 24th March, 1743–4."

Copy: MCh (Halliwell-Phillipps 770).

(b) 2° π², pp. *1.* Title, Conditions, and Johnson's *Account, 2* List of Contents of the Miscellany, *3* List of Subscribers, *4* Osborne's advertisements for *The Modern Husbandman.*

"they who think the Design worthy of their Encouragement . . . favour the Proprietor, Thomas Osborne, of Gray's Inn, Bookseller, or J. Robinson, on Ludgate-hill, with their Names, and Places of Abode. The first Number was published on Saturday the 24th of March, 1743–4."

Copies: CtY (*Tinker* 1295, ex R. H. Isham = IIm. J637.743p), Hyde (ex R. B. Adam, lacking 2d leaf); O (MS Carte 114 f.537–8).

The copy formerly owned by Jerome Kern (Anderson Galleries, 7 January 1929, lot 748a, *illus.*) is untraced, but it lacked the second leaf; another copy owned by the Duke of Devonshire was reported in *The Times Literary Supplement* 9 September 1939, 532. Philip Bliss's copy (Sotheby, 28 June 1858, lot 2026) was bound in a copy of the *Harleian Miscellany* and was bought by Booth for £4–18*s.*

(c) 2° π², (Blue paper wrappers to individual parts of James's *Medicinal Dictionary,* 1743–45), pp. *1* Title, Conditions, Johnson's *Account,* and advertisements for *Carribeana, 2* List of Contents of the Miscellany, *3* List of Subscribers, *4* Osborne's advertisements for *The Modern Husbandman.*

[Conditions as (b) above]: ". . . or J. Robinson, at the Golden Lion in Ludgate Street. . . ."

Copies: O (Vet A.4.b.20*).

(d) 4° π^2, (Blue paper wrapper to individual parts of the *Harleian Miscellany*), pp. *1* Title, Contents, and advertisements, *2–3* blank inner pages of wrappers, *4* Conditions, and Johnson's *Account.*

[Conditions as (b) above]: ". . . favour the Proprietor, Thomas Osborne, of Gray's Inn, Bookseller, with their Names, and Places of Abode."

Copy: O(JJ) (b.108a).

(e) 4° π^2, (Blue paper wrappers to individual part of John Smith's *Memoirs of Wool*, 16 January 1744–45), pp. *1–2* account of Smith's work, *3* Advertisement for part 9 of vol. 4 of the *Harleian Miscellany*, *4* Johnson's *Account.*

Copy: O(JJ) (b.112).

The Miscellany was published in 8 vols. 4°, 1744–46, with a second edition of vol. 1 only in 1753.

Courtney 15; *Supp.* 126–27; *Hazen* 50–52; *Wiles* 339; G. J. Kolb in *Papers of the Bibliographical Society of America* 48 (1954): 196–98.

The distinction of copies with or without the names of subscribers is of no significance save to mark the perfection of a copy. Kolb's textual argument is not supported in any of the above versions. The proposals were also printed as a final leaf to vol. 13 of *GM* 1743, in vol. 3 of *Catalogus Bibliothecae Harleianae*, pp. *1, 2–8,* and in the *London Evening Post,* 19 April 1744.

7. The Publisher   24 September 1744

Proposals for Printing every Fortnight, (Price Sixpence) The Publisher: containing Miscellanies in Prose and Verse. Collected by J. Crockatt, Bookseller.

2° π1, pp. *1* Title, Johnson's *Account of the Design,* Conditions, and list of coffee-houses where subscriptions and communications may be sent, *2* blank.

8°, 3 sheets, 6*d.* every fortnight; "The first Number to be published in November next."

Four parts only of the *Publisher* appeared, December 1744 to March 1745.

Life, 1 : xiv *n.; Supp.* 129; *Hazen* 193–95; *Rothschild* 1222.

Johnson's *Account* was reprinted as a preface to no.1 of the *Publisher.* A facsimile of the *Proposals* was published by R. W. Chapman at the Clarendon Press, 1930.

Copy: CTc(R).

8. Grey's Debates of the House of Commons [March 1745]

Proposals for Publishing the Debates of the House of Commons from the Year 1667 to the Year 1694. Collected by the Honourable Anchitell Grey, Esq;

GM 15 (March 1745): 135–42; (August 1745): 448; and n.s., 1(1856): 677 note c.

The March notice announced: "If it should be desired by a sufficient number of subscribers, part of the impression shall be printed in two volumes in folio." Apologies for the delay occasioned by the slowness of subscriptions appeared in May (226), July (338). The August notice stated that the proposals were "Just published" and gave details of the conditions:

8°, 10 vols., £2–10*s.:* £1–1*s.* + £1–9*s.*

The *Debates* were published in 10 vols. 8° in 1763. (See no. 24 below.)

Courtney 19.

No separate copy known.

9. A New Edition of Shakespear [April 1745]

Proposals for Printing a New Edition of the Plays of William Shakespear, with Notes Critical and Explanatory, in which the Text will be corrected: the Various Readings remarked: the Conjectures of former Editors examin'd, and their Omissions supply'd. By the Author of the Miscellaneous Observations on the Tragedy of Macbeth. . . . Subscriptions are taken in, and Receipts signed by E. Cave at St John's Gate; and by the Editor.

2° π1, pp. *1* Title, Conditions, and Specimen opening (pp. 11–12) of two pages of an annotated text of *Macbeth* 3.2.1–28, 2 blank.

[12°], 10 vols. £1–5*s.* in sheets; 10*s.* − 6*d.* + 14*s.* − 6*d.*

The projected edition was stifled by Tonson's threat of legal action (Giles E. Dawson, "The Copyright of Shakespeare's Dramatic Works," *Studies in Honour of A.H.R. Fairchild* [1946]: 11–35).

Courtney 18 (with facsimile in 1925, 1968 issues), *Life,* 1 : 175; *Supp.* 129; *Rothschild* 1225; C.W. Hart in *Modern Language Notes* 53 (1938): 367–68.

Published with Johnson's *Miscellaneous Observations on the Tragedy of Macbeth,* 1745, as a final inserted leaf, folded to fit the 12° size of that pamphlet; sometimes also found separately and perhaps so issued.

> *Copies:* (with *Misc. Observations*): CtY, DFo, HWL, Hyde, MB, MiU, PPRF, RHT, TxU; BM(Ashley), CTc(R), LVA (Dyce 5278, with note that the *Proposals* are an insertion), OPc, OWc; (as separate leaf): DFo; O, O(JJ).

10. Johnson's *Dictionary of the English Language*   [August] 1747

The Plan of a Dictionary of the English Language; Addressed to the Right Honourable Philip Dormer, Earl of Chesterfield; One of His Majesty's Principal Secretaries of State. London: Printed for J. and P. Knapton, T. Longman and T. Shewell, C. Hitch, A. Millar, and R. Dodsley.

(a) 4° π1 A–D⁴ E1, pp. *i* Title, *ii* Erratum, 1–34 Johnson's *Plan.*

This first issue is most readily distinguished by the presence of the drop-head title on p. 1 which bears the words: "To the Right Honourable Philip Dormer, Earl of Chesterfield; One of his Majesty's Principal Secretaries of State. My Lord, . . . &c." It is commonly called the "Chesterfield" state.

A facsimile of this issue was published by the Scolar Press in 1970.

> *Copies:* CtY (Tinker), Hyde (ex R.B. Adam), HWL, MH (Widener); BM (11630 e 10/8), BSB, CTc(R), NdNC (423.81297).

(b) 4° π1 A⁴ (± A⁴) B–D⁴ E1, pp. *i* Title, *ii* Erratum, 1–34 *Plan.*

In this second issue the first whole sheet has been canceled, and all the letterpress on p. 1 before "My Lord . . ." has been removed, leaving a noticeable blank space. There are other minor variants between the two, resulting from the resetting of the type for sig. A (see *Sledd & Kolb,* 80) which help to determine the priority of the two versions. For obvious reasons this issue is denominated the "Non-Chesterfield" state.

> *Copies:* AAH, CLU-C, CSmH, CtY³, DFo, DLC, HWL², Hyde³, ICN, ICU, IU, MH², NCU², NjP, NPM, NRo, PHi, PPRF, ViU; ANLW, BM³, BmP, CPc, CTc, CTc(R)², CU, ENLS², LU(S), LVA, O, OASc, OPc, YM.

This pamphlet neither solicits subscriptions nor offers conditions, but it is nevertheless a detailed account of a projected work, published with an eye to arousing public interest.

The *Dictionary* was published in 2 vols. 2° in April 1755.

Courtney 20; *Life,* 1:182ff.; *Supp.* 130, *Rothschild* 1228–30; *Sterling* 502; *Tinker* 1301; R. W. Chapman in *RES* 2 (1926): 216–18; R. F. Metzdorf in *The Library* xix (1938): 198–201, 363; *Sledd & Kolb,* 78–82; R. C. Alston, *Bibliography of the English Language* 5 (1966): 361 (recording 8 further copies).

In view of the relative scarcity of copies *(a)* it is possible that the cancellation of sig. A was effected at an early stage in the publication of the work.

For the 2d edition, see no. 14 below.

11. William Lauder's Edition of Grotius's *Adamus Exsul*

[5 September 1747]

Proposals for Printing by Subscription Hugonis Grotii Adamus Exsul, Tragoedia: With an English Version, and the lines imitated from it by Milton subjoined to the pages. By William Lauder, A.M. . . . Subscriptions are taken in by Mr. Davidson, in the Poultry; Mr. Vaillant, in the Strand; Mr Cave, at St John's gate; and by the Editor.

8°(¼) π1, pp. π1ʳ (2 pages side by side) *1* Title and Conditions, *1–2* Johnson's *Account;* π1ᵛ (2pp.) *3* Latin text of *Adamus Exsul* 1.1.1–16, *4* English version in parallel.

5*s.*: 2*s.* − 6*d.* + 2*s.* − 6*d.*

The *Adamus Exsul* was not published separately, but parts of it (with interpolations by Lauder) were quoted in his *Essay on Milton,* 1750, and used by Lauder to support his argument that Milton was a plagiarist.

Johnson's advertisement was reprinted in *GM* 17 (August 1747): 404, and again as the Preface to Lauder's *Essay* with some additional matter, probably by Lauder.

Courtney 36; *Life,* 1:230; *Supp.* 130; *Hazen* 78–82.

Copy: BM (11822 p. 1).

12. Charlotte Lennox's *Poems?*   [1749–52]

In William Strahan's Printing Ledger (British Library: Add MS 48800 f.72ᵛ) is the following entry:

Messrs Payne & Bouquet   £   s.   d.

1749

Octr. 1000 Proposals for Mrs Lennox, with paper   — 15 —

Mrs. Lennox had published her *Poems on Several Occasions. Written by a Young Lady,* 8° in 1747, but she issued proposals for printing by subscription, Poems on Several Occasions, in November 1752, which were also recorded by Strahan (Ledger, f.83ᵛ):

Mr Andrew Millar   £   s.   d.

1752

Novr. Proposals for Mrs Lennox, No 500   7   6.

It seems probable that the 1749 proposals were for an equally abortive venture.

Johnson made Mrs. Lennox's acquaintance about this time, and it is possible that he assisted in the writing of these proposals; he was certainly involved with her in some literary project (D. E. Isles, "The Lennox Collection," *Harvard Library Bulletin* 18 [1970]: 334–35.)

Johnson's part in the proposals remains conjectural.

No copy known.

13. Anna Williams's *Essays in Verse and Prose*   25 September 1750

Proposals for printing by Subscription, Essays in Verse and Prose. By Anna Williams. . . . Subscriptions are taken in by Mr Dodsley in Pall-Mall; Mr Robinson in Maidenlane, Covent-Garden; Mess.Payne & Bouquet in Paternoster-row; and E.Cave at St John's Gate.

1 vol. 8°, 5s. (2s. − 6d. + 2s. − 6d.) "in blue paper."

GM 20 (September 1750): p. "423."

The work was eventually published in 4° in 1766 (see no. 25 below).

Courtney 112; *Life,* 2:479; *Hazen* 213.

No separate copy known.

14. Johnson's *Dictionary of the English Language*   [April 1755]

The Plan of a Dictionary of the English Language; Addressed to the Right Honourable Philip Dormer, Earl of Chesterfield; One of His Majesty's Principal Secretaries of State. London: Printed for J. and P. Knapton, T. Longman and T. Shewell, C. Hitch, A. Millar, and R. Dodsley. MDCCXLVII.

$8°$ $\pi 1$ A–D^4 E^4 ($-$ E4 = $?\pi 1$), pp. i Title, ii blank, 1–37 Johnson's *Plan*, 38 blank.

Published with the *Dictionary* itself. Strahan's Ledger (British Library: Add MS 48802A f.10) records as part of the account for the whole work:

1755	£	s.	d.
April Reprinting y^e Plan, 2½ Sheets, No 1500 @£1:5:0	3	2	6

Sledd & Kolb, 82–83.

There are a few very slight press variants between copies, notably that the press-figure on A2^v (p. 4) may be 4 or 8.

> *Copies:* CSmH, CtY, HWL^2, Hyde^2, ICN, IU, MH, NjP, TxU^3; ANLW, BM^2, BSB, CTc^2, CU^2, DmD, GM, GU, MC (imperfect), O, YM, YwLB.

[Alston 5:361 records 6 more copies; see no. 10 above]

15. Johnson's *Dictionary,* second folio edition   [7 June 1755]

In Strahan's Ledger (British Library: Add MS 48800 f.97^v) is the entry for the second folio edition of Johnson's *Dictionary,* which includes the following:

Partners in Johnson's Dictionary D^{rs}	£	s.	d.
1755			
June Printing 5000 Proposals in Folio	3 –	8	– –
24000 D^o in Quarto @ 5s	6 –	– –	– –
250 Folio Titles to stick up		2–	6d.
50 Advertisements for Country Papers, with paper		5 –	–.

The ledger also records printing 50 reams of blue covers for the weekly parts, and it is probable that those wrappers bore advertisements and announcements and perhaps also reprints of the proposals (cf. nos. 4 and 6 above). Not a single item from Strahan's list is known to have survived.

The second folio edition of the *Dictionary* was published in sixpenny weekly numbers from June 1755, each number of three and four sheets alternately, or in shilling numbers of seven sheets each.

Sledd & Kolb, 112–13, 148.

Whether Johnson composed any announcement for these proposals is uncertain; no such notice appears in contemporary newspaper advertisements.

No copies are known of either the folio or the quarto proposals.

16. Charlotte Lennox's Translation of Sully's *Memoirs*   [September 1755]

In Strahan's Ledger (British Library: Add MS 48802A f.13ᵛ) is the following entry:

Partners in Sully's Memoirs	£	s.	d.
1755			
Sepr. Printing Dᵒ 211½ Sheets . . . &c.	179	7	– –
For 2000 Proposals for Dᵒ		15	– –

500 copies of the finished translation were published in 3 vols. 4° on 8 November 1755.

Hazen 110–16.

There is no list of subscribers in the published work, and it is possible that what Strahan described as "Proposals" were in fact only some kind of separate advertisements. Johnson's part in them is conjectured in the light of his known contribution of a Dedication to the work.

No copy known.

17. Johnson's edition of Shakespeare   1 June 1756

Proposals for Printing, by Subscription, the Dramatick Works of William Shakespeare, Corrected and Illustrated by Samuel Johnson. Subscriptions are taken in by J. and R. Tonson, in the Strand; J. Knapton, in Ludgate-Street; C. Hitch and L. Hawes, and M. and T. Longman, in Pater-noster-Row.

8° π⁴, pp. *1* Title, *2* Conditions, *3*, 4–8 Johnson's *Proposals*. 8 vols. 8°, £2–2*s*. (£1–1*s*. + £1–1*s*. in sheets).

The edition was published in 8 vols. 8° in October 1765.

Strahan's Ledger (British Library: Add MS 48802A f.20ᵛ) records printing 3,000 copies of the proposals in May 1756.

Courtney 78; *Life,* 1:318, 545; *Supp.* 140; *Rothschild* 1226–27; *Tinker* 1311.

A facsimile edited by R. W. Chapman was published at the Clarendon Press in 1923.

Signed receipts for the subscriptions are rare but examples are: CSmH (LO 9626), PPRF; O (G. A. Staffs. 4° 8, p. 487, but with the original signature cut away and a facsimile substituted).

Copies: CtY (Tinker: Im J637.756Pr), DFo (PR 2752.J5.1756), HBM, HWL, Hyde, ICN (ex L. H. Silver), RHT; BmP (559980), CU (Ddd 25.84/0), CTc (209 e.85.61/1), CTc(R)², NIBQU² (ex Thomas Percy), O (Don. e768), O(JJ) (imperfect: title leaf only, ex Thomas Percy), SSL. [Two or three more copies have passed through the salerooms and appeared in booksellers' catalogues during the past decade.]

18. Richard Rolt's *Dictionary of Trade and Commerce*   [January 1757]

In Strahan's Ledger (British Library: Add MS 48802A f.22ᵛ) is the following entry:

Partners in Rolt's Dictionary 1757	£	s.	d.
Janry Proposals for Dº in Numbers, Nº 16,000	4	10	— —.

The *Dictionary,* with a Preface by Johnson, was first published as a single folio in February 1756, and it was reissued with a cancel title in 1761. Strahan's account shows that an attempt was planned to dispose of the original stock (1,000 copies were printed), by issuing it in parts. Part 1 was advertised as published by the *London Chronicle,* 29 February–1 March 1757, but the scheme seems not to have continued beyond the first two numbers.

Hazen 199.

Johnson's connexion with the *Dictionary* is the only reason for supposing he might have been concerned with these proposals.

No copy known.

19. James Bennet's edition of Ascham   [December 1757]

Proposals for Printing by Subscription, the English Works of Roger Ascham, Preceptor to Queen Elizabeth. . . . With Notes and Observations, and the Author's Life. By Mr. James Bennet, Master of the Boarding-School at Hoddesdon in Hertfordshire. Subscriptions are taken in by R. and J. Dodsley, in Pall-Mall, and J. Newbery, in St. Paul's Church-Yard.

4º π², pp. *1* Title, 2 Conditions, and receipts form, 3 Johnson's *Advertisement, 4* blank.

1 vol. 4º about 50 sheets, 10*s.*–6*d.*

Strahan's Ledger (British Library: Add MS 48800 f. 86ᵛ) records this printing of the proposals:

1757	£	s.	d.
Decr. 24 Bennet's Proposals for Ascham's Works,			
No. 1000		15	— —.

Publication was delayed to "digest, and prepare for the Press, some Materials which have been communicated to the Editor by many learned Gentlemen." The edition eventually appeared in 1761. (See no. 22 below.)

Courtney 100; *Life,* 1:550–52; *Supp.* 141; *Hazen* 19–23.

The "Letters to Queen Elizabeth and others" that are included in the edition are not mentioned in these proposals, and it is likely that they formed the additional materials that held up publication. This, and the fact that the unique copy was sent by Bennet to the Duke of Newcastle on 7 March 1758, imply that the surviving copy is of the 1757 printing.

Copy: BM (Add MS 32878 f. 150).

20. Joseph Baretti's *Poems* [1758]

Proposals for Printing by Subscription, Le Poesie di Giuseppe Baretti. . . . Subscriptions are taken in by Messrs. Dodsley, in Pall-Mall; Mr Vaillant, in the Strand; and the Author, in Poland-Street, five Doors from the King's Arms.

4° π², pp. *1* Title, text of Johnson's advertisement, and conditions, *2,* 3–4 *Amor di Gloria, Oda,* as a specimen.

About 12,000 lines of verse, £1–1s.

The work was never published.

Strahan's Ledger (British Library: Add MS 48802A f.31) includes the following entry:

1758 Mr Baratti	£	s.	d.
Proposals for Poems n° 1000		15	— —
For a Ream of Royal Paper for D°	1	— —	— —
Receits N° 300 with Paper		7	– 6
	2	– 2	– 6.

Hazen 17–18.

Copies: CtY (Im J637. + A753); O (MS Bodl. Add. c.244/165).

21. John Newbery's *The World Displayed*   23 October 1759

> On the First of December next will be published, By J. Newbery, at the Bible and Sun in St. Paul's Church-Yard, in neat Pocket Volumes . . . illustrated and embellished with Variety of Maps. . . . The World Displayed; or, a Curious Collection of Voyages and Travels Selected from the Writers of all Nations. In which the Conjectures and Interpretations of Several vain Editors and Translators are expunged; Every Relation is made concise and plain, and the Divisions of Countries and Kingdoms are clearly and distinctly noted.

8° π1, pp. *1* Title, *1–2* Description of the work and the contents of vol. 1, 2 Johnson's address *To the Public.*

The World Displayed was published and republished from 1759 onwards in monthly volumes each of which seems to have been reprinted independently as demand required. The final set of 20 vols. 12° was commonly bound in 10 and in Newbery's "vellum manner." Few sets are wholly first editions, nor is it easy to determine what would constitute a completely first edition.

Hazen 216–17; S. Roscoe, *John Newbery and His Successors 1740–1814,* (London: Five Owls Press, 1974), A640(1).

Copy: O(JJ) (b.149).

22. Bennet's edition of Ascham   [August 1760]

Strahan's Ledger (British Library: Add MS 48800 f.120ᵛ) records a second edition of the proposals. (See no. 19 above.)

1760	£	s.	d.
Augst. Proposals for Ascham's Work			
No. 500 with Paper		17	–6.

The edition was published in a single 4° volume in January 1762, although the title bears the date "1761."

The presumption that the two versions of the Proposals do differ considerably, and that the later is larger, is enforced by the fact that Strahan's charge for 1,000 copies of the first edition was 15*s.* whereas for only 500 copies of the second he charged 17*s.* − 6*d.*

No copy known.

23. John Hoole's Translation of Tasso's *Jerusalem Delivered*   [April 1761]

In William Bowyer's Paper Stock Ledger (Bodleian MS Don b.4, f.175) the account for the printing of Hoole's translation of Tasso includes the following entry:

1761   Jerusalem Delivered, for Mr Hoole D[elivere]d to Mr Hoole 1500 Proposals (¼Sht) D^d to D° of the two first Sheets which were printed above the Number (by his order).

The translation of Tasso was published in 2 vols. 8° in June 1763.

Courtney 101; *Life,* 1:383; *Hazen* 62–63 (despite Johnson's encouragement of the venture, Hazen doubts his involvement in the Proposals).

C. Welsh, *A Bookseller of the Last Century* (1885), 237, reports that the Proposals were advertised in *The Public Ledger,* 10 April 1761.

Johnson was himself a subscriber to the work, and his copy is in the Hyde Collection; his part in the proposals remains conjectural.

No copy known.

24. Grey's Debates of the House of Commons   [?1762]

In the Beginning of May next, will be ready to deliver, In Ten Volumes, Octavo, Price Two Pounds Ten Shillings, in Sheets, The Debates of the House of Commons, From the Year 1667 to the Year 1694. (To which the Right Hon. the late and present Speakers, with many worthy Members, have been pleased to subscribe). Collected By the Hon. Anchitell Grey, Esq; who was Thirty Years Member for the Town of Derby, Chairman of several Committees, and decyphered Coleman's Letters for the Use of the House, Printed for Mess. Henry and Cave, at St John's Gate.

8° π1, pp. *1* Title, *1–2* Johnson's address *To the Public.*

The Debates were published in 10 vols. 8°, 1763.

Courtney 19. (See no. 8 above.)

The only known copy of this announcement bears the pencilled date "1762." The names of D. Henry and R. Cave appear in the imprint of the edition dated 1763, but when the *Debates* were reissued with cancel titles in 1769 the booksellers named in the imprint were T. Becket and P. A. DeHondt. This announcement therefore refers to the 1763 issue, and the date 1762 is probably correct.

Copy: O(JJ) (b.162).

25. Anna Williams's *Miscellanies in Prose and Verse*   [?1763]

Proposals for Printing by Subscription, Essays in Verse and Prose. By Anna Williams.

4° π², pp. *1* Title, Conditions, and receipt form, *2* Johnson's *Advertisement,* *3–4* The Petition, as a specimen.

1 vol. 4°, 5s.

The work was published as *Miscellanies in Prose and Verse*, 4°, in April 1766.

Life, 2:25; *Hazen* 213–14.

Strahan's Ledger (British Library: Add MS.48802A f.67) records the printing of the whole work:

	£	s.	d.
1766 Miss Williams			
March Poems 23½ Sheets N° 750 @ 14ˢ	16	9	–
Proposals for D° at Different times	1	1	–
For 37 R of Paper for D° @ 16/6	30	10	6
	48	0	6.

750 copies of 23½ sheets account for 34¼ reams of the 37; the remainder was presumably used for the proposals which, at ½ sheet each, implies 1,750 copies. The phrase "at different times" suggests there may be variant impressions, though the surviving copies are identical. (See no. 13 above.)

On 9 June 1759 Johnson wrote to Mrs. Montagu, "I am desired by Mrs Williams to sign receipts with her name for the subscribers which you have been pleased to procure" (*Letters*, 1:122, no. 132). Mrs. Carter wrote also to Mrs. Montagu on 8 July 1762, that "Poor Mrs Williams is endeavouring to get a subscription to some Essays which are to be published next spring, in the hopes of being able to buy an annuity. She had this scheme some time ago, and then I hear you were so good as to procure her several subscribers" (*Letters of Mrs Carter*, ed. M. Pennington [1817], 1:164). James Grainger wrote to Thomas Percy on 4 December 1766 and referred to the delay in the publication of the work, "I have not seen Miss Williams's Miscellany . . . I hope she had a numerous subscription. If I am not mistaken I subscribed a great many years ago" (J. Nichols et al., *Illustrations of the Literary History of the Eighteenth Century* [London: J. B. Nichols and Son], 7 (1848): 294). The two stages of the publication of the work are described in *Johnsonian Miscellanies*, ed. G. B. Hill (Oxford: Clarendon Press, 1897), 2:172–73, in the *Anecdotes* of Lady Phillipina Knight. Anna Williams got £150 for the work.

Johnson's letter of 12 February 1767 to Sir James Caldwell (*Letters*, 1:431) implies that the publication was not very successful and that efforts were then being made to involve members of the Irish book trade.

Copies: O(JJ)² (b.164, b.164a; both ex Thomas Percy, one lacking the receipt form, the other dated in MS "1763"; both annotated by Percy with names of subscribers).

26. Edward Lye's Saxon Dictionary   20 June 1767

Proposals for Printing a Dictionary, Anglo-Saxon and English. Also a Specimen of the Theology, Bequests, Grants, and Poetry of the Anglo-Saxons, Literally translated. . . . London. Printed for the Author, and sold by C. Marsh, at Charing-Cross, W. Owen at Temple-Bar, and G. Keith in Grace-Church-Street. M.DCC.LXVII.

4° π², pp. *1* Title, *2* Conditions, *3–4* Specimen.

One vol. 4°, in 4 parts, three monthly from time when subscribers number 200; 10*s.* − 6*d.* + 10*s.* − 6*d.* with 3d part; no more copies than subscribers.

Lye died 19 August 1767, and the undertaking devolved upon Owen Manning (1721–1801) who published new proposals in folio, dated January 1768, offering the work in 2 vols. folio, at 2½ guineas. The work was published in 2 folio vols. dated 1772 (Gough noted in his copy: "Vol.1. came out May 1st 1769"). The work was printed by Edmund Allen of Bolt Court, who was Johnson's friend and landlord during his residence there from March 1776 until his death.

Johnson advised Lye about the 1767 Proposals in his letter of 26 September 1765, but the advice is confined to details of the wording of the conditions, and unless there were proposals published earlier than June 1767, he seems to have had little to do with them. His name appeared among the subscribers as "Rev. *Samuel Johnson,* LL.D."

Letters, 1 : 176, 174.

Copy: O (Gough Saxon Lit. 217).

27. Charlotte Lennox's *Original Works*   14 February 1775

Proposals for Printing by Subscription, Dedicated to the Queen, A New and Elegant Edition, Enlarged and Corrected, of the Original Works of Mrs. Charlotte Lennox. . . . Subscriptions will be taken in, and Receipts delivered, by Mr. Dodsley, in Pall-mall; Mr. Becket, in The Adelphi; Mr. White, in Fleet-street; Mr. Wilkie, in St. Paul's Church-yard; Messrs. Dilly, in The Poultry; Mr. Prince, at Oxford; Mr. Woodyer, at Cambridge; Mr. Frederick, at Bath; Mr. Sprange, at Tunbridge; Mr. Balfour, in Edinburgh; and Mr. Faulkner, in Dublin.

4° π1, pp. *1* Title and Conditions, *1–2* Johnson's announcement, 2 Receipt form.

3 vols. 4° with frontispiece by Reynolds, £2–2*s.* (£1 − 1*s.* + £1 − 1*s.*) in sheets; to be delivered in October 1776.

The work was never published: see Johnson's letter to Lennox of 2 May 1775 for an account of the particular problems facing her venture, *Harvard Library Bulletin* 19 (1971): 172–76.

Courtney 117; *Life*, 2:289, 509; *Hazen* 90.

  Copy: CtY (ex James Boswell, MS P.35; marked for quotation in *Life*).

28. *A New and Elegant Edition of the Spectator*   30 November 1776

The Spectator. To be comprized in Twenty-four Weekly Numbers at Sixpence each. On Saturday, December 14, will be published, Number I. (Containing Five Sheets of Letter-Press) of a New and Elegant Edition of The Spectator; . . . Written by the late Mr. Addison and others. . . . Printed (by Assignment from Jacob and Richard Tonson) for the Proprietors, And sold by R. Baldwin, No. 47, Pater-noster Row, And may be had of all the booksellers in Town and Country.

8° π1, pp. *1* Title, *2* Johnson's address *To the Public*, Conditions, and advertisements for other editions of the *Spectator* in 8 vols. 8° @ £2; and 8 vols. 12° @ 12*s*.

109 Sheets (8 vols. 12°), 24 numbers, 3 numbers per vol.; engraved frontispiece by Grignion in each vol.

The edition was eventually published in 1788, the part publication apparently having failed. It was the first edition to contain notes on the text, and it included an "Advertisement" leaf in vol. 1, which throws light on the vicissitudes of the edition: "There being an immediate demand for an impression of the Spectator in this form, and two volumes having been printed some years ago with great accuracy, under the direction of a Writer of distinguished taste and talents; the other six volumes have been suitably adapted to them on the same improved but contracted plan. An accidental fire retarded the publication by destroying the antecedent volumes, when the other six were nearly finished. They are reprinted from a copy that escaped destruction, with additions which it is hoped the superintendant of them, and the publick at large, will not dislike."

Percy was the first editor but was succeeded by John Calder. The destruction of the first two volumes eliminated Percy's share, and it was probably John Nichols who edited them "with additions."

Life, 2:502–3; J. F. Woodruff in *Notes and Queries* 216 (February 1971): 61–62.

Johnson's address was also printed in the *Public Advertiser* 14 December 1776 on the publication of number 1, and reprinted by Isaac Reed in the *European Magazine* 16 (July 1789):5.

> *Copy:* BM (T 1563 [7], ex Isaac Reed: Alexander Chalmers; inscribed by Reed: "This Advertizement was drawn up by Dr. Johnson").

29. William Shaw's *Analysis of the Scotch Celtic Language*   March 1777

Proposals for Printing by Subscription, inscribed, by permission, To the Right Honourable the Earl of Eglinton: An Analysis of the Scotch Celtic Language. By William Shaw, native of one of the Hebrides. . . . The Books will be delivered in November 1777, by - J. Murray, Fleet-Street, J. Donaldson, Arundel Street, Strand, and Richardson and Urquhart, No. 91, Royal Exchange, London; C. Elliot, Edinburgh, and Dunlop and Wilson, Glasgow, where Subscriptions are also received.

4° π1, pp. *1* Title and Conditions, *2* Johnson's notice.

1 vol. 4°, 10*s.* − 6*d.*

The work was published in 4° in London, 1778, and in a second edition 8° in Edinburgh in the same year.

Courtney 129; *Life,* 3:107, 488; *Supp.* 154; L. F. Powell in *Johnsonian Studies* (Cairo, 1962): 9–13.

> *Copies:* CtY (ex Boswell, marked for quotation in the *Life*), Hyde (ex Boswell—Talbot de Malahide); O (Gough Gen.Top. 366 f.552), O(JJ) (b.237a, date cropped away).

30. John Hoole's translation of Ariosto   [1780–81]

In his letter of 29 January 1781 to Warren Hastings, Johnson wrote:

"Mr Hoole, a Gentleman long known and long esteemed in the India house, after having translated Tasso, has undertaken Ariosto. How well he is qualified for his undertaking he has already shown. He is desirous Sir, of your favour in promoting his proposals, and flatters me by supposing that my testimony may advance his interest (*Letters,* 2:409, no. 712).

The work was published in 5 vols. in 1783.

Life, 4:70; *Hazen* 60n.

Johnson's possible contribution is conjectural.

No copy known.

CONJECTURAL

31. Richard Bathurst's *Geographical Dictionary*   [March–April 1753]

This undertaking is described in a MS account that was sent to William Strahan by Johnson with a covering letter dated "March 22d" (*Letters,* 1:48–49, no. 47) which Birkbeck Hill assigned to 1753 on the grounds that Bathurst is described as "a Physician . . . of about eight years standing." Bathurst took his B.M. at Cambridge in 1745. Johnson's letter is concerned to secure a suitable contract for Bathurst. The so-called "Proposal" is in an unidentified hand that was probably Bathurst's but was manifestly composed by Johnson:

There is nothing more apparently wanting to the English Literature, than a Geographical Dictionary, which though its use is almost every day necessary, not only to Men of Study, but of Trade or publick employment, yet has been hitherto, not only unperformed, but almost unattempted among us . . .&c.

The document describes the projected work and the manner of its intended compilation; however, it is not a proposal for the publication of a work but simply a proposal to Strahan inviting his investment in the undertaking.

The work was never published and doubtless never performed. Bathurst "died at the Havannah" in 1757.

Boswell's Life of Johnson, ed. G. B. Hill (Oxford: Clarendon Press, 1887), xxii–xxiv.

Though not a proposal in the sense in which the preceding items may be so described, this piece is included here because it is often mentioned as a Johnsonian "Proposal" and accordingly merited some notice.

Copy: MS Hyde.

14

"Curious Eye": Some Aspects of Visual Description in Eighteenth-Century Literature

Rachel Trickett

In his essay "Is Verse a Dying Technique?" Edmund Wilson has an interesting paragraph on the relation of poetry to music and to the visual:

> It was not till after Alexander the Great that prosody was detached from harmony. The Greek name for "prose" was "bare words"—that is, words divorced from music. But what the Romans took over and developed was purely literary. This, I believe, accounts for the fact that we find so little exact visual observation in Greek poetry, if we compare it with Latin poetry. Greek poetry is mainly for the ear. Compare a landscape in one of the choruses of Sophocles or Aristophanes with a landscape of Virgil or Horace: the Greeks are *singing* about the landscape, the Romans are fixing it for the eye of the mind; and it is Virgil and Horace who lead the way to all the later picture poetry down to our own Imagists. Again, in the Elizabethan age, the English were extremely musical: the lyrics of Campion could hardly have been composed apart from their musical settings; and Shakespeare is permeated with music. When Shakespeare wants to make us see something, he is always compelling and brilliant; but the effect has been liquified by music so that it sometimes gives the impression of objects seen under water. The main stream of English poetry continues to keep fairly close to music through Milton, the musician's son, and even through the less organ-voiced Dryden. What has really happened with Pope is that the musical background is no longer there, and that the ocular sense has grown sharp again.[1]

Despite some unsupported generalizations—Milton's acute visual sense is conveniently ignored here—Wilson is saying something important about Dryden and Pope, and about those curious phases in the history of the human imagination when the oral or the visual sense alternately predominates in poetry.

Description has always been available to poets, and always, in one way or another, used by them: in imagery, in emblem (which might be called the visual epitome of an idea), or in the catalogue of sensuous and visible delights that, though it need not itself contain description, persuades the reader to visualize. But there is no doubt that the visual quality in eighteenth-century poetry is different in kind as well as in degree from that of earlier periods. When Wordsworth praised the Countess of Winchilsea, Dyer, and Thomson above their contemporaries, he was responding to their new attitude toward the visible world, especially the visible world of nature.

This new attitude has been variously attributed to the empirical approach to the natural world, to the need in science for accurate description and itemization, and to the status of post-Cartesian man as *spectator ab extra* with regard to his environment. More recently, James Turner has suggested that the growth of *topographia* from the seventeenth to the eighteenth centuries should be connected with social and political realities and causes.[2] Certainly by the eighteenth century the Horatian happy man was firmly located in the countryside with a new and contemporary air, the result of political as well as moral principles. But none of these factors, independently or even together, accounts for what is one of those curious shifts in the history of the imagination—the sudden emergence in this period of a descriptive visual idiom as the common currency for an increasing number of poems.

The *Ut pictura poesis* aesthetic had been thoroughly argued from Leonardo's *Paragone* (where the artist found it necessary to raise painting above poetry or music, since painting previously, in the Middle Ages, had not even been granted the status of an art), to the disputes over the picturesque at the end of the eighteenth century. Writers had concentrated especially—sometimes to the advantage of poetry, sometimes of painting—on the essential difference between the two arts, arguing that one is a temporal, the other a spatial medium. Consciousness of that difference enabled the poets of the eighteenth century to develop a descriptive rhetoric of varying degrees of subtlety but, paradoxically, gave no such impetus to the writers of prose fiction or discourse.

Examples of the development of descriptive rhetoric in verse can scarcely avoid beginning with Dyer. Himself a painter, his verse epistle to his mentor Jonathan Richardson, *To a Famous Painter* (1726), contains the stock in trade of Augustan landscape verse (first brought together in Dryden's "Elegy on Mistress Anne Killigrew," who excelled in "the sister arts" of poetry and painting): reflections in water, sylvan effects of open and shady vistas, nymphs, satyrs, and ruins. But Dyer presents them with a painter's feeling for light and with a sense of perspective conveyed in the first four lines of the following passage:

The beauteous shapes of objects near!
Of distant ones confus'd in air!
The golden eve, the blushing dawn,
Smiling on the lovely lawn!
And pleasing views of checquer'd glades!
And rivers winding through the shades!
And sunny hills!—and pleasant plains!
And groups of merry nymphs and swains!
    Or some old building, hid with grass,
Rearing sad its ruin'd face;
Whose columns, frizes, statues, lie,
The grief and wonder of the eye![3]

Richardson, in his *Theory of Painting* (1715), had made several observations on the effect of distance on shape and color, and Dyer has added this dimension of depth and distance to the conventional scene. Yet the poem failed to satisfy William Gilpin, the father of picturesque beauty, who, in his *Observations on the River Wye* (1782), wrote:

> Dyer was bred a painter; and had here a picturesque subject: but he does not give us so fine a landscape, as might have been expected. We have no where a complete, formed distance; though it is the great idea suggested by such a vale as this: no where any touches of that beautiful obscurity, which melts a variety of objects into one rich whole. . . . his distances are as all in confusion, and indeed it is not easy to separate them from his foregrounds.[4]

There is an innate absurdity in this criticism that should be exposed. Gilpin assumes that the technique Dyer acquired as a painter could be reproduced with a kind of transliterated accuracy in language, whereas this could in fact only be effected by some artifice to strip words of their conceptual overtones. In "Grongar Hill" (1726), Dyer does, in fact, make a distinction between the visual and the conceptual by separating his passages of description and of moralizing. The scene produces a state of mind, and the state of mind is summed up neatly in a well-turned commonplace:

A little rule, a little sway,
A sunbeam on a winter's day
Is all the proud and mighty have
Between the cradle and the grave.

This procedure is precisely the opposite, for example, of Vaughan's in the previous century. In Vaughan's verses the argument of the poem, the discourse, is the predominant vehicle, but it is illustrated by appropriate metaphors that sometimes have the felt quality of actual personal observation, often suggested by a use of the demonstrative, as here:

It glows and glitters in my cloudy breast
　　Like stars upon some gloomy grove,
Or *those* faint beams in which *this* hill is drest
　　After the sun's remove.

Dyer's concentration on the description of landscape, despite the appropriate moral reflections it evokes, seems to give the journey of the eye over the
prospect the same status held by discourse or argument in the poetry of the
previous century. Though John Wesley included "Grongar Hill" in his
Collection of Moral and Sacred Poems (1744), evidently thinking of it as a
discursive rather than simply topographical poem, its didacticism is less
striking, certainly less original, than its use of the movement of the eye over
the field of vision.

　The vogue for verse essays in which description leads to moralizing
merged in the course of the century with the fashion for excursion poems,
verses where the poet himself, not merely his glance, is moving through the
landscape. Thomson's *Seasons* (1726) introduces this motif. In *Spring,* the
beauty of flowers and the pleasure of scents are conveyed in the course of a
promenade:

　　　　　　　　Long let us walk,
　　Where the Breeze blows from yon extended Field
　　Of blossom'd Beans.[5]

Again in *Summer,* after elaborate preliminaries, we reach the excursion by
line 585:

　　　　THUS up the Mount, in airy Vision rapt,
　　I stray, regardless wither; till the Sound
　　Of a near Fall of Water every Sense
　　Wakes from the Charm of Thought. . . .

　　　　　　　　　　　　　　　　　　　　　(585–88)

In *Autumn,* one short digression from line 651 to 680, a compliment to
Doddington, involves a ramble round his estate. *Winter* (1726), composed
before the other seasons, opens retrospectively with a recollection of childhood walks in the Cheviots:

　　　　Pleas'd have I, in my chearful Morn of Life,
　　　　When nurs'd by careless Solitude I liv'd,
　　　　And sung of Nature with unceasing Joy,
　　　　Pleas'd have I wander'd thro' your rough Domain;
　　　　Trod the pure Virgin-Snows, myself as pure;
　　　　Heard the Winds roar, and the big Torrent burst;
　　　　Or seen the deep fermenting Tempest brew'd,
　　　　In the grim Evening-Sky.

　　　　　　　　　　　　　　　　　　　　　(7–14)

Here Thomson introduces movement in time as well as in space into his description. It is an important element which Cowper and Goldsmith both developed further in retrospects as well as prospects. Goldsmith's *Traveller* shows the poet wandering Europe to escape from melancholy recollections and filling his mind with observations on life in the countries he passes through. *The Deserted Village* (1770) more subtly exploits a complicated time scheme of recollection and anticipation which interacts skillfully with the descriptive and the didactic elements in the poem.

The debate between painting and poetry had often concentrated on the timeless quality of painting, to its advantage or disadvantage in the comparison. Richardson in his *Discourse on the Dignity of the Science of Connoisseur* (1719) writes:

> painting is another sort of writing . . . [but the pictures it produces] come not by a slow progression of words, or in a language peculiar to one nation only. . . . What a tedious thing it would be to describe by words the view of a country (that from Greenwich-Hill, for instance), and how imperfect an idea must we receive from hence! Painting shows the thing immediately and exactly. (247)

Sir Joshua Reynolds, on the other hand, admits the fact of temporal sequence in painting with regret in his fourth *Discourse* (1772): "A painter must compensate the natural deficiencies of his art. He has but one sentence to utter, but one moment to exhibit."[6] A limited effect of sequence may be conveyed by certain painterly devices, but the use of time-scheme in meditative verse can undoubtedly transform and enrich our sense of the scene. It provides precisely that depth and dimension which foregrounds and distances contribute to a painting.

The opening lines of *The Deserted Village* are an exercise in memory, the poet's recollection of a particular place. Three times he repeats the formula "How often": "How often have I loiter'd o'er thy green"; "How often have I paused on every charm"; "How often have I blest the coming day." The exclamation is a rhetorical device for intensifying feeling and encouraging visualization. A greater than Goldsmith, Wordsworth, adapted it from him in a yet more sophisticated form:

> If this
> Be but a vain belief, yet, oh! how oft—
> In darkness and amid the many shapes
> Of joyless daylight; when the fretful stir
> Unprofitable, and the fever of the world,
> Have hung upon the beatings of my heart—
> How oft, in spirit, have I turned to thee,
> O sylvan Wye! thou wanderer thro' the woods,
> How often has my spirit turned to thee!
>
> ("Tintern Abbey," lines 49–57)

Wordsworth's mounting sense of climax, with the two *how oft*'s modulating into the final *how often*, conveys an emotion and an urgency more intense than Goldsmith's pensive melancholy. But Goldsmith was skillful in handling the movement of *The Deserted Village* and its shifts of tone and scene. We emerge from the past in the first paragraph to the present in the second—leading to generalizations about the economic condition of the country and a traditional praise of retirement, couched here in more local and personal terms than had previously been common. Then follows the lovely evocative passage of recollection where a whole series of sounds, recalled "in sweet confusion" in lines from which the conventional caesura has been smoothed away, make up an idyll that few readers have not found themselves visualizing. Evocation is followed by brief description of the cottage and garden by the preacher's "modest mansion" and, more extensively, in almost novelistic style, of the characters of the preacher and the schoolmaster. Time again performs a useful function in the transition from character (the schoolmaster) to scene (the inn parlor):

> But *past* is all his fame. The very spot,
> Where *many a time* he triumphed, is forgot.
> Near *yonder* thorn, that lifts its head on high,
> Where *once* the signpost caught the passing eye,
> Low lies *that* house where nutbrown draughts inspired,
> Where greybeard mirth and smiling toil retired.
>
> (217–22)

I have italicized the words that carry the weight especially of the mingling of time and place in the passage, the two demonstratives "yonder" and "that" being particularly important in singling out past and present objects of the same scene.

The genial description of the inn parlor, which is markedly visual, is followed by exhortation in the Augustan mode, the long simile of the country girl turned harlot introducing a passage on corruption in the town, which again returns to the figure of the "poor, houseless, shivering female"—no longer a comparison but, instead, a real character in the scene. It is an easy transition from this to the question "Do thine, sweet Auburn, thine the loveliest train/Do thy fair tribes participate her pain?" and to the movement into an imagined nightmare future in the New World where Goldsmith's natural history joins his imagination to produce a tropical panorama "Far different from every former scene." These former scenes are at once identified by a brief inventory that recapitulates the sights and sounds previously evoked in greater detail:

> The cooling brook, the grassy-vested green,
> The breezy covert of the warbling grove,
> That only sheltered thefts of harmless love. . . .
>
> (360–62)

The "pictured scene" of the villagers' departure for foreign parts is a formal tableau of pathos, but the tone modulates to humor in the final exhortation to Poetry, made as a throw-away aside here so that the figure of the poet himself does not seem any different in scale and stature from the characters of the poem. A mood of humility and intimacy is projected back from the conclusion over the whole work.

The Deserted Village exemplifies the sophisticated techniques that had long been established for presenting scene in poetry during the century. These techniques are comparable in many ways to the new freedom and subtlety that the later landscapes of Gainsborough display. "Tintern Abbey," an even more complex work in the management of time and place, shows how completely Wordsworth had mastered this rhetoric and how skillfully he could exploit the new freedom to move about in the mental as well as the physical space of the poem. This poem's final disclosure is that Wordsworth is not alone and musing but, rather, addressing a companion, his sister, and the conclusion is an opening out, a movement of expansion and possibility rather than the dropping of a curtain, or a finale. Again, as in *The Deserted Village,* though the tone is more elevated and intense (indeed, Wordsworth thought of the poem as an ode because of its "impassioned language" and transitions), "Tintern Abbey" concludes in a grave mood of companionable intimacy rather than in solitary musing. Within the intricate structure of the thought, its movement between past and present and on toward the future, Wordsworth retains the visual elements of the scene and imprints them on our minds. Only one thing is conspicuously absent—Tintern Abbey itself. We have left the world of conventional landscape entirely, and there is no need even for the genuine ruin of the picturesque excursion in what Wordsworth has made of it.

Over the century, then, an entire idiom and rhetoric for relating the poet's discourse to his environment had been established. No comparable techniques exist in eighteenth-century prose. Neither in the novel nor in nonfictional prose is there any equivalent of the tradition of Thomson, Dyer, Cowper, and Goldsmith. We are so accustomed to description as the natural idiom of the novelist in the nineteenth century that the lack of it in Defoe, Richardson, Fielding, and Smollett is at first astonishing. In nineteenth-century history the great set-pieces of Macaulay and Carlyle come across with the confidence and authority of scenes from a novel. Every picture does indeed tell a story and it may even, as in Ruskin's marvelous descriptions, carry an argument. Yet the eighteenth century gave particular weight to the visual arts in its aesthetic theory. Gibbon writes in his *Memoirs,* speaking of the value of travel to a young man:

> A musical ear will multiply the pleasures of his Italian tour; but a correct and exquisite eye which commands the landskip of a country, discerns the merits of a picture, and measures the proportions of a building is more closely connected with the finer feelings of the mind.[7]

That his own eye was correct is shown often in *The Decline and Fall of the Roman Empire* where Gibbon inserts descriptive passages at appropriate moments, as when he gives an account of the Emperor Julian's winter quarters at Paris or his resort at Daphne, or of the location and artifices of Constantinople. Vivid detail intersperses the measured flow of the narrative:

> But in remarkable winters, the Seine was deeply frozen; and the huge pieces of ice that floated down the stream might be compared, by an Asiatic, to the blocks of white marble which were extracted from the quarries of Phrygia.[8]

The description of the temple of Apollo at Daphne is one of Gibbon's finest, but, as in the entire history, every visible item is subordinated to the dialectical process of cause and effect. The fact that the temple was raised to Apollo is more important than the posture of his statue (though this is accurately described); the myth of his pursuit of Daphne is recalled to make the historical point that the Syrian poets had transferred the story "from the banks of the Peneus to those of the Orontes"; the growth of the village is the result of "the stream of prophecy" emanating from the oracle, and of its attraction of so many pilgrims to the area. It is only after all this has been established that Gibbon allows himself a purely sensuous and visual account of the beauties of the place.

The subordination of visual detail to argument is an almost universal practice in eighteenth-century prose. Hervey's *Meditations among the Tombs* (1746), that most popular and influential document of religious sensibility, seems to offer the same occasion for description as similar settings in the "graveyard school" of poetry. But there is no paragraph in it that could be used as the basis of an illustration, nor is any particular tomb described. The vast travel literature of the period is informative rather than descriptive. Smollett's relation of his residence at Nice in *Travels through France and Italy* (1766) gives us a detailed account of climate, local habits, food, and occupations, but there is not one description of vegetation and fruit. To some extent this is understandable, the intention of such works (though not of Hervey's) being to inform rather than to affect. But the novel offers a greater opportunity for exploiting description.

Scott, apologizing for Fielding's comparative failure as a playwright, observes:

> But we know not any effort of genius which could successfully insert into a good play those accessories of description and delineation which are necessary to dilate it into a readable novel. It may thus easily be conceived, that he whose chief talent lies in addressing the imagination only, and whose style therefore, must be expanded and circumstantial, may fail in a kind of composition where so much must be left to the efforts of

the actor with his allies and assistants, the scene-painter and the property man.[9]

Defoe, Richardson, Fielding, and Sterne are all, indeed, "expanded and circumstantial," but they are not descriptive in the full sense Scott means, or, indeed, in the way in which as a novelist preeminently he is. Defoe and Richardson are both careful to use itemized details to verify the setting or atmosphere of an incident. The gold necklace Moll Flanders steals from the child in the alley is one example, the famous footprint of *Robinson Crusoe* another. Richardson's details animate all his novels—Pamela's round-eared cap and ribbons bought from the pedlar, Clarissa's sister Bella's high complexion, the windows of the many rooms in which Clarissa is imprisoned; the cedar parlor in *Sir Charles Grandison* where the ladies sit in the bow window seat, tilting up their hoops to make room for him. But there are no memorable landscapes in Richardson's work. Austin Dobson, writing on Richardson in the English Men of Letters series, speculates on what a nineteenth-century novelist would have made of Mr. B.'s Lincolnshire house where Pamela is kept prisoner; Richardson makes no attempt to "realize" it.

There is one exception to this rule in both Richardson and Fielding—their treatment of the ideal country squire's estate. Both indulge in pictorial description here. Allworthy's house in *Tom Jones* and Grandison Hall in *Sir Charles Grandison* are given full visual treatment. The account of Grandison Hall, purporting to be from an independent correspondent and set in inverted commas to mark it off from the rest, reads like a National Trust brochure, and this in itself betrays the reason for their use of visual detail. Such description is intended to underline the ethos of the benevolent country gentleman, ruling his domain, improving his estate, caring for his garden and exercising his power with responsibility and compassion. Fielding's comparable passage is the account in book 1, chapter 4 of *Tom Jones* of Squire Allworthy at home, under the title "The Reader's Neck brought into Danger by a Description." This self-consciousness itself warns us that Fielding is thinking of such a description as a convention, but a high poetic convention, like the epic battle, not a convention of simple narrative. His attempt at it is clumsy and confusing; he is ill at ease with description, with any attempt to depict natural beauty:

> In the midst of the Grove was a fine Lawn sloping down towards the House, near the Summit of which rose a plentiful Spring, gushing out of a Rock covered with Firs, and forming a constant Cascade of about thirty Foot, not carried down a regular Flight of Steps, but tumbling in a natural Fall over the broken and mossy Stones, till it came to the bottom of the Rock; then running off in a pebly Channel, that with many lesser Falls winded along, till it fell into a Lake at the Foot of the Hill, about a quarter of a Mile below the House on the South Side, and which was seen

from every Room in the Front. Out of this Lake, which filled the Center of a beautiful Plain, embellished with Groupes of Beeches and Elms, and fed with Sheep, issued a River, that for several Miles was seen to meander through an amazing Variety of Meadows and Woods, till it emptied itself into the Sea, with a large Arm of which, and an Island beyond it, the Prospect was closed.[10]

There is no evidence to support a reading of this passage as ironic, there being no genuine tradition of accounts of country houses worthy of Fielding's satiric attention. And he had no desire to raise a smile at the expense of Prior Park, Ralph Allen's home, on which Squire Allworthy's grounds are based. He was clearly fond of scenery and proud of his patron's achievement, as we may see from a less well-known passage in book 11, chapter 9, where the narrator follows Sophia and Honour on the last stages of their journey to London.

This is a subtle and interesting passage because of the way Fielding exploits time and movement in it, and it tells us something about his attitude to narrative and description:

> We will therefore take our Leave of these good People, and attend his Lordship and his fair Companions, who made such good Expedition, that they performed a Journey of ninety Miles in two Days, and on the second Evening arrived in *London,* without having encountered any one Adventure on the Road worthy the Dignity of this History to relate. Our Pen, therefore, shall keep Pace with the Travellers who are its Subject. Good Writers will indeed do well to imitate the ingenious Traveller in this Instance, who always proportions his Stay at any Place, to the Beauties, Elegancies, and Curiosities, which it affords. At *Eshur,* at *Stowe,* at *Wilton,* at *Eastbury,* and at *Prior's Park,* Days are too short for the ravished Imagination; while we admire the wondrous Power of Art in improving Nature. In some of these, Art chiefly engages our Admiration; in others, Nature and Art contend for our Applause; but in the last, the former seems to triumph. Here Nature appears in her richest Attire, and Art dressed with the modestest Simplicity, attends her benignant Mistress. Here Nature indeed pours forth the choicest Treasures which she hath lavished on this World; and here Human Nature presents you with an Object which can be exceeded only in the other.
>
> The same Taste, the same Imagination, which luxuriously riots in these elegant Scenes, can be amused with Objects of far inferior Note. The Woods, the Rivers, the Lawns of *Devon* and of *Dorset,* attract the Eye of the ingenious Traveller, and retard his Pace, which Delay he afterwards compensates by swiftly scouring over the gloomy Heath of *Bagshot,* or that pleasant Plain which extends itself Westward from *Stockbridge,* where no other Object than one single Tree only in sixteen Miles presents itself to the View, unless the Clouds, in Compassion to our tired Spirits, kindly open their variegated Mansions to our Prospect. (612–13)

To Fielding (or "the ingenious Traveller") the picturesque landscape is a sylvan one. Bagshot Heath is gloomy, Salisbury Plain a bore. For the most part art prevails over nature in his taste for the visual, until at Prior Park nature asserts her ultimate superiority. This superiority is the final compliment; it is this that required the tribute of art—the description over which the reader broke his neck, since a suitable tribute is inevitably beyond the author's powers. But in the later passage Fielding's skill is more than up to his task. Ostensibly seeing Sophia into London, he is at the same time mentally tracing back a journey to Bath where at the improved grounds of Esher, Stowe, Wilton, Eastbury, and (home again) Prior Park, the ingenious traveler (with "ravished Imagination") pauses to admire the civilized estates of the country gentry and the handiwork of William Kent. The same to-and-fro movement is repeated in the next paragraph, where we are moving eastward over Bagshot Heath and westward again from Stockbridge to Salisbury Plain. There is an almost Sterneian virtuosity about this trick that Fielding emphasizes in the last paragraph of the chapter, by inviting the reader "to apply all this to the *Boeotian* Writers, and to those Authors who are their Opposites"—in other words, to cooperate in the art of narrative and of imagining, to fill in for himself the beauties on the way:

> for tho' we will always lend thee proper Assistance in difficult Places, as we do not, like some others, expect thee to use the Arts of Divination to discover our Meaning; yet we shall not indulge thy Laziness where nothing but thy own Attention is required. (614)

Fielding intends the reader to provide his own description by visualizing the scene for himself. To hold up the pace of the narrative by breaking into description would be to destroy the peculiar relationship between author and reader, teasingly parodied here in the reminder that the reader has a job to get on with as well. So we find no scenery in Fielding, only scenes, often of exquisite dramatic point, like the moment when Tom meets Sophia in London, when she is just glancing at herself in the looking glass and suddenly sees his reflection. The reader of Fielding—and of Richardson—constructs a picture from the circumstances with which they choose to provide him. In the picturesque and the epistolary novel the development of description as a function of the narrative found little room.

Yet Scott's wonderful manipulation of scene painting, his powerful and dramatic sense of the visual, was not entirely without precedent. In his *Life of Smollett,* he writes:

> Every successful novelist must be more or less a poet, even although he may never have written a line of verse. The quality of imagination is absolutely indispensable to him: his accurate power of examining and embodying human character and human passion, as well as the external face of nature is not less essential.[11]

Scott read generously into Smollett's cold but vigorous and detailed narrative this particular imaginative power, but it was in the Gothic romances of

Mrs. Radcliffe that the description of landscape and scene especially struck him:

> Indeed the praise may be claimed for Mrs. Radcliffe, of having been the
> first to introduce into her prose fictions a tone of fanciful description and
> impressive narrative, which had been hitherto exclusively applied to
> poetry. . . . Mrs. Radcliffe has a title to be considered the first poetess of
> romantic fiction, that is, if actual rhythm shall not be deemed essential to
> poetry.[12]

The lack of a descriptive rhetoric in eighteenth-century prose, at a time when so much of its development in verse was taking place, suggests that the writers of the period were peculiarly attentive to the function of the new genre, the novel, in contradistinction to that of poetry. The intention of history was already established—it was to be exemplary, veracious, and informative. The novel was to be in some sense a history, but it partook of the nature of drama as well and, in ironic reversal, of the epic narrative. But what distinguished it from poetry or from the drama was emphasized both by the deliberate mock-heroic form of Fielding, and by the assumed intimacy and privacy of the epistolary mode. Description of scene could only be developed in a genre where the individual voice of the poet, expressing his sensations as well as his opinions, might find a new function for the traditional use of natural scenery in imagery and for the growing interest in the appearance of the external world. Only when truth to human nature was not the first concern of the novelist, when writers of fiction could return to the freedom of romance rather than the veracity of history, when imagination rather than observation was given priority, did a form of fiction develop in which some of the relationships between the figure and the landscape, the subject and the physical environment, could be attempted, however crudely.

In his *Philosophical Enquiry into the Origin of our Ideas of the Sublime and the Beautiful* (1759), Burke devoted the fifth and final section to a consideration of words and to what extent they are associated with or may evoke the visible recollection of the objects they represent. He divides words into three categories: aggregate words, simple abstract words, and compounded aggregate words. Examples of the first are *man, horse, tree, cattle.* Of the second, *red, blue, round, square.* Of the third, *virtue, honor, persuasion.* As a general principle he remarks:

> If words have all their possible extent of power, three effects arise in
> the mind of the hearer. The first is, the *sound;* the second, the *picture,* or
> representation of the thing signified by the sound; the third is, the *affec-
> tion* of the soul produced by one or by both of the foregoing. *Compounded
> abstract* words, of which we have been speaking, (honour, justice, liberty,
> and the like,) produce the first and the last of these effects, but not the
> second.[13]

On the whole, Burke finds it improbable that most speakers *visualize* or entertain a picture even of the simple objects that some words may connote. In section 5 of this last part of his *Enquiry,* entitled "Examples that WORDS may affect without raising IMAGES," Burke takes the example of the poet Blacklock, blind from birth, and maintains that his descriptions, though of objects and scenes he never saw, are as spirited and affecting as those of men who have always had their sight. Blacklock's descriptions are characteristically conventional in the idiom of the eighteenth century and emphasize Burke's belief that association rather than the power of sight or the capacity to visualize is the basis of our response to language. Burke concludes: "Indeed so little does poetry depend for its effect on the power of raising sensible images, that I am convinced it would lose a very considerable part of its energy, if this were the necessary result of all description" (170).

To some nineteenth-century aestheticians—Ruskin and Arnold especially—contemporary poetry *had* lost much of its energy, though neither ascribes this loss to the prevalent idiom of description. It seems, however, to be related to meditation, to musing as opposed to action, and there is no doubt that the meditative essay in verse gave rise in the eighteenth century to the rhetorical techniques through which visual description began to dominate poetry. Contrarily, prose discourse, or the novel dealing with human passions and human action, was much later in admitting the description of scene or landscape as an affective and persuasive element in its construction. By the end of the eighteenth century aesthetic criticism was almost entirely dominated by arguments over the picturesque—what Wordsworth was to call later in *The Prelude* "the tyranny of the eye," until he and Coleridge rescued it from this limited perspective. Yet there must be few readers today who fail to prefer the visual authenticity of Keats, or Tennyson, or Hopkins to the descriptions of Blacklock or any conventional eighteenth-century pastoralist.

This particular episode in the history of the imagination, however, was necessary to effect an entirely new literary conception of the relationship between the subject and the object, between man and his environment, between the writer and his material. Simple as the domination of the eye may now appear in eighteenth-century poetry, it nevertheless provided a means whereby a poet like Wordsworth or a novelist like Scott could discover new and more intense presentations both of human sensation and of human experience and action.

NOTES

1. Edmund Wilson, *The Triple Thinkers* (New York: Harcourt, Brace, 1938), 37–38.

2. James Turner, *The Politics of Landscape: Rural Scenery and Society in English Poetry 1630–1660* (Cambridge, Mass.: Harvard University Press, 1979).

3. John Dyer, "An Epistle to a Famous Painter," in *Minor British Poets 1660–1780,* ed. David P. French (New York: Benjamin Blom, 1967), 4:311.

4. William Gilpin, *Observations on the River Wye* (London, 1782), 59–60.

5. Lines 498–99: all quotations from *The Seasons* are taken from the recent edition by James Sambrook (Oxford: Clarendon Press, 1981).

6. Sir Joshua Reynolds, *Discourses on Art,* ed. Robert R. Wark (New Haven: Yale University Press, 1975), 60.

7. Edward Gibbon, *Memoirs of My Life,* ed. Georges A. Bonnard (New York: Funk and Wagnalls, 1969), 136.

8. Edward Gibbon, *Decline and Fall of the Roman Empire,* chaps. 23 (Julian's resort at Daphne), 53 (location of Constantinople), 19 (description of the river Seine, from which my quotation comes).

9. *Miscellaneous Prose Works of Sir Walter Scott, Bart.* (Edinburgh: Cadell, n.d.), 255.

10. Henry Fielding, *The History of Tom Jones; A Foundling,* ed. M. C. Battestin and F. Bowers (Oxford: Clarendon Press, 1974), 42–43.

11. Scott, *Miscellaneous Works,* 276.

12. Ibid., 324.

13. Burke, *Philosophical Enquiry,* ed. J. T. Boulton (Notre Dame: University of Notre Dame Press, 1968), 166.

15

Sentimental De-education

G. A. Starr

Locke's chief contribution to the novel may have been that by doing away with innate ideas, he introduced a conception of man as the protagonist of a *Bildungsroman*—as the product of certain formative, educative experiences which it became the task of the novelist no less than the philosopher to trace. By the beginning of the nineteenth century Mary Brunton could flatly declare, in her *Self-Control* of 1811, "It is the fashion of the age to account for every striking feature of a character from education or external circumstance."[1] The sentimental novel resists this fashion, at least when its subjects are male. It denies both the formative influence and the explanatory power of education and external circumstance, so that its heroes, far from learning and growing and maturing as they would in a *Bildungsroman*, remain fixed in a pattern of attitudes and behavior that eighteenth-century society associates with infancy or femininity, but not with masculine adulthood.

To be impervious to the lessons of experience is the fate of many characters in nonsentimental novels as well, but such characters usually serve as grim or comic foils to heroes and heroines whose superiority lies in their greater educability. The margins of a typical *Bildungsroman* are thus strewn with unteachables, rigidly set in their ways. Sentimental heroes aren't simply impervious to experience, for they react to everything with tremulous acuteness. They are unaffected in a different sense: failing or refusing to change, they develop no more "manly" response to vicissitudes but steadily retain the childish simplicity they set out with. Unlike the cumulative, forward-moving progress of the *Bildungsroman*, the structure of the sentimental novel is static or backward-moving, as the transformation of boys into men ordinarily brought about through education is thwarted or undone. Education is a gradual, incremental process, but in the sentimental novel nothing is gradual, nothing is incremental, and process itself is anathema, implying as it does the impermanence of Edens inhabited by innocent Adams.

Not that education proceeds in an altogether additive or expansive fashion in the *Bildungsroman,* or in the nonsentimental eighteenth-century novel generally. The author of *Tom Jones* recognizes, just as clearly as the author of *Civilization and Its Discontents,* that education involves learning to relinquish, curtail, or redirect certain of our wishes, and that the goal of education is not a simple increase in power over our circumstances but a compromise between our own demands and those imposed upon us. The usual view is that this repressive or sublimative aspect of education was what sentimentalists, with Rousseau leading the way, sought to eliminate, substituting self-realization for social accommodation as their ideal; and educational reform does appear to have moved in this direction, both in theory and practice, at the end of the eighteenth century. But in English fiction, these attitudes and aspirations tended to be expressed in books like *The Fool of Quality* (1764–70) or *Sandford and Merton* (1783–89), both of which have more in common with the *Bildungsroman* than the sentimental novel.

Even writers committed in theory to the Lockean doctrine of character-formation through education and experience are known to hanker after less "realistic" explanations of character, especially where their heroes and heroines are concerned. The alternative explanations can be even more deterministic than those based on social conditioning: examples from before, during, and after the eighteenth century might be pagan destiny; divine election or reprobation; ruling passions or humors; and the pattern of phrenological bumps on someone's head. Fatalistic or mechanistic as such explanations may be, they are all paradoxically unfettering in a more important sense, in that they challenge the tyranny of actual social experience over one's essential nature. This tendency, often associated with the romance rather than the novel, is a vital ingredient in even the most resolutely social novels, and the very ascendancy of the Lockean experiential explanation of character probably intensified a later eighteenth-century impulse to deny or escape the force of circumstance.

In any case, the sentimental novel richly exemplifies this impulse, whether we associate it with the romance or some other literary, psychological, or mythic mode. The sentimental hero is subjected to ordeals and stresses of various kinds, but not to the pressure of having his character made dependent on training, habit, and the other contingencies of experience that Lockean psychology regards as decisive. A devoted nurturer himself, the sentimental hero owes everything to nature.

On the other hand, he is also something of a romance-figure in his reticence and uneasiness over the question of his paternity. The very title of R. S. Crane's "Suggestions toward a Genealogy of the 'Man of Feeling'" contains an oxymoron, because the man of feeling has no genealogy.[2] The ethical values he represents do have historical antecedents, but the individual man of feeling, as a literary personage, finds it hard to acknowledge what Beckett's Hamm calls his "accursed progenitor" or, indeed, any form of male authority. Just as he displays an aversion or incapacity to beget offspring, so too he minimizes the agency of any human father in bringing him into the world or making him what he is. He thus poses as self-made, just as his text purports to be self-generated: keenly aware of the analogies between sexuality and authorship, he repudiates both as links between himself and the world. When, as in Sterne's case, attention is drawn to either kind of procreative gesture, the whole affair is invested with a whimsicality that tends to dissociate it from ordinary acts of generation.

We are told by Freud and his followers that boys' identification with their mothers and with women in general is broken down during and after the Oedipal phase. The sentimental hero is regressively intent on restoring this lost link with a portion of himself. The image of adult masculinity that prevails in eighteenth-century society offers him little support in this project, so the hero looks back with special fondness and regret to a period of childhood before he was exhorted to "be a man" and give up womanish traits and associations. He shies away from roles and attitudes that his culture sanctions as masculine—from the public, purposive activities that only males engage in, and from the rationality and aggressiveness with which men are expected to pursue them. He does not go in for blood sports, or seek economic, political, or social advancement in competition with other males. He gravitates toward relationships that are assigned to women in his society or that involve figurative mothering. Most at ease with the very young and the very old, traditional objects of feminine care, he feels special kinship with those who have been reduced to similar helplessness, like lunatics and the victims of sexual, legal, economic, or colonial male oppression. Even his attachment to animals has a distinctly maternal quality: his role is always that of nursing, tending, or playing with them, never (for example) that of breeding or marketing them.

Why not regard this as learned behavior—as a matter of rejecting one set of formative experiences and "role models" in favor of another? For one thing, the sentimental hero's "feminine" traits are simply not acquired: they are his donnée, his birthright, innate and fundamental to his identity. Far from being shaped by his experience, the sentimental hero can't be coerced or seduced away from his original state; immune to the formative influences that would ordinarily submerge or eradicate the "feminine" side of his nature, his development is not so much deflected as never begun.

The sentimental hero is thus an exception to the Popean principle that as the twig is bent, the tree is inclined. Nor is it merely that he is a human bonsai whose normal growth has been artfully stunted, although a Harley never does seem to eat or drink like a Tom Jones, and is always being severely pruned and clipped. The metaphor finally will not hold, for the sentimental novel calls into question the very concept of normal growth, offering a root-and-branch critique of the assumption that tender saplings

should become toweringly erect trees. (The only image drawn from arboriculture that the sentimentalist would endorse is that of Sir Thomas
Browne, who wishes that we might procreate like trees, and thus avoid a
sexuality that Browne deems foolish and the sentimentalist finds threatening.)

Another objection might be that eighteenth-century England and
nineteenth-century America provide abundant and depressing evidence
that sentimentalism can be culturally induced, learned behavior. Where
young women are concerned, there is no doubt that sentimentalism has
from the beginning reinforced prevailing sexual stereotypes, perpetuating
the role assigned to women in a male-dominated society. In their case,
sentimentalism could be taught and learned. Furthermore, there are English books in the wake of *Emile,* such as *The Fool of Quality* and *Sandford and
Merton,* that appear to assume that sentimental values can be inculcated.
Within these works, humane mentors like Mr. Fenton and Mr. Barlow are
portrayed as educing a benevolent sensibility in their young charges, and
the stories themselves are evidently designed to have the same educative
effect on young readers. Even though they concern boys, both Brooke's
and Day's tales about preserving and strengthening the innocence of youth
thus approximate the pattern of continuity that marks the career of the
sentimental heroine. But there are difficulties with such a scenario for the
sentimental hero.

One problem is that by denying a fundamental opposition between sentimental values and the reigning image of masculinity, or by attempting to
show that they are readily reconcilable in the person of the hero, these
stories condemn themselves to a fatal unreality. They initiate that long line
of impossible prigs who were to be mocked so tellingly in Mark Twain's
"Story of a Good Little Boy." Even more false is their pretense that such
goody-goodies are tolerated—let alone cherished and rewarded—in the
actual world. On this matter the true sentimental novel, like Mackenzie's
Man of Feeling, tends to be more realistic.

Another problem with lads like Henry Moreland and Harry Sandford is
that they themselves lack the sense of loss, of being exiled from paradise
into a fallen world, that seems to be a distinguishing mark of the sentimental hero. Sentimental novels sometimes begin like these works, with a ten-
der-hearted young man setting out to find his place in society as he would
in a *Bildungsroman;* but before long the world reveals its antagonism to his
simple, spontaneous goodness, and he must either withdraw from it altogether or retreat to the company of other victims and outcasts like himself. In other words, *The Fool of Quality* could be read as a very lengthy first
installment of a sentimental novel, in the sequel to which Henry Moreland
would come to grief as young Benignus does in Samuel Jackson Pratt's
("Courtney Melmoth's") *Liberal Opinions, upon Animals, Man, and Providence*
(1775). But where there is growth or development there is no longer a

sentimental hero, for such a figure isn't merely spontaneous and innocent and benevolent, but is in full possession of such traits from the outset and clings to them despite one realization that they disable him from (rather than qualifying him for) an active, useful role in existing society.

The distinction can perhaps be clarified by a brief comparison between passages from *The Prelude* and *A Sentimental Journey*. Wordsworth speaks of early days "In which, a Babe, by intercourse of touch,/I held mute dialogues with my Mother's heart," and he notes as one object of the poem "to display the means/Whereby this infant sensibility,/Great birthright of our Being, was in me/Augmented and sustain'd."[3] Yorick also carries on "mute dialogues" by "intercourse of touch," enactments and proofs of the sensibility that he too regards as the birthright of our being. Wordsworth, who has never lost this birthright, matter-of-factly traces sensibility back to maternal contact during earliest infancy, and calmly reflects on all that subsequently "augmented and sustain'd" it. But Yorick's Quixotic quest hinges on his birthright being lost: time and time again he tries to reconstitute his idyll, but its being "augmented and sustain'd" is in his case unthinkable. (Imagine Yorick and Maria in housekeeping together—or for that matter, any silent converse in the book prolonged another instant.) Yorick's "intercourse of touch" recapitulates and parodies infant sensibility; each mute dialogue revives the possibility of immediate communion between innocent hearts, yet perfect sensibility is always being fatally "augmented" by erotic quickenings of pulse. At several points in *The Prelude* mothers and infants do figure sentimentally in the conventional sense, but the passage just cited is distinctly *un*sentimental in assigning positive value not only to an original "birthright" but to the educative processes that it later undergoes. The self-as-"Babe" is an object not of wild regret but of keen yet dispassionate interest, a "Mother's heart" not the sole or last but the first of many boons of nature.

Another way of illustrating the incompatibility of the sentimental novel with the *Bildungsroman*, with education, and with process generally is to consider briefly the convention of love at first sight. The sentimental ethos, prizing instantly formed bonds of sympathy between strangers, tends to regard such moments of heightened sensibility as both possible and creditable to the parties involved: what better example could there be of benign directness and spontaneity in human affairs? The adversaries of sentimentalism, however, not only challenge the substance and worth of sudden attachments, but also put forward an alternative conception of love as something gradual and cumulative, to be established only over time. According to this view, one does not *fall in* love but *learns to* love. (Austen's *Sense and Sensibility* embodies both aspects of the latter position: on the one hand, it satirizes the giddy and groundless infatuation that Willoughby inspires in Marianne; on the other hand, it presents Edward Ferrars as an unhandsome hero whose manners required intimacy to make them pleasing.) In love as in other matters, the *Bildungsroman* insists on our constantly testing and revising what Austen calls first impressions, and like any educative process, this takes time. Only through a careful monitoring of their unfolding experiences can heroines come to know what others and they themselves are really like, and we are expected to read their stories in the same spirit. The sentimental novel demands something quite different from its heroes and its readers: we are expected to react instantly to good and evil with appropriate degrees of sympathy or abhorrence, but there is little question of our having to learn better how to tell them apart, since there are no gradations between innocence and depravity in the morally melodramatic world of sentimentalism. The kind of ethical and epistemological workout so edifying to characters and readers alike in the *Bildungsroman,* and so central to the educative pretensions of most eighteenth-century novels, is largely absent from the sentimental novel.

Taking a dim view of supposed progress in all spheres, the sentimental novel not only casts doubt on processes of individual growth and development, but displays considerable pessimism over the prospect of general social betterment through education. The world at large is irredeemable, and the root of the trouble lies less in political or economic or religious institutions, which might be amenable to reform, than in the very nature of organized society, which demands that men assume active, public roles and relegates passivity and privacy to the realm of the feminine. From this perspective, even the rationality prized so highly by Godwin, Holcroft, and other late eighteenth-century radicals is hopelessly tainted. In Ann Murry's *Mentoria: or The Young Ladies' Instructor* of 1778, a governess tells her pupils, who have been urging her to teach them some science, that "Knowledge, like power, beyond a certain degree subjects those who possess it, to many temptations and inconveniences."[4] A thoroughgoing sentimentalist endorses this principle, without any such qualification as Mentoria's "beyond a certain degree": all knowledge is power, and its possession no mere temptation but a token of one's already having fallen from a state of innocence.

The fullest literary expression of this equation between knowledge and power, and of the incompatability of either with goodness of heart, is found in the late writings of that arch-sentimentalist Mark Twain—in the somber conception of Hank Morgan in *A Connecticut Yankee* or of Satan in *The Mysterious Stranger.* But it is also present in eighteenth-century works like *The Man of Feeling,* the heroes of which are exempted from acquiring the knowledge and power that betoken adult masculinity. In this respect the sentimental hero is even more of an outsider than the picaro, who is usually a very apt learner, forced by circumstances to exercise his talents against society but wanting nothing more than to gain admittance to it. The sentimental hero, who learns nothing and forgets nothing, is more akin to the harmless madman. Mackenzie's Harley has been rightly called a "saintly fool,"[5] and Sterne's characters are all genially touched. In *Tristram Shandy* we may have a Lockean demonstration of necessitarian psychology, of character-formation through accidents of individual experience, so that in some ways people in the Shandean world are products of their educations. But at bottom Sterne's characters, and the sentimental hero generally from Harley to Huck Finn, are all oddities on whom education hasn't "taken," originals blithely or tearfully beyond the reach of adaptive socialization. In this respect they are liberated and liberating: they hold out the possibility that one can slip through the net of education—both formal instruction and the more pervasive conditioning of family and society—with all one's native, precious, quirky individuality intact.

One major exception to the pattern sketched in the preceding pages has been acknowledged already: when sentimental values happen to coincide with those of society at large, as in the case of women, there can be a convergence of the otherwise opposed structures of the *Bildungsroman* and the sentimental novel. But what about other exceptions? Aren't there books, for example, in which male characters embrace the ideology of sentiment after a period of callous selfishness or downright misanthropy? If so, can't sentimentalism be thought of as learned behavior, and don't such books suggest a compatability between the sentimental novel and the *Bildungsroman?* Or again, even if there were no characters within books that experienced this kind of learning, couldn't it be argued that most sentimental novels are designed to bring about some such process in the reader? That is, don't these novels all assume a marked degree of worldliness on the part of their audience and yet have as their implicit goal a sentimental education of the reading public, leading to a new sympathy with traditional objects of indifference or contempt such as slaves, madmen, animals, and "fallen women"?

"I converted Mr. Scrooge," Dickens says in a letter, "by teaching him that a Christian heart can not be shut up in itself, but must . . . be a link in the great human chain, and must have sympathies with everything." That an un- or anti-sentimental male character can be brought to understand and adopt sentimental values would appear to be demonstrated once and for all by a work like *A Christmas Carol.* In the sentence just quoted, however, "converted" is a more crucial term than "teaching," for what takes place in such episodes is a secular form of classical Christian conversion and has little to do with teaching or learning in any familiar sense. Scrooge's transformation is an abrupt rebirth rather than a gradual growth, a sudden regression rather than a cumulative progression. As to the result, heroes of the *Bildungsroman* do not invariably grow sadder but wiser, yet an advance toward rueful maturity is more typical of them than the reversion to cheerful childishness that Scrooge undergoes ("I'm quite a baby. Never mind. I don't care. I'd rather be a baby. Hallo! Whoop!"). To be born again in the sentimental sense is to put off not merely the old man, as St. Paul expresses it (Colossians 3:9), but manhood itself.

The main difference, though, is not in the product but the process: not in Scrooge's taking a great leap backward, but in the rapidity and completeness of his break with previous habits of mind. The pattern of years is reversed in a night. Traditionally, conversion may be the work of an instant but regeneration takes time. In *A Christmas Carol*, Dickens collapses the two, implying that a change of heart will make for a full and effectual change of behavior. His conviction that the ills of society can be remedied through individual transformations and do not require an alteration of the existing political or economic system has been criticized on ideological and pragmatic grounds, most notably by Orwell. My point is that by basing social on individual reformation, and by basing individual reformation in turn on a model of Christian conversion rather than regeneration, Dickens can be regarded as a thoroughly sentimental reformer: not in the colloquial sense that he indulges in wishful thinking or exaggerates the role of feelings and emotions in practical human affairs, although he may do both, but, rather, in the sense that he envisions change as occurring spontaneously and totally if at all, as unpredictably as the working of grace in Calvinism— something neither earned nor achieved, but divinely and mysteriously given. The latter-day chief of sinners does not grope or grow toward (let alone "learn") saintliness but has it thrust upon him, overnight. More could be said about "change of heart" as a sentimental version of the transformation chronicled in earlier works like Bunyan's *Grace Abounding*, with the instant of conversion displacing the painful, protracted processes of confirmation and regeneration. For present purposes, however, it is sufficient to acknowledge that Dickens's Scrooge acquires sentimental traits rather than possessing them all along; yet his melodramatic metamorphosis tends to bear out the contention that sentimental tales lack the element of gradual, incremental growth and discovery typical of the *Bildungsroman*, and that even when change does occur, it is apt to be spontaneous and regressive rather than prolonged and progressive. In short, whatever "teaching" of his hero Dickens did in *A Christmas Carol* must be thought of as very different from, if not contrary to, ordinary processes of education.

A second possible exception to the pattern occurs in works having sentimental education not as their internal subject but as their rhetorical object. Such novels have existed since the eighteenth century, but their aim can be labeled "educational" only if that term is qualified along the lines suggested in my discussion of *A Christmas Carol*. There is no question that many such novels have sought to broaden their readers' sympathies and to show them that jaded and Scrooge-like as they may have become, they can still be made to feel benevolence, pity, and other pleasurably humane sensations through reading. This depends, however, on a transformation like

Scrooge's taking place in the reader. After a lifetime's education into anti-sentimentalism, Scrooge is converted at last by witnessing a series of visionary tableaux of his own past, present, and future. The reader, responding to images of Scrooge responding to images of Scrooge, must be moved to abandon his own habitual worldliness and callousness.

To precipitate the desired conversion, it may help but is not necessary to depict an exemplary change of heart within the story. In *Uncle Tom's Cabin*, Augustine St. Clair's fatally delayed conversion and Simon Legree's satanically rejected conversion are as effective for this purpose as George Shelby's successful one. Yet none of these dramatizations of potential or actual change is as forceful as the immutability of Uncle Tom himself, who is a model sentimental hero not only in his childlike, Christlike, or "feminine" simplicity and vulnerability, but also in his utter self-consistency: he sustains his original character to the point of martyrdom rather than learning, adapting, or evolving through his ordeals.

The difference between what characters and readers "learn" from sentimental novels and what is involved in ordinary education is articulated in Matthew 10:16, "Behold, I send you forth as sheep in the midst of wolves: be ye therefore wise as serpents, and harmless as doves." Modern criticism has found the first half of Christ's command a fitting gloss on the careers of characters like Tom Jones, who must learn to temper their genial impulses with serpentine prudence if they are to take their rightful places in the world. But can a Blifil ever really be "taught" the innocence of a dove? Some sentimental authors appear to believe that deep inside the world's Blifils there may linger traces of simple goodness; they also tend to assume, however, that such goodness cannot be brought back to the surface through a gradual shedding of harmful integuments, but can be retrieved and revived only through a kind of conversion. The majority of sentimental novels chronicle the fate of sheep amidst wolves—of characters whose original dovelikeness remains intact; those that deal with characters like Scrooge, who have lost it, portray an abrupt reversion from serpent back to dove rather than an achievement of the union between the two that Christ enjoins. Within the sentimental novel, these qualities are treated as irreconcilable: hard-headedness is fatal to good-heartedness.

Yet the narrators of sentimental novels often prove more capable than their characters of joining the serpent and the dove: this is a major difference between Mackenzie's manner and Harley's, Dickens's and Stephen Blackpool's, even Stowe's and Uncle Tom's. The consequences of authors transacting their essential business with readers over the heads of their heroes cannot be explored here, beyond noting that most sentimental characters are sadly deficient in prudence, manipulativeness, and humor, but that their creators need not be. The fact that authors can combine such worldly traits with the keen sensibilities of their heroes holds out the possibility of the reader's doing so, too; that is, of his undergoing a change of heart without having to break totally with his old way of life. The danger in this possibility, as critics of sentimentalism have insisted since the eighteenth century, is that the sensations of sympathy, benevolence, and the like can become substitutes for exertion rather than spurs to it, impulses that spend themselves on imaginary objects of distressed virtue rather than finding their proper outlets in social action. Whatever the validity of such charges—whether a sentimental change of heart secularizes and updates or merely burlesques St. Paul's experience on the way to Damascus—it should by now be clear that this process has little in common with what we ordinarily think of as education.

NOTES

1. Mary Brunton, *Self-Control; a Novel* (1811; rpt. London: Colburn and Bentley, 1836), 5.

2. R. S. Crane, "Suggestions toward a Genealogy of the 'Man of Feeling,'" *ELH* 1 (1934): 205–30.

3. William Wordsworth, *The Prelude*, 2.267–72.

4. Ann Murray, *Mentoria: or the Young Ladies' Instructor*, 4th ed. (London, 1785), 38, quoted by Josephine Kamm in *Hope Deferred: Girls' Education in English History* (London: Methuen, 1965), 115.

5. See Robert Platzer, "Mackenzie's Martyrs: The Man of Feeling as Saintly Fool," *Novel* 10 (1976): 59–64.

IRVIN EHRENPREIS: A Handlist of Published Works

BOOKS AND EDITIONS

The "Types" Approach to Literature. New York: King's Crown Press, 1945.

Editor, with Herbert Davis. John Percival, Earl of Egmont. *Jonathan Swift, a Brief Memoir.* Oxford: privately printed, 1951.

Editor, with Herbert Davis. Jonathan Swift. *Political Tracts 1713–19.* Oxford: Blackwell; Princeton: Princeton University Press, 1953.

Editor. Jonathan Swift. *An Enquiry into the Behaviour of the Queen's Last Ministry.* Bloomington: Indiana University Press, 1956.

The Personality of Jonathan Swift. London: Methuen; Cambridge, Mass.: Harvard University Press, 1958. Reprint. New York: Barnes and Noble, 1969.

Swift: The Man, His Works, and the Age. Vol. 1. London: Methuen; Cambridge, Mass.: Harvard University Press, 1962.

Fielding: Tom Jones. London: Edward Arnold, 1964. Chapter 1 reprinted in *Fielding: A Critical Anthology,* edited by Claude Rawson, 528–37. Harmondsworth: Penguin Books, 1973.

Editor, with Anne H. Ehrenpreis. *Boswell's Life of Samuel Johnson.* New York: Washington Square Press, 1965.

Editor. *American Poetry.* London: Edward Arnold, 1965.

Editor, with Howard Anderson and Philip B. Daghlian. *The Familiar Letter in the Eighteenth Century.* Lawrence: University of Kansas Press, 1966.

Swift: The Man, His Works, and the Age. Vol. 2. London: Methuen; Cambridge, Mass.: Harvard University Press, 1967.

Editor. Jonathan Swift. *Prose Works.* Vol. 14 (index). Oxford: Blackwell, 1968.

Editor. *Wallace Stevens: A Critical Anthology.* Harmondsworth: Penguin Books, 1972.

Literary Meaning and Augustan Values. Charlottesville: University Press of Virginia, 1974.

Acts of Implication: Suggestion and Covert Meaning in the Works of Dryden, Swift, Pope and Austen. Berkeley and Los Angeles: University of California Press, 1980.

Swift: The Man, His Works, and the Age. Vol. 3. London: Methuen; Cambridge, Mass.: Harvard University Press, 1983.

Essays and Notes

With B. C. Friedl. "The Classics Fight Back in France." *The Nation* 152 (1941): 671.

"English Literature and the Humanities." *News Letter of the College English Association* 4 (1942): 6.

"Swift and Mr. John Temple." *MLN* 62 (1947): 145–54.

With B. B. Cohen. "Tales from Indiana Students." *Hoosier Folklore* 6 (1947): 57–65.

"Swift's Father." *N & Q* 192 (1947): 189–91.

"Swift's 'Little Language' in the *Journal to Stella*." *SP* 155 (1948): 80–88.

"Swift's *Enquiry*." *N & Q* 194 (1949): 360.

"Southey to Coleridge, 1799." *N & Q* 195 (1950): 124–26.

"Swift's Voyages." *MLN* 65 (1950): 256–57.

"Moving Pictures." *N & Q* 195 (1950): 162.

"Lady Betty Butler to Swift." *TLS* (15 December 1950): 801.

"Swift and Satire." *CE* 13 (1952): 309–12.

"Swift on Liberty." *JHI* 13 (1952): 131–46. Reprinted in *Swift: Modern Judgments*, edited by A. Norman Jeffares, 59–73. Nashville and London: Aurora Press, 1969.

"Swift's History of England." *JEGP* 51 (1952): 177–85.

"The Date of Swift's *Sentiments*." *RES* 3 (1952): 272–74.

"Swift's April Fool for a Bibliophile." *The Book Collector* 2 (1953): 205–8.

"Swift and Esther." *TLS* (8 January 1954): 25.

"Swift's First Poem." *MLR* 49 (1954): 210–11.

"Four of Swift's Sources." *MLN* 70 (1955): 95–100.

With James L. Clifford. "Swiftiana in Rylands Eng. MS 659 and Related Documents." *Bulletin of the John Rylands Library* 37 (1955): 368–92.

"The Pattern of Swift's Women." *PMLA* 70 (1955): 706–17.

"William Carlos Williams." *Departure* 4, no. 11 (1957): 5–10.

"Orwell, Huxley, Pope." *Revue des Langues Vivantes* 23 (1957): 215–30.

"The Origins of *Gulliver's Travels*." *PMLA* 62 (1957): 880–99. Reprinted in *Fair Liberty Was All His Cry*, edited by A. Norman Jeffares, 200–25. London: Macmillan; New York: St. Martin's, 1967.

"Why Literature Should be Taught." *Proceedings of the Philosophy of Education Society* 14 (1958): 93–103. Reprinted in *On Teaching Literature*, edited by J. S. Hawley and E. B. Jenkinson, 101–4. Bloomington: Indiana University Press, 1967.

"A Survey of Eighteenth-Century Anthologies." *CE* 20 (1958): 147–51.

"Readable Americans." *Revue des Langues Vivantes* 25 (1959): 416–19.

"Joseph Moxon." *TLS* (22 May 1959): 305.

"Swift's Grandfather." *TLS* (12 June 1959): 353.

"Fielding's Use of Fiction: The Autonomy of *Joseph Andrews*." In *Twelve Original Essays on Great English Novels*, edited by Charles Shapiro, 23–41. Detroit: Wayne State University Press, 1960. Reprinted in *Joseph Andrews*, 299–312. New York: New American Library, 1961; and in *Henry Fielding und den englische Roman des 18. Jahrhunderts*, 236–50. Darmstadt: Wissenschaftliche Buchgesellschaft, 1972.

"The Literary Side of a Satirist's Work." *MR* 2 (1962): 179–97.

"Four Poets and Others." *MR* 2 (1962): 397–410.

"The Meaning of Gulliver's Last Voyage." *REL* 3 (1962): 18–38. Reprinted in *Swift: A Collection of Critical Essays,* edited by Ernest Tuveson, 123–42. Englewood Cliffs: Prentice-Hall, 1964; and in *The Personality of Jonathan Swift,* by Irvin Ehrenpreis, 148–68. New York: Barnes and Noble, 1969.

"Introduction." *Joseph Andrews.* New York: Washington Square Press, 1963.

"Personae." In *Restoration and Eighteenth-Century Literature: Essays in Honor of A. D. McKillop,* edited by Carroll Camden, 25–37. Chicago: University of Chicago Press, 1963. Reprinted in *Literary Meaning and Augustan Values,* by Irvin Ehrenpreis, 49–60. Charlottesville: University Press of Virginia, 1974; and in *Satura: Ein Kompendium moderner Studien zur Satire,* edited by Bernhard Fabian, 308–20. Hildesheim: Georg Olms Verlag, 1975.

"The Age of Lowell." In *American Poetry,* by Irvin Ehrenpreis, 69–96. London: Edward Arnold, 1965. Translated into Polish and reprinted in *Literatura Na Swiecie,* 86–121. Warsaw: Grudzien, 1979.

With Howard Anderson. "The Familiar Letter in the Eighteenth Century: Some Generalizations." In *The Familiar Letter in the Eighteenth Century,* edited by Irvin Ehrenpreis, Howard Anderson, and Philip B. Daghlian, 269–82. Laurence: University of Kansas Press, 1966.

With James L. Clifford. "New Light on Swift and his Family." *TLS* (21 April 1966): 356.

"The Cistern and the Fountain: Art and Reality in Pope and Gray." In *Studies in Criticism and Aesthetics, 1660–1800: Essays in Honor of Samuel Holt Monk,* edited by H. Anderson and J. S. Shea, 156–75. Minneapolis: University of Minnesota Press, 1967. Reprinted in *Pope: A Collection of Critical Essays,* edited by J. V. Guerinot, 111–23. Englewood Cliffs: Prentice-Hall, 1972; in *Literary Meaning and Augustan Values,* by Irvin Ehrenpreis, 76–93. Charlottesville: University Press of Virginia, 1974; and in *Pope: Recent Essays,* edited by Maynard Mack and James Winn, 502–26. Hamden, Ct.: Archon Books, 1980.

"Dr. S***T and the Hibernian Patriot." In *Jonathan Swift: 1667–1967: A Dublin Tercentenary Tribute,* edited by R. McHugh and P. Edwards, 24–37. Dublin: The Dolmen Press, 1967.

"Swift and the Comedy of Evil." In *The World of Jonathan Swift,* edited by Brian Vickers, 213–19. Oxford: Blackwell, 1968. Reprinted in *Jonathan Swift: A Critical Anthology,* edited by Denis Donoghue, 207–15. Harmondsworth: Penguin Books, 1971.

"Letters of Advice to Young Spinsters." In *The Lady of Letters in the Eighteenth Century,* 3–27. Los Angeles: William Andrews Clark Memorial Library, 1969. Reprinted in *Stuart and Georgian Moments,* edited by Earl Miner, 245–69. Berkeley and Los Angeles: University of California Press, 1972.

"Jonathan Swift." Lecture on a Master Mind, *Proceedings of the British Academy* 54 (1970): 149–64.

"The Style of Sound: The Literary Values of Pope's Versification." In *The Augustan Milieu: Essays Presented to Louis A. Landa,* edited by H. K. Miller and others, 232–46. Oxford: Clarendon Press, 1970. Reprinted in *Literary Meaning and Augustan Values,* by Irvin Ehrenpreis, 63–75. Charlottesville: University Press of Virginia, 1974.

"Poverty and Poetry: Representations of the Poor in Augustan Literature." In *The Modernity of the Eighteenth Century*, edited by L. T. Milic, 3–35. Cleveland: Case Western Reserve University Press, 1971.

"Swift's Letters." In *Focus: Swift*, edited by Claude Rawson, 197–215. London: Sphere Books, 1971. Reprinted in *The Character of Swift's Satire*, edited by Claude Rawson, 227–44. Newark: University of Delaware Press, 1983.

"The Life of the Modern Poet." *TLS* (23 February 1973): 193–95.

"Meaning: Implicit and Explicit." In *New Approaches to Eighteenth-Century Literature*, edited by Phillip Harth, 117–55. New York: Columbia University Press, 1974. Revised and reprinted in *Literary Meaning and Augustan Values*, by Irvin Ehrenpreis, 1–48. Charlottesville: University Press of Virginia, 1974.

"Viewpoint." *TLS* (8 February 1974): 132.

"The Arts in America." *NR* 1, no. 4 (1974): 38.

"Yucktalk: Literary Style in the Oval Circus." *NR* 1, no. 6 (1974): 5–14.

"Destination America—Some Bicentennial Reflections." *NR* 3, no. 27 (1976): 3–11.

"Continuity and Coruscation: Dryden's Poetic Instincts." In *John Dryden II*, 3–26. Los Angeles: William Andrews Clark Memorial Library, 1978.

"Jane Austen and Heroism." *NYRB* (8 Feb. 1979): 37–43. Revised and reprinted in *Acts of Implication: Suggestion and Covert Meaning in the Works of Dryden, Swift, Pope and Austen*, by Irvin Ehrenpreis, 112–45. Berkeley and Los Angeles: University of California Press, 1980.

"Strange Relation: Wallace Stevens' Nonsense." In *Wallace Stevens: A Celebration*, edited by Frank Doggett and Robert Buttell, 219–34. Princeton: Princeton University Press, 1980.

"*Rasselas* and Some Meanings of 'Structure' in Literary Criticism." *Novel* 14 (1981): 101–17.

"Swiftian Dilemmas." In *Satire in the 18th Century*, edited by J. D. Browning, 214–31. New York: Garland, 1983.

"Homage to Schubert the Poet." In *David Schubert: Works and Days*, ed. Renée Karol Weiss (Princeton: *Quarterly Review of Literature*, 40th Anniversary Issue, Poetry Series 29, 1983), 310–21.

REVIEWS

The Satire of Jonathan Swift, by Herbert Davis. *PQ* 28 (1948): 404.

The History of the Four Last Years of the Queen, by Jonathan Swift, edited by Herbert Davis. *JEGP* 51 (1952): 108–9.

The History of the Four Last Years of the Queen, by Jonathan Swift, edited by Herbert Davis. *PQ* 31 (1952): 303–5.

Political Tracts 1710–1713, by Jonathan Swift, edited by Herbert Davis. *JEGP* 51 (1952): 599–601.

The Text of Gulliver's Travels, by Harold Williams. *PQ* 32 (1953): 279–99.

Jonathan Swift and the Anatomy of Satire, by John Bullitt; *Swift's Rhetorical Art*, by Martin Price. *PQ* 33 (1954): 300–301.

Swift and the Church of Ireland, by Louis Landa. *JEGP* (1955): 122–24.

Jonathan Swift, by John Middleton Murry. *PQ* 34 (1955): 322–23.

The Masks of Jonathan Swift, by W. B. Ewald. *MP* (1955): 134–36.

Swift and Carroll, by Phyllis Greenacre. *PQ* 35 (1956): 33–32.

My Darling Clementine (film). *The Oxford Magazine* 74 (24 May 1956): 443.

Le Jour Se Leve (film). *The Oxford Magazine* 74 (14 June 1956): 510.

A Tale of a Tub, by Jonathan Swift, edited by A. C. Guthkelch and D. Nichol Smith (2d ed.). *MLR* 54 (1959): 89–90.

The Achievement of Marianne Moore, compiled by E. P. Sheehy and K. A. Lohf. *The Library* 14 (1959): 73–74.

The Poems of Jonathan Swift, edited by Harold Williams (2d ed.). *MLR* 54 (1959): 73–74.

English Satire, by James Sutherland. *MLR* 54 (1959): 247–48.

Eugene O'Neill and the Tragic Tension, by Doris V. Falk. *MLR* 54 (1959): 603.

Wallace Stevens, by Robert Pack. *MLR* 54 (1959): 426–27.

Pope's Iliad, by William Melmoth, edited by G. Cronin and P. A. Doyle. *CJ* 56 (1960): 42.

"Recent Poetry": *The Crow and the Heart (1946–1959),* by Hayden Carruth; *The Happy Birthday of Death,* by Gregory Corso; *Form of Women,* by Robert Creeley; *The Year of the Green Wave,* by Bruce Cutler; *On the Way to the Island,* by David Ferry; *A Water Walk by Villa d'Este,* by Jean Garrigue; *Graffiti,* by Ramon Guthrie; *The Gazabos: Forty-one Poems,* by Edwin Honig; *Wallace Stevens,* by Frank Kermode; *Songs,* by Christopher Logue; *Wage War on Silence,* by Vassar Miller; *Apples from Shinar,* by Hyam Plutzik. *MR* 1 (1961): 362–72.

Richard Steele's Periodical Journalism 1714–16, edited by Rae Blanchard. *RES* 12 (1961): 299–300.

The Power of Satire, by Robert C. Elliott. *CJ* 57 (1962): 34–36.

"Four Poets and Others": *Disorderly Houses,* by Alan Ausen; *Changes,* by Michael Benedikt; *A Broadsheet against the New York Times Book Review,* by Robert Bly; *The Islanders,* by Philip Booth; *Companion to Your Doom,* by Richard Emil Braun; *Journey to a Known Place,* by Hayden Carruth; *In the Stoneworks,* by John Ciardi; *Starting from San Francisco,* by Lawrence Ferlinghetti; *Landcastle,* by Albert and Helen Fowler; *Abraham's Knife,* by George Garrett; *The Many Islands,* by William Goodreau; *A Harlot's Hire,* by Allen Grossman; *The Mother of the Amazons,* by Albert Herzing; *Halfway,* by Maxine W. Kumin; *Imitations,* by Robert Lowell; *Horatio,* by Hyam Plutzik; *Fires of Home,* by John M. Ridland; *The Linen Bands,* by Raymond Roseliep; *Initial A.,* by David Shubert; *Suits for the Dead,* by David R. Slavitt, *Twenty Poems,* by Georg Trakl, trans. by James Wright and Robert Bly; *Advice to a Prophet,* by Richard Wilbur. *MR* 2 (1962): 397–410.

"Poetry without Despair": *About the House,* by W. H. Auden; *The Lost World,* by Randall Jarrell; *The Carnivore,* by David R. Slavitt. *VQR* 42 (1966): 163–68.

"Solitude and Isolation": *Questions of Travel,* by Elizabeth Bishop; *West of Childhood: Poems 1950–65,* by Isabella Gardner; *The Puritan Carpenter,* by Julia Randall. *VQR* 42 (1966): 332–36.

Defoe and Spiritual Autobiography, by George A. Starr. *PQ* 45 (1966): 551–52.

Berryman's Sonnets, by John Berryman. *TLS* (4 July 1968): 699.

A Small Desperation, by Dannie Abse; *The Light around the Body,* by Robert Bly; *Masks,* by Edward Brathwaite; *Stoats in the Sunlight,* by Stewart Conn; *The Sorrow Dance,* by Denise Levertov; *Selected Poems,* by Kenneth Patchen; *The Signs among Us,* by W. W. Robson. *TLS* (15 August 1968): 868.

The Ordinary Universe, by Denis Donoghue. *TLS* (3 October 1968): 1134.

The Body, by Michael Benedikt; *Spring Journal,* by Edwin Honig; *Onions and Roses,* by Vassar Miller; *Shall We Gather at the River,* by James Wright. *TLS* (17 October 1968): 1172.

In, On or About the Premises, by Paul Blackburn; *Selected Poems,* by Paavo Haaviko, trans. by Assia Gutman; *Kitchen Poems,* by J. H. Prynne; *Two Voices,* by D. M. Thomas; *A Trampoline,* by Gael Turnbull. *TLS* (24 October 1968): 1202.

Perspectives on Poetry, by J. C. Calderwood and H. E. Tolliver; *Modern Poetry: Essays in Criticism,* edited by John Hollander. *TLS* (26 December 1968): 1457.

Collected Poems, by Basil Bunting; *Shifts of Being,* by Richard Eberhart; *Plans for an Orderly Apocalypse,* by Harvey Gross; *North Central,* by Lorine Niedecker. *TLS* (27 February 1969): 212.

Selected Poems, Vol. 1: The First Decade, by Robert Duncan. *TLS* (1 May 1969): 467.

Selected Poems, by A. R. Ammons; *The Wise Old Wicked Man,* by Archibald MacLeish; *The Lice,* by W. S. Merwin. *TLS* (29 May 1969): 585.

Lecture de la poésie américaine, by Serge Fauchereau; *"A" 13–21,* by Louis Zukofsky. *TLS* (17 July 1969): 770.

Selected Poems, by John Crowe Ransom; *Incarnations,* by Robert Penn Warren. *TLS* (23 April 1970): 446. Reprinted in *TLS: Essays and Reviews 9* (1971): 79.

Mortal Fire, by Peter Dale; *Neighbours,* by Glyn Hughes; *The Visit,* by Ian Hamilton; *The Burning Cone,* by George MacBeth. *TLS* (2 July 1970): 703. Reprinted in *TLS: Essays and Reviews 9* (1971): 90.

The Maximus Poems, by Charles Olson. *TLS* (13 November 1970): 1315.

The Finger, by Robert Creeley; *Letter to an Imaginary Friend,* by Thomas McGrath; *Beyond Power,* by M. L. Rosenthal; *Short History of the Fur Trade,* by Adrien Stoutenburg; *Working against Time,* by David Wagoner. *TLS* (11 December 1970): 1436.

Complete Poems, by Elizabeth Bishop; *Collected Poems,* by Alan Dugan; *The Fire Screen,* by James Merrill; *Snapshots of a Daughter-In-Law,* by Adrienne Rich. *TLS* (22 January 1971): 92.

The Eye-Beaters, by James Dickey; *Nerves,* by John Wieners; *Walking to Sleep,* by Richard Wilbur. *TLS* (21 May 1971): 580. Reprinted in *TLS: Essays and Reviews 10* (1972): 158.

St. Martin's, by Robert Creeley; *Bending the Bow,* by Robert Duncan; *Adventures of the Letter I,* by Louis Simpson. *TLS* (23 July 1971): 855.

Collected Poems and Epigrams, by J. V. Cunningham. *TLS* (22 August 1971): 1024.

Love and Fame, by John Berryman; *Breaking and Entering,* by X. J. Kennedy; *Regarding Wave,* by Gary Snyder. *TLS* (27 December 1971): 1602.

The Complete Poems, by Randall Jarrell. *TLS* (31 March 1972): 360. Reprinted in *TLS: Essays and Reviews 11* (1973): 149–52.

Internal Colloquies, by I. A. Richards. *TLS* (23 June 1972): 710.

Suggestion and Statement in Poetry, by Krishna Rayan. *TLS* (8 December 1972): 1481.

Collected Poems 1950–1970, by Donald Davie. *TLS* (22 December 1972): 1548. Reprinted *TLS: Essays and Reviews 11* (1973): 155–57.

The Bear on the Delhi Road, by Earle Birney; *Earle Birney,* by Frank Davey; *Cry Ararat!,* by P. K. Page. *TLS* (26 October 1973): 1306.

Recovery, by John Berryman. *TLS* (30 November 1973): 1465.

The Poetry of John Crowe Ransom, by Miller Williams. *SAQ* 72 (1973): 169.

"Poetry by the Yard?": *Cruelty,* by A; *Uplands,* by A. R. Ammons; *The Uncorrected World,* by Kenneth O. Hanson; *Letters to a Stranger,* by Thomas James; *Departures,* by Donald Justice; *The Anonymous Lover,* by John Logan; *Breaking Open,* by Muriel Rukeyser; *The Beasts and the Elders,* by Robert Siegel; *The Story of Our Lives,* by Mark Strand; *Between Two Lives,* by Frederick Turner; *Merciful Disguises,* by Mona Van Duyn; *Hard Freight,* by Charles Wright. *TLS* (29 March 1974): 339–40.

A Closer Look at Ariel, by Nancy Hunter Steiner. *TLS* (12 April 1974): 391.

Wallace Stevens and the Symbolist Imagination, by Michael Benamou. *MLR* 69 (1974): 159–61.

Buchanan Dying, by John Updike. *NYRB* (8 August 1974): 6–8.

Ross and Tom, by John Leggett. *NYRB* (31 October 1974): 19–20.

Love-Hate Relations, by Stephen Spender. *NYRB* (14 November 1974): 32–34.

Long Distance, by Penelope Mortimer. *NYRB* (12 December 1974): 42–43.

"Dickinsons in Love": *The Life of Emily Dickinson,* by R. B. Sewall. *NYRB* (23 January 1974): 3–4.

"A Misunderstood Genius": *The Treasure of Auchinleck,* by David Buchanan; *Samuel Johnson,* by John Wain. *NYRB* (20 February 1975): 3–6.

"Bloomsbury Variations": *Personal Record, 1920–1972,* by Gerald Brenan; *The Loving Friends,* by David Gadd; *The Bloomsbury Group,* edited by S. P. Rosenbaum. *NYRB* (17 April 1975): 9–12.

"Teacher": *The Twenties,* by Edmund Wilson. *NYRB* (12 June 1975): 3–6.

"Boysenberry Sherbert": *Self-Portrait in a Convex Mirror,* by John Ashbery; *Departures,* by Donald Justice. *NYRB* (16 October 1975): 3–4.

"The Rescue of Edith Wharton": *Edith Wharton,* by R. W. B. Lewis. *NYRB* (13 November 1975): 4–9.

"The State of Poetry": *Somewhere Is Such a Kingdom,* by G. Hill; *Collected Poems,* by G. Oppen; *Turtle Island,* by Gary Snyder. *NYRB* (23 January 1976): 3–6.

"Love, Hate, and Ezra Pound": *Ezra Pound,* by Donald Davie. *NYRB* (22 May 1976): 6–12.

"Swift's Sting": *Jonathan Swift,* by A. L. Rowse. *NYRB* (24 June 1976): 3–6.

"Lowell's Comedy": *Selected Poems,* by Robert Lowell. NYRB (28 October 1976): 3–6.

"Inside Auden's Landscape": *Collected Poems,* by W. H. Auden, edited by E. Mendelson. *NYRB* (3 February 1977): 10–12.

"The Moral World of Robinson Crusoe": *The World of Defoe,* by Peter Earle. *NYRB* (28 April 1977): 9–11.

"The Triumph of Dr. Johnson": *Samuel Johnson,* by W. J. Bate. *NYRB* (10 November 1977): 3–6.

"Mr. Eliot's Martyrdom": *Eliot's Early Years,* by Lyndall Gordon; *T. S. Eliot's Personal Waste Land,* by J. E. Miller; *T. S. Eliot: The Longer Poems,* by Derek Traversi. *NYRB* (9 February 1978): 3–8.

"The Music of Suffering": *The Composition of Four Quartets,* by Helen Gardner; *Remembering Poets,* by Donald Hall. *NYRB* (7 December 1978): 16–19.

"Lit in Trouble": *Literature Against Itself,* by Gerald Graff; *Celestial Pantomime,* by Justus Lawler. *NYRB* (28 June 1979): 40–43.

"The Powers of Alexander Pope": *Alexander Pope and the Arts of Augustan England,* by M. R. Brownell; *Alexander Pope: The Poet in the Poems,* by D. H. Griffin. *NYRB* (20 December 1979): 48–51.

"The Long and the Short of It": *Brother to Dragons* and *Now and Then,* by Robert Penn Warren. *NYRB* (21 February 1980): 27–28. Reprinted in *Robert Penn Warren's Brother to Dragons: A Discussion,* edited by James A. Grimshaw, 184–90. Baton Rouge: Louisiana State University Press, 1983.

"Disaffected Writers": *American Writing Since 1945,* by Warner Berthoff. *New York Times Book Review* (6 April 1980): 10, 20.

"The Powers of Sympathy": *Harvard Guide to Contemporary American Writing,* edited by Daniel Hoffman; *Part of Nature, Part of Us,* by Helen Vendler. *NYRB* (29 May 1980): 12–14.

"Otherworldly Goods": *Scripts for the Pageant,* by James Merrill. *NYRB* (22 January 1981): 47–51.

"All-American Bard": *Walt Whitman: A Life,* by Justin Kaplan. *NYRB* (2 April 1981): 10–14.

"Digging In": *Poems 1965–75,* by Seamus Heaney; *A Coast of Trees: Poems,* by A. R. Ammons; *Selected Poems,* by Mark Strand. *NYRB* (8 October 1981): 45–47.

"Continuity and Change": *Rumor Verified: Poems 1979–1980,* by Robert Penn Warren. *Atlantic Monthly* (December 1981): 88–91.

"The Other Sylvia Plath": *Sylvia Plath: The Collected Poems,* edited by Ted Hughes. *NYRB* (4 February 1982): 22–24.

"Whose Life Is It, Anyway?": *Katherine Anne Porter: A Life,* by Joan Givner. *NYRB* (20 January 1983): 13–14.

"The Two Robert Brownings": *Robert Browning: A Life within Life,* by Donald Thomas. *NYRB* (29 September 1983): 41–42.

"Three-Part Inventions": *The World, the Text, and the Critic,* by Edward W. Said. *NYRB* (19 January 1984): 37–39.

"Unheard Melodies": *The Odes of John Keats,* by Helen Vendler. *NYRB* (12 April 1984): 33–34.

"The King of Correspondence": *The Yale Edition of Horace Walpole's Correspondence. NYRB* (26 April 1984): 19–21.

"Art, Life, and T. S. Eliot": *T. S. Eliot: A Study of Character and Style,* by Ronald Bush. *NYRB* (28 June 1984): 5–9.

"Human Wishes": *Samuel Johnson,* by W. J. Bate; *A Preliminary Handlist of Copies of Books associated with Dr. Johnson,* by J. D. Fleeman; *Samuel Johnson 1709–1784: A Bicentenary Exhibition,* edited by K. K. Yung; *Samuel Johnson,* by Donald Greene. *London Review of Books* (20 December 1984): 5–6.

"The Seductive Journalist": *James Boswell: The Later Years,* by Frank Brady. *NYRB* (28 March 1985): 3–6.